Improving Accounting
Reliability

IMPROVING ACCOUNTING RELIABILITY

Solvency, Insolvency, and Future Cash Flows

HENNING KIRKEGAARD

Foreword by C. Torben Thomsen

Q

Quorum Books
Westport, Connecticut • London

Library of Congress Cataloging-in-Publication Data

Kirkegaard, Henning, 1938–
   [Dynamiske regnskab. English]
   Improving accounting reliability: solvency, insolvency, and
future cash flows / Henning Kirkegaard.
      p.   cm.
   Includes bibliographical references and index.
   ISBN 1-56720-143-1 (alk. paper)
   1. Bankruptcy—Accounting I. Title.
   HF5686.B3K5713   1997
   657'.48—dc21   97-8855

British Library Cataloguing in Publication Data is available.

Library of Congress Catalog Card Number: 97-8855
ISBN: 1-56720-143-1

First published in 1997

Quorum Books, 88 Post Road West, Westport, CT 06881
An imprint of Greenwood Publishing Group, Inc.

Printed in the United States of America

The paper used in this book complies with the
Permanent Paper Standard issued by the National
Information Standards Organization (Z39.48-1984).

10 9 8 7 6 5 4 3 2 1

Copyright Acknowledgments

CONTENTS

FOREWORD

In the summer of 1993 during a visit to Denmark, I had one of those "once-in-a-lifetime" experiences of making an exciting discovery. I was browsing through the public library in the town of Hillerød when I came across Henning Kirkegaard's book *Det Dynamiske Regnskab*, which has since been given the English title *Improving Accounting Reliability*.

Here was a book written in the passionate conviction that accounting not only could change but must change—its focus should move from the "past" to the "future." Moreover, the book was written in a style hoping to bridge the gap between the professional and the user of financial information. Kirkegaard also sought to lay a solid foundation for his new approach by using concepts of Karl Popper from the philosophy of science.

Breaking with tradition, the book comes as a breath of fresh air to stimulate thoughtful debate and critical examination of propositions taken for granted. It invites the reader to participate in making judgments as to the validity of the new views in an interdisciplinary setting.

While I wish that Kirkegaard might have been less polemic in his presentation, that style makes for more interesting reading. Even when he presents his views, with which you may not agree, you are the final judge.

Yes, the book is one of the most innovative and provocative works on accounting in this century. And while it is only a beginning, it could be the start of a fruitful and productive trend of thought that will invigorate, rejuvenate and strengthen the accounting profession, as accounting becomes more relevant to a larger public.

C. Torben Thomsen
Fresno State University, California

PREFACE

Can *future payments* appear from balance sheets?

This simple question is the key to this entire book, and the answer has wide ranging consequences for accounting practice. The question is direct, and the way it is expressed is in itself a challenge to traditional thinking, habits and prejudice. The question is worded so it can and must be answered with a clear and well-founded "yes" or "no," instead of with a vague "perhaps" or "I don't know."

This key question is also new—as far as I know it has never been asked before. This may surprise readers, but in fact basic ideas about current phenomena are very rarely questioned. And until now no one seems to have been in any doubt about the nature of financial statements. They have always been regarded as *a tool for use in writing financial history*.

So in both traditional accounting theory and the accounting practice used all over the world the question is always answered with a clear "no." No one doubts that financial statements show us the financial consequences of *past events*. Financial statements are historical documents, and if you want to learn anything about the payments of the future you have to consult budgets, not financial statements.

However, very few scientific truths last forever, and this book has been written to enable interested readers to doubt, think for themselves, acknowledge the potential of an entirely new viewpoint and then on their own terms learn how to answer our key question with a resounding and well-founded "yes."

The question about the basic nature of financial statements is of vital importance, both for accounting specialists and for nonspecialist users of financial statements. Because if it is possible to predict future payments, it is also possible to *predict any future suspension of payments* instead of allowing such events to surprise us. So there can be no doubt that if we can answer our key question with a "yes," there will be great practical consequences in the world of accounting in the future.

Until 1986 there were no theories or ideas indicating that financial statements could be regarded in themselves as predictions, as systems of information concerning future payments.

The target group for this book consists of readers who are *interested* in accounting. But would it not be better to address a new theory about accounting to readers who are *accounting specialists*? New scientific ideas about accounting should surely be addressed primarily to researchers and specialists in the field of accounting. What can nonspecialist readers be expected to learn from reading such a book?

The answer is that financial statements are widely used in modern society. Accounts are kept and used by everyone, no matter what their educational background. So accounting should always be a profession with an open boundary between theory and practice, between research and the use of the results of research.

Someone once said that war was far too important a business to be left to generals; similarly, we can say that accounting is far too important a business to be left to accountants.

The world of accounting is currently facing great changes and upheaval. In such situations, there will always be some people who look for new solutions and improvements, and others who seek only to hang on to traditions. The people looking for new solutions are the ones who are interested in the future, so it is possible to narrow down this book's target group even further. Readers who are interested in improvements are not all accounting specialists, and not all accounting specialists are interested in improvements.

My two basic premises are that accounting desperately needs new solutions and improvements, but that new solutions and improvements can only be created by people who are genuinely interested in and thus motivated for taking on a task that might prove both long lasting and difficult. So the aim of the book is to build a communicative bridge between nonspecialist users of financial statements and accounting specialists who are not tied by prejudice or restricted by force of habit.

In other words, I adopt the principle of the open system of scientific theory, which states that researchers should never try to take out a patent on theories and philosophies. We shall only perceive each other's actions as being sensible if we are able to obtain and exchange meaningful information across the professional barriers that divide us. And communication is not accounting's strong suit—generalists are often unable to understand the language used by accounting specialists.

The lack of understanding of traditional financial statements is a major problem in modern society. So any attempt to produce comprehensible financial statements will be of interest to a far wider circle than accounting specialists alone. This is why I have chosen to write this book as openly, clearly and accessibly as possible, constantly seeking to achieve the simplest and most straightforward way of expressing my message. Special terminology is only used when absolutely necessary. There is a certain amount of repetition, but I regard this as unavoidable, since new concepts are always difficult to grasp at first sight, and we need all the examples, explanations and repetition we can get. I have done my best to produce an accessible and reader-friendly book. The world of accounting has always been regarded as closed, difficult to understand and boring. But I believe the opposite is also possible—it really is possible to see accounting as open, easy to understand and interesting.

There is no doubt that accounting is of great importance with regard to economics, due to the fact that the basic material of economics consists of sums and accounts from enterprises in the public and private sectors. So new ideas in the world of accounting will have an immediate and direct impact on the world of economics, too.

But does the world of economics need new ideas? Readers must answer this question themselves. Let us assume that only readers who answer "yes" or "perhaps" will continue to read this book. And if we say that new ideas are necessary, what chance do such ideas have of gaining acceptance amongst professional economists? Professor John Kenneth Galbraith has pointed to both the chains to tradition and the aggressive dullness of the traditional theory on economics. And accounting professor Vernon Kam has stated that the inexactness of our attempts at defining the very word *Accounting* is an indication of the primitive state of accounting theoretical development today. No accounting theorist has yet been able to demonstrate logical connections between basic postulates, sound principles and relevant procedures. This explains why the Financial Accounting Standards Board (FASB) still prefers to speak about a "conceptual framework" rather than about a good theory.

There are probably few economists or accountants who remember their student days as an intellectually invigorating experience. But does economic theory really need to be so boring? Many years of teaching have taught me that the best way of retaining people's interest is to surprise them every now and then. As a result, this book contains a good number of strange and surprising elements. For instance, there are doctors treating appendicitis by bloodletting, there is a world famous attorney asking a question about one of the basic tenets of Roman law; and there is a ship that sails fast and almost reaches its destination safely. These strange elements may surprise readers, but there is method in the apparent madness. The book deals with a serious topic that is of vital significance for society. But in my view it is perfectly possible to write serious nonfiction without necessarily making it difficult, depressing or boring to read. And that is why I have decided to adopt a straightforward and informal style—out of consideration for my readers.

I hope readers find this book easy to read, even though the contents may not always be easy to swallow. As far as critical method and choice of concepts are concerned, I have deliberately adopted a critical attitude and aimed to achieve the sharpest possible formulation of criticism and scientific method. Researchers have no other option if they wish to avoid vague, indefinite results. For instance, when our new scientific theory claims that *the future cannot be predicted by referring to the past*, all scientifically viable accounting theory must be based on this fact. And all attempts to calculate and interpret financial ratios based on old financial statements must be rejected as being entirely lacking in scientific interest. When scientific theory discovers that predictability as a philosophical concept has new limits, and that *it is naive and foolish to believe that linear mathematics can be a useful tool in making financial predictions*, then no scientifically viable accounting theory can be based on the financial ratios produced by traditional accounting, which relies on linear mathematics. Instead, it must be accepted that the calculation and study of financial ratios and so-called "tendencies" or "trends" are nothing but simple and unrealistic speculation. Traditional so-called "accounting analysis," involving the study of old financial statements, must be banned forever from the field of serious science, where it has never really belonged.

Obviously, the new accounting theory will be provocative simply because it is different from traditional accounting theory. So there is no reason to imagine that debate and professional argument can be avoided. The new theory will cause trouble—there is little doubt about that.

My weapons in the debate will be my knowledge of accounting theory and practice, my knowledge of scientific theory and logic, and last but not least, a wish for openness. All criticism, philosophy, concepts and reasons are presented openly, allowing readers to judge for themselves. Naturally, I am absolutely certain that the new concepts hold water, and that they are far superior to the old ones. But my opinion should carry no weight—after all, my theories might be nonsense. Readers must decide for themselves whether the new ideas are useful. No pressure will be exerted to accept my theories, since I regard myself as a researcher, not a missionary.

One word of warning to readers of a delicate disposition. The dogma and myths of traditional accounting are exposed to attack in this book. The years that have elapsed since the discovery of the new theories, as well as a great deal of discussion, have convinced me that traditional accounting theory should certainly not be treated as sacred. I am not the only one to be dissatisfied with accounting traditions, so there is no reason to be angry about my criticism. This book is an attempt to solve the problems facing the world of accounting instead of denying their existence. On completion of my book on the "rebus" concept, one experienced certified public accountant wrote to me that "Your great achievement is not the demonstration of weaknesses, but the indication of solutions."

I already know that there is bitter opposition to my ideas in many quarters. So of course I expect to be contradicted. The guardians of tradition are invited to try and argue convincingly against me, and if they succeed I shall withdraw the views put forward here.

I started to write this book almost by chance following a conversation with one of my neighbors. Good neighbors are a great blessing, and in this respect I have indeed been blessed. One of my good neighbors is Poul Lodberg, a judge in the Danish High Court (Eastern Division) in Copenhagen. When I finished a book on the management accounting of the future in 1987, I started to focus on the pair of concepts *solvency/insolvency*, which are familiar in commercial law but somewhat less familiar in accounting theory. In recent years there have been an unfortunate number of unforeseen financial collapses in the business community, all resulting in legal action being taken. I asked Poul Lodberg what such occurrences looked like seen from the point of view of a judge. He answered my questions with great patience, and his interest was aroused when I mentioned that the accounting specialists of the future would be able to use modern technology to provide early warnings of incipient suspension of payments.

I explained my ideas, and Poul Lodberg said "That sounds very interesting. In fact, if you can write a book about how to predict insolvency in such a way that lawyers can understand it and accept its usefulness, then you will have produced nothing less than a sensation."

I asked him whether he was serious, and he said he was. He meant it quite literally. We parted, and I spent several days pondering the issue. I knew other lawyers who did not consider themselves to be accounting experts, and I knew they understood the term "owners' equity" to be a direct expression of the value present in enterprises.

I had long been aware of the fact that people simply misunderstand each other when talking about the financial position of enterprises. Professional managers, lawyers and accounting specialists often apply entirely different meanings to exactly the same terms. This alone is the cause of a huge amount of confusion. But my conversation with Poul Lodberg was decisive.

My conclusion was that if competent, realistic lawyers really felt that it would be a sensation to be able to systematically and scientifically predict insolvency, then it was certainly worth my while to spend a couple of years working on the subject. Sensations are like miracles—ordinary people find them difficult to produce, and they take time. But every now and then new ideas make a breakthrough and acquire importance. After more than five years of testing the new theory, I am now convinced that insolvency can be discovered at a very early stage, providing that proper accounts are kept.

But readers must judge for themselves whether this book really is a sensation. Sensation is a big word, and it is easy to be afraid of it. In this book I describe, criticize and suggest improvements of a system of information that has remained unchanged for 500 years. I base my theories on modern scientific theory, and in particular on Russel L. Ackoff (definitions and measurements) and Karl Popper (testing of hypotheses). The book outlines a method used to describe solvency. The method is reproducible—in other words, it produces the same results in identical conditions no matter who uses it. And this is certainly not true of the procedures currently used in accounting all over the world.

Readers must now decide for themselves whether the accounting theory presented here is of any use. My suggestions come with the best intentions, and naturally I hope that readers will feel them convincing. I should like to express the warmest thanks to everyone who has shown interest in my efforts, and spent their valuable time and energy on commenting and discussing the points raised.

And now: Welcome to an attempt to describe a new era in the history of accounting.

Improving Accounting Reliability

1 INNOVATION DEPENDS ON KEEN DEBATE

Without courage there cannot be truth, and without truth
there can be no other virtue.

—*Sir Walter Scott*

The French philosopher René Descartes wanted to base his theories on
foundations that were absolutely reliable, so he started by denying everything apart from the phrase "Cogito Ergo Sum" ("I think therefore I am").
And Karl Popper, a more modern philosopher, may well have found inspiration in Descartes when expressing his skepticism and criticism of scientific methods. Popper presents researchers with the apparently paradoxical
demand that they should seek to contradict their own theories. But on
closer study, Popper's rigid demands appear to be not paradoxical after all,
but rather an expression of a sound, logical attitude. Theories or methods
that are incapable of withstanding criticism probably contain defects. Researchers must be more critical than anyone else. Far too many so-called "scientific" explanations have reflected delusions and wishful thinking, at the
cost of enormous human and material resources. Consequently, we shall
start by denying that there is any such thing as scientific accounting theory.
The accounting theory that we know at present has been in a state of what
can only be described in brief as deep, dogmatic torpor. It is currently
bogged down in a system of thought that is sterile, closed and stagnant. But
the world around us is changing fast, and the limits of accounting and
other branches of science are constantly being expanded. The accounting
theory with which we have been familiar until now could well be a theory
that (as a science) is still *primitive* and *confused*.

This assessment of current accounting theory may well sound too cate-
gorical, harsh and destructive, and may even give offense to many people
involved in the world of accounting today.

But the assessment is necessary nonetheless. It is the inevitable conclusion that readers with knowledge of (and respect for) logic must surely
draw when they consider the views propounded by two greatly respected
researchers. These two views about accounting and the theory of science
and cognition are described forthwith, and readers are invited to use them
as premises from which to draw their own conclusions.

The first view represents the world of accounting itself, and is propounded by an internationally oriented (and internationally respected) theorist. It concerns the theory of accounting, its practice and the nature of its
doctrine, and it runs as follows:

1. *The practice* of accounting primarily serves the purpose of meeting formal legal (and particularly fiscal) requirements, but provides no objective
   scale of values for the choice of optimum or satisfactory decisions. The
   structure of modern accounting serves to protect company shareholders
   very little, but to a greater extent it is designed to meet the financial (and
   often personal) interests of small groups of people such as trade and
   employer associations, majority shareholders and individual members of
   the management, and to suit the convenience of accountants.

2. *The theory* of accounting is constructed in the form of dogmatic
   scaffolding rather than a scientific framework. The common foundation of microeconomic and macroeconomic aspects of income and
   capital has not been given proper attention or presented adequately,
   and empirical hypotheses have not been tested satisfactorily. As a
   result, accounting theory is now unable to provide the most appropriate systems of registration and control at any time to meet specific, well-defined purposes.

3. *The academic/educational aspects* of accounting place far too much
   emphasis on technical issues, and fail to include modern scientific
   results in traditional theories of the circulation of capital. Students
   are given no help to interpret the theory of accounting using recent
   contributions from behavioral and organizational research, modern
   logic, cognitive theory and mathematics. Students are given knowledge that is related to the past, but that is not sufficiently flexible to
   make it satisfactory for use in the future, with all its analytical models, computers and simulation systems.[1]

The third item in this sharply worded and highly critical assessment
makes the point that the focus of current accounting is placed on yesterday,
on *the past*. Naturally, attempts have been made to practice accounting as
a science for many years, but unfortunately these attempts have largely
been in vain until now. Quite simply, there is no connection between

accounting and the theory of cognition. Accounting still lacks basic theories and concepts, and as a result the language of accounting cannot be viewed as a logical and consistent language that realistically describes the world we live in.

The second view expresses the idea that there are mutual connections between the theory of cognition and the sciences, and tells us something fundamental about the importance of philosophy for science, and for the eternally vital distinction that needs to be made between sciences and pseudosciences. This view is brief and extremely precise: "Theory of cognition without contact to science becomes an empty shell. And science without theory of cognition is (insofar as it can be conceived at all) primitive and confused."[2]

The first view is propounded by Professor Richard Mattessich in *Die Wissenschaftlichen Grundlagen des Rechnungswesens*, a book whose contents we shall return to later. And the second view is that of the physician and philosopher Albert Einstein, one of the greatest geniuses of the twentieth century.

The two views can be summarized as follows:

1. Until now, accounting as a science has lacked a foundation in the theory of cognition.
2. Science without the theory of cognition is (insofar as it can be conceived at all) primitive and confused.

Readers can draw their own conclusion, and are welcome to contradict the premises on which this conclusion is based if possible. It certainly seems unlikely that this assessment of accounting theory and practice will be acceptable to everyone.

This is the first (but by no means the last) time readers may feel challenged by the contents of this book, which goes directly against the accounting theory that has prevailed until now, and directly against the helpless, powerless practice of modern accounting that is the result of the primitive and confused theory on which it is based.

Nobody can deny that the lack of an accounting theory that cannot be called primitive and confused represents an extremely serious practical problem. In particular, accountants themselves suffer from this lack, and are frequently exposed to criticism when events reveal that financial statements that have been presented are entirely inadequate and untrustworthy.

Such criticism of financial statements is often directed at the people involved rather than at the actual problems of accounting, and the question is whether this is entirely fair. Accounting specialists have been called untrustworthy, but this is probably too hasty a condemnation. It is probably more likely that it is *the current practice of accounting itself* that is untrustworthy, not necessarily the accountants involved. And if certain individuals *do* need to be criticized, then perhaps the researchers who are the theorists of accounting should shoulder part of the responsibility for the fact that things have so often gone wrong in the world of accounting in recent years. The problem may well have its roots in the primitive and confused theory of accounting that has prevailed until now.

This book is based on a single new, basic idea that was discovered in 1984. The idea can be expressed as a hypothesis: Financial statements represent systematic assertions that can and should logically be regarded as a *prediction of payments*, instead of being regarded as "financial history" (as accounting theory has suggested until now). In other words, financial statements should be regarded as representing systematic statements regarding payments of *the future*, not payments of *the past*.

Making statements about the future means making predictions, and in order to make predictions you have to act in relation to whatever is being predicted. Action in relation to something that has been predicted implies helping to ensure that certain future events come to pass if they are desirable, and are avoided if they are undesirable. Financial statements that say something about the future thus become an instrument for the actions of management, making it possible to use them for *accounting for responsible management*.

As mentioned earlier, this new theory of accounting basically offers a prediction of payments, *not* "financial history."

Please note the use of the word "not." It indicates that battle is soon to be joined—but it is to be hoped that we shall find ourselves on the same side! In logic the word "not" is used to distinguish between things, to make limits and reveal differences. In saying "A is not B" you are making a precise, clear distinction with no exceptions. Three is not five. Night is not day. A prediction is not a description of the past.

A new theory of accounting which says that financial statements should be a prediction contradicts the old theory. And the fact that the theory being contradicted is well-established and time-honored all over the world means that it is probably impossible to avoid conflict.

The guardians of accounting tradition will probably be outraged at the following claim, which may well seem highly provocative, but which is in fact a simple description of the current situation: It is possible to claim and prove that in terms of scientific cognition and method, the accounting theory of today is still at the same stage of development as medicine was more than 200 years ago. Accounting exists, and it is recognized as a branch of science. It is also regarded as an important science for society. Systematic research and teaching in accounting take place. There is also an extensive amount of literature on accounting, and a great many accounting theories and procedures have been developed. Accounting has branched out into specialist areas, and special theories and procedures have been designed for each of these areas.

But the theories and procedures of accounting are all partial. They only cover certain limited areas. The theories are often expressed in unclear terms, and often contradict each other. The procedures are apparently rational and logical, but lack a precise, reliable base in scientific method. There is an obvious and widespread doubt and lack of clarity with regard to the basic theories and definitions of accounting. And it is possible to claim and prove that problems that are still regarded extremely seriously by accounting theorists are actually hollow pseudoproblems that no one should be wasting his time on.

Society develops and changes very rapidly, and accounting specialists are constantly being faced with new tasks and problems. But we accounting theorists have not even been able to suggest good solutions to old, painfully familiar problems. There is no point in denying that the situation is characterized by powerlessness.

The terrible credibility crisis currently facing the world of accounting can only be explained by blaming the impotent theory on which modern accounting is based. Quite simply, accounting has lost its relevance, its contact with reality. The accounting theorists who are still satisfied with the old theories are like people discussing the correct color of the wallpaper while their house burns down around them. And the few accounting theorists with the courage to apply traditional theories in practice are sometimes badly hurt by the result. The fact is that accounting theory and the real world have drifted very far apart. Accounting theory does not fit reality, and reality does not fit accounting theory. But many accounting theorists still seem to believe that it is reality which has something wrong with it.

In the course of this book, readers will discover that a number of analogies are drawn to other branches of science. Let us try drawing such an analogy now, using the medical science of the past and its lack of insight and method as our example. As late as the cholera epidemic of 1853, doctors were still debating whether cholera was a disease that was *contagious* or *miasmatic*. Contagious diseases were defined as diseases that were transmitted by physical contact, while miasmatic diseases were transmitted by "toxic" or "bad" air.

Doctors believed that it was vital to clear up the issue of whether cholera was contagious or miasmatic, because clarification might make it possible to treat this serious but inexplicable disease. Doctors could see that people fell ill owing to cholera, that it spread rapidly and that it cost a great number of lives. But no one knew the cause of the disease, so no one knew how to treat it.

A description of cholera was regarded as vital, and this description had to be expressed using the familiar, respected terminology of the time. For instance, doctors already thought they knew that malaria was miasmatic (mal aria equals bad air). Discussions among doctors had been going on for centuries, and were documented by a great number of penetrating theories and extensive literature. Some doctors believed that cholera was contagious, others miasmatic, and naturally the two parties denied the truth of each other's claims. There were also many different ways of treating patients suffering from cholera. The cures were applied with great enthusiasm and care, but unfortunately the patients still died.

Then in 1883 it was discovered that cholera was spread by the cholera bacillus present in contaminated drinking water, and for the first time the disease had a scientific, straightforward and comprehensible explanation. The microscope enabled people to study cholera bacilli, and experiments proved that the new explanation was correct. But the most important thing was that the explanation indicated an easy course of action to solve the problem. Boiling drinking water killed the bacilli, thereby preventing cholera.

It was also discovered that malaria was not after all miasmatic, but that it was transmitted by mosquitoes. Once again a scientific, straightforward and comprehensible explanation had been found, and once again action could be taken to solve the problem (eradicate mosquitoes, and you eradicate malaria).

Medical science gradually achieved new understanding. Fewer and fewer doctors spent their time discussing the contagious/miasmatic nature of diseases. It was realized that these words actually reflected *speculations* about reality, instead of focusing on *observations* of reality. Instead of being certain of knowing anything, doctors started learning new things that contradicted old knowledge. This is what happens every time scientific progress is made. The old "knowledge" crumbles, and is given a new name: "dogma." Dogma is belief that is accepted without criticism.

The accounting practice that is accepted and applied internationally at present is still a fertile field of dogma. The business of accounting, in the words of Richard Mattessich, is characterized by its use of "dogma and myths, masks and cosmetics" to an extent that is fortunately not encountered in many other fields in which professional knowledge is formed, maintained and used.

Doctors took cholera very seriously because it cost a lot of human lives. It was seen as a big and important problem for society. And recently, accounting specialists have been noticing an increasing number of inexplicable deaths among companies in the private sector—companies that died even though they seemed healthy enough. The financial statements that were supposed to reflect the situation of these companies turned out to be completely misleading, and a great number of human and financial resources were lost. Like cholera, this situation is a major problem for society.

For centuries, doctors debated whether diseases were contagious or miasmatic, and the accounting theorists of the present day debate "concepts of profit" and the "information value" of these concepts. It is assumed that interim financial statements are more or less "informative" in relation to various "information requirements" attributed to various "interested parties." The choice of the term "concept of profit" excludes other terms, and the appearance of the balance sheet is thus affected by this choice.

Here is an example. Various forms of "fixed assets" are included in balance sheets, and these are traditionally divided into "tangible," "intangible" and "financial" fixed assets. When you vary the "profit" you also vary these assets, and vice versa.

As we shall see, the most serious problem in the world of accounting in terms of cognition is that no one has yet been able to define the concepts of "assets" and "liabilities" in a scientifically reliable way. No one has yet been able to present a *complete, consistent, necessary* and *sufficient* definition of the concept we call an "asset." And concepts "fixed assets" that are not defined must be regarded as being undefined.

In other words, current accounting theory tells us that the balance sheets included in financial statements contain something undefined and "tangible," something undefined and "intangible" and something undefined and "financial."

Unfortunately, these terms are not suitable tools for solving problems—and yet they are used as such. Naturally, students are forced to learn all about the concepts used in a balance sheet, because they are part of time-honored accounting theory. If you are unable to repeat the names of the concepts mentioned in your textbook and repeat the comments contained therein, you will fail your exam. And if you fail your exam, you will never be regarded as an accounting specialist. It is that simple.

But students who try to apply the aforementioned, undefined concepts to formulate and solve problems will not get very far. There are many examples of frustrated students of accounting trying bravely but in vain to learn concepts, understand them and apply them in practice.

But at the moment the theorists are still engaged in considering theories about "interim financial statements," "profit," and other "interim result" concepts. As accounting experts know, there are many different "profit concepts." Many different terms are used to describe the items in a balance sheet, and a wealth of literature is available to document all these subtle terms and concepts. The concepts mentioned here have been in use for many years, and are still taken seriously by theorists.

However, these "profit concepts" and names of balance sheet items all have the same qualities as contagious and miasmatic diseases: *They are products of speculation and belief, not of scientific cognition and observation of reality.*

It is reasonable to call accounting theory primitive and confused, and this assessment can be supported. Accounting theory has not yet demonstrated (or even hinted at) any clear, logical and comprehensible connection between concepts and procedures, for example, between ideas about the nature of problems and ideas about specific activities to solve these problems.

Some readers may regard this assessment as unduly harsh, but anyone in disagreement should be able to disprove the statements previously made, and disprove them convincingly. Where in accounting theory is there any description of the connection between basic concepts, descriptions of reality, and procedures?

Actually, it seems strange that a subject like accounting should give rise to such enormous problems and place people at such a loss. Most nonaccountants probably wonder why it has been possible to turn the idea that *in the long run company income should preferably be larger than expenses* into a branch of science.

But no one can deny that practicing accountants are facing major unsolved problems, and no one can deny that accounting theory has not yet been convincing in its attempts to solve these problems by developing increasingly sophisticated definitions of the concepts of profit and interim results.

Sometimes the simplest of statements and questions are the best. Let us therefore repeat what most accounting theorists and practicing accountants have agreed about for many years: Unless you sell your entire company, it is logically impossible to obtain a precise (i.e., a scientifically reliable) expression of the "profit" or "result" for a given period in terms of an amount of money. So it is also meaningless to continue to speculate about traditional "interim financial statements" and their degree of "information value." Quite simply, it is a waste of time.

Let us ask the following simple question: Could we survive without the concept of profit? This book gives the answer "Yes, easily." And we would actually be better off without this concept, because there would be less to discuss and disagree about. In the future we can replace traditional, unclear delayed interim financial statements with something that is far preferable: Modern management accounting. We can replace the flat, lifeless, static picture of accounting that we have grown accustomed to with analogous, dynamic management accounting that shows us the financial situation *right now*, not the financial situation as of January 31st last year. And we can base this new type of accounting on a few clear, comprehensible basic concepts with which almost all readers will already be familiar. The old pen and paper that used to be sufficient to make double entry bookkeeping work in practice are no longer good enough. Nowadays we need tools that are far more powerful, because a great amount of calculation is necessary, and a great amount of data involved. So we must use the new information technology. We need modern, basic registration and updating techniques, and we need rapid and unambiguous communication.

How is it possible for the equity capital in company financial statements to disappear like dew before the sun from one moment to the next, leaving a considerable negative balance? It is no answer to say that this is due to a change in accounting principles from "going concern" to "realization value." The fact is that this "answer" does not solve the problem. It simply describes the problem using different, more complicated words.

Attorneys use the concept of *solvency* to express a company's ability to pay its bills. As we shall see later on in this book, it is no contradiction to claim that a solvent company is also a financially problem-free company for its creditors. The problems of creditors arise only when a company becomes *insolvent* instead of being *solvent*. The sooner the onset of insolvency can be discovered, the better the chances of avoiding or restricting the losses incurred. It must be possible to express the concept of solvency precisely as the difference between assets and liabilities, and this point will be amplified in a later section. The concept of solvency and its logical opposite, insolvency, are absolutely key issues in both accounting and company law.

And yet the problem of solvency/insolvency is not described in depth anywhere in traditional accounting theory. In fact, the problem is only dealt with in relatively neutral descriptions and unprocessed texts copied from the language of the law.

Some accounting theorists may claim that they have dealt with the concept of insolvency in reports claiming to be able to predict future insolvency using more or less sophisticated mathematical/statistical reproductions of figures taken from previous periods. But such "predictions" are impossible to carry out, claims modern philosophy. The figures can be worked out, of course. But they are meaningless for the simple reason that the world outside (and thus the conditions on which the predictions are based) unfortunately changes constantly in ways that cannot be predicted.

Traditional accounting theory is completely helpless when the world changes, and when the object of the description is changing, developing, alive and dynamic. There is something basically wrong with the "knowledge" we claim to possess in accounting theory. The "knowledge" possessed by accounting specialists is purely professional in nature. It is expressed in professional language using words and expressions that are virtually incomprehensible to the layman. And it has been kept within a closed system for far too long. It is high time we removed the boundaries between the world of the accounting specialist and the world of other professionals, who have such an acute need for knowledge about the financial situation of both the public and private sectors. Everyone who needs such financial knowledge also needs knowledge of financial statements.

The use of modern technology and a gradual transition to the "information society" lie ahead. This change, which we are witnessing during the second half of the twentieth century, will pave the way for entirely new opportunities when it comes to rapid, practical problem solving in the world of accounting. These exciting new opportunities can be expressed precisely as follows: We have been used to taking our problems to specialists who have the necessary knowledge and information. In the future, the reverse process will be possible: We shall be able to bring the necessary knowledge and information to the problems.

Traditionally, a classic distinction is made between so-called "expert" knowledge and "general" knowledge. But the problem of the modern world is that the amount of available information (and thus the amount of available knowledge) is growing all the time at increasing speed. The old world picture is rapidly becoming outdated. The myth of "the omniscient specialist" must now be abandoned, and specialists themselves should be the ones most grateful for this.

The aim of this book is to make a resolute, energetic attempt to break the closed, rigid and professionally barren mold of traditional accounting theory. The result of the attempt may be negative, but this risk has been carefully considered and allowed for.

But the attempt may have a positive outcome, and if so a new era in the history of accounting will begin. We need to establish an accounting theory that cannot be described as primitive and confused. Consequently, we need to establish a cognitive foundation for accounting, a branch of science that will continue to describe the financial consequences of our actions in the international society of the future.

After all, even a child can see that the financial statements that we are still forced to accept as the only legislative (and thus the only systematic) source of information about the financial situation of a company *simply cannot be reliable* (and could indeed be directly misleading) at the time when they are presented. The balance sheet that people claim reflects the assets and liabilities of a company is drawn up by taking a copy of the updated financial accounts on a specific date (the end of the accounting period). This copy is described as the "trial balance," and following a number of so-called "subsequent items," the financial statements are claimed to give "a true and fair view" at the balance sheet date. But even if it were possible to produce a completely true and fair picture on a given date, the figures obtained would be meaningless because the day after the trial balance is calculated, the financial situation of the company concerned is different. Everyone knows that the world around us is changing fast, and huge and significant changes in outside circumstances often occur extremely quickly.

So naturally, the balance sheet is out of date the day after it is produced, and a couple of weeks later the situation of the company may well be completely different. The strategy of the company may have changed, and new purchase/sale contracts may have been signed. New opportunities and risks that were not predicted on the balance sheet date may have arisen.

The most important tasks of the management are to make well-founded decisions about the opportunities of the future, and to formulate strategy. We live in an age in which change and development must be regarded as the normal state of affairs. So it is no longer possible to claim (with any basis in logic and science) that the static accounting theory and practice of today provide any information that is of the slightest value to anyone.

Accounting specialists are aware of this fact. In practice, accountants seek to compensate for the out-of-date nature of company financial statements by drawing up rules stating that the annual report must contain information about any significant changes occurring since the balance sheet date. But accountants who try to apply these rules are only placing the rope of untrustworthiness around their own necks. The day after they have visited a company and ascertained with great care that a new situation has arisen, this situation has changed once again.

If you ask a scientist how to describe *change* and *development* reliably, the answer will be that any such description must be *dynamic*. Time is the decisive element, without which no such description is possible. And the variable elements in a dynamic model do not coincide in terms of time.

So *time* is the vital element of all financial control. And this vital element is completely lacking in traditional accounting models. In the rest of this book we shall take a closer look at the practical and theoretical potential of *dynamic management accounting*. Economics involves metabolism, life, growth and change. The "true and fair picture" of a company's financial position should be a realistic reflection of the actual situation. Therefore, the true and fair picture must also be a *living* picture.

NOTES

1. R. Mattessich, *Die Wissenschaftlichen Grundlagen*, p. 17.
2. J. Witt-Hansen, *Filosofi*, p. 5.

2   ACCOUNTING AND THE LOSS OF REALITY

For Time will teach thee soon the truth,
There are no birds in last year's nest.

—*Henry Wadsworth Longfellow*

The word "relevance" can be defined as "importance" in a given context. And if this definition is accepted, then accounting (which should be one of the most practical subjects of all) has lost its relevance. International accounting researchers claim that the connection between accounting and reality has been lost beyond recall, and that the traditional accounting model has outlived its usefulness and demonstrated its impotence on more than one occasion. The tragic consequence of this fact is that managers (i.e., users of financial statements) often have to make decisions blindfolded. Traditional accounting systems are inadequate. They provide no useful, up-to-date information at all, which is why managers have to act without the benefit of such information, resulting all too often in disaster. The financial statements with which we are currently familiar are incomprehensible, and they are always presented too late. They are incomprehensible because they are based on incomplete or entirely absent logic, and they are too late because they are tied to specific bookkeeping procedures that force accounting specialists to delay the information they contain. One leading accounting theorist claims that despite its huge importance for modern society, accounting is still being practiced blindfolded, with no basic principles, without logic and without a scientific foundation. Managers are expected to take responsibility, and yet they are forced into a pattern of behavior that has been aptly described as short-term and opportunistic. There is an acute, even desperate need for new ideas.

Accounting has lost its relevance, its connection with reality. There is an urgent need to reconsider the basic (but unfortunately largely unsolved) problems of accounting in a new and critical light, using modern scientific theory and modern information technology. There is also an urgent need to draw up new, up-to-date management accounting systems for use in practice. This is the basic message of a book published in 1987 and written by H. Thomas Johnson and Robert S. Kaplan, two American professors of accounting (the latter at the prestigious Harvard Business School).

The title of the book, which claims this loss of relevance and connection with reality combines the titles of two world famous books.

The first of these is John Milton's *Paradise Lost*. Milton (1608–74) was one of the most famous Renaissance poets in England. In his book, published in 1667, he tried to give his readers new awareness about the times they were living in by comparing the loose or absent morals of the mid-seventeenth century with the situation that led to the expulsion from Paradise in the Bible.

The other world famous book is far more recent, and deals with a period of the twentieth century that only lasted twelve years, but which led to a war that cost incalculable suffering and more than 50 million lives. Its title is *The Rise and Fall of the Third Reich*. It was written by the American journalist, radio correspondent and historian William Shirer, and published in 1960.

The titles of these two famous books have been combined in the title of Johnson and Kaplan's book about the problems of modern accounting, thereby influencing the expectations of readers. It is called *Relevance Lost. The Rise and Fall of Management Accounting*.

It is interesting that the authors have thought up this unusual and highly descriptive title, which uses two familiar descriptions of huge problems and processes to describe the world of accounting. Most people regard accounting as being necessary for modern society, but also as being unfortunately complicated, bound by tradition, with an authoritarian and dogmatic image, bone-dry, closed, lifeless, extremely boring and thus of absolutely no interest to anyone other than those who practice it.

In an article published in 1984 entitled "The Evolution of Management Accounting," Robert S. Kaplan points out that the world of accounting is rigid, stagnant and barren, and he underlines this state of affairs in the following statement: "Virtually all of the practices employed by firms today and explicated in leading cost accounting textbooks had been developed by 1925." In 1925 almost all data processing was done manually. There were a few primitive mechanical calculators and typewriters, but these machines were relatively expensive, and few could afford them. Modern data processing techniques lay far in the future. Most people were forced to depend on the mathematical and writing skills of trusted individuals. Punch card machines had been invented in the United States before the turn of the century, but the development of these machines took a long time, using the primitive technology available at the time. So in 1925 punch card machines were only used by the very few, and the electronic data processing and data communication that would develop in the second half of the twentieth century were naturally quite unknown.

Most readers will surely agree that it is preferable that accounting specialists (i.e., accounts managers or accountants) be good at counting and writing. After all, the very word "accounting" is derived from the verb "to count." But the theories of accounting—the foundations on which the subject is based—have remained largely unaffected by the revolutionary developments in information technology witnessed during the past 40 to 50 years. These developments, and the new opportunities they have brought to the world of accounting, could well mean that the old, traditional theories of accounting are now outdated.

The following excerpt from the aforementioned article published in 1984 shows clearly that in Kaplan's view there is a basic misconception in current accounting theory. And misconceptions are problems of cognition. This excerpt shows the impotence of current accounting theory in the modern world: "It is unlikely that our current accounting graduates will have any understanding of the complex production environment in which cost accounting must be applied today. Future manufacturing processes will be even more unfamiliar to them as firms invest in computer controlled machinery, including Flexible Manufacturing Systems, (Computer Aided Design/Computer Aided Manufacturing) CAD/CAM and robots, for their production processes."[1]

Let us now turn our attention to Kaplan and Johnson's new book on the loss of relevance of accounting. The unusual, distinctive title gives the reader associations with the loss of something important that might be regained on new, modern terms (Relevance Lost), and also indicates that the reality known until now has had its day, and has now fallen so far that no one wishes it back (The Rise and Fall). The title may well indicate that a complete rethink is necessary.

We need look no further than the preface of Kaplan and Johnson's book for an assessment of traditional accounting. The preface states that the accounting systems known today are completely inadequate. The requirements made on accounting these days are far too great for the systems used, and accounting systems can no longer meet these requirements: "In this time of rapid technological change, vigorous global and domestic competition, and enormously expanding information processing capabilities, management accounting systems are not providing useful, timely information for the process control, product costing, and performance evaluation activities of managers."[2]

This sentence alone is a crushing condemnation of traditional accounting. It points out that managers need information that is useful and up-to-date, and underlines the fact that accounting systems do not provide this useful and up-to-date information for managers, who are thus forced to act without it.

This problem is not new, but it has grown increasingly visible and incontrovertible in recent years. Many different requirements have been made of accounting systems over the years, and it hardly seems strange that such practical requirements have also had a great impact on the development and prioritization of new theories. The fact that users of accounting systems have had different requirements over the years has forced accounting theorists to define a great number of different "accounting objectives," and to relate these objectives to each other. But the task has been far from easy, and misunderstandings have been unavoidable.

European (and particularly Scandinavian and German) developments in the accounting theories of the twentieth century have been influenced greatly by the German theorist Eugen Schmalenbach, who established his *accounts code theories* as long ago as the 1920s (theories that are still in use and in evidence in modern German accounting literature). The basic assumption of these theories is that accounting material is a necessary— and therefore indispensable—source of information in dealing with a wide range of tasks (monitoring and control of payments from customers, calculation and control of payments to suppliers, lenders, the tax authorities, shareholders and so on). But accounting data can also be a valuable source of information for the management itself (calculation and pricing, planning, control of financial results and so on).

In other words, Schmalenbach described a number of accounting tasks that *had to be dealt with* (exchange of payments with people outside the company), as well as a number of tasks that *could and should be dealt with* (information useful for the company management). In order to meet the information requirements of managers, it was necessary (as a minimum) to adjust and develop the basic registration used to ensure that all necessary payments were made and documented. But naturally, one system could not simply be replaced by the other. The information needed to control and document payments was indispensable. The basic registration used to provide this absolutely vital information was (and still is) always arranged according to the rules of double entry bookkeeping.

As mentioned earlier, data processing technology was still in its absolute infancy in the 1920s. So in order to meet the information requirements of management, Schmalenbach was forced to suggest *copying* the basic data of "financial accounting" in a special, new "management information system," which was given the name "cost accounting." This new system always used the basic data of financial accounting, but organized this data in new ways aimed at covering the aforementioned specific management requirements.

Naturally, it is vital that data is copied accurately from one system to the other. But in those days there were no reliable automatic means of doing this. The solution to this problem was inevitable. The distinguishing feature of the rules of double entry bookkeeping was that they ensured excellent "built-in" data security by balancing the books by means of the T-shaped debit/credit account. So it was decided that the data of management accounting should also be presented in the form of an account. In this way two comparable (but not always equally common) accounting systems arose:

1. The eternally necessary (and thus indispensable) *financial accounting*, kept in order to control and document the exchange of payments between the enterprise concerned and the outside world. This system was given the name of "financial accounting" in the accounting literature of Scandinavia, and ever since 1494 financial accounting has been organized according to the rules of double entry bookkeeping.
2. Supplementary *management accounting*, which can be drawn up and presented specifically with a view to covering the requirements of management for data in connection with financial control. This system was given the name of "cost accounting" (and subsequently "internal accounting") in Scandinavian accounting literature. A great number of attempts have been made to establish the theoretical and practical basis of management accounting.

Let us repeat that these two subsystems are identical in terms of the basic data used, and that the division into two separate systems was originally due solely to the lack of sufficiently advanced techniques of data processing. And then let us return to Johnson and Kaplan and their views on the lost relevance of traditional accounting: "it is the decline in relevance of corporate management accounting systems that is the recent phenomenon. Accounting systems for managerial decisions and control can be traced back to the origins of hierarchical enterprises in the nineteenth century. Unencumbered by any demands for external reporting, management accounting practices developed and flourished in the wide variety of nineteenth century corporations. Only in the past sixty to seventy years have external auditing and financial reporting systems come to perform the original function of management accounting systems."[3]

Naturally, Americans also use double entry bookkeeping, a system that has such formal strength that accounting experts quite simply regard it as a necessary, indeed indispensable, tool for all accounting, no matter whom the information is intended for. Another important question worth asking is whether double entry bookkeeping is logically sufficient as a measuring tool. We shall return to this question later on.

Johnson and Kaplan summarize the inadequacies of traditional accounting in the following succinct, damning fashion: "Today's management accounting information driven by the procedures and cycle of the organization's financial reporting system, is too late, too aggregated, and too distorted to be relevant for managers' planning and control decisions."[4]

This is the same as claiming that financial statements are out-of-date, unclear and incomprehensible, which is why traditional accounting in general is unreliable. This kind of judgment certainly says something significant about the impotence of traditional accounting. Three important consequences of this impotence are mentioned by Johnson and Kaplan.

The first consequence is the paradox that traditional accounting uses the management, instead of the management using accounting, which must have been the intention of drawing up financial statements in the first place: "Management accounting reports are of little help to operating managers as they attempt to reduce costs and improve productivity. Frequently, the reports decrease productivity because they require operating managers to spend time attempting to understand and explain reported variances that have little to do with the economic and technological reality of their operations. By not providing timely and detailed information on process efficiencies or by focusing on inputs such as direct labor that are relatively insignificant in today's production environment, the management accounting system not only fails to provide relevant information to managers, but it also distracts their attention from factors that are critical for production efficiencies."[5]

Accounting reports are thus presented as being *directly harmful* because they distract the attention of managers. In general, managers are not interested in the so-called "management information" provided by traditional financial statements, which are difficult or even impossible to interpret. Managers are not, in general, accounting experts themselves, so they do not usually determine the design of accounting reports or the period covered. And if nonspecialist managers ask for certain figures from a financial statement, and suggest the figures they need, they are often met with polite refusal and an explanation that "The information you want is not what you need." Trained accountants are naturally regarded as experts in their field, and they even have the weight of tradition on their side. Financial statements observe the guidelines with regard to form and content that have been the only ones available since 1925 (and even since 1494).

But the information required by managers cannot be found in traditional financial statements. The second of the three consequences of the impotence of traditional accounting is described by Johnson and Kaplan as follows: "The management accounting system also fails to provide accurate product cost data. Costs are distributed to products by simplistic and arbitrary measures, usually direct-labor based, that do not represent the demands made by each product on the firm's resources. Although simplistic product costing methods are adequate for financial reporting requirements—the methods yield values for inventory and for cost of goods that satisfy external reporting and auditing requirements—the methods systematically bias and distort costs of individual products. The standard product cost system typical of most organizations usually leads to enormous cross subsidies across products. When such distorted information represents the only available data on "product costs," the danger exists for misguided decisions on product pricing, product sourcing, product mix and responses to rival products. Many firms seem to be falling victim to the danger."[6]

This is a real condemnation of the familiar, so-called "standard cost accounting." The term "standard costs" implies norms of time and material consumption that have already been studied, measured and commented upon. These norms are now regarded as "standard" elements of cost in financial statements, particularly those of industrial companies involved in series or mass production. By combining the "old" and "new" prices of materials and wages, it is now possible, after production has been completed, to present a completely itemized production cost report, making it possible to trace discrepancies between predicted and actual events. Such reports make it possible to locate such discrepancies and discover whether they were due to price deviations, waste, defective production or other factors.

Kaplan and other authors have indicated that these ideas can be traced right back to the start of this century, when production processes, although standardized, were still largely manual or only partly mechanized. This meant that production processes were characterized by a lack of homogeneity and frequent defects or breakdowns. But in the 1990s and the future, production processes are not merely automatic, but actually controlled by computers that make virtually no errors at all once they have been properly installed and adjusted.

Modern technology is characterized by CAD/CAM, production robots, automatic quality control, and the "just-in-time" production philosophy. In this brave new world, standard cost accounting is a thing of the past, and is of little interest. And yet Kaplan writes that this obsolete accounting system is still regarded as being useful in research and teaching circles, that it produces "distorted" information when used in practice and finally, that this distorted information is the only information available to managers. The consequence of this is that vital decisions regarding price and discount policy, the composition of product ranges and the replacement of old products by new ones are made blindfolded. The information given to managers is useless, but it is the only information they have at their disposal.

The third consequence of the impotence of traditional accounting is that the current structure of accounting systems forces managers into what Kaplan elsewhere describes as *short-term, opportunistic behavior.* Demands are made for better financial results in both the private and public sectors. In the private sector the demand is for better "profitability," which can be achieved by increasing income and/or reducing expenses. In the public sector, as most people know, the demand is that "cuts" should be made. But what exactly are "profitability" and "cuts"? Is short-term or long-term profitability the aim? This distinction, where time is the critical factor, is not entirely without significance: "Finally, the manager's horizons contract to the short-term cycle of the monthly profit and loss statement. The financial accounting systems treat many cash outlays as expenses of the period in which they are made even though these outlays will benefit future periods. Discretionary cash outlays for new products and improved processes, for preventive maintenance, for long-term marketing positioning, for employee training and morale and for developing new systems can produce substantial cash inflows for the future. Managers under pressure to meet short-term profit goals can, on occasion, achieve these goals by reducing their expenditures in such discretionary investments. Thus, short-term profit pressures can lead to a decrease in long-term investment. Yet monthly accounting statements using the practices mandated for external reporting can signal increased profits even when the long-term economic health of the firm has been compromised."[7]

As the reader will realize, Johnson and Kaplan are not seeking merely to identify a few minor ailments in the theory or practice of accounting, or to present a new variation of (or new additions to) current accounting theory to enable it to fit a large, familiar frame of reference. No, the authors are actually preparing for an all-out assault on the accounting traditions of more than half a century. Revolution and innovation in the world of accounting are called for. These are no mere minor details. The entire framework and world picture of accounting have been fundamentally mistaken. It is high time that theoretical and practicing accountants realized that researchers in a subject whose very essence is the art of computing really should start working on the hypothesis that computers and electronic information technology in general must be incorporated into modern accounting. It is inadvisable to continue using a frame of reference whose entire world picture is anchored solidly in more than 60 years of authoritarian belief, tradition and dogma, and whose most advanced concept of tools is still the idea that the best way of performing two of the four known types of arithmetic (addition and subtraction) is by employing the services of a great number of people and large quantities of paper, pens and ink. Because these are all the tools needed to master the art of double entry bookkeeping.

Johnson and Kaplan are not the only modern theorists who have recently started to speak out openly in order to bring about innovation in the world of accounting, even though the price of such innovation may be strife and confrontation with many supporters of traditional methods. Such confrontation and strife are probably unavoidable. After all, the traditions of accounting are extremely strong.

Professor Richard Mattessich wrote of the "failure of accounting as a science" back in 1970 in his book *Die Wissenschaftlichen Grundlagen des Rechnungswesens*. In a later chapter we shall also see how the Harvard professor Robert N. Anthony demonstrates that accounting still lacks reliable basic concepts.

But even though the problems caused by the defects of accounting are serious (indeed extremely serious), there is room in Johnson and Kaplan's book for somewhat less depressing comments on the subject of the lost connection with reality. Appealing to people's sense of humor is a good way of promoting new understanding. For instance, Hans Christian Andersen's famous story of "The Emperor's New Clothes" is often used to knock figures of authority off their pedestals. In "The Emperor's New Clothes" a child is heard to remark "But he's got no clothes on," after which everyone realizes the truth of the remark and starts to see the world as it really is.

Johnson and Kaplan certainly do not lack a sense of humor. And in the midst of all their serious comment one feels they have a gleam in their eye. Anyone who is familiar with the current rules for reporting "work in progress" (and who has thought about these rules and tried to discover the sense in them) will surely derive pleasure from the following description of the information value of monthly and quarterly statements. All the people involved are anonymous, which prevents the description from being threatening to anyone. First we have to go back 500 years in time, then we must journey from Venice to India and back again with a caravan. Hopefully, the reader will be able to see the camels in his or her mind's eye: "If we go back five hundred years to the publication of perhaps the original accounting book by Frater Luca Bartolomes Pacioli, we can ask what kinds of events were occurring in fifteenth-century Venice that led to a demand for accounting information. Undoubtedly, merchants were trading goods with other countries. Consider a group of investors who acquired goods produced in northern Italy and chartered an expedition to sell them in India. With the proceeds the traders purchased tea, traveled back to Venice, and then sold the tea. At the end of the expedition, the accountant subtracted the costs of the caravan and of acquiring the initial load of merchandise from the revenues received from the sale of tea in Italy to compute a profit for the entire trip, a profit to be distributed among the investors in the venture."[8]

At a safe distance from the events of the present day, this striking example of the caravan ensures that any similarity with contemporary people and events can be regarded as accidental. No one could possibly feel insulted. And yet virtually all the characteristics of modern management are present in this story. Someone has discovered a demand and found out how to meet it in a new way. One or more merchants have seen the chance to exchange one type of goods or services with another. Demand in one place can be met by production in another, and vice versa. The business project being launched carries a considerable risk, and many people will certainly refrain from proceeding as a result. It is also certain that a lot of people will be ready to shake their heads and say "I told you so" if the project fails.

However, the risk involved can be computed to some extent, and if the project succeeds everyone will profit, including buyers, sellers, employees and investors. A capital outlay is necessary, and the best path seems to be to share the risk among several investors so any losses will be bearable for the individual. This is where the art of computing, and thus accounting itself, becomes relevant: "To compute overall profitability of the venture and to distribute the net proceeds (the retained earnings) among the initial investors was a worthwhile role for accounting. One has to wonder, however, whether the investors or the Venetian version of the Securities and Exchange Commission or Financial Accounting Standards Board also asked the accountant to compute the expedition's profits during the third quarter of 1487 when the caravan was traversing the Persian desert en route to India. Probably not. Because even 500 years ago, investors likely understood that allocating the total profits of expeditions to periods as short as three months was not a meaningful exercise. Yet is not the value of preparing monthly income statements for many of today's organizations not unlike an attempt to allocate the profits of a long venture to every month within that venture?"[9]

Who can take the so-called interim accounting theories seriously after reading this example? There is no logic in such interim statements, and therefore no sense. Let us try to make this lack of logic clear.

> Is it possible to say that a 50-year-old man living in a country in which men live an average of 75 years is 66.6 percent dead? No, such a statement would be completely nonsensical.
>
> Is it possible to say that a pregnant woman halfway through her term is bearing a child that has 50 percent of human rights? No, such a statement would be completely nonsensical.
>
> Is it possible to say that a project that is 50 percent finished in technical terms has earned 50 percent of its contribution margin? No, such a statement would be completely nonsensical.

These statements can all be tested by observation, and can be declared either true or false. Either the man is alive, or he is dead. The pregnant woman is carrying either a child or a fetus. And either the project is finished, or it is not finished.

However, it is possible to regard these examples as *predictions*, and we can try to estimate the probability of such predictions without losing a clear meaning. It is likely that the man aged 50 will live at least 25 years more if he continues to enjoy good health. It is likely that the woman will give birth to a healthy child in four and a half months' time, providing nothing is observed to indicate the reverse. And finally it is probable that the project will be completed as expected, registering a financial reward when it does so.

The statements acquire meaning when presented as predictions, because we are talking of future events, that is, events that we expect to take place, but about which we cannot be realistically certain.

But although the statements about the 66.6 percent dead man and the fetus with 50 percent of human rights are immediately recognizable as pure nonsense, it is an undeniable fact that the same kind of nonsense is taken extremely seriously by traditional accounting. Anyone doubting the truth of this claim should check the worldwide IASC (International Accounting Standards Committee) standards regarding the treatment of "work in progress" in financial statements. No questions are asked in these standards as to their logical basis. Everything seems to be permitted. It is hardly surprising therefore that people who are not accounting experts find it difficult to understand interim financial statements. Indeed, it is surprising that *anyone at all* can actually claim to understand them.

But of course we cannot do without financial statements. We need financial information, even though we appreciate that the current form of such statements is meaningless: "Arguing that it is meaningless to allocate project profitability to short periods within the life of a project does not imply that we believe it fruitless to obtain indicators of short-term progress. Returning to our Venetian expedition, there were probably many measures of the caravan's performance during the third quarter of 1487 that the investors would have been interested in knowing. For example, what distance did the caravan cover and in what direction? How many provisions were left? What was the condition of the inventory being transported? Were the workers content or rebellious? There were many potentially useful indicators of the caravan manager's performance during the third quarter of 1487. But quarterly profits was not one of them!"[10]

The current accounting models for interim reports are meaningless for the simple reason that they are based on an unclear, fictitious situation, on a proportional calculation that has no basis in reality. The conclusion must be that the prototype of the accounting model currently in use all over the world to calculate the item known as "work in progress," as well as the foundations on which so-called "interim accounts theories" are based, are clearly and logically contradictory because they assume the truth of the statement: *"The future event designated X has already partially taken place."*

In the rest of their book about the lost relevance of accounting and the rise and fall of its traditions, Johnson and Kaplan give a great number of convincing examples showing that current accounting systems are obsolete, and that they do not work as intended. They are intended to function as a tool for managers in their efforts to gain an overview of the present financial situation, and thereby to establish a basis for reliable financial control.

Johnson and Kaplan make the following significant statements, which clearly indicate that accounting theorists (i.e., researchers) must bear a good deal of responsibility for the fact that the accounting practice observed worldwide is still detached from reality and unsatisfactory. There is something fundamentally wrong in the basic attitudes of accounting theory. In order to explain reality in theoretical terms, we have been forced to simplify it. But the process of simplification itself means that the result becomes detached from reality.

Theorists can handle simplified pictures and models of reality, and in communicating their knowledge to students they have therefore been content to use refined versions of these simplified pictures. In this way the tools of accounting have become the central issue, instead of the tasks the tools are expected to perform:

One might wonder why university researchers failed to note the growing obsolescence of organizations' management accounting systems and did not play a more active or more stimulating role to improve the art of management accounting systems design. We believe the academics were led astray by a simplified model of firm behavior. Influenced strongly by economists' one-product, one-production-process model of the firm, management accounting academics found little value in the cost allocations imposed on organizations by financial accounting procedures. Sixty years of literature emerged advocating the separation of costs into fixed and variable components for making good product decisions and for controlling costs. This literature, very persuasive when illustrated in the simple one-product settings used by academic economists and accountants, never fully addressed the question of where fixed costs came from and how these costs needed to be covered by each of the products in the corporations' repertoire. Nor did the academic researchers attempt to implement their ideas in the environment of actual organizations, with hundreds or thousands of products and with complex, multi-stage production processes. Thus, the academic literature concentrated on increasingly elegant and sophisticated approaches to analyzing costs for single-product, single-process firms while actual organizations attempted to manage with antiquated systems in settings that had little relationship to the simplified model researchers assumed for analytic and teaching convenience.[11]

The conclusion must be that theorists should face up to reality and start afresh. And this time they should try and retain a healthy respect for the real world in which accounting is to be practiced. In his article entitled "The Evolution of Management Accounting," Kaplan himself argues that accounting theorists should take a fresh look at the real world and start the urgent process of innovation in their profession after more than 60 years of blindfolded, unimaginative wandering in the wilderness. He expresses this as follows:

I suspect that researchers will not learn about the production and organization problems of contemporary industrial corporations by reading economics and management science journals. Researchers will need to leave their offices and study the practices of innovating organizations. Companies are responding to changes in their environment by introducing new organizational arrangements and new technology for producing their outputs. . . . The research will be more inductive than deductive, but likely productive, both for the individual researcher and for the management accounting discipline. . . . The research, in its intensive nature, has ensured that systematic data is supported by anecdotal data. More and more we feel the need to be on site, and to be there long enough to be able to understand what is going on. For while systematic data creates the foundation for our theories, it is the anecdotal data that enables us to do the building. Theory building seems to require rich description, the richness that comes from anecdote. We uncover all kinds of relationships in our "hard" data, but it is only through the use of this "soft" data that we are able to "explain" it, and explanation is, of course, the purpose of research. I believe that the researcher who never goes near the water, who collects quantitative data from a distance, without anecdote to support it, will always have difficulty explaining interesting relationships (although he may uncover them). Those creative leaps seem to come from our subconscious mental processes, our intuition. And intuition apparently requires the "sense" of things—how they feel, smell, "seem." Increasingly in our research, we are impressed by the importance of phenomena that cannot be measured—by the impact of an organization's history and its ideology on its current strategy, by the role that personality and intuition play in decision-making. To miss this in research is to miss the very lifeblood of the organization. And missed it is. Research, by its very design, precludes the collection of anecdotal information.

Let us conclude this chapter with Johnson and Kaplan's multi-faceted, precise definition of the new challenge facing all practical and theoretical accountants. Once again, we quote from *Relevance Lost*. The trumpet of innovation is at last being sounded:

The challenge and the opportunity for contemporary organizations . . . are clear. Management accounting systems can and should be designed to support the operations and the strategy of the organization. The technology exists to implement systems radically different from those being used today. What is lacking is knowledge. But this knowledge can emerge from experimentation and communication. The innovative spirit evident one hundred years ago at the outset of the scientific management movement can be recaptured by innovative managers and academic researchers who are committed to developing new concepts for designing relevant management accounting systems.[12]

It is hard to imagine how anyone could express the need for innovation in accounting theory and practice in a better way.

NOTES

1. Kaplan, "The Evolution of Management Accounting," 1984.
2. Kaplan and Johnson, *Relevance Lost*, preface, p. xii.
3. Ibid., preface, p. xii.
4. Ibid., p. 1.

5. Ibid., p. 1.
6. Ibid., p. 2.
7. Ibid., p. 2.
8. Ibid., p. 16.
9. Ibid., p. 16.
10. Ibid., p. 17.
11. Ibid., p. 14.
12. Ibid., p. 17.

3 DO WE UNDERSTAND FINANCIAL STATEMENTS?

Concepts without observation are empty.
Observation without concepts is blind.

—*Immanuel Kant*

The answer to this simple question is a shocking, resounding and irrefutable "no." Laypersons have often complained that economics is difficult to understand, but have comforted themselves with the thought that other sciences such as astronomy and psychology were difficult, too. In modern society we are all forced to depend on specialists to conceptualize their own particular areas of concern. But there are still no basic concepts to use about accounting, which is why no one has yet been able to conceptualize financial statements, not even the so-called experts. Quite simply, no one has yet been able to define the basic concepts of accounting in scientific and irrefutable fashion. It is not yet possible to say what "assets" or "liabilities" really are, which is why no one really understands what "equity" is, either. In practice, this makes it impossible to draw up accounting standards, and any attempt to do so must therefore be meaningless, and, at best, without effect. If the current definitions of assets, liabilities and equity are taken seriously they can do a lot of damage, because they mislead people into thinking that their problems are solved. Concepts that *can* be misunderstood *will* be misunderstood, which is why accountants can sometimes be compared to healers who use a wide range of linguistic rituals and treatment procedures, but who may have considerable difficulty in actually producing concrete results. One internationally recognized professor of accounting concludes that we have a desperate need for a basic conceptual framework that is capable of withstanding criticism, and that can thus be used as a genuine problem solving tool. And until basic accounting concepts are found, no one can claim truly to understand financial statements.

The question posed as the title of this chapter may irritate a number of people, in particular accounting experts, who may regard the question as bordering on the tactless. Nonetheless, this risk must be run, because the question must be asked. The fact is that key executives interpret financial statements very differently when using them as a vital ingredient in the process of decision making and control. And in recent years there has been distinct and widespread dissatisfaction with the quality of the financial statements provided. Nowadays, the users of financial statements are making demands that preparers of financial statements feel themselves incapable of meeting.

In January 1987 Professor Robert N. Anthony contributed an exceptionally accurate and clearly worded article to the *Harvard Business Review*. The title of this article was extremely revealing: "We Don't Have the Accounting Concepts We Need."

The preface to Anthony's article indicates clearly what its conclusion will be. The preface states that the issue of whether the world of accounting needs a new, general frame of reference has been discussed for many years. Since the 1930s a good number of earnest attempts have been made to provide such a framework, but none of the organizations making the attempt has met with any success. Several barriers (some political, others to protect special interests) have been erected to hamper these attempts. But in Anthony's view the failure of these attempts does not mean that the search should be discontinued. He insists that accounting needs definitions, a valid theoretical foundation on which to base future procedures.

The most recent attempt in this search was made by the Financial Accounting Standards Board (FASB), an organization that is widely known and respected in the United States, and that assumed the task of establishing a framework for American accounting guidelines in the mid-1970s, after which several million dollars were spent in the attempt to perform the task.

The work of the FASB is outlined in a total of six statements concerning the concepts of accounting, which were drawn up and published during the period from 1978 to 1985. The titles and dates of publication of these statements are as follows:

- Statement No. 1: "Objectives of Financial Reporting for Business Enterprises" (Nov. 1978).
- Statement No. 2: "Qualitative Characteristics of Accounting Information" (May 1980).
- Statement No. 3: "Elements of Financial Statements of Business Enterprises" (Dec. 1980).

- Statement No. 4: "Objectives of Financial Reporting by Nonbusiness Organizations" (Dec. 1980).
- Statement No. 5: "Recognition and Measurement in Financial Statements of Business Enterprises" (Dec. 1984).
- Statement No. 6: "Elements of Financial Statements" (Dec. 1985).

All the evidence indicates that the FASB did its best, but in Anthony's opinion the attempt was in vain. The most important reasons why the FASB failed are as follows:

- The FASB avoided the most important issues, and thus only managed to increase the confusion that it was trying to clear up.
- The FASB confused accounting managers and accountants by drawing up pointless distinctions between the private and public sectors.
- The FASB compromised so much when drawing up definitions that the final text is meaningless.
- The FASB failed to answer the basic, fundamental questions in accounting (the meaning of the terms assets, liabilities, profit and loss, the distinction between writing history and describing the future, the distinction between the owner's point of view and the all-round point of view and the question of the objects of accounting measurements).

Anthony recommends in his article that the FASB acknowledge that its attempt has failed, that the entire project be shelved without further comment, and that a fresh attempt be made resulting in a valid proposal for a theoretical frame of reference for accounting.

Anthony writes with great lucidity and perspicacity, as well as with great directness. He describes the lack of a set of comprehensible basic definitions of accounting: "Accounting doesn't really have a satisfactory conceptual framework—a broad outline of what financial accounting practices should be. And none of the groups that have taken on responsibility for articulating the framework has been able to do so."

Anthony then goes on to list a number of serious but unsuccessful attempts to solve the problem of a lack of accounting definitions, and he praises the FASB for making a brave attempt. The process required is difficult—so difficult that many managers and accounting specialists may well feel that it is best not even to attempt it, and instead be content to solve the day-to-day problems in conventional, pragmatic fashion.

One reason that practical people—whether they're accountants, financial analysts, or business executives—feel this way is that they are uneasy about the development of concepts. They understand how a particular accounting standard will affect their work; a standard helps solve specific business problems in a very direct way. These people have difficulty, however, understanding how a concept can affect them or their business. So they argue that either we don't need to worry about a statement of concepts, or that we can go slower in the process of conceptual development.

Although they generally won't oppose the discussions, neither do they support them enthusiastically. Moreover, practical people tend to be bored by what they consider to be an academic discussion of ideas.

The guidelines in question are the practical regulations available for use in approaching specific accounting issues (e.g. the issue of assessing the value of stock in the balance sheet). It is easy enough to consult written accounting standards and find a rule that recommends the use of the principle of "lower of cost or market." But in the practical world of accounting, such principles tend to blow in the wind without any comprehensible reference to generally applicable concepts. It has proved impossible to find a scientifically viable justification for the use of the "lower of cost or market" principle, or indeed for the use of similar accounting principles or standards. As Anthony points out, a conceptual framework is lacking.

This lack is extremely serious. In order to understand various phenomena, you need to possess the appropriate concepts. If you have no basic conceptual framework for accounting, you will not be able to comprehend the statements of which accounting consists. As a result, accountants are forced to accept that the discussion about the basic concepts of financial statements and accounting will continue until the problem seems to have been solved in a convincing fashion. But in Anthony's view, this is no reason for accountants to despair:

The discussion is not academic. Standards are developed within the framework provided by concepts. Unsatisfactory concepts lead to unsatisfactory standards. . . . Financial accounting practices are governed by generally accepted principles, or standards, which are derived from a conceptual framework. Accounting needs this framework for the same reason a country needs a constitution to guide the development of its laws. . . . Without it, debate over the issues bogs down because arguments are based on individual frames of reference that are rarely made explicit, with no common basis for analysis. If some geologists accept the concept of evolution and others do not, arguments about the significance of a certain fossil formation are likely to get nowhere.

Anthony then goes on to explain in his article:

- that the FASB has failed to perform the task intended,
- why we need better practical accounting procedures, and
- what a proper, appropriate and acceptable system of accounting guidelines should look like.

In the rest of this chapter we shall present and comment upon the main points of Anthony's argument. And it is worth remembering that the basic and, in practice, still unsolved cognitive questions about accounting as a concept are of course international questions. They need to be discussed and solved all over the world.

What is the purpose of financial statements? We shall return to this question later. The FASB answers as follows: "Financial reporting should provide information that is useful to present and potential investors and creditors and other users in making rational investment, credit and similar decisions. . . . The primary focus in financial reporting is information about an enterprise's performance provided by measure of earnings and its components."

In other words, financial statements are regarded as an information system. They are intended to *provide* information. But in order to provide information you need to *have access to* the information required. And in order to obtain this information you need to carry out measurements. This method of reasoning seems banal, but is in practice often overlooked. Naturally, it is meaningless in any connection to demand "further information" unless you know that such information exists. In order to obtain meaningful answers, you must of course ask meaningful questions. When you define something you need to define it clearly, and you also need to solve the problem of measurement.

Anthony comments on the FASB's attempt to define the purpose of financial statements as follows: "This is an excellent beginning, but it is only a beginning. Because most accounting controversies center on how to measure events that should be included in a period's net income, concepts on these matters are necessary."

Thus, we are on the right track, but we still need a clear and stringent definition, as well as the solution of the problem of measurement that is connected with it.

The next key concept analyzed critically by Anthony is the concept of "owners' equity," or simply "equity," which is generally taken to denote the difference between assets and liabilities in the balance sheet.

The word "equity" generally means "fairness," but it can also be used to denote a difference in value (e.g., the value of property after all debts have been cleared). And it is the latter definition that applies when the word is used to describe the difference between assets and liabilities in financial statements.

However, we should be careful not to attribute any particular separate significance to this difference. After all, the difference is no more than a residual result. Statements are made about assets and liabilities in the balance sheet, and the extent to which assets exceed liabilities is described as being the owners' equity. But this difference is not in itself of great interest. It would actually be more interesting to describe the components that make up the assets and liabilities instead.

Anyone with a rudimentary knowledge of bookkeeping knows that the result of a given period is formally identical with the difference in the items on the balance sheet for the period in question. We say that a financial statement "balances." So in practice we can decide ourselves whether to explain the result as a difference in the balance sheet, or to explain differences in the balance sheet by referring to the result. The information given is the same; the only difference is in the way this information is explained.

But in defining equity the FASB seeks to define an interim result that is described as "comprehensive income"—an attempt that is not entirely successful. The following excerpt shows clearly that Anthony indeed has the courage of his convictions. A genuine authority on the subject speaks out, and the new but imprecise concept of comprehensive income is thoroughly crushed: "the board introduces the concept of 'comprehensive income,' which is simply the change in equity from nonowner sources during an accounting period. Comprehensive income is a meaningless term. I have not seen it before and I doubt that I will see it again."

We have just seen that the difference between assets and liabilities for a given period is logically identical with the result for the same period, which means that the problem of definition could be solved in this respect if only we are able to define assets and liabilities precisely. But here, too, certain problems arise. Anthony points out that "Statement No. 3 defines assets as "probable future economic benefits" and liabilities as "probable future sacrifices of economic benefits." It then waffles by saying that these conditions are necessary but not sufficient to classify an item. In other words, no item can be an asset unless it has probable future economic benefits, but not all such items are assets. The statement terms this difficulty in classifying assets "the problem of recognition" and leaves it at that. The board addresses the matter again . . . but it never resolves the problem."

As revealed later in this book, this cognitive problem is not necessarily insoluble. It can be claimed and proved that assets and liabilities can be defined clearly by changing one's cognitive standpoint completely and regarding financial statements as a system of statements that consist of *well-founded predictions of payments* and nothing else.

However, we are putting the cart before the horse now, and must first allow Anthony to have his say. He is clearly dissatisfied with the fact that the problem has not been solved, and he also knows what scientifically viable taxonomy actually involves. He has the following to say about the FASB's attempts to draw up definitions of assets and liabilities: "This is a cop-out. It is no more helpful than defining voters as adult human beings. All voters are adult human beings, but aliens, felons, and certain other adults are not voters. Unless an accounting definition indicates both the necessary and the sufficient conditions for classifying an item in the accounts, it is inadequate. This is a fundamental rule of taxonomy."

Let us now return to the FASB's attempt to define the concept of equity, and to Anthony's criticism of this attempt: "Defining equity as the difference between assets and liabilities perpetuates an unrealistic concept that is prevalent in both textbooks and practice. The amounts reported as equity in a business entity are actually the amounts of capital obtained from two quite different sources: investments by equity investors and the entity's profit-making activities. In present practice, they roughly correspond to paid-in capital and retained earnings, respectively."

It is worth adding that concepts that are only defined as the difference between two other concepts can hardly have any independent meaning apart from this. You can call such differences what you like—the name you give them is not significant in itself. The main thing is to retain a healthy skepticism about them, and to try and give the concepts of *assets* and *liabilities* a precise and well-defined content. If we succeed in doing so, new and more meaningful designations for the difference between these two key concepts may well be easier to find.

Our problem is related to recognition and measurement. The FASB states that definition is a question of recognition, and then shelves the entire matter. Anthony describes this sin of omission with his characteristic precision and clarity, leaving the reader in no doubt about his message: "From the outset of the concepts project, the board deferred the resolution of tough issues. It justified the deferrals by maintaining that these issues related to "recognition and measurement," the subject of a later statement. . . . The result was Statement No. 5, . . . which became a catchall for unresolved issues. In tackling these issues some of the board members became more set in their opinions. To get something out, they had to make all sorts of compromises. . . . Because of this, Statement No. 5 is seriously flawed and raises more questions than it answers."

We note that Anthony does not criticize the FASB for its failure to describe the problem of recognition and measurement, or for describing this problem as being unsolved. What he is dissatisfied with is the fact that the board apparently seeks to solve the problem of definition by yet another reference to the way things are done in practice. But serious deficiencies in practical procedure are precisely the reason why work on new definitions is necessary, so we must agree with Anthony that the FASB ought not to give up and seek to explain or conceal the unsolved problems simply by referring once again to the world of practical accounting, which has no conceptual framework. The whole point in seeking to draw up accounting definitions is to avoid referring to current practice. "The purpose of a concepts statement is to assess what financial reporting should be, not to describe what current practices are. Statement No. 5, however, deals primarily with the board's perception of current practices, with no guidelines for improvement. . . . This is no way to resolve issues, unless you accept the premise that accounting standards are already perfect."

Accepting this premise is very far from easy. Surely neither the preparers nor the users of financial statements would claim that the distinguishing feature of current accounting procedure is its perfection.

The next paragraph in Anthony's article is short, but will surely be regarded as provocative by a number of people. The question it poses is whether evolution (i.e., the stable, gradual development of concepts) is at all possible based on the existing accounting system, or whether the world of accounting needs to discard the current system entirely and seek a veritable revolution instead: "The statement does say in several places that the concepts are subject to "gradual change or evolution," but it gives no indication of the desirable direction. The FASB can thus use Statement No. 5 to support any future standard, as long as it isn't revolutionary. In some disciplines, an occasional conceptual revolution is the most important way of making progress."

This short paragraph provides an excellent description of the tension and unease that prevails in the world of accounting today. Highly regarded accounting theorists are now insisting that in many major respects the practical work carried out by accountants currently takes place blindfolded. And naturally, the accounts managers and accountants working in the field who are accused of working blindfolded are forced to defend themselves. In many cases, they are unhappy about the criticism leveled at their work. Some may even feel that their own former teachers are now criticizing them for using methods that these teachers themselves once presented as being the best available.

Naturally, practitioners who do their best to apply the best available methods feel that they are doing a good job. Their problems have to be solved here and now, using imperfect methods if necessary. As long as there is no convincing alternative to current methods, these methods will continue to be used. So the message practitioners should send to theorists is that they should cease their negative and destructive criticism, and instead provide a constructive alternative to the current unsatisfactory methods. Practitioners should answer the criticism of theorists by saying "If you are really that dissatisfied with the methods we are using at present, and which we actually learnt from you originally, then why not tell us how to replace these methods with something better? And please speak the same language as us when you do so!"

Accounting researchers are required to produce definitions and methods that solve problems, and to describe these definitions and methods clearly enough to enable practicing accountants to understand the reasons for the changes, and to apply them without needing to repeat their entire course of training.

It may seem strange that the task of defining basic concepts is so difficult. After all, accounting itself is a measurement system. As Anthony puts it:

Accounting is a measurement system that uses the arithmetic operations of addition and subtraction. You add individual asset items to obtain totals for classes of assets and total assets, and subtract expenses from revenues to arrive at net income. It is a simple fact that numbers cannot be added or subtracted unless they have the same attribute. To put it another way, you can't add apples and oranges—but if you call them "pieces of fruit," or if you express both apples and oranges in terms of their cost or some other attribute, then you can add the resulting numbers. Statement No. 5 disregards this basic fact about measurement systems. Instead of settling on a single attribute, it discusses five of them—historical cost, current cost, current market value, net realizable value, and present value—and says that each has particular cases for which it is appropriate. The single attribute that is necessary to make sense of the additions and subtractions used in accounting does exist; otherwise accounting numbers would be a meaningless mishmash. The attribute is "financial resources"—the flow of financial resources into, through, and out of the entity, and the status of these resources as of a particular moment.

Our comment on this point must be simply that accounting numbers *are* actually regarded as a "meaningless mishmash" by the nonaccountant. Or to put it more diplomatically, conventional financial statements are impossible to understand. The difference between these two statements is only a matter of politeness—the meaning is exactly the same.

However, the question is whether Anthony's proposal for a key definition is completely precise and clear, and thus whether it meets the demands he himself makes earlier in the article. Definitions must be *both* necessary *and* sufficient in order to give basic accounting concepts logical content. And it is by no means certain that the term "financial resources" is the clearest term available.

As previously mentioned, a point that will be amplified later, financial statements should be regarded as being *dynamic* in order to attain clear meaning. Anthony concludes the preceding excerpt by using the term "as of a particular moment," and the moment he is thinking of is undoubtedly the closing date of financial statements (i.e., the end of the period concerned). This shows that Anthony sees financial statements as being an expression of "net income," expressed "as of a particular moment." Dynamic financial statements aim to replace the term "as of a particular moment" by the term "as of any particular moment."

The difference between using the word "a" and the word "any" may seem slight, but the actual difference reflected (i.e., between static and dynamic accounting) is huge, as will be revealed later.

Anthony concludes his article by patting the FASB on the back for their attempt, and by outlining what he calls a "new approach." It is not easy to draw up a new theory, because the theory required must be practical, and practice is based on a well-founded frame of reference. The following remarks should provide food for thought both for accounting researchers and for those interested in obtaining the results of such research. Is the teamwork between researchers and practicing accountants good enough? Could we achieve more simply by investing modest resources if we worked in new ways, with no dividing walls between the worlds of ideas and reality?

Developing a conceptual framework for financial accounting is not easy. . . . Part of the trouble is the theoretical nature of the job. Many disciplines recognize the distinction between theory and practice; medicine, for instance, generally acknowledges the difference between a practicing physician and a theoretical biochemist. No one expects a physician to make breakthroughs in biochemistry; and no one expects a biochemist to heal patients. . . . In accounting the distinction is not as clear. Most accountants are practitioners, as preparers of accounting information, auditors or teachers. Only a handful are interested in making a career as theorists, and for those few the opportunities are limited to the largest public accounting and investment firms and a few university positions. . . . Moreover, accounting requires a special kind of theorist: a person who has a thorough knowledge of both the real world and accounting concepts.

There are only a few fundamental issues in financial accounting: the asset and liability versus the revenue and expense approach, the historical exchange value versus the inflation-adjusted approach, the proprietary versus the entity theory, and the question of which attribute accounting should measure. Unless a concepts project resolves these issues at the outset, the subsequent debate over a framework will be interminable and the resulting statements inconsistent. The FASB did not resolve the first three issues until statement No. 5, and even there it equivocated; it has not addressed the attribute question at all.

Unfortunately, it seems that many practicing accountants are still ignoring or trying to deny that there are any problems at all.

Is Robert N. Anthony the only one of his kind? Or are there other respected accounting theorists who also support his views?

The answer to this question is that Anthony is definitely *not* the only one to propound such views. A great number of other theorists have expressed their doubts concerning the same serious, unresolved problem. To confirm that this is the case, let us now quote a couple of excerpts from Richard Mattessich's book *Die Wissenschaftlichen Grundlagen des Rechnungswesens*.

After Mattessich's book, 17 years elapsed before Anthony addressed the problem. But there is a striking similarity in the basic views expressed, the argument used, and the description of the consequences of the lack of clarity. Regarding the lack of good concepts (i.e., the lack of a scientifically viable theoretical frame of reference), Mattessich wrote the following in 1970: "We seek to create a 'theory' which will not arouse the passions of practicing accountants, a theory which makes compromise possible, but which may perhaps be accepted as a theory nonetheless. We lack the courage to adapt the world of accounting to suit new scientific viewpoints, perhaps because we are afraid of incurring the wrath of practitioners. We are looking for the basic concepts of accounting, and yet we do not dare to look further than financial bookkeeping. We have theoretical ambitions, and yet we believe that in seeking for postulates we may end up without basic concepts, without formal logic, and without scientific perception."[1]

We saw earlier that Anthony criticized the FASB for mentioning no less than five concepts for such a simple concept as "cost price," and then claiming that each has particular cases for which it is appropriate. Mattessich claims that clarity can only be achieved by refraining from thinking in terms of specific, situation-oriented, single-purpose systems, which are often no more than sheer opportunism. Instead, attention should be focused on formulating a general basis, in other words on the construction of a general, multitask system. "The development of various single-purpose systems only makes a general basis for accounting even more indispensable. The fact is that if there is no general framework from which a specific accounting model can be developed for a specific purpose, then separate theories will have to be developed for each individual purpose. This will ruin the original objective, which was to achieve variety with a view to achieving flexibility." [2]

The following excerpt from Mattessich is of interest to anyone who views the concepts of accounting as being a potential instrument of communication between the theory, legislation and practice of accounting. No one really seems to accept responsibility for solving the problem, and everyone seems to be passing the buck on to someone else. Accounting experts say that the legislators should express themselves clearly about the rules to be observed in practice, and legislators say that accounting experts should express *themselves* clearly. Owing to the lack of basic concepts, the end result is confusion and lack of clarity, even though this was not the intention. The wearisome and futile task continues.

Like Anthony, Mattessich is good at expressing himself clearly, and there is also bite in his remarks. We are informed that the world of accounting is still bogged down in the scholastic and dogmatic philosophy of the Middle Ages:

There are very few areas of science which avail themselves of the number of masks and amount of cosmetics used in accounting. . . . Despite many serious attempts, compromise based on convention has been the result on far too many occasions. Instead of formulating a general theoretical framework for accounting, in which the legislation applying at any time could be incorporated and thereby in the form of special hypothetical sentences make up a specific model among many others, instead of this our science of accounting has continually placed the focus on a legalistic model, or at best sought to derive other models from such a legalistic model. . . . In this way the same thing happened to accounting as happened to medieval scholarship—critical, inquisitive philosophy was replaced by obedience and orthodoxy. Nothing is more dangerous to a branch of science than this. [3]

Can anyone really still think that current accounting practice is distinguished by its high standards? Anyone who claims this should be able to answer Anthony and Mattessich's questions concerning the lack of scientifically viable concepts on which to base accounting. But no one has done so yet.

We conclude this chapter by turning to Robert N. Anthony for a final remark: "Financial accounting desperately needs an authoritative conceptual framework. Without it standard setters will continue to approach each issue on an ad hoc basis and argue from their own premises and concepts."

Anyone unable to answer the points raised in this chapter convincingly should probably consider accepting that the task of drawing up a good, basic conceptual framework for accounting has not yet been performed satisfactorily. Practical progress is not possible without a good theory, and any attempts to ignore or deny the truth of this will fail in the long run.

The task in hand involves drawing up a basic conceptual framework. And until this task has been performed, all serious accounting theorists and practitioners will probably have to accept that the answer to the question posed at the beginning of this chapter may well be "No, no one really understands financial statements and what they say."

NOTES

1. R. Mattessich, *Die Wissenschaftlichen Grundlagen des Rechnungswesens*, p. 16.
2. Ibid., P. 20.
3. Ibid., P. 23.

4 SOLVENCY AND LIQUIDITY, INSOLVENCY AND ILLIQUIDITY

To be conscious that you are ignorant is a great step to knowledge.

—*Benjamin Disraeli*

What do lawyers mean when they talk about solvency and insolvency? What do accounting specialists mean when they talk about liquidity and illiquidity? How should responsible business managers use these concepts? Is there a connection between them, and if so, what is this connection? Each of the two pairs of concepts is complementary—each pair forms a whole. And when we search for scientifically viable definitions of these basic concepts, we discover that a debtor who is illiquid is a debtor who is *temporarily* unable to pay his or her debts, whereas the insolvent debtor is *permanently* unable to pay his or her debts. Time is thus an element in these definitions, and time is also necessary in order to distinguish between the concepts. A problem of invisibility arises with regard to solvency/insolvency because the solvency or insolvency of business enterprises is not apparent in traditional financial statements, even though such statements claim to give a "true and fair view." Consequently, traditional financial statements are worthless as a means of describing the financial position of business enterprises.

This chapter should be seen as an attempt to create a linguistic link between three different fields in which the key concepts for which this chapter is titled are widely used. The concepts of *solvency* and *liquidity*, *insolvency* and *illiquidity* are regarded as being of central importance in all three fields. But there may be a number of relatively important differences in the logical content of these concepts in practice. And if such differences in interpretation do exist, we must face up to the fact that they may make communication more difficult. There is a familiar rule in the world of information systems that says that if something *can* go wrong, it *will* go wrong. So any concept that *can* be misunderstood, *will* be misunderstood.

In practice, these three different fields are populated by *lawyers* (attorneys, judges and so on), *accounting specialists* (chief accountants and financial managers, accountants and so on) and *business managers* respectively.

Lawyers and accounting specialists are generally so highly trained that they are regarded as experts in their fields, both by themselves and by others. Their theoretical training and practical field of operations are both seen as parts of a whole. In their specialist roles they have an understanding and appreciation of the theory and practice of their subject, and they are described as "specialists," "professionals," "experts" and so on. But this is not the case with regard to business managers. The main requirement made of business managers is that they should act, lead, be able to take the right steps and do things correctly. This is a general requirement, made of managers with no reference to any specific training they may have received. Business managers are expected to be more than mere professional specialists. They are also widely expected to be generalists.

In practice, managers are of course often trained just as thoroughly as lawyers and accounting experts. But for one thing, not all managers have attended a theoretical course of further education. For another, such a theoretical course is not always necessary. And finally, any theoretical training acquired by managers may focus on areas that have little or nothing to do with the law and accounting. Many entrepreneurs were originally trained as craftsmen or technicians, and most industrial managers were originally engineers.

The primary requirement made of business managers is that they should have a general knowledge of management in practice. But in order to have such knowledge, they also need good insight into the practice of both law and accounting. So there is little paradox in the claim that responsible business managers should have at least some specialist knowledge of law and accounting.

For instance, as parties to legal proceedings, company presidents must always be able to explain their actions, even in questions of current law and accounting. In this chapter we shall seek to describe and illustrate the demands that can and should be made on business managers in terms of their understanding of financial statements in the most important area, corporate finances.

In terms of their logical content, the four key concepts mentioned in the title of this chapter have a number of very important similarities. As mentioned, it is remarkable that the four concepts are used in the daily terminology of lawyers, accounting specialists and business managers.

But there are also significant differences in the frequency with which these concepts are used. Lawyers generally refer to solvency and insolvency, whereas business managers and accounting specialists are more interested in liquidity and illiquidity. Why is this so? What are the similarities between the four concepts, and what are the differences?

We shall now attempt to achieve absolutely clear and unambiguous definitions of the two basic concepts of solvency and liquidity, and thereby of their opposites insolvency and illiquidity.

We use the term "clear and unambiguous definitions" to mean scientifically viable definitions, and we use the term "scientifically viable definitions" to mean that each individual concept must be fixed and defined in terms of an action that can be carried out and that can be observed to take place in the real world.

It is important to establish the meaning of these terms in order to reject all concepts based purely on assumption, speculation and belief. Our aim is to achieve clarity, which is why we insist on establishing concepts based on observations of reality.

Professionals and professional groups are often able to reach agreement on how to define scientifically viable concepts—concepts based on observations of actions in the real world, and they then begin describing and using such concepts in similar ways. But it is not possible to achieve clear definitions of concepts based on assumption, belief, assessment, speculation or faith. Anyone who tries to do so will discover that force in one form or another is always needed to prevent the concept from being attacked. But force does not help in the long run. Sooner or later, unclear concepts will come under attack by people who are annoyed by the lack of clarity. But if unclear concepts are simply replaced by other unclear concepts, the discussions will continue endlessly.

For instance, a "decision" is not a scientifically viable concept because it does not describe an action that can be carried out, but rather an abstract imitation or pretense of action. Like "souls," "decisions" cannot be observed in the real world. One simply has to accept that they exist. However, a concept such as an "agreement" is scientifically viable, because agreements consist of actions that can be observed in the real world. People believe and say that they make decisions, but there is no documentary proof of the fact until the resulting agreements are made.

It is true that the word "decision" is given a certain meaning in daily language, and it is also regarded as a significant concept by lawyers: "The General Meeting decided that. . . ." But the word "decision" cannot be regarded as a scientifically viable concept owing solely to its daily or special use. It is still founded on an idea or theory, not on an action that can be observed. General Meetings are believed and said to make decisions, but they can only be observed to elect and make statements.

According to the aforementioned interpretation, the use of the expression "the General Meeting decided that. . . ." means that the General Meeting made first a decision, and then a statement. What we observe is that a choice is made between several predefined alternatives, and a statement is issued undertaking to carry out or refrain from carrying out certain actions. The proof that this choice and statement have been made can be seen in the minutes of the General Meeting. But the debate regarding exactly what the concept of a "decision" is could continue for a very long time with little prospect of achieving a clear conclusion.

Let us now consider the definitions of solvency and liquidity. Actually, it would be preferable to start by defining the complementary concepts of insolvency and illiquidity, since in the world of accounting we are primarily interested in these logical opposites of solvency and liquidity. The fact is that in one respect, business enterprises that are always solvent and liquid are of little interest to the world of accounting, since they never give rise to any problems. They simply go on working, dealing with their business, and paying all their bills. But observations of the real world teach us that there are also enterprises that are *not* always solvent and liquid.

The problems we wish to describe and help to solve here are the problems that arise when an apparently solvent and liquid enterprise turns out to be insolvent or illiquid, contrary to all our expectations. So naturally, it is the key concepts of insolvency and illiquidity that interest us most.

However, both these key concepts are expressed as logical negations, and it is not possible to define the negation of a concept without first defining the concept from which it is derived. So we have to establish the content of the concepts of solvency and liquidity first. Let us define the latter concept first, since it is the easier of the two.

The concept of liquidity is extremely familiar in the theory of accounting and financing. It is defined as having a direct relationship with the action of "paying." Enterprises or individuals are said to be liquid at a moment or within a period when they are able to pay their due debts at the moment or within the period concerned.

It is important to note that the concept of *time* is of decisive importance in order to give our definition meaning. In other words, we can only talk of being liquid with reference to a given moment in time. We can also talk of being liquid within a given period, in which case a series of payments must be made during the period concerned.

Naturally, the necessary means of payment must be available to make it possible to make such payments. Payment can be made either in cash or by using references to cash. The daily language of accounting contains expressions such as "liquid capital" or simply "liquidity," terms that simply refer to means of payment that are easily accessible.

In practice, "liquid capital" and "liquidity" can have three and only three forms. The ability to pay can be demonstrated by the presence of means of payment in the form of:

1. cash holdings
2. deposits in bank accounts of various kinds
3. prearranged rights to draw on credits of various kinds

It is important to make the following point, since it is very often misunderstood. You do not need to own anything in order to be liquid. You can pay your debts using money you have borrowed. The individual who pays debts with other people's money is just as liquid as the person who pays with his or her own. The expression "to be liquid" simply means "to have the ability to pay."

The concept of illiquidity is simply the logical negation of the concept of liquidity. You are illiquid when you *cannot* pay your debts at a given moment or within a given period. The transition from a state of liquidity to a state of illiquidity that is more than just temporary is stated in the familiar (and for most interested parties unpleasant and fatal) expression "X has suspended payments."

So much for the definition of liquidity/illiquidity as a pair of concepts. Let us now turn our attention to solvency/insolvency. We have already seen that the logical negation of a concept gives no meaning until the concept from which it is derived has been defined. Nevertheless, a thoroughly tried and tested definition of the concept of insolvency can be found in section 17 subsection 2 of the Danish Bankruptcy Act: "A debtor is insolvent when he is incapable of meeting his obligations as they fall due, unless his inability to pay can be regarded merely as a temporary phenomenon."

The concept of insolvency is the logical negation of the concept of solvency, so the definition of solvency can be obtained by simply negating the definition of insolvency as follows: "A debtor is solvent when he or she is capable of meeting obligations as they fall due."

This sentence is clear, generally applicable and without conditions or reservations. Consequently, the word "always" can also be applied to it: "A debtor is solvent when he or she is *always* capable of meeting obligations as they fall due."

What is the difference between solvency/insolvency and liquidity/illiquidity? It is immediately apparent that the meanings of the two expressions "inability to pay" and "illiquidity" are identical. Replacing the expression "inability to pay can be regarded merely as a temporary phenomenon" by the expression "illiquidity can be regarded merely as a temporary phenomenon" makes no difference to the meaning of the excerpt from the Act quoted earlier.

The legislative powers that laid down the Danish Bankruptcy Act presumably used the term "inability to pay" because it is easy for the nonspecialist to understand, whereas concepts such as "liquidity" and "illiquidity" belong more to the specialized world of accounting.

It now appears that the basic criterion for distinguishing between the concepts of insolvency and illiquidity is *time*. The key to the distinction lies in the word "temporary." The opposite of "temporary" is "permanent." Is it possible to say that "permanent illiquidity" means the same as "insolvency"?

There is no doubt that this question must be answered in the affirmative. Insolvency exists if it is certain that an enterprise owes money to someone else and equally certain that the enterprise concerned is unable to pay this debt.

Having described the content of the two positive concepts of liquidity and solvency, and having described the logical negations of these two concepts, we can continue. It is now apparent that the two key concepts of illiquidity and insolvency must be seen in their proper context in order to acquire true meaning, and that in this context they should be defined as follows: Illiquidity means that a debtor is *temporarily* unable to meet obligations as they fall due. Insolvency means that a debtor is *permanently* unable to meet obligations as they fall due.

Once again, time is of decisive importance for the distinction made, and it becomes apparent that the problem now is to find out what we understand by the words "temporary" and "permanent." We shall never be able to distinguish between illiquidity and insolvency unless we succeed in understanding "temporary" and "permanent."

In order to analyze this problem, let us first see how the key concepts described until now can be combined, and how phenomena in the real world become apparent to us when we use such terms to describe them. Combining the two key concepts and their logical negations produces four (and only four) possibilities. These four possibilities describe four different logical states, which in turn describe four (and only four) different situations in which enterprises can find themselves as debtors. To help us in our analysis, we shall start by regarding the four possibilities as absolutes, describing the situations they reflect in black and white with no shades of gray. Once this stage of the analysis has been completed, we shall consider the possible shades of gray in greater detail.

The first stage of analysis reveals that a given enterprise (legal person, debtor) at any given moment can be:

1. solvent and liquid
2. solvent and illiquid
3. insolvent and liquid
4. insolvent and illiquid

State 1 reflects a situation in which enterprises are solvent and liquid. It also reflects a situation in which enterprises are unnoticed by anyone for the simple reason that everything is normal at such enterprises, no problems being apparent. Such enterprises pay all their creditors as claims are made. We have already pointed out that this state of affairs is actually of little interest. If all enterprises were in this state at all times, creditors would never incur losses, claims for payment would never be advanced through the courts and consequently legislation in this area would not be necessary. But in the real world, of course, there are enterprises that are not always in state 1, which is why legislation in this area is necessary.

State 2 reflects a situation in which enterprises are solvent and illiquid. We recall that the concept of illiquidity means that an enterprise is temporarily unable to pay. To illustrate state 2, let us consider an enterprise whose only asset at the time in question consists of a claim of $100 that will be paid by a debtor within 30 days. The enterprise's only debt is $50, which must be paid within 20 days. This means that the enterprise will be illiquid for ten days, but this illiquidity is only a temporary phenomenon. Such cases of illiquidity are extremely common in practice, occurring in many different situations and many different forms. But the problem of temporary inability to pay can always be solved by solvent enterprises. The management is often able to obtain deferral by approaching the enterprise's creditors, who may require the payment of interest during the deferral period. And even if deferral is not granted by creditors, the problem can still be solved. Enterprises that are undoubtedly solvent can take out a loan with collateral in their assets, or they can sell these assets, even though this may take some time. Such a step restores the ability of such enterprises to pay their debts, and no one suffers a loss as a result.

State 3 reflects a situation in which enterprises are insolvent and liquid. The debts of such enterprises are definitely larger than their assets, so someone is bound to suffer a loss. But this problem is invisible to outsiders, because despite their insolvency such enterprises are still able to pay their debts, even though this ability is only temporary. In practice, insolvent but liquid enterprises occur in many different situations and many different forms. The most straightforward example is that of an enterprise that has acquired capital in the form of a loan, the proceeds of which are used to finance a loss-making operation. It is only a question of time before payments will have to be suspended and creditors will realize that their claims have been lost either partially or completely. The size of the losses may vary, but there is never any doubt that someone will suffer a loss owing to insolvent (and thus only temporarily liquid) enterprises.

Finally, state 4 reflects a situation in which enterprises are insolvent and illiquid. Payments have been suspended, and it is apparent to all observers that the debts of such enterprises are larger than their assets. Enterprises that are definitely insolvent and illiquid have no chance of continuing to do business, and must be put out of their misery like wounded and suffering animals. Their story ends in bankruptcy, or in another solution involving the transfer of any assets to new owners and new managers, whereby creditors suffer losses of various dimensions with no realistic chance of recovery.

Let us now summarize the lessons learned from consideration of the four logical states outlined. In state 1 solvent and liquid enterprises do not create problems, and are therefore of little interest to us here. In state 2 solvent and illiquid enterprises are capable of solving their own problems, causing only temporary concern to their creditors. It is thus possible to conclude that solvency is the decisive criterion in determining whether enterprises are sound, and whether the creditors of such enterprises can sleep soundly in their beds.

In state 4 enterprises have suffered definite losses, and it is too late to do anything about the situation.

In other words, some of the states outlined are virtually problem-free. And yet problems do exist in the real world, so we are forced to conclude that such problems must be found and solved in the types of situation that cannot be analyzed as being problem-free.

Solvent enterprises cause only temporary concern to their creditors, and insolvent enterprises that have suspended their payments result in losses, and often large losses, when it is too late for their creditors to do anything about it.

But in state 3 we should be able to see the problems in time to enable creditors to avoid (or at least limit) their losses. We can now conclude that *enterprises that are already insolvent but not yet illiquid are dangerous to their creditors.*

Anyone giving credit to an insolvent but not yet illiquid enterprise will suffer a loss. Anyone giving large amounts of credit will suffer a large loss.

This analysis clearly reveals that the problem here arises due to *invisibility*. Creditors are forced *to believe* that they are dealing with a solvent enterprise. In general, they have no chance of *knowing* whether this is in fact the case. Nor do they have any reliable means of confirming any suspicions they may have that the enterprise concerned is, in fact, insolvent.

The reader may now be wondering what the purpose of financial statements and accounting is. Surely it is possible to consult financial statements to discover whether enterprises are solvent or not. What about the concepts of assets and liabilities? Surely accounting specialists can provide the information needed about solvency and insolvency. Let us now follow this line of thought and find out how traditional accounting provides information about solvency using its own traditional concepts.

The question of lack of solvency is undoubtedly important for many interested parties. The term "interested parties" is used in accounting theory to describe people and organizations within the enterprise concerned and in its immediate environment, such as managers, employees, customers, suppliers, lenders, shareholders, the customs and tax authorities, journalists and so on.

The characteristic feature of these interested parties is that they all interact with each other either temporarily or permanently.

This interaction amounts to "business," a word that originally meant "the state of being busy" or "activity." In other words, enterprises can be characterized in general by the fact that these interested parties are involved in an open, interactive system. The issue of whether they are "external" or "internal," of whether they are to be found inside or outside the enterprise concerned, is not of decisive importance. The decisive factor is their actions. We can observe that these interested parties are constantly engaged in the exchange of information and resources, involving the communication of various types of information and the exchange of goods, services and payments.

It is now easy to see why interested parties are almost always concerned with the continued existence of the enterprises in which they are involved. The fact is that they all risk suffering losses of various kinds if such enterprises become insolvent and are therefore forced to close.

The management and employees are hit very hard when enterprises become insolvent, and they often lose their jobs. Customers lose their usual source of supply of goods and services. They also lose the chance to obtain service and fulfillment of guarantee commitments concerning products that have already been supplied, which means that they in turn may experience problems. Creditors in the form of suppliers, lenders, shareholders and the customs and tax authorities clearly run the risk of suffering financial losses if their claims on enterprises are lost owing to insolvency.

Most of the interested parties mentioned here are located outside the enterprises that they are involved with, which means that they are forced to try and obtain information about the financial situation of the enterprises concerned by reading financial statements. Current legislation states that the information needed must be available in annual financial statements, and in traditional financial statements the reader seeks information about solvency by considering the balance sheet, which contains a specification of assets and liabilities. Let us now consider these two terms.

It is common knowledge that financial statements consist of two sections—a profit and loss account, and a balance sheet. These two sections must be considered in their proper context in order to give meaning. The profit and loss account is supposed to show the income and expenses of the preceding period, which means that it is also supposed to explain the connection between the balance at the start of the period concerned (the initial balance) and the balance at the end of the period (the end balance). The logic behind all financial statements is as follows:

initial balance + profit and loss account = end balance.

In other words, the profit and loss account is believed to express *the changes* occurring since the old balance was drawn up, whereas the new balance is believed to express the new financial *situation* or status.

As mentioned in an earlier chapter, the rules controlling the formal content of balance sheets are based on the definitions of double entry bookkeeping. Originally, enterprises were said to have a certain number of holdings of various kinds, and these holdings were given the name "assets." Enterprises were also said to have a certain number of obligations of various kinds, and these obligations were given the name "liabilities."

The original intention of double entry bookkeeping was to define the size of two figures:

1. Holdings, or "things at our disposal" (assets)
2. Obligations, or "things we owe to others" (liabilities)

Naturally, these two figures are hardly ever of equal size in the real world. And yet financial statements persist in claiming that the figures in the balance sheet "balance" by using the following equation:

$$\text{holdings (assets)} = \text{obligations (liabilities)}$$

However, anyone with only a rudimentary knowledge of the rules of double entry bookkeeping knows that for practical and technical reasons this equation must in fact be expressed as follows:

$$\text{holdings} - \text{obligations} = \text{"difference"}$$

which means that

$$\text{holdings} = \text{obligations} + \text{"difference"}$$

or, as these concepts are known in current accounting practice:

$$\text{assets} = \text{liabilities} + \text{equity}$$

The two sides of the equation now balance logically. What you have at your disposal is the same as what you owe to others plus the difference between these two figures.

Traditional accounting has chosen to call the difference between holdings and obligations "equity." In a later chapter we shall seek to explain why "equity" is not the best term that might have been chosen. For now, we shall concentrate on the concepts of assets and liabilities with a view to determining whether they can be used to shed any light on the issue of an enterprise's solvency/insolvency.

One apparently simple and clear way to define the distinction between solvency and insolvency is simply to say that a state of insolvency exists when total liabilities are greater than total assets, and that a state of solvency exists when total assets are greater than or equal to total liabilities.

As mentioned earlier, the concept of solvency describes not the act of making payments, but the difference between what you claim to have at your disposal and what you claim to owe to others. If you buy something and pay with someone else's money, you increase your debt (liabilities). But if you pay with your own money you reduce the size of your holdings (assets). In other words, we need to explain the concept of solvency by considering the two concepts of assets (holdings) and liabilities (obligations). If we apply these concepts, the following definition of solvency can be obtained:

Enterprises are solvent when their assets are greater than or equal to their liabilities. And enterprises are insolvent when their liabilities exceed their assets.

However, in two important respects this definition is unsatisfactory. First, there is no mention of the time at which assets and liabilities are considered. And second, the definition is only clear and meaningful if the content of the two key concepts of assets and liabilities is perfectly clear.

We have already seen that time is a necessary factor in defining the concepts of assets and liabilities and the relationship between the two. The concepts are quite simply meaningless unless time is incorporated into their definition. Unless we incorporate time, we can neither understand the concepts of assets and liabilities, nor distinguish between them.

So anyone wishing to say anything about the solvency or insolvency of an enterprise based on financial statements must also consider the time in question, by stating (for instance), "This data proves that enterprise X was/will be solvent/insolvent at time *t* or within a defined period." In other words, in order to retain meaning, we must modify our earlier definition by saying that:

Enterprises are solvent at a given time or within a given period when their assets are greater than or equal to their liabilities at the time concerned or at any time within the period concerned. And enterprises are insolvent when their liabilities exceed their assets.

Time has now been incorporated into our description of assets and liabilities. Can we now use traditional financial statements to shed light on the issue of solvency/insolvency?

No, unfortunately we cannot. Even if we define assets and liabilities in terms of time, we cannot solve our problem until the concepts of assets and liabilities have been given a unambiguous content. And so far this task has proved to be impossible.

Anyone with only superficial knowledge of accounting practice is perfectly aware that traditional financial statements are actually characterized by distinct lack of clarity when it comes to making definitions.

It is easy to provide an example of this lack of clarity. After all, the meaning—and thereby understanding—of the concepts of "holdings" and "obligations" must logically concern *the future*, and yet traditional financial statements only describe *the past*.

These definitions incorporate time, but it is common knowledge that traditional financial statements are claimed to describe the financial consequences of actions occurring in the past, whereas warnings about insolvency must of course be directed towards the future.

So far our theoretical analysis has revealed that it should be possible to detect incipient insolvency by consulting the traditional accounting figures for assets and liabilities, but that there still seems to be a "problem of invisibility"—that is, the whole picture is not yet clear to us.

It must be obvious that the transition from certain solvency to certain insolvency hardly ever occurs suddenly at a certain moment, but is instead a process occurring over time.

But even though this is the case, surely it must be possible to design a financial early warning system based directly on the data contained in financial statements.

Let us now try to progress from here by drawing an analogy to the world of medicine. The *symptom* we observe in a patient can be compared with the actions of payment and the temporary or permanent termination of these actions. The *illness* we wish to diagnose in order to provide effective treatment in good time is insolvency. But symptoms are very often uncertain indicators of illnesses, and the problem is that when symptoms are finally confirmed, they tend to occur at a very late stage of the illness concerned.

We desperately need a better technique of diagnosis. And a considerable problem would be solved if accounting specialists were able to provide a reliable diagnosis when enterprises were "in danger of insolvency" or exhibited "incipient insolvency."

As a basis for the next stage in our analysis of concepts, let us now recall the four possible states that enterprises find themselves in at any given moment.

As mentioned before, enterprises can be:

1. solvent and liquid
2. solvent and illiquid
3. insolvent and liquid
4. insolvent and illiquid

In dealing with these concepts until now, we have been simplifying the situation, and we shall now try to explain the simplification involved, and then remove it. Until now, we have been examining these concepts at a given moment in time and in certain theoretical conditions. The result is a series of snapshots showing that "the enterprise is in this situation at the moment." All other factors are regarded as being irrelevant, and analysis of various combinations of solvency/insolvency and liquidity/illiquidity can then be carried out using such snapshots as our tool.

But such snapshots only provide *static* descriptions. A static description is a description in which time is not incorporated as a variable factor. In our analysis so far we have studied various combinations of solvency/insolvency and liquidity/illiquidity, revealing that the interesting combination for us is that of the insolvent enterprise that is still liquid.

But in order to continue our analysis, we must examine the transitions between the various states. This can only be done if we supplement our snapshots by incorporating time into our description. And when time is incorporated as a variable in a description, the description becomes *dynamic*.

Naturally, in real life enterprises are never in a quiet, static state. In practice, enterprises can best be described as living organisms that are subject to ongoing development and change, and that are constantly exchanging resources and information with the world outside.

Traditional financial statements contain a balance sheet describing the financial situation of enterprises on specific dates, in specific circumstances—that is, they provide a static picture. But in order to obtain an early warning about incipient insolvency, of course we need to describe the transitions between the various states. And in order to describe these transitions, we need dynamic financial statements.

So the conclusion of our analysis until now must be that *if we want an early warning system capable of identifying incipient insolvency, we need dynamic financial statements.*

Let us now conclude this chapter by summarizing the most important defects in traditional accounting.

The most important defects of traditional financial statements are that they are:

1. *static*, instead of being dynamic
2. *out-of-date*, instead of being up-to-date
3. *unclear*, instead of being clear
4. *incomplete*, instead of being complete

Our analysis has already demonstrated that time must be incorporated into our descriptions in order to provide our basic concepts with any real content.

We also claim that traditional financial statements are often available too late in relation to the incipient insolvency that we wish to predict. This means that traditional financial statements are out-of-date.

We also claim that we lack an unambiguous (i.e., scientifically viable) definition of the key concepts of assets and liabilities to enable nonaccountants to understand financial statements without difficulty. Traditional financial statements are unclear.

Another defect that is extremely serious in this connection is that traditional financial statements are incomplete, failing to show us all the rights and obligations of enterprises. One simple, typical and extremely clear example of this incompleteness is the potential debt in connection with salaries paid to employees who are entitled to lengthy periods of pay when they are fired. Enterprises whose employees all have the right to six months' notice actually have a permanent salary debt amounting to 50 percent of their total annual salary payments, which is normally a pretty hefty sum. Annual salaries are entered in traditional financial statements under the heading "wages and salaries," but the potential salary debt is invisible to the reader. It is described as a "contingent liability," and is not included in traditional financial statements.

Financial statements that are static, out-of-date, unclear and incomplete must surely also be unreliable. It is therefore reasonable to claim that traditional financial statements are unreliable, and reasonable to add a fifth point to our list of defects in traditional financial statements. And once this fifth point has been added, traditional financial statements can be said to be financial statements that are:

1. static, instead of being dynamic
2. out-of-date, instead of being up-to-date
3. unclear, instead of being clear
4. incomplete, instead of being complete
5. *unreliable*, instead of being reliable

Let us conclude by saying that the traditional financial statements that the whole world is still forced to regard as a vital source of information about the financial situation of enterprises are actually based on a cognitive foundation that has been regarded as completely invalid for more than 200 years from a philosophical point of view. Quite simply, this foundation is made of mud.

In order to believe the figures and statements contained in old financial statements, we have to believe that the enterprises concerned and their surroundings are stable and static. If the situation inside and outside these enterprises is stable and static, we can predict and trust the tendencies that we observe when studying old financial statements. But if there are constant and frequent changes in the situation of these enterprises and their surroundings, we are forced to accept the consequences of this fact and regard the study of old financial statements as a waste of time.

We have already seen that it can be claimed and proved that traditional financial statements are static, out-of-date, unclear, incomplete and thereby unreliable.

So it is surely no exaggeration to say that the traditional accounting model is "probably not entirely satisfactory," or that it "probably could be improved in certain ways," to use a diplomatic turn of phrase.

But anyone accepting that change is the rule rather than the exception in the real world, and that development and change depend on the availability of useful financial information, is forced to be honest and accept the consequences of this fact.

Karl Popper, a modern philosopher, says that all efforts should be made to "falsify" theories or ideas, to prove that they are untenable. Ideas can only be regarded as scientifically viable and currently useful if it proves impossible to falsify them.

At the moment the whole world seems to accept that traditional financial statements are useful in evaluating the solvency of any given enterprise. Let us now test the tenability of this attitude by applying Karl Popper's "falsification" technique.

Let us try to falsify the following working hypothesis:

Traditional financial statements are worthless as a means of evaluating the solvency of any given enterprise.

The most important basis of this hypothesis is that in our theoretical analysis we have seen that none of the four key concepts we have analyzed and defined in this chapter is comprehensible or distinctive without incorporating the concept of time. And time is not incorporated into traditional financial statements, which are regarded as being static descriptions or snapshots of the financial situation of business enterprises.

Traditional financial statements consist of a balance sheet and a profit and loss account. The balance sheet is claimed to reflect the assets and liabilities of an enterprise at the last moment in the period the statement is claimed to cover. And the profit and loss account is regarded as "economic history," which is also dated and regarded as the total sum of information about the financial consequences of actions considered to be irrevocably concluded on the last day of the old accounting period.

We stated earlier that the concept of time is not incorporated into the definition of traditional financial statements. Actually, until recently there have been no scientifically viable definitions of accounting as a concept.

Let us now try to consider the issues described in theory in this chapter from other angles, and then try to find valid arguments to demonstrate that our working hypothesis can be falsified. If it can be falsified, we shall be forced to accept that traditional financial statements are not after all worthless, and that the accounting traditions currently respected all over the world are the best of all possible accounting traditions.

But if it proves impossible to falsify our hypothesis concerning the worthlessness of traditional financial statements, we shall be forced to consider a number of possible improvements to current accounting practice. And we may be forced to conclude that in order to *present* appropriate financial statements, we need to start *keeping* appropriate financial accounts.

5 TRADITIONAL ACCOUNTING REGISTRATION

Ubi non est ordo, ibi est confusio.
Where there is no order, confusion reigns.

—*Frater Luca Bartolomes Pacioli*

One basic method is still used all over the world to measure financial inter-actions between business enterprises and their environments. This method was developed by merchants in Renaissance Europe, and it is familiar to everyone, although few understand it. It is known as double entry book-keeping, and it enabled merchants in the Middle Ages to predict and mon-itor patterns of payments in the immediate future, as well as to predict the precise time at which suspension of payments might occur. This ability to predict future events enabled them to take preventive action in order to avoid such undesirable occurrences. But the skills apparently mastered by medieval merchants seem to have been lost today, even though we now have computers enabling us to make calculations far more accurately and rapidly than ever before. The T-shaped account used in bookkeeping and the primitive data processing techniques of the past always place account-ing information in one specific logical order that might be excellent when monitoring payments from specific accounts, but that is extremely unsuit-able when monitoring earnings and liquidity. Double entry bookkeeping has a number of excellent features when used as an information system. Its weaknesses have not become apparent until recently.

In this chapter, which caters perhaps in particular to readers who are not accounting specialists, we intend to take a closer look at double entry bookkeeping, a special technique used to register the financial consequences of actions. This technique is widely used today as a basic and unchallenged method of registration by accountants all over the world. Anyone wishing to acquire or communicate systematic knowledge about the financial situation of an organization needs to be familiar with this old method of registration and the main features of its application in practice.

Basically, double entry bookkeeping can be described as a method or set of rules used to register or process data. Precisely formulated sets of rules for data processing are called "algorithms" by modern computer scientists, so double entry bookkeeping can also be regarded as a system of *measurements* and *algorithms*.

The method was invented and developed in the Middle Ages, and was described scientifically for the first time in 1494. However, despite its venerable age and apparent simplicity, double entry bookkeeping has been surrounded by a shroud of incomprehension bordering on mystery ever since. It is hardly surprising that people who are not accounting specialists have been forced to abandon the attempt to understand financial statements, since even among the most highly respected of accounting specialists there has been a good deal of doubt regarding the actual nature of the rules governing double entry bookkeeping. As late as 1969, the American professor Yuri Ijiri, a specialist in accounting measurements, wrote that "it is not possible to say that we have exploited the mathematical, philosophical, and behavioral aspects of the double entry bookkeeping system completely."[1] And we recall that Robert N. Anthony's criticism of the lack of good basic concepts and comprehension despite the apparent simplicity of double entry bookkeeping appeared as recently as 1987.

Let us start by considering one of the best-known expressions in the world of bookkeeping. The word "account," like double entry bookkeeping itself, is Italian in origin. The Italian "il conto" originally meant quite simply "bill" or "calculation." So a system of accounts should basically be regarded as a system used to calculate the financial consequences of the actions of organizations. This kind of calculation is necessary for the very good reason that the end result (a financial statement) consists of a combination of all the individual calculations made (the individual accounting items).

Naturally, financial statements for given periods consist of a great number of *different* items. Traditionally, these items (income, expenses, assets, liabilities) are divided into different types according to what is known as a *chart of accounts*, which simply means a list in which each account is named, described and organized in a specific order. The chart of accounts controls the systematic order used. Items that are logically connected in terms of type are placed in the same section of the system, itemized in the same account. This enables us to add up the expressions contained in the accounts by aggregating the data provided. These aggregations consist of sums and balances, and in principle they can be calculated at any time to cover periods of varying length.

For instance, if the sales account for any given period contains three items of $5, $7 and $8 respectively, we can calculate and then refer to a *sum*, which represents the "total sale" in the period in question of $20. If a customer owes us $25 at any given time, and if he then pays us $10, we refer to a new *balance* of $15.

Basically, a distinction is made between two logical divisions of the accounts contained in a financial statement. The financial statement for any given period consists of a balance sheet and profit and loss account. These two main elements have been given various names over the course of time, but the clearest and best name may well be that obtained from German accounting theory, which refers to two parallel lists of accounts, one showing "Leistungen" (services, products), and one showing "Zahlungen" (payments). In other words, the basic distinction denotes the financial consequences of the interaction between an organization and its environment seen in terms of the logical connections between services given and services received (buying and selling in the broadest sense), and the payments arising from such transactions. Consequently, the dual purpose of financial statements is that the profit and loss account (the list of services given and received) is intended, as its name implies, to show the financial result of a period expressed in terms of *income* and *expenses* (sales and purchases), whereas the balance sheet (the list of payments) is intended to show the financial, or *purely monetary situation* at a given time. This dual form of registration is summarized in figure 5.1.

The sight of the words debit and credit may cause some readers to recall their own brave but futile efforts to understand double entry bookkeeping. Most people who have encountered this system during the course of their education no doubt remember that the rules and their application simply had to be learned by heart. It might be possible to learn how to use the rules correctly with a good deal of hard work and patience, but it was very difficult to see the purpose of the exercise during the process of debiting/crediting.

In order to increase our understanding of double entry bookkeeping, it is worth pointing out that this 500 year old set of rules can be traced back to a period in which trade on organized markets was still at a very early stage of development, when merchants seldom did business with the same person twice in a row.

But then some merchants took the daring step of doing business on credit. This practice was, of course, rather risky—but it was also risky to walk around in public carrying large sums of money. The merchants had to weigh one risk against the other, and since they were used to calculating in order to carry on their affairs, they also used their calculation skills to work out the risk involved in granting credit. The expression "the calculated risk" is of more recent date, but it describes a tool that has always been used by those in business.

Balance Sheet Account (payments)		Profit and Loss Account (services)	
Assets	Liabilities	Expenses	Income
Debit	Credit	Debit	Credit

Figure 5.1. Division into accounts of payments and services.

The wish to do business on credit meant that entirely new demands were made on the way people went about their affairs. New ideas and concepts were required, as well as entirely new methods of trading and calculating. Naturally, payment in cash was logical and simple, and made few demands on data processing systems. Merchants could, of course, manage without bookkeeping, as long as they took care to conclude all deals and pay in cash both when buying and when selling. People who always do business in cash have no difficulty in obtaining a precise idea of their financial situation at any time. They simply need to sell their stock and then count how much money they have.

For instance, merchants who went to market with 100 identical coins, then did their business and came home with 130 identical coins, had no difficulty in calculating the profitability of their journey. *The change in liquidity* (i.e., the change in their cash holding) was a convincingly direct and tangible expression of *profitability* (i.e., the profits or losses made on the journey).

This simple connection between liquidity *(L)* and the financial result *(R)* of each business journey or project can be expressed as follows, where the symbol Δ represents "increase":

$$R = \Delta L$$

To be more specific, the profit of 30 coins could be said to arise as the result of specific purchase and sale transactions. If the merchant concerned had allowed one of his assistants to trade on his behalf, he would probably have asked for a specification of each individual transaction. Such a specification could have been given by providing a summary over time of the individual purchase and sale transactions and the payments made *(U)* and received *(I)* associated with them. The precise mathematical expression or algorithm for this summary of transactions from the start of a period *(T)* to its end can be formulated as follows:

$$R_p(T) = \sum_{t=0}^{T} (I_p(t) - U_p(t))$$

Actual payments made and received are marked by a lower case *p*. If this algorithm is used to produce a list of the individual transactions, the result of the trade journey can be explained as shown in figure 5.2. The list shows us the individual cash purchases and sales day by day, and each transaction is indicated by a progressive *T* number (*T*-No.).

We repeat that our merchant had 100 coins when he started his journey to market, and figure 5.2 shows that he purchased goods costing a total of 50. The 100 coins can thus be regarded as a liquidity reserve, an unutilized capacity to pay, which cannot be seen in figure 5.2.

As a result, we must now alter figure 5.2 so that it expresses the development of both profit and liquidity over time. This can be achieved by combining payments made and received into a single column, in which payments made are indicated by a minus sign and payments received have no sign. Thus altered, the table in figure 5.3 shows us the development in both profit/loss and liquidity item by item.

These simple examples show that the idea of an economic result is intrinsically linked to money and the payment of money. The simple identification of a "change in liquidity" as being the same as a "profit" can also be expressed as follows:

Assertions of profit and assertions of changed liquidity are assertions about the same set of actions.

The concepts dealt with so far in this chapter are extremely simple, and thus very easy to understand. Our imaginary merchant only does business in cash, and always sells his stock to find out his financial position. But how can our merchant say anything convincing about his profit or loss if some of the income that should have been received has not yet arrived because he has granted credit? And what happens if certain cash holdings were present in one sense but not in another because he had incurred a debt during his journey, and thus owed a certain proportion of his income to someone else?

Day No.	T-No.	Payment Received	Payment Made	I-U
1	1		− 40	− 40
1	2		− 10	− 50
2	3	15		− 35
4	4	40		5
4	5	25		30

Figure 5.2. Cash Flow used as a direct explanation of profit/loss.

Day No.	T-No.	Payment	Profit	Liquidity
				100 *
1	1	− 40	− 40	60
1	2	− 10	− 50	50
2	3	15	− 35	65
4	4	40	5	105
4	5	25	30	130

* Initial cash holding

Figure 5.3. Profit/loss and liquidity over time.

The change in cash holdings would then no longer be a direct expression of the profitability of his journey. And an acute and highly relevant problem would arise in such circumstances if our merchant had no available logic or language to use in describing the precise connection between profitability and liquidity when trade took place on credit.

The first steps towards the solution of this problem were taken with the introduction of *bills of exchange*. Bills of exchange are documents in which one person states that he owes another person a specific sum of money that will be paid on a specific date stated in the bill. If the debtor is known to the claimant as a prosperous and honorable person, the possession of the bill is regarded as being almost as good as the possession of cash. The bill can be described as a reliable prediction of payment. If the claimant needs the money before the date stated, it is of course possible to cash the bill and thus achieve liquidity, although the price of doing so involves the payment of interest to the bank.

A bill in which you are named as the debtor is known as a *bill of acceptance*. A bill of acceptance defines your debt, so like a bill of exchange it can be described as a reliable prediction of payment. Thanks to the use of bills of exchange, bills of acceptance and cash, it was now possible to draw up a logical calculation capable of replacing the lost but extremely important connection between *profitability* ("this is how much money I have earned/lost") and *liquidity* ("this is how much money I have available to pay with").

This new knowledge about the use of bills of exchange as a means of providing a reliable prediction of payment made it possible to understand something that had previously been impossible to understand. Merchants could now go on business trips without goods and money, and return without goods and money. But they could still be pleased with the trade they had done. If asked about the result of his trips, a merchant could answer "I have earned 90, and I'm pleased about that." And if they were asked where the money was, they could answer "It is on its way, I'm certain about that." The certainty was based on the possession of bills of exchange.

Bills of exchange and *bills of acceptance* enabled medieval merchants to do things they had never been able to do before, things that must have filled their contemporaries with amazed disbelief. They were able to predict future payments with a certainty which both they and others could regard as being reliable. Let us consider a simplified example of the kind of transaction involved.

In this example our imaginary merchant allows his cash holding of 100 to stay at home. He knows his customers and suppliers very well, which means that he is able to buy and sell on credit. On arriving home after his journey, during which he has sold everything he has bought, he brings no cash with him. Instead, he has three bills of exchange and two bills of acceptance that he now organizes according to the dates on which they are to be paid. See figure 5.4. He now has documentary evidence of his profit of 90, but he also realizes on making the calculation that *he can now predict his own suspension of payments*. If payments are made as agreed in the documents, he will be forced to suspend his payments on the 21st day.

Day No.	Document	Payment	Profit	Liquidity
				100*
20	Accept 1	– 80	– 80	20
21	Accept 2	– 60	– 140	– 40
30	Bill 1	70	– 70	30
35	Bill 2	50	– 20	80
40	Bill 3	110	**90**	190

* Initial cash holding

Figure 5.4. Prediction of own suspension of payments.

Clearly, the two bills of acceptance of 80 and 60 must be paid *before* any money is received from the bills of exchange. But the calculation is a prediction that shows that he has insufficient liquidity. The profit is 90, so the journey has undoubtedly been profitable. But our merchant has forgotten to include his liquidity as a factor. However, he now makes up for this slip by drawing up the prediction contained in figure 5.4, a prediction that enables him to prevent the problem of illiquidity from causing him to suspend his payments.

The prediction of events makes it possible to act in relation to the events predicted. Our merchant visits his bank and discounts bill 2. Bill 2 has a nominal value of 50, but the bank charges 2, leaving the merchant with proceeds of 48. He can then repeat his calculation of the financial consequences of his journey (see the new prediction of profit and payment in figure 5.5).

It is apparent that our merchant could have waited until the 20th day before discounting bill 2, since payment of the second bill of acceptance was not needed until the 21st day. But the main thing is that discounting the bill made the merchant liquid, and that the transaction took place before his creditors started to approach him in vain to obtain their money. If you are liquid you can pay your debts, and do not lose reliability in the eyes of others. If you are not liquid you cannot pay your debts, and you risk losing reliability in the eyes of others.

Figure 5.5 tells our merchant that the profit from his journey is now 88 instead of 90. It also confirms the statement made earlier to the effect that expressions of profit (financial results) and changed liquidity are expressions of the same thing. Financial results can only be expressed meaningfully if they are expressed in terms of payments.

The use of bills of exchange and acceptance meant that people gradually grew accustomed to the fact that changes in wealth owing to trade ("I have grown richer/poorer") were connected with a moment in time that did not necessarily have to correspond to the time payment was made ("the money

Day No.	Document	Payment	Profit	Liquidity
				100*
10	Bill 2	48	48	148
20	Accept 1	− 80	− 32	68
21	Accept 2	− 60	− 92	8
30	Bill 1	70	− 22	78
40	Bill 3	110	**88**	188

* Initial cash holding

Figure 5.5.   Adjusted calculation of profit for liquid enterprise.

is in the box"). This new realization was regarded as a step of great importance, and the use of the bill of exchange as a means of payment was described enthusiastically as the sea in which the vessels of trade sail, without which all trade would be impossible.

Previously, changes in wealth ("I have grown richer/poorer") could only be explained in direct connection with payments that had been made ("the money is in the box"). But now marginal changes in prosperity could be described in terms of a *reliable prediction of payment* ("the money will be in the box as soon as the customer pays"). Bills of exchange and acceptance thus became logical instruments making it possible to exchange goods at one time and money at another systematically. Bills of exchange and acceptance both contain *two financial points of measurement*. The first point is when bills are issued. Delivery is declared to have taken place, and the claim concerned has thus come into existence. We will call this first point of measurement Realized *(R)*. The second point of measurement is, of course, when payment is made. The prediction of payment is confirmed when payment is made, and we will call this point of measurement Paid *(P)*.

Figure 5.6 shows a simple model that enables us to see the financial consequences of four sales transactions. These days, of course, financial statements are consulted, in which descriptions of a great number of "business trips" and other projects are combined in a single picture of financial consequences. But modern financial statements are in fact no more than an attempt to present a complete description of the financial consequences of a large number of individual transactions whose logical content is identical with the simple and therefore more easily understood purchase and sale transactions on which our models are based.

The sales transactions in figure 5.6 are drawn up using the bill of exchange as a means of description, and the model enables us to calculate the financial consequences of the transactions of any given period. This can be done in two different ways, and these two ways are integrally connected with the two points of financial measurement described earlier. We can calculate both the payment result and the realization result for the period N.

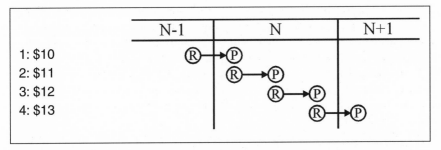

Figure 5.6. Connection between points of measurement designated "Realized" and "Paid."

The *payment result* for the period is identical to the change in liquidity. This is the result that our merchant would regard as being both necessary and sufficient if he always dealt in cash. It is calculated by adding the payments made over time, and is defined, as mentioned earlier, as the payments received during the period minus the payments made during the period. Figure 5.6 clearly shows that the payment result for period N is $33. The basic statement that can be made about the payment result is "This is the financial result for the period. The money is in the box."

Nowadays, the payment result for a period is generally referred to as the change in liquidity or cash flow during the period, thus expressing the difference between the amount of money available at the start of the period and the amount available at the end of the period.

The concept of the realization result appeared about 500 years ago, and expresses the result that is necessary and sufficient when bills of exchange are received on delivery instead of cash, provided that such bills of exchange are regarded as being a reliable prediction of payment. The financial point of measurement known as "Paid" uses the pair of concepts known as *payments made/payments received* for the cash flow being described, but as early as the Middle Ages it was acknowledged that a different but logically equally precise pair of concepts was needed for the financial point of measurement known as "Realized." The names given to this pair of concepts were *income/expenses*, and today we use these concepts to describe new amounts owed and debts arising due to the fact that the seller supplies goods on credit to the buyer. The logical content of the expressions "income" and "expense" is thus as follows:

An income is a reliable prediction of payment received.

An expense is a reliable prediction of payment made.

These days, of course, financial statements express the "result" of a period using the terms "income" and "expenses." The time of realization is preferred by merchants able to operate with calculated risks, because such merchants have one eye on the future when they act. They calculate the probability of making a loss on their claims as accurately as possible, and summarize the result over time using the financial point of measurement known as "Realized." The sense of growing richer or poorer is now associated with this point, which can be identified *earlier* than the point of measurement known as "Paid." However, the realization result is not quite as reliable as the payment result. Errors in prediction may occur occasionally, and such errors have been given the now familiar name "loss on debtors."

Specifications of individual transactions are also desirable when doing business on credit, and such specifications are easy to obtain by summarizing individual purchase and sale actions over time in terms of predictions of the payments received and made, which they reflect. The precise expression or algorithm of this sum over time T is as follows, where "I" still represents payments received, and "U" payments made:

$$R_r(T) = \sum_{t=0}^{T} (I_r(t) - U_r(t))$$

As mentioned, any growth in amounts owed or debts is exactly the same as income and expenses. Changes in prosperity can be expressed in terms of predictions of payments, and this applies both to individual business trips and to periods involving several business trips and other projects. Such predictions of payments are now expressed in the preceding algorithm by a lower case r (realized) instead of the lower case p (paid) used in the earlier algorithm.

Logically, the realization result must be regarded as a prognosis—as a prediction of the payment result. And naturally, the realization result is unreliable if payments are not made as predicted. By their very nature, predictions cannot be confirmed as being true or false until a later date, when their accuracy becomes apparent.

The new concept of realization result allows for errors in prediction between the points of measurement known as "Realized" and "Paid." Naturally, if a claim previously regarded as being good turns out not to be good, a loss will be made, and this loss must be noted as soon as it can be registered for the sake of reliability. However, for simplicity we shall omit such losses from our examples for the present, returning to this problem in a later chapter. Let us continue our analysis of basic concepts.

The use of the algorithm with the point of measurement known as "Realized" has already been demonstrated in figures 5.4 and 5.5, which show the economic result for a period as being identical with the predictions of payments acquired during the period. The two figures prove that merchants as long ago as the Middle Ages had a reliable method of predicting their liquidity and thereby predicting any possible suspension of payments.

Figure 5.6 shows that the payment and realization results for any given period are not the same. The payment result for period N is 33, whereas the realization result for the same period is 36. But the figure also shows that if we describe the financial consequences of the four chains of action without considering what are known as "accruals," naturally two identical results will be obtained, which are staggered in relation to each other. There is no error of prediction in the example shown in figure 5.6. In other words, the difference between payment and realization results has only arisen due to convention. It is the demand for interim financial statements that forces us to regard two identical phenomena as being different.

As mentioned, the realization result can be calculated systematically before the payment result is available, but this calculation requires an estimate of the prediction error—that is, an advance calculation of the risk of incurring a loss on debtors. The basic definition of the realization result for any given period is: "This is the economic result for the period. The money will be in the box, when and if the payments in question are made as agreed."

The fact that we can see that the realization result is a logical statement composed of payment predictions now makes it possible to adjust our definition of the concepts of result and liquidity as being identical. The adjusted definition is as follows: *Assertions about economic results and assertions about changed future liquidity are assertions about the same set of actions.*

Until now we have seen that expressions of changes in prosperity ("I have become richer/poorer") can be linked logically with two clearly different financial points of measurement. But which point of measurement is the "best" or "correct" or "true" one? The question is which expression should be chosen. Should one be chosen and the other abandoned? Or could the two types of statement be combined in one and the same information system?

The idea of having two financial points of measurement for any given purchase or sale was originally regarded as being such an obvious advantage that experiments were carried out involving forms of registration other than that provided by bills of exchange. Even though merchants had good reason to wish that trade should take place on credit in many situations, cash transactions were, of course, by far the most common. And naturally, it was preferable to identify the results of both forms of transaction in the same system of information, using the same logic. But how could this be achieved when cash and credit transactions both took place on the same business trip? How could it be achieved when merchants returned from their trips carrying bills of exchange, bills of acceptance, and cash? Let us consider an example of the problem involved.

Figure 5.7 shows a typical example of the simple chronological form of notation devised by medieval merchants following a number of experiments.

R-Day	T-No.	Description	P-Day	$
1	1	Buy on credit from merchant A	11	−10
1	2	Cash sale	1	20
1	3	Cash purchase	1	−10
2	4	Buy on credit from merchant B	12	−25
4	5	Sale on credit to customer C	15	40
4	6	Sale on credit to customer D	20	30

Figure 5.7. An original financial record.

We recognize the two financial points of measurement known as "Realized" and "Paid" for each individual transaction, and we can also see that each transaction has been given an individual designation by using a transaction number. This list, containing each individual purchase, sale and payment transaction in chronological order, is quite simple. But it is nonetheless of central importance with regard to the purely formal reliability of modern day financial statements. These days, this primary measurement of the financial consequences of purchase and sale transactions is known as a *record*. But other names are also used, such as "list of items," "list of transactions," "log," "audit trail" and so on.

This primary data carrier, with its unbroken, chronological record of the financial consequences of transactions, will always be a vital tool for accounts managers and accountants wishing to confirm the purely formal reliability of a given financial statement. If there is no such record, it will not be possible to see and trace the unbroken, chronological sequence of transactions. And the consequence of this will be that it will not be possible to know for certain whether any items are missing, or whether certain items have been included in a financial statement twice or more.

In other words, such records make it possible to check the formal *completeness* and *consistency* of any given financial statement. Naturally, financial statements that lack certain items are incomplete. And financial statements that include the same item several times are inconsistent, since they contain statements that contradict each other.

But do such records provide an accurate impression of economic results and liquidity? The reader will observe that figure 5.7 contains six items that say nothing about the profitability of the trip or the liquidity of the merchant involved. There is no overall view of the result of the trip. The calculations that were easy to carry out using bills of exchange and acceptance no longer seem possible. Bills of exchange, bills of acceptance and cash represent a loose-leaf system, but the record in figure 5.7 is a fixed list containing data that is tied to a chronological order.

Naturally, medieval merchants wanted knowledge of the financial situation of their enterprises. So they insisted that their need for information be met. But this was by no means an easy task. The record provided reliable data, logical completeness and consistency. But the price paid was high— there was no longer any clear idea of profitability and liquidity. The loose-leaf system involving bills of exchange, bills of acceptance and cash helped to calculate profitability and liquidity at points chosen at random. But the data provided was not particularly reliable. Documents might easily disappear or be included more than once. And there was an even more serious problem to contend with. Even if maximum care was taken with the original documents, the accuracy of the calculation itself could not always be relied on. The reader will no doubt recognize this uncertainty concerning the addition of figures. Addition carried out without the aid of machines always needs to be carried out twice, and the results compared. Anyone who has ever tried to add up a great number of figures taken from several different documents without the aid of a calculator will surely agree that the task takes a long time, and that mistakes can easily be made. Figures 5.4 and 5.5 also show that calculations involving several different figures have to be made for each individual line, which is hard enough in itself. But it is also important to note that the figures show that if only one of the bills of exchange or acceptance changes its validity (i.e., if it is paid or extended), the entire calculation has to be repeated.

Medieval merchants were faced with an extremely down-to-earth and problematic dilemma. Which system should be chosen, and what could they most easily do without? Was data reliability, completeness and consistency more important than the meeting of their need for information? Was it possible to achieve a regular flow of information regarding profitability and liquidity?

As time went by, merchants and their assistants realized that they needed what is referred to nowadays as a reliable information system.

As the merchants discovered, the greatest problem was the provision of a general answer to the following question: "How can we convert chronological information about transactions systematically into figures that are capable of providing us with a good general picture of both profitability and liquidity? And how can this be done to ensure that transactions involving both credit and cash can be included in the same system?"

In the course of the fifteenth century, this problem was solved by the merchants of Venice using a method that was so simple, general and convincing that it was subsequently regarded as nothing less than a stroke of genius. Two inventions were needed to construct the system required. One was taken from the world of trade, and the other was found in the world of mathematics.

First, the invention taken from trade. The solution of the problem was made much easier by the discovery of the fact that sales on credit and sales in cash were remarkably similar in the sense that credit sale transactions changed and resembled cash sale transactions as soon as customers paid their debt on expiry of the term of credit. Payment meant that claims no longer existed, and that the money was in the box. Saying that a claim no longer exists is logically the same as denying and therefore cancelling a previous statement regarding the existence of such a claim.

At some point (no one knows exactly when), someone had the straightforward but inspired idea of regarding what was familiar and simple as being a variation on what was new and more complicated, in other words of regarding cash sales as being a logical variation of credit sales. Any statement about purchases or sales could be regarded logically as containing two pieces of information: one concerning changes in prosperity, and the other concerning method of payment. And all statements concerning payments would then either be connected to a statement regarding changes in prosperity, or be a confirmation of a prediction of payment stated previously.

The medieval merchants now realized that two logical statements could be made both at the moment of realization and at the moment of payment for the same transaction, statements that were always simultaneous, and thus could and should always be viewed in connection with the other pair of statements in order to be meaningful.

Figure 5.8 shows this double pair of statements as expressions of being richer/poorer, combined with simultaneous statements concerning not paid/paid. At the time of realization the pair of statements contained an expression of change in prosperity plus an expression of documentation: new claim or cash. If payment was made in cash at the same time as realization, the transaction had been fully described. If not, the other double entry came into force. At the time of payment the pair of statements contained a negation of a claim plus a statement either of payment, or of loss if it was discovered that a claim was worthless.

The following system of registration was chosen: An income is logically identical with a claim that has been acquired, and similarly an expense is logically identical with a new item of debt. Then (sometimes simultaneously) payments are made, which cancel (equalize) items of claim and debt, thereby confirming the predictions of payments.

The information system needed was expected to cope with all the types of statement mentioned. Consequently, a calculation (or account) was needed for each of the following transactions:

1. Income ("richer statements")
2. Expenses ("poorer statements")
3. Claims equals predictions of payments received (known nowadays as "debtors")
4. Debt equals predictions of payments made (known nowadays as "creditors")
5. Cash (known nowadays as cash in hand or at bank, autowithdrawal and so forth)

We have already seen that statements of result are logically connected to the act of supplying goods, and thus to the financial point of measurement

	Richer	Poorer
Not Paid	New Claim = Income	New Debt = Expense
Paid	Payment Received	Payment Made

Figure 5.8. The logical content of double entry registration.

known as *Realized,* i.e., to the pair of concepts known as "income" and "expenses." The other three accounts describe predictions of payments and confirmations of these predictions.

The method of calculation chosen (the account form) is still generally used. Experiments revealed that the task of addition, which naturally took place without calculators in the Middle Ages, meant that the easiest technique was to draw up independent columns of positive and negative figures. The account was thus shaped like the letter T, with the vertical line separating the two columns of figures. After further experiments, it was discovered that it was a good idea to separate statements about changes in prosperity from statements about payments systematically. The same figure was thus registered simultaneously in two different accounts when items were entered.

The basic form of these accounts consisted of four types of account only: "Predictions of payments received" (claims), "Predictions of payments made" (debt), "Income" and "Expenses." Over the course of time, these four main items have been given many different names, and these days they are known as "Assets," "Liabilities," "Profit" and "Loss" respectively. *Predictions of payments* are included in the *balance sheet,* and statements concerning *changes in prosperity* are known as the *profit and loss account.*

The two sides of these first simple accounts were called "debit" and "credit." The two words come from Latin, and simply mean "owed by me" and "owed to me" respectively. Customers who owed anything were known as "debtors," and suppliers who were owed anything were known as "creditors."

The idea that finally made this system complete, and that ensured data reliability and provided merchants with the information regarding profitability and liquidity that they needed, was taken from the world of mathematics. Quite simply, it was agreed to reverse the sign in front of corresponding items so that the sum of each double entry item was always zero. The entire accounts consisted of individual items, so the total sum of the accounts as a whole was also zero. Nowadays, we say that such accounts "balance." But this simply means that we are sure that the accounts contain exactly the same data *after* the record has been organized as *before* the record was organized.

The system was given its time-honored and worldwide name based on the principles outlined. Figure 5.9 shows the simple but inspired basic registration system of double entry bookkeeping as it still exists today. After more than 500 years, there have been no fundamental changes in the logic of this system, either with regard to the rules of measurement or with regard to the rules of data processing. Double entry bookkeeping has undoubtedly worn well.

The nonspecialist may be surprised to see that the sign in front of "loss" is positive, and that the item "profit" has a negative sign. It should surely be the other way around. Losses are generally regarded as being negative, whereas profits are positive.

But it is easy enough to explain this apparent inconsistency, which is due to the simple but inspired data processing rule that ensures the purely formal reliability of this system of information. The rule of double entry bookkeeping is that each item should be entered simultaneously using the same figure on both the debit side (+) and the credit side (–). If this rule is observed, the sum of the figures contained in the system will always be 0. The sum of the positive figures is identical with the sum of the negative figures. We say that the accounts "balance."

Figure 5.9 shows an example of the way the system works when applied to a single sales transaction on credit. The two staggered financial points of measurement are shown in the books. At time $t(r)$ the prediction of payments received is registered in the form of a claim of 100, and the seller here declares that he has become more prosperous. And at time $t(p)$ the statement of the claim is canceled, because payment has been made. If the transaction described in figure 5.9 had taken place in cash, no time would elapse between the two financial points of measurement, and any change in prosperity would thus have been entered in the form of a single double entry item set off directly in the account for cash holdings (the cash account).

The claim is noted in figure 5.9 as being paid at time $t(p)$. But if the claim had not been met, the seller would have been forced to register not payment, but a debit in the account for losses (expenses): "I have become poorer," and a credit in the buyer's account: "claim cancelled."

Balance Sheet Account		Profit and Loss Account	
Buyer's Account		**Loss and Profit**	
Debit (+)	Credit (–)	Debit (+)	Credit (–)
$t(r)$ 100			$t(r)$ 100
	$t(p)$ 100		
Cash Account			
Debit (+)	Credit (–)		
$t(p)$ 100			

Figure 5.9. The registration system of double entry bookkeeping.

The formulation of these rules was a great leap forward for the art of accounting. On arriving home following a business trip, or on conclusion of a project, merchants were now able to obtain a clear impression of profitability and liquidity, and to inform others of this impression, by studying each individual item in their records, counting their cash holding and then using double entry bookkeeping. The items in the record could be copied one by one into a book containing preprinted accounts.

Thanks to this copying and organization of data, it was always possible to balance the books and thus remain certain that the data used was reliable. The rule stating that the sum of all items should always be zero meant that the books could be balanced at any time. And if "consolidated accounts" were needed (i.e., if several sets of data needed to be combined) the simple balancing rule was vital in terms of data reliability. It still is. There is still no such thing as a trial balance that is *more or less* correct. Either the books balance, which means that the figures are reliable and the organization and copying have been accurate. Or the books do not balance, in which case the figures are not reliable because it is apparent that one or more mistakes have been made.

Following copying, organization and balancing, it was now possible to obtain data in which chronological measurements appeared in the form of *management accounts*, providing systematic coverage of the needs of merchants for information.

Figure 5.10 shows this economic model, which was new in the Middle Ages, following conversion of the chronological measurements already outlined in the record of a business trip (figure 5.7).

Readers will no doubt observe the control figures underneath the table in figure 5.10. The rule is as follows: The sum of assets minus the sum of liabilities is always numerically identical with the sum of income minus the sum of expenses. This means that data reliability, and thus logical completeness and consistency from chronological measurements, can now be said to exist following systematic organization. Nonspecialist readers can confirm the data reliability of the system by carrying out a control check after each individual item in the example shown in figure 5.10. But readers who are familiar with the world of accounting will have no need of such measures, since they already know and accept the formal reliability of this set of rules.

Nonspecialists studying the individual items in figures 5.9 and 5.10 will discover that the phenomenon of "an account" can simply be regarded as a combined register of figures specifying positive and negative sums. No time need be spent on speculating about the strange words "debit" and "credit." Instead of using the word "debit," we can say "add to the positive figures" (assets, claims, predictions of payments received) whenever you register a sale (an income). And instead of using the word "credit," we can say "add to the negative figures" (liabilities, debts, predictions of

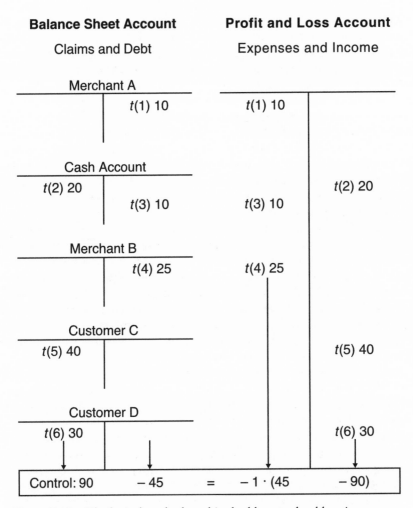

Figure 5.10. The logical method used in double entry bookkeeping.

payments made) whenever you register a purchase (an expense). Whenever a claim is met by payment, one of the assets of the seller (cash holdings) increases, and another asset (debtors, predictions of payments received) decreases accordingly. Naturally, this kind of balancing has no effect on the result for the period, since the result is expressed using concepts such as income and expenses.

A simple task will enable the nonspecialist reader to confirm his or her understanding of the system. If the business trip shown in the record in figure 5.7 was carried out by one of the merchant's assistants, and if this assistant carried 50 coins with him when he started the trip, how many coins would he have to give the merchant on his return? The answer can be found easily by studying the movements shown in the cash account in figure 5.10. The merchant, of course, will ask for 60 coins from his assistant.

Figure 5.10 also shows us that double entry bookkeeping was a huge leap forward in the world of accounting. Merchants could now obtain a precise idea of their claims and debts. Individual items in the record could now be organized and divided into accounts for debtors (claims) and creditors (debts) respectively. My customer regards me as a supplier, and my supplier regards me as a customer. So the figure described in my books as a claim on customer D will appear in customer D's books as a debt. The same phenomenon is thus interpreted differently, depending on one's point of view. The respective roles and the situation affect one's point of view and the concept in question.

This realization meant that merchants now found it easy to agree with both customers and suppliers regarding the size of the figures they owed each other at any time. The balance of any account could be determined immediately, and if two parties arrived at two different figures, the balance could be itemized and the reason for the disagreement revealed. Apart from the initial plus or minus sign, the balance of the merchant's account should always be identical with the balance of the customer's account, and this identity could be checked. The two accounts always consisted logically of the same chronological list of claims and payments.

Figure 5.10 shows that the accounts of the balance sheet are divided into individual accounts that permit itemization of the accounts of each individual debtor and creditor. Readers will have no difficulty in imagining an individual supplier or customer account in which several purchase and sale transactions are itemized. A calculation of the balance in such an account reveals how much is owing and still requires payment. Consequently, we can say that the division demonstrates that double entry bookkeeping represents an information system that supports the *systematic control of payments*. Monitoring of the correct entry of payments and control of the dispatch of one's own payments can be supported by information provided by the system, and it is actually rather difficult to imagine that these tasks could be carried out reliably without the use of the data items shown in the figure.

Naturally, in practice accounting systems are a good deal more complicated than the small-scale model system shown in figure 5.10. In practice, individual debtor, creditor and cash accounts in the balance sheet have their own data carriers, and balancing can only be carried out by studying and combining figures from many different individual accounts.

The items of the profit and loss account are also combined in a single account in figure 5.10, whereas in practice a number of sale and purchase accounts would be involved, divided into type and location. The account items also need to be counted and combined in order to balance them against the items in the balance sheet.

The simplified account for expenses and income (loss and profit) in figure 5.10 shows another great advantage introduced by double entry bookkeeping. It is apparent that merchants could now not only check their payments systematically, but also satisfy their need for information regarding profitability in the form of a calculation of the realization result, which is composed of statements concerning the income and expenses of a period. Even though figure 5.10 is highly simplified and only contains six items, it is still sufficient to show that users are free to choose any accounts period using this system. The realization result of 45 shown in figure 5.10 is found by calculating the difference between an income of 90 and expenses of 45 during the period concerned, which is defined as the time interval $t(1)$ to $t(6)$.

All transactions are measured in the record at a given time (i.e., within a specific time interval), which means that any given transaction number interval provides an unambiguous description of the period concerned. But as mentioned earlier, the choice of period is quite arbitrary. For instance, if you want to know the result of the period $t(2)$ to $t(5)$, it is easy enough to calculate the figure required: $60 - 35 = 25$.

In other words, there is no systematic requirement or natural law stating that you have to operate with specific, predefined accounting periods. The fact that many accounting systems are designed to produce fixed, predefined interim reports, for which users must wait until they have been finalized, is not the result of any natural law. The reason for this disadvantageous practice is rather the lack of sufficiently advanced information processing techniques.

The definition of double entry bookkeeping as an information system is as follows:

Double entry bookkeeping is an information system whose measurements and algorithms support the chronological, systematic and reliable processing of predictions of payments.

In a subsequent chapter we shall return to a further discussion of the logic behind the measurement and itemization methods used in accounting. And we shall see that the old, time-honored and illustrious information system known as double entry bookkeeping reached and overstepped its logical limits some time ago.

NOTE

1. Y. Ijiri, *The Foundations of Accounting Measurement*, p. 102.

6   FINANCIAL STATEMENTS— THE CONFUSING IMAGES OF PAST EVENTS

There are very few areas of science in which masks and cosmetics are used to the same extent as in the world of accounting.

—*Richard Mattessich*

The presentation of financial statements by business enterprises is always regarded as an important event worthy of considerable attention and interest. Financial statements are required by the law, and are subject to the law. They represent the only source of financial information that is accessible to the many interested parties outside the enterprises concerned. The law states that the impression of an enterprise's financial situation conveyed by financial statements must be "true and fair," and undoubtedly regards the content of financial statements as being more important than the way they are presented. *But the truth is that it is impossible to describe the financial position of a business enterprise using traditional financial statements.* All attempts to do so are doomed to failure. The practical presentation of financial statements is based all over the world on seven apparently sound, so-called "basic principles." But these principles are in fact based on nothing more than traditional practice and custom. It would actually be more honest to describe traditional financial statements as "unfounded dogma," as a logically dubious tradition whose continued use results in the loss of great material and human resources every day of the year. As tools for describing the financial situation of a business enterprise, traditional financial statements are worthless, because it is impossible to describe something that is constantly changing using something that only changes once a year.

In chapter 5 we described the main features of the logic behind the registration and data processing techniques of accounting—the more than 500 year old method of double entry bookkeeping, which is still used all over the world to organize and carry out regular registration of the interaction of enterprises with their outside environments (purchase, sale and payment transactions). Chapter 5 also showed that the use of the two pairs of concepts, income/payments received and expense/payments made, meant that it was possible to measure a "marginal change in prosperity" for each individual transaction, regardless of whether payment was made at the same time as each transaction or at a later date. In double entry bookkeeping, marginal changes in prosperity are thus linked to the realization time of each individual purchase or sale transaction. In general, it is assumed that payment is made either when transactions take place (payment in cash), or at a specified later date (payment on credit).

We can now claim familiarity with the logic of this basic registration technique. We are also now aware of the main features of financial accounts kept to control payments and provide documentation of activities. Double entry bookkeeping is regarded all over the world as an indispensable means of registration. And the following statement is so obvious that it is never discussed: "Naturally, anyone *disclosing* financial statements must also *keep* financial accounts."

In this chapter we shall take a closer look at the special way in which the basic registration techniques of double entry bookkeeping are used to draw up the special accounting reports that we call traditional financial statements.

Apart from the words "financial statements," the title of this chapter also contains three words that describe three important features of the traditional world of accounting. These features can all be traced back to the way annual and interim financial statements are currently understood.

The first of these three words is "confusing," which refers to the fact that traditional financial statements simply *cannot be understood* by the reader. They cannot be understood in relation to the real world without appearing to be self-contradictory. And when any information such as that contained in financial statements is incomprehensible but claimed to be important, the result will undoubtedly be confusion and frustration. We remind the reader of the title of chapter 3.

The second word is "images," which refers to the fact that financial statements always contain a figure that is claimed to give an impression of the *financial result* for the period concerned. This figure is supposed to show something about the efficiency of the enterprise concerned during the period, and is included in the so-called "profit and loss account." The figure is generally referred to as the "result for the period," but also as the "profit," "deficit" and so on. Accounting theorists and practitioners have long been aware that it is logically impossible to express a "financial result" using a single figure alone. But no better alternative has yet been found, so the practice continues.

The third word is "past," which refers to the fact that financial statements are primarily regarded as a form of *financial history*, as reports describing the financial consequences of events that have already occurred. But the word also refers to the banal but significant fact that financial statements are always published some time after the date on which they closed. It often takes three months or more to draw up a financial statement, so enterprises whose accounting year is the same as the calendar year are not usually able to present their annual financial statements until April or May the following year.

In 1983, the Danish Institute of Certified Public Accountants (DICPA) published a pamphlet outlining five "basic accounting principles," but in the "Danish Accounting Standards," 1987, this figure was increased to seven. We shall now list these seven so-called principles, and comment upon them in brief.

1. Enterprises should be regarded as "going concerns"
2. Continuity is important
3. Accruals
4. Substance over form
5. Materiality (Relevance)
6. Separate valuation of assets and liabilities
7. Prudence

The first principle, known as the "going concern" principle, is expressed in the language of *religious belief*. It states clearly that certain external conditions will remain unchanged in the future, that the future can be predicted, and that consequently certain undesirable events will not take place:

Enterprises are normally regarded as being going concerns, i.e., they are expected to continue operations in the foreseeable future. Among other things, this implies that enterprises neither intend nor need to liquidate or make material reductions in their operations.[1]

It is a widely accepted fact that in the real world enterprises cannot necessarily be expected to continue operations, and that the future is far from foreseeable. But this fact is ignored in the first principle. There have been many examples in recent years of enterprises being *forced* to "liquidate or make material reductions in their operations." But such events are regarded by the DICPA as being unpleasant surprises, the exception rather than the rule.

Modern scientific theory is based on the concept that the future is not at all foreseeable, so it is surely no exaggeration to claim that the "going concern" principle is entirely out of step with modern research and science, and that it reflects a somewhat naive, oversimplified and obsolete view of reality. Anyone interested in obtaining an accounting practice that is scientifically reliable must surely reject any claim that the future is "foreseeable."

The unrealistic "going concern" principle should be abandoned forthwith, and could be replaced by a principle containing the following statement: *The future is unpredictable, and the future financial situation of an enterprise can never be predicted by statistical forecasting.*" This statement would be in accordance with current scientific theory, and the notion of predictability is dealt with in chapters 8, 11 and 12.

The second principle outlined by the DICPA deals with the notion of consistency. The Danish text has the word *continuity*, which is certainly not the same as consistency:

The same accounting principles are applied from one financial year to the next, just as the opening balance for each year is the same as the closing balance for the previous year. The principle of continuity (consistency) also implies that the same accounting policy is applied to all items with a similar content in a financial year.[2]

Professional behavior is very rarely based on the recommendation that you should simply do what you normally do. And yet this is clearly what the DICPA recommends. The message to accountants is "Don't think! Just do what you normally do." No reason is given for the recommendation that continuity is in itself of any value when it comes to presenting financial statements.

Once again, the DICPA seems to assume that the world is calm and stable, governed by continuity. If current accounting practice were the best possible accounting practice, then no one would mind continuing to apply it. However, it is surely unwise to continue the use of an accounting practice that has already had disastrous results for a great number of business enterprises. The principle of continuity is surely dubious and even dangerous. If professional people simply close their eyes and automatically do what they normally do, then serious problems will soon arise. Because the world, of course, is constantly changing in the most unexpected ways.

The third DICPA principle states that income and expenses must relate to specific periods, a principle that traditional financial statements regard as being extremely important: "Revenues and costs relating to the year which the annual accounts cover are recognized, irrespective of the time of payment."[3] The problem with this principle was illustrated in chapter 2, where Johnson and Kaplan's entertaining example of the caravan in the Persian desert showed how difficult it could be to estimate revenues and costs for individual quarters of the year, a task that is logically impossible. The entire traditional theory of periodic accounting is based in general on the statement "The future event designated X has already partially occurred," which is a logical contradiction in terms.

The fourth DICPA principle has already been referred to in this chapter, and states that "Substance is more important than form": Transactions and other events should be accounted for and presented according to their substance and financial reality and not only with regard for their legal form.[4]

Everyone will surely agree that substance and meaning are the most important things, and that form is no more than a language in which a given substance can be expressed precisely and clearly. The structure given to our methods and descriptions must be adapted to suit our wish to communicate logical substance, and this must apply to all professional communication. For instance, if a surgeon has discovered and successfully tried a new operation technique, it is of course important to ensure that there are no spelling mistakes or omissions in the description of the technique. But the most important thing is that other surgeons are able to learn how to use the method correctly. And this will depend on whether they accept and understand the reasons for the new method. This is the only way to introduce the method and enable surgeons to use it whenever it is superior to traditional methods and refrain from using it when it is not.

In other words, it is difficult to contest the statement that substance is more important than form. It must be regarded as a general statement applying to all types of professional communication and teaching. And the fact that it is a general statement means that it is difficult to use as a specific accounting principle. It is, after all, what can best be described as a *truism*, a banal matter of course. It is always true to say that substance is more important than form. But if something is always true, there is no reason to draw attention to it.

The fact that the statement is included as one of the DICPA's accounting principles is probably due to the wish of practicing accountants to agree on a fundamental issue. The message of the DICPA may well be as follows: "We know that current accounting practice leaves much to be desired, because otherwise we would not spend time drawing up new principles. We also agree that it is the substance of financial statements that is the important thing."

The fifth DICPA principle is that all information in financial statements must be relevant:

In the preparation and presentation of the annual financial statements, special emphasis should be given to factors which are material for the understanding of the undertaking's assets and liabilities, its financial position and profit and loss. Neither the Accounting Standards nor the Annual Accounts Act are concerned with factors which are immaterial for the understanding of the annual financial statements.[5]

The DICPA emphasizes that some information is important, but does not specify why. Consequently, this principle is rather difficult to understand. How can anyone claim that emphasis should be attached to certain information that is important without specifying why it is important? At the heart of this DICPA principle lies another truism. Professionals in all walks of life have to distinguish between what is material for understanding and what is not. But what does "material for understanding" actually mean?

Let us study this point in greater detail. The meaning of the expression "material for understanding" or "importance in a given context" is the same as the meaning of "relevance" (the word relevance may remind readers of the title of Johnson and Kaplan's *Relevance Lost*).

Can the DICPA principle be interpreted as an admission that anyone drawing up a financial statement and communicating its content to others must be aware of the problem of understanding and its possible solution before anything else? Is this an admission of the need for a clear basic framework of concepts? How can specialists explain what "assets" and "liabilities" are unless they are certain that they can define these key concepts unambiguously themselves?

Here, too, there may be a chance for development and progress. Practicing accountants who wish to give special attention to factors that are "material for the understanding of the undertaking's assets and liabilities, its financial position and profit and loss" must need a clear and noncontradictory theory of accounting. Definitions are needed as tools to establish this kind of understanding.

The sixth DICPA principle explains that financial statements must be itemized to a certain degree, which must surely reflect the wish to prevent any concealment of details. The principle states that items should be valued individually:

The individual items under assets and liabilities must be separately valued, and the netting off of assets and liabilities or costs and revenues is not allowed. The fact that assets and liabilities are valued separately implies that an asset must not be overstated because another asset is understated. Correspondingly, an asset must not be understated because a liabilitiy is not included or is understated in the balance sheet.[6]

This principle may seem perfectly plausible, indicating a concern for detail that may reassure the reader of the reliability of financial statements. Each item must be valued individually, which should mean that the sums of different items are correct and reliable. However, the fact is that this principle is quite meaningless, owing to two very important and well-known reasons.

The first reason is that there are no scientific methods for evaluating individual items. And the second reason is that the requirement that attention should primarily be paid to details tends to shift the emphasis of evaluation away from the most important thing, which is to view the enterprise concerned as a whole. The legal requirement for a "true and fair picture" emphasizes the importance of an overall view.

In chapter 10, we shall note how an experienced certified public accountant describes the practical effect of traditional so-called evaluation principles in very critical terms. He uses the word "elasticity," and claims that it is impossible to prevent the creation of so-called secret reserves. In chapter 12 we shall see that current evaluation principles have absolutely no scientific foundation, which means that no comprehensible criteria for the selection of such "principles" can be given. In other words, it is no use pretending to make evaluations of assets and liabilities when no well-defined scale of measurement for such evaluations exists.

For instance, the sixth DICPA principle will result in considerable, insurmountable practical difficulties if the object being valued is a single, large-scale, coordinated project consisting of several separate projects, each of which involves elements of production, research, ongoing control and development. Engaging new professional staff in such projects is time consuming, and the loss of a single key member of staff during the project may be a major catastrophe. In many cases, it may take new members of staff six to nine months to acquire sufficient knowledge to contribute effectively to the project. How can an accountant then be expected to enter such an enterprise from the outside and quickly evaluate or even describe such a project by considering each item individually? The idea is simply preposterous. So it is preposterous to require that it should be carried out.

The final principle in DICPA's list is also the best known of them all. It states that all due prudence should be exercised, and is described by the DICPA as follows:

Uncertainties inevitably surround many of the items which are included in the financial statements accounts. Therefore, prudence must be exercised in the preparation of financial statements. However, prudence does not justify the creation of secret or hidden reserves.[7]

The principle of prudence, that losses should be accepted when they seem likely, but income only when it is certain, is well-known to anyone with a rudimentary knowledge of accounting. It is reasonable to claim that this particular accounting principle is *the most dangerous* of them all. It can be regarded as a direct and extremely serious threat to the reliability of the accounting profession.

This claim is based on the fact that the principle of prudence is a logical contradiction in terms, because it requires behavior in direct contravention to the behavior regarded as natural by managers. Managers are used to operating in a world that is expected to change unpredictably. It is a world that contains a risk that does not exist in a world that has a "foreseeable future."

The only people who can conceive of risk, adjust to risk and describe it as a "calculated risk" are those who accept the very existence of risk. *And there is no risk in a future that is predictable.*

The principle of exercising prudence is so well-known in accounting practice that it is automatically regarded as being correct. This problem is so basic and significant that we have decided to deal with it separately in chapter 10. For the moment we shall merely indicate a single obvious example demonstrating that the principle of prudence contradicts another of the DICPA's principles. The reader may note that the preceding quotation implies that only realized profits should be included in financial statements. This means that the "production principle" may not be used. Naturally, projects that are still "in progress" have not yet been realized. And yet it is still not forbidden to use the "production principle." Indeed, it is widely used and recognized. In other words, accountants are allowed to be *imprudent*, as long as they are *prudent*. The logic of this situation is not easy to pinpoint.

Actually, it is surprising that people can be persuaded to believe that financial statements can be presented either "prudently" or "imprudently." Of course managers may be more or less cautious in their actions, since caution in relation to actions can be measured in terms of the consequences of such actions. Enterprises either survive and flourish, or they wither and die.

But it is not possible to conceive of prudence in relation to financial statements. Is it possible to present a prudent financial statement that describes the actions of an imprudent manager? We refer the reader once again to chapter 10.

The conclusion must be that what the DICPA chooses to call "Fundamental Accounting Principles" can actually be regarded from two points of view—a traditional/authoritarian point of view, and a skeptical, scientific point of view. And if the latter point of view is adopted, the following statement ensues: *Traditional so-called accounting principles are nothing but names given to traditional procedures that are logically empty of content, and therefore without effect.*

Let us now consider the DICPA's seven so-called accounting principles once again, but this time we shall describe them in a manner reflecting the open, skeptical/scientific point of view. The seven principles now reveal the lack of scientific foundation for the accounting practices adhered to all over the world as the twentieth century draws to its close. Current accounting practice is based on an authoritarian demand that we should respect the following:

1. An unrealistic claim (enterprises are regarded as "going concerns")
2. Force of habit (continuity is important)
3. An unnecessary irritant (income and expenses must relate to specific periods)
4. A truism (substance over form)
5. Another truism (materiality)
6. A utopian idea (separate valuation of assets and liabilities)
7. Nonsense (the principle of prudence)

Perhaps this presentation of traditional accounting principles has angered my readers, and if so it is worth adding that traditional accounting principles may well be the best possible accounting principles. But in order to prove that this is the case, such readers must answer the critical viewpoints presented here by revealing the scientifically viable foundation and concepts of traditional accounting. For this is the only way of satisfying the demands of skeptical accounting theorists.

The fact that the practice and theory of accounting have drifted so far apart that they are now in direct contradiction to each other is a paradox with alarming practical consequences. It is a disturbing fact that the following statement can be made to describe current accounting practice all over the Western world: "Traditional accounting practice is contrary to common sense, and common sense is contrary to traditional accounting practice."

Let us now consider the way traditional financial statements are drawn up in terms of their main items. Financial statements, of course, consist of three main sections:

1. A profit and loss account
2. A balance sheet
3. A report and notes

These three sections are regarded as forming what is described as "a whole." The first two sections make up the actual financial statement, and the third consists of comments, specifications and additional details. It is assumed that the profit and balance for any given period can be stated "correctly."

As all accounting specialists know, the process of drawing up a financial statement starts by making a copy of all the sums and balances entered in accounts organized according to the principles of double entry bookkeeping. This copy is known as a *trial balance*. It is drawn up at the *end of a period*, which means that it should include all the items from the first day of the period up to and including the last day. Naturally, this trial balance cannot be drawn up until after the end of the period concerned. In practice, and assuming that the necessary bookkeeping has been performed efficiently, trial balances can be drawn up the day after the period ends.

But after this date a certain amount of time has to elapse to ensure that all necessary items from the previous period have been included. Naturally, some suppliers send invoices more slowly than others for services rendered. So in practice a certain delay is always required, a delay that is irritating but necessary to ensure that the trial balance really does contain all relevant items.

The delay is generally spent in calculating what are known as "accruals," a name given to items regarded as describing the "value" of an enterprise's stock, its "work in progress," and what are known as its "fixed assets." Items regarded as having a value are entered under assets in the balance sheet. Otherwise, items are "written down," "depreciated" or itemized as a loss made during the period concerned.

Calculating accruals is time consuming work. For instance, stock is often evaluated by finding out what its original price was. As long as stock has not been in store too long, its "historic cost price" is regarded as being an expression of its value. Otherwise it is "written down." The precise meaning of the expression "historic cost price" is quite unknown, and no one knows why goods are claimed to have a value identical with the price originally paid for them. In chapter 12 the reader will find a list of all the different so-called "stock evaluation principles," and will realize that there is no good reason to use these "principles" other than the fact they have always been used. There are a good many different "principles" (last-in first-out (LIFO), first-in first-out (FIFO), and so forth) to choose from, and the final "stock value" often varies considerably depending on the "principle" used. So this practice causes a great deal of confusion. The literature on accounting contains no explanation of when it is reasonable to use any of these "stock evaluation principles," or when to refrain from using them. It seems to be up to the individual to decide. The only thing accountants must remember is that they should do what they normally do, otherwise they will no longer be obeying the requirement for continuity.

What are known as "work in progress" and "fixed assets" also have to be accrued. For these items, too, the fact is that accruals are completely meaningless for anyone requiring a scientifically viable explanation. To be blunt, the process of establishing their value is based on illogical ritual.

No one knows better than accounting specialists themselves that depreciation, write-down, revaluation and so forth are merely games with figures—not expressions of anything real. But everyone continues to go through the motions of calculating such figures, referring to the fact that the law says that we must do so.

Once all these accruals have been discussed, they are entered as "post entries" in the trial balance, after which various linguistic adjustments are carried out, and the enterprise concerned is ready to present its *annual financial statement*, a document that is boldly claimed to give a "true and fair view of the company's assets and liabilities."

But the accrual ritual actually enables enterprises to shape this document according to their own wishes and interests. If the management wishes to show a relatively large, impressive "accounting profit" for the year, it behaves accordingly and seeks to maximize its assets. And if the management wishes the opposite, it seeks to maximize its liabilities. There are no scientifically viable methods of evaluating all these accruals, so naturally the result is that the profit and loss account expressed in terms of "profit," and "loss," is completely impossible to interpret, and thus completely *unreliable*.

The management can fix the profit as it wishes within a very wide margin. The figure described as the "profit for the year" by the management cannot be accepted or rejected based on common sense. Managers can ask their accounts manager and accountant "What was the profit for the year?" And the accounts manager and accountant can answer "What would you like it to be?" The language of accounting is a weak, flexible and imprecise tool that can be used to great effect by unscrupulous opportunists all over the world.

The worst thing about this situation is that accounting specialists with practical experience are perfectly aware of the fact that traditional financial statements do not give a true and fair picture of anything at all, that they are simply incapable of doing so. Accounts managers and accountants are all aware that the traditional balance sheet model is not and never can be a realistic description (a true and fair picture) of the company's financial situation (assets and liabilities) at any given time.

The situation is absurd. Accountants spend a lot of time trying to do a job that they know is impossible. This claim is very easy to prove. We simply have to quote the following excerpts from the DICPA's pamphlet on financial statements. The DICPA says that the profit and loss account is regarded as reflecting history, so this statement is of little interest to us here. The pamphlet states that "The purpose of the profit and loss account is to inform readers of a company's level of activity and earnings during the previous year."

But the description of the balance sheet is somewhat more interesting. We take the liberty of quoting the revealing sentence in italics:

The main purpose of the balance sheet is to provide a clear view of a company's assets, debts, provisions and equity capital. . . . *The balance sheet is not a precise expression of the value of a company on a given date.*[8]

The DICPA could just as easily have written "The balance sheet is not a reliable expression of the assets and liabilities of a company on a given date," since owing to the lack of a concrete definition of the term "value of a company," this value must be expressed as the difference between assets and liabilities—the difference between holdings (what we have) and debt (what we owe to others), at the time in question. The preceding italicized sentence can thus be written as follows: "The balance sheet is not and can never be a reliable expression of the assets and liabilities of a company on a given date." The conclusion of this reasoning must be that practicing accountants themselves regard it as being impossible to meet the requirements of the law.

The reason why it is impossible to give a "true and fair picture" in the balance sheet is straightforward and well-known. Quite simply, the main items in the balance sheet are not all defined in the same way. In chapter 3, which concerned the lack of basic concepts in accounting, we saw Robert N. Anthony emphasizing that it is meaningless to add up items that do not have the same properties. The DICPA expresses this problem as follows in its pamphlet:

The balance sheet contains a number of items such as cash holdings and bank deposits which can be stated precisely, whereas the value of other items such as stock, operating plant, property, and so forth, must always be based on an estimate of their value for the company in its future operations.[9]

The reader may recall that the concepts of *solvency* and *insolvency* were used and analyzed earlier, which led us to the conclusion that *these two concepts were most important.* "Solvency" means the absence of risk for creditors, and "insolvency" means the presence of risk for creditors. Solvent companies cause no financial problems for the simple reason that the creditors of such companies are in no danger of incurring any losses. Consequently, *insolvency is the only decisive accounting concept describing risk*. If only incipient insolvency owing either to "lack of profitability" in "primary operations" or other factors could be predicted, then it could truly be claimed that *a vital problem in theoretical accounting had been solved.*

These concepts of solvency and insolvency are both defined using the well-known basic concepts of assets and liabilities that are prominent features of financial statements. We also saw that solvency and insolvency are the only concepts that are really of vital importance to people interested in the situation of business enterprises. And we saw that the two concepts are defined using assets and liabilities, *And yet the concepts of solvency and insolvency are not mentioned anywhere in the DICPA pamphlet about financial statements, nor are these two key concepts mentioned or dealt with anywhere in the 700 page long Danish Company Accounts Act with its appurtenant comments.*

Why is it that the only accounting concepts of real and decisive importance for people interested in the situation of business enterprises, and that are defined as the difference between assets and liabilities, are also the only concepts systematically ignored by accounting specialists? This must surely be regarded as something of a $64,000 question.

One important element in the answer is undoubtedly the dogmatic statement that enterprises should be regarded as going concerns. If financial statements have to be drawn up according to this unrealistic principle, the effect is that any consideration of risk is systematically ignored. The Act actually gives accounting specialists prior forgiveness for any sins of omission that they may be forced to commit. In practice, attention is fully concentrated on a phenomenon called a "financial statement" containing the concepts of "assets" and "liabilities" as its two most important logical elements.

The only thing people interested in the situation of business enterprises really need is information concerning solvency, a concept that is also formed by comparing the concepts of "assets" and "liabilities." And yet financial statements say nothing about the solvency of enterprises. The concept of solvency is almost unknown in accounting theory and practice—in other words, a concept of decisive importance is virtually ignored by accounting specialists.

Anyone who believes that solvency is revealed by traditional financial statements will encounter severe difficulty. The unexpected financial catastrophes of recent years in trade and industry show beyond a shadow of doubt that traditional financial statements do not contain information about the solvency and insolvency of business enterprises.

In chapter 4 we presented the following hypothesis, which we intend to consider in greater detail. We tried to refute the statement that "Traditional financial statements are worthless as a means of describing the financial situation of business enterprises."

So far we have definitely not been able to refute this statement. In fact, the statement seems to have been confirmed. Let us now briefly repeat the logical defects that must be attributed to traditional financial statements. Unfortunately, the financial statements that people outside business enterprises are still forced to accept as their only source of information about the financial situation of such enterprises are:

1. *static*, instead of being dynamic
2. *out-of-date*, instead of being up-to-date
3. *unclear*, instead of being clear
4. *incomplete*, instead of being complete
5. *unreliable*, instead of being reliable

At best, balance sheets give us a logically incomplete picture of the life of an enterprise at a random moment. And this momentary picture, which is already incomplete, is distorted and made even more artificial by what are known as accruals, which lack all possible logical basis.

The reader may now agree that it would be a good idea to try and reach clear, scientific definitions of the concepts of assets and liabilities. An attempt to do so will be made in a subsequent chapter. In a previous chapter we saw that Robert N. Anthony regarded these definitions as representing the most important scientific problem facing the world of accounting.

If the attempt to reach reliable definitions succeeds, we may open the door leading to *dynamic* accounting practice in the future, which will mean that we no longer have to wait for the confusing images of past events, but will be able to obtain an immediate measure of the solvency of enterprises. This measure will always be real-time, *up-to-date*. And the fact that the new accounting practice will be based on a solid foundation will also make future financial statements *clear* (i.e., immediately comprehensible). Finally, the new accounting practice will make it possible to draw up logically *complete* financial statements describing all the financial consequences of the actions of management. If we succeed in achieving a model for accounting that has these properties, we shall be able to draw up what can be regarded as *reliable* financial statements.

The financial statements with which we are familiar at present are actually meaningless. So when drawing up guidelines for future accounting practice it would be a good idea to focus on clarity, logic and comprehension to a greater extent, instead of on dogmatic belief.

We can thank the philosopher Ludwig Wittgenstein for the last three sentences in this chapter, sentences that we use to conclude our description of the logically empty and therefore worthless financial statements drawn up at present. Wittgenstein's comments can be used as both a serious reminder and an auspicious sign for anyone who feels that the reliability of accounting specialists is currently open to considerable doubt, and that this problem must now be confronted and a solution sought.

Very few would disagree that accounting is in need of a new approach, a new theoretical base capable of providing us with an accounting practice supplying clear, comprehensible and thus reliable financial statements.

And perhaps even more important, the principles used today for the want of anything better should immediately be condemned as being unreliable, and should be described as "the old accounting dogma." Ludwig Wittgenstein's sentences are as follows:

> Anything that can be thought, can be thought clearly.
>
> Anything that can be expressed, can be expressed clearly.
>
> If there is nothing to say about something, say nothing about it.[10]

NOTES

1. DICPA, *Regnskabsvejledning nr. 1*, p. 11.
2. Ibid., p. 11.
3. Ibid., p. 11.
4. Ibid., p. 11.
5. Ibid., p. 12.
6. Ibid., p. 12.
7. Ibid., p. 12.
8. DICPA, *Årsregnskabet*, p. 14.
9. Ibid., p. 14.
10. J. Witt-Hansen, *Filosofi*, p. 174.

7 THE GOOD MANAGER AND THE PROBLEM OF RESPONSIBILITY

It is bad to pay with other people's money.

—Danish proverb

If traditional methods of describing the financial situation of business enterprises are worthless, then anyone using such methods faces serious difficulties. What the world of accounting needs is the kind of early warning system used by doctors when they become aware of symptoms in their patients. We need to predict the onset of financial illnesses at an early stage. The law requires business managers to be *responsible*. They are naturally expected to be so, and to be able to answer for their actions if events occur that inflict losses on others. One of the incontestable examples of the worthlessness of traditional financial statements can be seen in the concept known as *"contingent liabilities."* Lawyers and accounting specialists interpret this concept in different ways, which does little to improve the clarity of financial statements. But actually it is impossible to describe payment liabilities that have not yet occurred using traditional financial statements. It would be possible to describe payment liabilities that already exist; but traditional financial statements fail even to do this. The problem of lack of clarity rears its ugly head again, this time with potentially distressing consequences. Switching from one "accounting principle" to another is often a major shock to both managers and creditors. And even the most conscientious and knowledgeable manager risks incurring considerable personal loss. Even a *bonus pater familias* (a careful and decent manager) can fall victim to the danger of relying on traditional financial statements.

We started chapter 4, which dealt with the concepts of solvency and liquidity, with the following sentence: "This chapter should be seen as an attempt to create a linguistic link between three different fields in which the key concepts mentioned in the heading above are widely used."

The same is true of this chapter. Once again, our starting point is three roles, specialist points of view, or concepts of reality. The problem of incipient insolvency can be considered from these three different points of view:

1. that of the responsible manager (director, professional executive)
2. that of the accounting specialist (accounts manager, accountant)
3. that of the lawyer (attorney, judge, civil servant)

In this chapter we intend to take a closer look at the basic concept of responsibility for financial statements, and thus of responsibility in accounting issues. A number of legal cases have occurred in recent years owing to instances of unforeseen suspension of payments and bankruptcy, thereby showing with great clarity that there is certainly no general agreement concerning the content and importance of financial statements. The very occurrence of such legal cases is sufficient evidence of the fact that the theme of responsibility needs to be reconsidered.

In view of the fact that repeated mistakes are made using traditional financial statements as a method of registration, is anyone prepared to take any responsibility at all for such financial statements? Is it possible to even consider attributing responsibility to anyone when financial statements dealing with the past are regarded as being relevant for the present and future, which means that decisions are made blindfolded? Any talk of responsibility is surely meaningless in such circumstances. Myths and conventional dogma continue to block the pathway to true assumption of responsibility. Let us now consider the way in which current legislation and legal practice regard the concept of responsibility.

In legal theory and practice, anecdotes are used extensively as a means of understanding situations. In order to explain specific concepts or distinctions, it is the rule rather than the exception to use examples in the form of small-scale, concise descriptions taken from real-life situations. For instance, in the cartoon series "Peanuts," Snoopy the dog often appears in the guise of a world famous lawyer. In one cartoon one of his small friends quotes one of the basic concepts of Roman law, lifting his finger and saying "Ignorantia legis neminem excusat" (ignorance of the law is no excuse). Snoopy the lawyer then asks "What if you have no idea at all about what's going on?"

This is a very sensible question, and should certainly not be ignored. During the last decade or so there have been so many unexpected financial collapses and so-called financial scandals that key persons involved in many of these events must surely have had no idea about what was going on. The explanations given by such key persons vary. Some claim to have been surprised by the events that took place; others that they were victims of a financial crisis. But naturally, professional individuals cannot really expect to be relieved of their responsibility by claiming to have no idea about what's going on. And lawyers also regard this as an inadequate defense.

The word *responsibility* is derived from the word "response," indicating that in its original meaning it contained an element of communication between two or more individuals. In its current use, according to *Webster's New Twentieth Century Dictionary*, responsibility is defined as *the condition, quality, fact or instance of being responsible, answerable, accountable or liable, as for a person, trust, office or debt*. For instance, person A might say to person B "I blame you for the event leading to the loss that I have documented. The loss could have been avoided if you had performed action X or refrained from performing action Y in good time." In other words, person B is *held accountable* for his or her actions. Parties A and B will then be represented by their laywers, and following presentation of the case a judge will reach a decision by applying the law to the case in question.

Being responsible for your actions also means being the person rewarded or punished for the actions concerned. Business managers make up their minds independently and then choose to take actions that may be uncertain or risky. If all goes well, managers are regarded as "clever," "enterprising" or "creative," and it is assumed that their next decision will meet with success, too. The value of such people rises accordingly on the headhunter market. But if things go wrong, such managers risk being described as "imprudent," "over-adventurous" and so on. And the rewards such unfortunate managers originally expected turn into the opposite. "Imprudent" managers may be held *liable to pay compensation*, and may even incur *criminal liability*.

Responsibility can also be equated directly with duty, and may imply the *duty to stand accountable for your actions*. And finally, responsibility can be used to imply liability for the legal consequences of your actions. In the world of business, responsibility is linked to specific roles, and everyone knows that *managers bear responsibility*.

This book is concerned with accounting theory, so it is necessary to draw a distinction between the world of accounting and the legal world. In this chapter we shall study a number of situations in which criminal liability is the issue in financial affairs, where the question of responsibility is linked directly to financial statements. The reason for this is that financial statements and the information they convey are decisive elements in legal cases dealing with financial affairs.

We shall also ignore all the many cases in which crimes are committed intentionally, concerning ourselves only with cases arising owing to negligence. Naturally, intentional financial crimes can be just as serious for the victims affected, but they are of little interest within the scope of this book.

The reason for our lack of interest in intentional fraud is that the rules and practice applied in judging such cases should have no influence on managers and accountants who have a clear conscience. Of course the details of embezzlement and other forms of fraud may well have considerable entertainment value. Such cases often reveal amazing inventiveness and creativity in avoiding the letter of the law. It may also be interesting to consider such cases from the point of view of data security ("How can we design information systems to make it difficult or even impossible to commit intentional crimes?"). This is an extensive subject that is beyond the scope of this book, but the issue of data security will nevertheless be dealt with briefly in a later chapter.

People who commit intentional crimes can hardly regard themselves as *bonus pater familias*, an expression used in Roman law and originally meaning "careful and decent manager." The expression is used in current law to describe any person who acts sensibly and carefully, and who knows the rules of the game he or she is involved in. The title of this chapter includes the expression "the good manager" in order to emphasize that we are only considering the role model of a *bonus pater familias*. In other words, the business managers and accountants we consider here are people who wish to act sensibly and carefully. They want to know the rules of the game they are involved in, and they wish to be regarded as professional specialists who would never dream of breaking the law.

But why are managers and accounting specialists unable to say much about the financial situation of business enterprises?

This question can be expressed even more clearly by considering the *connection between responsibility and information.* A book written by Jan Carlzon from Sweden, entitled *Riv Pyramiderne ned!* (Tear the Pyramids Down!), contains the following two highly revealing sentences: "If you possess no information, you cannot assume responsibility. But if you do possess information, you cannot avoid assuming responsibility."[1]

Jan Carlzon clearly believes that the necessary and sufficient condition that must be fulfilled before responsibility can be assumed is that people are adequately informed. But what happens if no information is available? Are we no longer responsible in such circumstances?

If you approach the manager of a business enterprise that is growing or in a state of flux and ask "What is the financial situation of your company at the moment?" the answer will often be "I only wish I knew. In fact, I desperately need to know. But I can't find out until our financial statement has been completed, and that won't be for a while yet. But by the time it is ready it will be out of date, which means I will have missed the opportunity of taking any necessary action."

In practice, business managers *never* possess complete and up-to-date information about the financial situation of their enterprises. There is always a delay owing to the process involved in bookkeeping, and there is always obscurity owing to the lack of consistent accounting concepts. Financial statements are *always delayed, incomplete and ambiguous.* Several surveys carried out in recent years show clearly that, in general, managers do not understand traditional financial statements, and that as a result they are not particularly interested in them. And even managers who *are* interested in the financial situation of their enterprises only have access to financial statements that are out of date. The consequence of this is that, in practice, business managers are never able to claim full insight into the financial situation of their enterprises at any time. At best, they can consult a financial statement that is only slightly delayed, which means that their options for taking action are also "only slightly delayed." But does the phrase "only slightly delayed" have any meaning? Surely the decisive point here is that either options for taking action are delayed, or they are not delayed. If you miss a train, surely it matters very little whether you miss it by three minutes or 63 minutes.

If Jan Carlzon's comment quoted above is taken literally, then managers are entitled to say "I had no reliable information about the financial situation in the form of an up-to-date, reliable financial statement for my enterprise. So it is not reasonable to expect that I should be held responsible for the consequences." And if the blame is then directed at the accountant, he is entitled to reply "It's not my responsibility, but the management's. I merely audit and sign the financial statements. I always observe the law, so no one can blame *me.*"

But what would a judge say in response to such claims of lack of responsibility in a court of law?

Quite clearly, it is not sufficient for managers to claim that they lacked information. The judge would simply say that they should have obtained the information they needed.

In such circumstances, judges always ask the key question "Were manager A and accountant B aware of the financial situation when action X was performed, or when action Y was not performed?" This is not the same as asking "Did manager A have access to a good financial statement when action X was performed?" When judges ask whether manager A was aware of the financial situation, what they really mean is "Was manager A aware of the situation, or should manager A have been aware of the situation?" Ignorance of the law was no excuse under Roman law. And as we approach the end of the twentieth century, ignorance of your situation cannot be used as an excuse, either. Modern lawyers talk of both mistakes of law and mistakes of fact.

So managers cannot escape responsibility by claiming that their financial statements were in disarray or kept incorrectly, or indeed by offering any other excuses. The law states that financial statements must be kept. Judges assume that they *are* kept, and failure to do so means incurring responsibility.

The responsibility for ensuring that financial statements are kept adequately lies with *the manager*. The responsibility for ensuring that financial statements describe the actual financial situation correctly also lies with *the manager*. But in practice this responsibility for financial statements and their contents should be shared by *the accountant*. After all, the accountant is the one who signs financial statements, thereby appearing as a professional witness in the eyes of all interested parties outside the enterprise concerned, including the creditors.

In other words, if a financial statement is misleading, or if it simply does not exist, *there are no excuses*. Indeed, if managers are also accounting specialists, judges may regard this as making the matter worse. Neither the manager nor the accountant can escape responsibility in the event of a financial scandal.

One of the problems on which Danish accountants have focused attention is the so-called "expectation gap," a term that reflects the difference between the services provided by accountants and the *expectations* users have with regard to these services. How can this expectation gap be explained, bridged and removed? Could the professional methods used by accountants be improved by considering financial statements from a different point of view?

Let us now seek to explain the expectation gap by considering a concept that is of central importance to enterprises that are threatened by bankruptcy, or that have already gone bankrupt. The concept is already well known to both accounting specialists and lawyers, but the two professions interpret it very differently. And whenever a concept with the same name is interpreted differently by different specialists, the result is bound to be confusion and misunderstanding.

The dubious concept in question is known as *contingent liabilities*. Not surprisingly, such liabilities and their correct treatment are of particular interest to accountants and lawyers dealing with enterprises threatened by bankruptcy. And naturally, the fact that lawyers and accountants disagree about the interpretation of the term is extremely unfortunate.

What, exactly, are "contingent liabilities"? In "International Accounting Standards" no. 10 point 3, the International Accounting Standards Committee (IASC) makes the following attempt at definition:

A contingent liability is a factor or situation whose final outcome, whether profit or loss, can only be confirmed by the occurrence or nonoccurrence of one or more future events about which uncertainty exists.

The reader has already been shown several examples of the fact that the basic concepts of traditional accounting are either absent, or defined inadequately or in self-contradictory fashion. The concept of contingent liabilities is not defined clearly and strictly, either, and unfortunately the definition quoted above is useless. If situation B can only be confirmed by the occurrence or nonoccurrence of event A, then situation B can either always be confirmed, or never be confirmed. Definitions that allow for any logical conclusion exclude nothing, and therefore say nothing. Unfortunately, the definition of contingent liabilities offered by the IASC allows for anything, and is therefore empty of logical content. Clarity must be sought down other channels.

Let us take our starting point in the familiar division of financial statements into assets and liabilities. Contingent liabilities, of course, belong under liabilities. And practicing and theoretical accountants will also agree that the term "assets" is used to describe all the "rights to receive payment" of a specific organization, and the term "liabilities" to describe the "liability to make future payments." But when is the liability to make a future payment a "contingent liability," and when is it not? Why are some "liabilities to make future payments" invisible in "going concern" financial statements? When and how are such liabilities expressed in the balance sheet? How can (or how should) we distinguish between "contingent liabilities" and other liabilities? And why is such a distinction necessary anyway? In short, if we want financial statements that are complete, should we not include *all* types of liability?

Is a contingent liability a liability to make future payment based on a "certain" event, or only on a "probable" event? Is a contingent liability an item of debt that will always fall due for payment sooner or later? Or might it never actually be paid?

The nonaccountant might well reply that the answer to the problem is simple and obvious. "Certain" payment liabilities should be included in the balance sheet, whereas "uncertain" ones could be excluded. Lawyers might reply that payment liabilities that are bound to fall due should be included in financial statements. Liabilities that are only "contingent" (e.g., guarantee liabilities) should of course be described systematically as well, in order to make risk evaluation possible. But they do not need to be included in the balance sheet. Why is this advice not followed in traditional financial statements?

This might be an awkward question, but it is also an important one. It may be the case that the problem of invisibility in financial statements is due to *the existence of certain payment liabilities that simply do not appear in traditional financial statements.*

In current accounting practice there are plenty of examples of certain payment liabilities that cannot be found in the balance sheet. It is also possible to identify two types of invisible payment liability—those that were already agreed to and therefore certain on the balance sheet date, and those that were only likely to fall due. So the vital question is "Can contingent liabilities be regarded as being certain sooner or later, or will they only fall due in certain circumstances?" The discussion and solution of this problem is of crucial importance in both Danish and international accounting practice.

Let us now repeat the attempt to regard contingent liabilities as "payment liabilities arising due to events that have occurred." The statistical way of calculating the risk that such liabilities to make future payments will actually fall due is as follows:

$$risk = probability \times consequence$$

The probability of an event occurring is assessed separately. In some cases, the probability is one, and in others it is somewhat less. The financial consequence in the equation above can be described as being one or more sums of money that must be paid on one or more occasions in the future. So contingent liabilities can be described as a systematic calculation of risk with three logical elements:

1. An estimate of the probability that an event will occur
2. An estimate of the size of the payment involved
3. An estimate of the time at which payment must be made

Some events are certain (e.g., if employees entitled to a certain period of notice are fired, their salaries will have to be paid for a specific period of time), and in such cases the probability of payment being necessary is 1. The risk can now be calculated by describing the consequence (i.e., the size of the payment concerned and the date on which it falls due). This task is easy, since all the data required is easily available.

Let us now include the events that are not "certain" in our description. A description of a "future payment caused by the occurrence of an event" is shown in the logical table in figure 7.1. The table reveals that the concept of contingent liabilities can be regarded basically as *a systematic and logically complete calculation of risk.*

CONTINGENT LIABILITIES	The liability is certain. The event has occurred.	The liability is uncertain. The event has *not* occurred.
The consequence (sum and date) can be described with reasonable certainty	Leasing contracts. Salary and wage agreements. Holiday pay, etc. Deferred tax.	Product guarantees. Loan guarantees.
The consequence and date) can *not* be described with reasonable certainty	Certain so-called contingent taxes.	Major legal cases, product liability, environment, etc.

Figure 7.1. Logically complete distinctions between contingent liabilities.

It is immediately apparent that figure 7.1 contains a logically complete description of payment liabilities. It describes all possible payment liabilities, in other words, all liabilities arising from both certain and uncertain events. It also includes both the easy and the difficult descriptions of consequence. This means that figure 7.1 actually describes all the liabilities of business enterprises, regardless of what these liabilities are traditionally called.

Accounting specialists wishing to regard the liabilities of an enterprise as a single figure reflecting an overall, systematic calculation of risk must be prepared for the fact that some of the items listed in figure 7.1 are not currently shown in traditional "going concern" financial statements. We have already seen that such statements contain undeniable conflicts and ambiguity.

But what should be our main consideration—our respect for tradition or our respect for reality? Why should we accept invisibility in financial statements and run the risk of experiencing unfortunate financial shocks if this is not necessary? We have seen that contingent liabilities can be described using a model producing a *systematic calculation of risk*. Perhaps this model could be used to launch a debate aimed at clarifying the content of current financial statements. If the attempt succeeds, the current form of financial statements will change over time. The Danish so-called accounting standards state that substance is more important than form. And this must be regarded as a truism. No professional specialist would ever claim anything else.

Let us assume that the best definition of contingent liabilities is the one used by the legal profession. After all, in cases of bankruptcy this is the definition that will be applied. But there is a clear difference in the way the legal profession and the accounting profession define contingent liabilities. The Danish Company Accounts Act of 1981 says that annual financial statements should be "a true and fair view of assets and liabilities." Our conclusion must be that if the Danish legislators meant "true and fair" to mean "realistic" or "true to reality," *then current accounting practice is clearly in contravention of the law.* Because at the moment the accounting and legal professions interpret the concept of contingent liabilities very differently.

Taking a closer look at this serious paradox, which also has serious consequences, there can be little doubt that the core of the problem lies in the fact that double entry bookkeeping is regarded all over the world as being the necessary and sufficient tool for registration purposes. *But double entry bookkeeping is logically incomplete as a method of registration.* The realization of this fact may be the turning point that makes accounting theorists and practitioners start looking for new tools to use in carrying out the necessary and sufficient basic registration and calculation of consequences.

To illustrate this point, let us now consider the example of a contractor who has built a bridge and sent a bill for payment of the final installment. Two weeks later he receives a letter from his client. There can be little doubt that the picture of our contractor's situation depends very much on the content of this letter. The letter might contain a check for the amount owing, and the thanks of the client. On the other hand, it might contain a brief statement to the effect that the client refuses to pay a single cent until certain specified defects in the bridge have been remedied. The contractor's liquidity may already be somewhat strained, and if no payment is received the contractor may be unable to pay his subcontractors. These subcontractors now risk incurring a loss, even though they have done nothing wrong.

Assume that our imaginary contractor has an accounting year that is identical to the calendar year, and that the events described above occur in May. How on earth can traditional financial statements be used to describe such changes in financial circumstances? The answer, of course, is that they are useless in such cases, because the event causing the drastic change could not have been predicted.

But it is possible to describe the events that have occurred in *management accounts* that are kept on a day-to-day basis. As we shall see in a later chapter, the *project accounts* that describe the bridge-building project can be seen as a separate system, a subsystem. The latest information about the case can be used as basic data, and new calculations of financial consequences can be produced quickly. Ideally, these new calculations can be made available as soon as the new situation becomes apparent.

A contract with "open ends" is a contract whose final outcome is not yet known owing to the fact that the events, actions and payments described therein all lie in the future. Any attempt to describe future events and call this description precise is doomed to failure. But it is possible to describe future events, actions and payments as *logical what-if calculations*.

The prototype of a logical calculation about the future is as follows:

1. We assume or expect that event or events X will occur no later than time or time period A. Data describing such future expected events is represented by *expectation variables* in our calculation.
2. Based on these expectation variables, and following calculation and evaluation of the financial consequences, we reach a statement about *decision variables*. At time B we will perform action or actions Y. In doing so, we consciously refrain from performing certain other actions, and refrain from performing the so-called "zero alternative" (i.e., taking no action at all).
3. The *control basis* of our hypothesis is that we expect payment or payments Z arising from the actions that have been performed to become apparent at time or time period C.

This basic formulation contains a set of statements about the future, but naturally the calculation does not claim certainty. It is by definition open to change and correction. It can always be revised.

Future calculations, which are based on the question "What happens if?" and which are clearly defined in terms of conditions, calculations and data, can always be kept ready for use in making new calculations of consequences with no significant waste of time (and ideally with no waste of time at all) as soon as the presence of new information makes the original assumptions irrelevant.

It is now easy to imagine the questions that our contractor will ask himself and seek to answer. It is also obvious that he wants the new answers as quickly as possible after receiving the letter from his client. We recall that there were two possible contents of the letter, resulting in two entirely different outcomes in terms of the contractor's contingent liabilities. One of these is the expected, undramatic outcome that confirms the hypothesis of payment. The other is far more dramatic, surprising the contractor by the occurrence of an unexpected event. He may believe that he has acted sensibly and carefully, but the contents of the letter clearly reveal that the client does not believe the same.

The contractor must now ask and try to answer two vital questions as quickly as possible:

1. What are the financial consequences of the new information in this particular case?
2. What will the financial consequences then be for my company as a whole?

We note that there are two questions: one relating to the project at issue, and the other relating to the overall situation. They both require answers, and the answers must be seen in relation to each other to give any meaning, because the meaning of the answers will depend on the consequences of the particular case in relation to the consequences for the company as a whole. We can demonstrate this mutual interdependence between the two answers with an example involving throwing a die and gambling on the result, assuming that gambling is legal.

A wealthy gambler called A says to a person called B (who is also wealthy), "Here is an unbiased die. You are only allowed to throw the die once. If you throw a 1, 2, 3 or 4, I will double your current fortune. If you throw a 5 or 6 you have to give me everything you possess."

If she is sensible, B will quickly refuse the offer—even though the chance of winning is two to one. B's problem is that the consequences of losing are unbearable. But if A makes the same proposal again, changing the stakes to payment for dinner at a restaurant, B will probably accept unless she has any specific reasons for refusing again. The chance of winning is still good, but this time any loss will be bearable.

The striking thing about this example is that the statistical chances of winning and losing are exactly the same in both cases. But although the probability of losing in both cases is identical, the consequences of loss are very different. B accepts the risk of paying for a dinner, but refuses the risk of losing her entire fortune. At which point on this scale does the risk become too great for her to accept the gamble? Naturally, this point is not predefined. It will be defined by B based on at least two factors—her willingness to take risks, and the size of her fortune. These two factors must always be seen in conjunction, since they are closely related to each other.

Naturally, people's attitude towards an uncertain future varies considerably, as does their ability to bear losses. Depending on your temperament, there are two ways of describing the uncertain future. Some people say, "You're running a risk," while others prefer to say, "You're taking a chance." People's willingness to take part in the die-casting gamble just described will undoubtedly vary a great deal, and lawyers would tell us that this is perfectly natural. The evaluation of risk is a highly individual affair, and will always depend on the circumstances involved (as a judge would say). In this connection, two issues must be evaluated:

1. The risk/chance of the project in itself
2. The risk/chance facing the enterprise as a whole

What is the calculated risk in the real world? How can we describe *the probability* of a future event occurring, and how can we describe and evaluate *the consequences*? Let us now apply our theoretical example to the real world of professional management and ask these vital questions once again. Everyone knows that there is always a certain risk involved in running a company. But what is the point at which a "normal" risk becomes an "abnormal" risk? What is the size of the loss that managers are allowed to suffer or inflict on others without anyone complaining? Where is the borderline for managers wishing to avoid incurring unexpected responsibility and the risk of being punished?

We shall refrain from giving details of the law relating to bankruptcy offenses, but simply point out that the thing managers are not allowed to do, the thing for which they may be subject to legal punishment, is to inflict a loss or significant risk of loss on others. In other words, one vital criterion involved in reaching a judgment is *the risk of loss*. If no risk of loss is incurred, no crime will have been committed. This means that the same action may be judged differently, depending on whether it is carried out by a wealthy company or a financially fragile company.

Once again, the importance of managers' understanding the financial situation of individual projects and their companies as a whole is apparent—otherwise managers cannot know where the borderline between the criminal and the legal runs.

We have already decided that this chapter should take no account of intentional financial crimes. But we still need to identify the most important distinctions between the legal concepts of *intent* and *negligence*. The fact is that even managers who believe they have acted sensibly can be judged guilty of intentional crimes in certain circumstances. Judges may regard their actions (or their failure to act) as being intentional.

Let us conclude this chapter by returning to the concept of responsibility and its importance for managers and accounting specialists, whom we regard as sensible and conscientious individuals. Criminal law as we know it has its roots in religious concepts of the "good" and "evil" actions of humans. Such actions can be described, and their consequences calculated. In a democracy it is the task of each individual citizen to address these difficult and important questions.

Let us now make one more attempt to clarify the concept of responsibility, this time taken from the world of *behavioral psychology*. In a short article about the nature of individuals, Professor Anders Munk draws a clear and highly relevant distinction between "moralistic" and "responsible" attitudes. Professor Munk's view is that managers must be held responsible for the consequences of their actions:

In our society we still have a *primitive moralistic* attitude that says "It doesn't matter as long as you didn't do it deliberately." This allows our politicians to say "I didn't know what I was doing, I didn't know the consequences of my actions, so no blame can be attached to me." Surely everyone agrees that it would be better to adopt a *responsible* attitude, the acceptance of which would force the same politician to say in the same situation "I didn't even try to find out what I was doing. I didn't consider the consequences. So I have made a grievous error." The responsible attitude is based on the fact that "Consequences are consequences, whether they were intentional or not, and consequences are the only things that count."[2]

Consequences are the only things that count, and an attempt must be made to calculate these consequences in advance, even though precise calculation is not possible.

Accounting is the science of the financial consequences of the actions of organizations. Assuming financial responsibility means knowing the financial consequences of your actions. We conclude with a definition of the concept of the responsible manager:

A responsible manager is a manager who knows or should know the consequences of his or her actions. A financially responsible manager is a manager who knows or should know the financial consequences of the actions of the organization.

Managers and accounting specialists need to know the financial consequences of their actions, which is why it is necessary to calculate these consequences, which is why we need to be able to calculate. And in order to calculate, we need up-to-date, reliable data. *Management accounts* have the data and calculation programs required, and differ significantly from traditional financial statements because they are oriented towards the future, towards the systematic measurement and calculation of financial risk both in terms of individual cases, and in terms of enterprises as a whole.

If legislation is required to ensure that traditional financial statements are replaced by management accounts, the German version of the Fourth European Union Accounting Directive could be adjusted to read as follows:

Financial accounts must be kept in a way that ensures that they provide a realistic impression of the solvency, liquidity and results of business enterprises at all times.

The true and fair picture would then become a dynamic, living picture. The emphasis would shift from *static financial statements* presented once a year to *dynamic management accounts that are updated on a real-time basis*. There is one significant difference between the two. Management accounts enable all interested parties to describe, gain insight into and share real responsibility for the financial consequences of the management's actions. Management then becomes a process, the result of communication between the interested parties involved.

Traditional annual financial statements can never be used for this purpose. They are always published too late, and metaphorically represent *a ticket for a train that has already left the station.*

NOTES

1. Jan Carlzon, *Riv Pyramiderne ned!*, p. 14.
2. Anders Munk, *Om menneskets natur*, p. 122.

8 OOPS, ANOTHER UNPLEASANT SURPRISE

> I realized that any physical system that behaved non-periodically would be unpredictable.
>
> —*Edward Lorenz*

Revolutionary discoveries in the history of science often look like mistakes when they are first made. But strokes of genius often require no more than a bright idea by a researcher, or a new question by a single man or woman about a specific subject. The discovery of penicillin by Alexander Fleming in 1928 is one of the best examples in the history of science of a mistake leading to interesting consequences. A mistake seemed to have been made when a bacterial culture was ruined by mold. But it proved to be a very interesting mistake, and Fleming's surprise was the first step leading to a new era in the history of medicine. It might have looked like a happy coincidence, but Louis Pasteur once said "A happy coincidence only occurs to those who are prepared for it." Perhaps a happy coincidence occured to the American scientist Edward Lorenz. Alexander Fleming discovered penicillin on an ordinary day in 1928, and Edward Lorenz discovered the concept of *unpredictability* on an ordinary day in 1961. This discovery was a culture shock for accounting theory, and probably for the entire science of economics. Until now, many economists have claimed that the financial position of a business enterprise or society can be predicted. But the truth is that this is only possible within certain narrow and clearly defined limits. Beyond these limits chaos rules. The new theories of chaos force us to carry out a thorough revision of our economic theories. Some of these theories can be disposed of without a qualm, but there are also new forms of order in what used to be regarded as disorder. And herein lies the hope of gaining new insight.

Ever since the end of the 1950s, entirely new scientific insight has been gained into the concept of *predictability,* an insight that revolutionizes all our previous ideas. The new knowledge will probably mean that a large proportion of current accounting literature, particularly literature relating to budgeting, will have to be abandoned in the near future because it is obsolete and no longer reflects reality.

The new scientific insight claims new limits to predictability, and outlines new procedures for use in predicting events. As a result, this insight is of great interest to the world of accounting, in which predictability is assumed to exist to make "budgeting" or "long-term strategic planning" possible.

In this chapter we shall describe the main ideas contained in the new insight, and discuss its possibly revolutionary importance for the procedures used in financial planning. It should not really be necessary to point out the deficiencies of the current procedures, but let us describe one of these deficiencies all the same, in order to set the ball rolling.

Throughout accounting theory one particular assumption has always been made in more or less visible fashion, an assumption we shall call *the postulate of inertia.* This postulate claims that there is a close connection between the past, present and future, and that changes tend to follow certain patterns and only take place slowly. The postulate of inertia can also be expressed as follows: *the future will resemble the past, unless new evidence appears.* So the postulate of inertia makes it possible to predict financial events based on current evidence, and then later to ask whether any special circumstances have arisen in the interim that make it impossible to regard this passive prediction as being valid. If the answer is "yes" the prediction must be modified, but if the answer is "no" the passive prediction is regarded as an active prediction. Such "active" and "passive" predictions are known as budgets. In large enterprises the procedures for budgeting are organized formally. Budgets are "coordinated," "accepted" or "approved" using special rituals in which managers function rather like priests. Once the ritual has been completed, the enterprise concerned believes it has said something about its future financial situation.

If subsequent events fail to develop as predicted in the budget, managers tend to feel that there is something wrong with the events rather than with the budget. If major discrepancies between predictions and actual events become apparent, managers react with surprise, perhaps with the words used as the title of this chapter (Oops, Another Unpleasant Surprise). The budget expresses an enterprise's expectations regarding the future, and budget procedures have a powerful effect, persuading people to believe in budgets rather than in their own observations of reality.

But many managers who are not accounting specialists express doubts about the rituals surrounding budgets. The budget procedures outlined in accounting textbooks are very often useless in practice, and are often rejected on the grounds that future financial situations cannot be predicted. But practical objections of this kind are treated with an indulgent smile by many economists, who believe that of course financial situations can be predicted as long as you proceed systematically.

But can they? What would a scientist say? What do we *believe* about the future, and what do we actually *know* about it? What is the difference between the art of prophecy and the art of scientifically viable prediction?

The English philosopher and logician William of Occam (1275–1349) achieved immortality thanks to the Latin phrase "Entia nun sunt multiplicanda praeter neccessitatem." This famous phrase has been given the name "Occam's Razor," and has been used for centuries to distinguish between knowledge and belief by using logical evidence. Some people choose to explain their observations as the work of gods or demons, whereas others prefer to identify simple, natural, scientifically based explanations without making more assumptions than strictly necessary.

The principle in Occam's Razor states that a person should not increase, beyond what is necessary, the number of entities required to explain anything, or that the person should not make more assumptions than the minimum needed. Since the Middle Ages this principle has played an important role in eliminating fictitious or unnecessary elements from explanations.

Occam's Razor was regarded by Bertrand Russell as an extremely useful instrument for logical analysis. Despite its venerable age the Razor is still sharp, and it is very useful when passing criticism or analyzing basic concepts. And there are a great number of basic assumptions in economic theory, the worst being those that are invisible.

The main distinction between belief and knowledge is probably that people who possess certain types of knowledge are able to *describe, explain* and *predict* things in a systematic way that is sufficiently persuasive to inspire belief in other people who know either less than they do, or nothing at all, about the subject in question.

At this point the reader might object that it seems odd to describe the difference between belief and knowledge by saying that knowledge is distinguished by the fact that it is capable of inspiring belief. Surely it is illogical to describe the concept of knowledge in terms of the concept of belief.

Actually, this is not necessarily illogical. Things that are capable of inspiring belief are worth believing in. Things that are capable of inspiring belief in professional circles are worth believing in among professionals. The professionals who regard themselves as scientific are the ones who are the most skeptical when it comes to testing the knowledge they claim. So it can safely be claimed that whatever science regards as knowledge about a given phenomenon is the most reliable information currently available about that phenomenon. Knowledge is not constant over time. It may change and develop. And in some research environments the door is always kept slightly ajar to allow for the appearance of new ideas that can then be tested critically. If the test is passed, "new scientific knowledge" has been obtained.

Knowledge however, can never be regarded as definitive or eternally valid. Events, criticism and research often reveal new points of view that make established knowledge look rather outdated. The concepts, interpretations and so-called knowledge that seemed irrefutable yesterday may seem incomplete and outdated today on closer inspection. Knowledge changes and develops constantly. The history of science is a stage on which many different truths have played a role, many authorities have been challenged, many new questions asked and many new doors opened—often in spite of bitter opposition to change.

People who possess knowledge can make systematic predictions about future events. For instance, doctors can predict the future treatment required and results expected once a diagnosis has been finalized. Engineers can estimate the amount of material needed to build a bridge that is expected to carry a given maximum weight. In such circumstances, doctors and engineers can be regarded as experts or specialists. We all have faith in such experts and specialists, and we believe the predictions they make. We have little choice—the alternative would be chaos.

Sometimes events do not match the predictions made about them. Sometimes events may even be in direct contradiction to predictions. Despite all their hard work, doctors may lose their patients; engineers may have to watch their bridges collapse only a short time after they were built. Depending on the extent of the consequences of such unexpected occurrences, they are described as events, accidents or catastrophes.

When such occurrences affect *other people*, accounting specialists are surprised and say that they are *abnormal*, by which they mean that such events lie outside the norm, beyond the expectations they had in advance. But we do not lose our faith in the experts as a result. In abnormal circumstances everyone wants an explanation. Patients who die unexpectedly are examined, and doctors then explain to each other and to the public that the cause of death was unexpected, or that the death was inexplicable. Collapsed bridges are examined, too, after which the engineers report that the foundations were not strong enough, or that the wrong materials and procedures were used. Engineers may give up altogether, like doctors are sometimes forced to, and admit that events are sometimes inexplicable.

But naturally, the individuals who are personally involved in such events regard them in a completely different light. How does a doctor feel when the patient dies unexpectedly? And how does the engineer feel when a bridge suddenly collapses? They are probably profoundly affected, and may feel a sense of guilt.

Accounting specialists can stand back and consider such questions regarding other people's catastrophes at a safe distance from both the events and the experts concerned. But what do other people think of accounting specialists? Are we regarded as reliable experts in other people's eyes when our patients die or our bridges collapse? Can we provide persuasive explanations when such things occur? Are our procedures really good enough? Are we sufficiently concerned? Do we share any responsibility?

We can and should ask such uncomfortable questions about our own specialist role, and we ought to be able to provide convincing answers. Research into the world of accounting should focus on the question "What goes through the minds of other people when unexpected catastrophes occur that are not medical or technical, but financial? What do our explanations of such catastrophes sound like to others? Can we explain such events at all, or are they inexplicable?"

The job of accounting specialists is *to reliably describe, explain and predict the financial position of business enterprises*. But at the moment accounting specialists do not enjoy a reputation for reliability in other people's eyes, because there have been too many accounting catastrophes in recent years. The reputation of accounting specialists is under considerable threat, and can only be saved by the development of methods that can solve the problems. Anyone can make a mistake, of course, but analysis and explanations are necessary in order to prevent such mistakes from recurring. To err is human, but it is discreditable to continue making the same mistakes.

People who suffer financial losses always want to find out who was responsible. The question asked is "Can these so-called abnormal events and consequences be explained as normal events and consequences that deviated from their normal course owing to misguided actions or the failure to perform correct actions? Did anyone do anything wrong? Or did anyone fail to do what should have been done?" If the answer is yes, the people who made the mistakes or failed to do what they should have done will be liable to suffer condemnation and demands for compensation or punishment. When financial statements are part of the information given, demands are made for the allocation of responsibility for the financial consequences of the actions concerned. This point is dealt with in chapter 7, which shows that legislation and the law courts already make such high demands on the keeping of accounts that even managers who are expert accountants can make mistakes without feeling that they should be condemned or judgment passed on them.

In order to emphasize the connection between the concepts of responsibility and predictability, let us now briefly quote a number of phrases taken from the world of law. In an article entitled "Er tiden moden til en ny straffelov?" (Is the Time Ripe for a New Penal Law?), the Danish professor Vagn Greve starts by outlining the concepts of punishment and guilt. Vagn Greve illustrates how the law is based to a large extent on religious and philosophical viewpoints. One of the sections of the article, headed "A New Concept of Guilt," makes it clear that even a concept as fundamental as guilt is unclear and therefore open to discussion:

Punishment depends on guilt. There is disagreement about what guilt is, but everyone agrees that it is a key concept in all debates on crime policy. Punishment must be defined as a conscious addition of evil. It can only be justified . . . if applied to guilty persons. . . . In former times the guilt for any damage caused by a member of a family was placed at the door of the entire family. This view is still apparent in international politics and in the moral codes of gangs—as it is in current views of Hell's Angels, multinational companies, and other such collective organizations. But standard penal law abandoned this way of looking at things a long time ago. . . . The concept of guilt that now prevails . . . is highly influenced by the Christian and in particular the Lutheran view of Man. In this connection, it is significant that Luther emphasized the "purity of the heart." . . . The Protestant ethic is thus based on the concept that evil comes from free will.[1]

Many readers may be surprised to see how narrow the gap is between the law and ethics/religion. In other words, everyday citizens can and should take part in the debate concerning the concepts of justice and guilt. The importance of this debate for the world of accounting is obvious. In German, the same term, *die Schuld,* is used for both "guilt" and "debt."

The demand that individuals should be able to predict the consequences of their actions or neglect is expressed by Vagn Greve as follows:

So modern man may incur guilt by attempting to achieve reprehensible goals, or by consciously using reprehensible means, or by failing to live up to standard requirements concerning acting in a way that is at least reasonably acceptable.

In other words, you can be adjudged guilty either owing to intent or owing to negligence. Modern individuals need to know exactly what the situation is. And modern managers need to know that their audience consists of a society with both written and unwritten standards, with an alert press and with open channels of communication:

The conclusion . . . is that we have left behind us the period in our history in which guilt depended on the intentions of the individual. Today, guilt depends (and should depend) on society's general evaluation of the actions concerned (negligence).

This is a big change, but it is remarkable that there are no contradictions between these conclusions presented by the lawyer, and the views about responsibility presented by Anders Munk, the biologist. You can assume responsibility when you know the consequences of your actions. So the key issue for accounting theory in general is whether or not a given event that has occurred, and its financial consequences, *could have been predicted.*

Let us now proceed with the problem of predictability by proposing a small experiment. Let us assume that a person known as A approaches a person known as B and says, "Here are my careful calculations of temperature, air pressure, wind strength and wind direction measured at midnight on New Year's Eve each year during the period 1992–96. Please tell me what the weather will be like on 1 July 1998." B answers that it is impossible to make such a prediction based on this data, so A asks B to make a weather forecast for New Year's Eve the next year instead. What will be B's answer?

If B is a scientifically trained meteorologist, her answer will be clear: the prediction is simply impossible. But if B is an accounting specialist, she may attempt to make the prediction all the same. She may carry out a number of calculations involving tendencies, averages and distributions. She may use a mathematical procedure known as exponential smoothing to gaze into the crystal ball of the future. She may even work out a number of financial ratios to show "the direction of developments" and "the strength of developments" with regard to certain key parameters. Finally, it is probable that the prediction will be accompanied by a great number of reservations.

The reader has probably noticed that this weather data consists of measurements or descriptions of reality on New Year's Eve. The same applies to traditional financial statements. They, too, are regarded as descriptions of reality, or the "true and fair view" on New Year's Eve, if the accounting period is identical with the calendar year.

Naturally, it is quite meaningless to imagine that the weather can be predicted by using this data. And yet old financial statements are believed to contain "valuable signals," and are "attributed a certain value as the basis of prediction." The postulate of inertia is used in traditional financial statements, reflecting the belief that next year will be more or less the same as this year.

Meteorologists would not dream of presenting weather forecasts based on old data, but approach their job quite differently. We refer to a book written by a Danish professor of meteorology, Aksel C. Wiin Nielsen, entitled *Forudsigelighed. Om grænserne for videnskab (Predictability. The Limits to Science)*. In this book, Wiin Nielsen describes the revolutionary development in concepts of predictability that has taken place in recent times. And the new scientific insight gained into the new limits is of great interest to economists and other scientists alike:

Most people who received their formal education before the middle of this century have been brought up to believe that the part of the world that can be described by classical dynamics is deterministic, i.e., predictable. It is true that this view was revised completely following the development of quantum mechanics, but at the same time it was pointed out that classical physics lies on the borderline with quantum mechanics. In other words, deterministic physics was still correct, as long as people remembered to apply it only to phenomena that were on a sufficiently large scale in terms of time and space.[2]

The basic working hypothesis used by meteorologists has always been that:

if you had a sufficiently accurate view of the initial situation based on observation, and if you learned to describe the physical processes in the atmosphere with sufficient accuracy, the atmosphere would also be predictable in principle for very extensive periods. Inaccurate predictions only had to be accepted because the available observations were still too few and too inaccurate, and because we still had not learned the right way to describe all the physical processes involved.

Economists will no doubt see a clear parallel between this situation and that of their own profession. The same basic thought processes apply to both the two fields, a claim that can be tested easily by replacing the word "atmosphere" by the word "economy" in the preceding quotation. It should then be possible to say that the basic working hypothesis of economists, and certainly of accounting theorists, has been:

if you had a sufficiently accurate view of the initial financial position based on observation, and if you learned to describe the physical processes in the economy with sufficient accuracy, the economy would also be predictable in principle for very extensive periods. Inaccurate predictions only had to be accepted because the available observations were still too few and too inaccurate, and because we still had not learned the right way to describe all the physical processes involved.

There was never any serious doubt in accounting theory about this basic hypothesis, only about its possibly incomplete application.

And now for the shock. Perhaps it is far too optimistic to claim that things can be predicted in this way:

it came as something of a shock to all indoctrinated "classical" physicists when a couple of American colleagues . . . in the late 1950s and early 1960s put forward a point of view that could lead to the conclusion that the details of the atmosphere were in principle unpredictable for sufficiently lengthy periods of time, or in other words that there is a theoretical limit to the time within which the atmosphere is predictable.

This must give food for thought to accounting theorists and practitioners alike. If scientific meteorologists have discovered a limit to predictability, perhaps there is a similar limit to the predictability of financial affairs. Perhaps it is just as meaningless to talk about long-term financial planning as it is to talk of long-term weather forecasts. Experienced readers will surely agree that many of the procedures currently used to make financial predictions are inadequate with regard to their effect, and unclear with regard to their scientific justification. Who ever said that humans are able to look into the future anyway?

Let us now underline the impossibility of prediction. In the following quotation, the reader will clearly see that the issue at stake is very far from trivial. The expression "epoch-making" is used, meaning the start of a new era in which what we believed in yesterday is no longer scientifically reliable. It is also significant that the conclusion that changes our conception of predictability once and for all is based on a very obvious and simple idea, on *nonlinearity as a principle*.

This epoch-making conclusion rests largely on the fact that all basic laws are non-linear. But nearly all laws describing problems in classical physics are nonlinear, so it is no surprise that these conclusions had a profound effect on the deterministic working hypothesis, not only with regard to meteorology but almost everywhere. The definition of the upper limit to the predictability of the atmosphere became an important issue for meteorologists, and proved to be far larger than the practical limit to predictability known today. So there is still good reason to improve our observation systems and methods of prediction. On the other hand, the limited predictability of all nonlinear phenomena introduced completely new dimensions to natural physics. The limit to predictability is now being studied intensively in many areas ranging from biology to economics.[3]

Naturally, the realization of the impossibility of predicting beyond a certain limit does not mean that prediction is completely impossible. It simply means that predictions can only be made within certain acknowledged limits that may well be wider than anyone believed in the past. The realization may even be something of a relief. The fruitless search for predictability is over, and researchers are now studying "intensively." There is new hope, and there is even a reminder to economists:

Meteorologists who have spent most of their professional working lives preparing predictions of the future state of the atmosphere, i.e., presenting the weather forecast, cannot help wondering how other predictions are made. Is pure guesswork used? Are the predictions made based on a system that has been tested at an earlier date? Is it possible to make predictions about systems as complicated as the economy of an entire country?[4]

At this point it may be appropriate to recall the Danish aphorism "Even the ancient Romans wondered how two economists could ever keep a straight face when they met."

This book deals not with the economy of entire countries, but only with microeconomics, or the description of the financial situation of individual enterprises. But the question of predictability is the same in both instances, and there is a connection between microeconomics and macroeconomics. Even macroeconomists need to make measurements, and to the extent that these measurements describe the payment of money, they are derived from the financial statements issued by business enterprises. The system known as "the financial situation of an enterprise" is regarded here as a subsystem of the total system known as "the financial situation of a society." The question of predictability applies to both systems, but in this book we shall ask it in a slightly different way in order to restrict its scope and to avoid annoying macroeconomists. Is it possible to predict a (sub)system as complicated as that of the financial situation of a business enterprise? Perhaps the aforementioned aphorism can be transferred to the microeconomic scale and to the present day, in which case it would read as follows: "A great number of levelheaded people wonder how two accountants can ever keep a straight face when they meet."

Let us now emphasize two points drawn from these quotations and examine them in greater detail:

1. The deterministic working hypothesis
2. The issue of linearity/nonlinearity in economics

Determinism is the belief that so-called acts of will, natural events and social changes are settled by earlier causes. A given event known as A is regarded as being the cause of the subsequent event B, which is known as the effect. Naturally, if you want to make predictions you need to be able to say that A is the cause of B. Anyone believing that strict determinism exists in economics leaves little scope for management and free will.

For readers who are not economists, it may be worth pointing out that in the world of economics we operate with both *deterministic* and *stochastic* models. In the deterministic model the probability of an effect occurring is one. A always causes B. But the stochastic model predicts effects using calculations of probability. For example, if I sit at a table with a shaker in my hand containing a die and turn the shaker on its head, the die will *always* fall onto the table. This is a deterministic prediction. If anyone asks me to predict the result of the throw, my answer must be that I can, but only with a certain probability of 1:6 for any given result. In other words, the stochastic model enables us to operate with predictions of phenomena that we regard as being deterministic but uncertain. The result cannot be predicted, but the set of results can.

Let us now continue our scientific description of predictability. It is apparent that the problems of reality can be divided according to their suitability for description and solution using mathematical procedures:

Scientific and many other problems can be divided into linear and nonlinear problems. Linear problems can be described using linear equations, and nonlinear problems by nonlinear equations . . . in linear systems the results are proportional to the efforts invested in solving the problems, but this is not the case in nonlinear problems.[5]

In other words, the effect of calculations will always be proportional to the cause in question. If the cause is small, the effect will be small, and if the cause is large, the effect will be large. Accounting theory is familiar with such proportional calculations in what is known as the rate of turnover of the items in the balance sheet called debtors, stock and creditors. Predicted increases in purchases and sales are assumed to cause proportional increases in these items.

There is a remarkable reason for the division into linear and nonlinear problems:

This division is not only formal but also extremely practical, because linear equations always have solutions, whereas it is rare for nonlinear equations to be solved by classical mathematical methods, and if they can be solved they often describe quite uninteresting problems. The fact is that the vast majority of important scientific problems are described by nonlinear equations, whereas only a minority belong to the straightforward linear category. By and large it is possible to say that before the age of computers science had to stick to linear problems. Approximate (and not always valid) methods were found to simplify nonlinear problems into linear ones. . . . In other words, the attempt to solve nonlinear problems was abandoned.

Corresponding considerations are already evident in the theory of business economics. The American organizational theorist and Nobel Prize winner Herbert A. Simon wrote of "mathematician's aphasia," the loss of ability to speak about the real world. Mathematics is deceptively seductive, and it is easy to forget reality in one's enthusiasm for figures and procedures. Simon describes the symptoms of mathematician's aphasia in the following ironic and highly accurate fashion:

The victim abstracts the original problem until the mathematical intractabilities have been removed (and all semblance to reality lost), solves the new simplified problem, and then pretends that this was the problem he wanted to solve all along. He expects the manager to be so dazzled by the beauty of the mathematical results that he will not remember that his practical operating problem has not been handled.[6]

The message is that researchers and practitioners must remain highly alert and skeptical. There are two subconclusions:

1. It is better to admit that you have given up trying to solve a problem than to fool yourself and others into believing that you have solved it using unrealistic methods.
2. People who believe that a given problem has been solved can no longer be persuaded that it still exists.

Economists would do well to remember Wiin Nielsen's remark that the vast majority of problems belong to the difficult, nonlinear category, and that problems that are soluble are often quite uninteresting. In order to underline the new insight, an analogy to the animal world shows that we actually know very, very little when it comes to the point:

Incidentally, it is worth pointing out that it is rather inconsistent to use the negative term "nonlinear" to describe the largest category of problems . . . we might as well divide animals into "elephants" and "nonelephants" respectively, which is not a particularly accurate definition.[7]

Why, and how long, must we accounting theorists continue to entertain our students with linear (but irrelevant) methods of solving problems? Our students will undoubtedly see through us.

Readers who are familiar with microeconomics and accounting theory will also be familiar with the magical formula that helps transform difficult, nonlinear problems into more straightforward linear ones. All you have to say is "all else being equal," and Eureka! Both business enterprises and the world in which they operate are immediately frozen in time. This magic trick then makes it possible to study the financial situation of such enterprises under the microscope and regard them as absolutely stable, unchanging systems, whose aim is to optimize results (i.e., to earn as much money as possible), and in which there are no problems of information or communication because the "decision makers" are in full possession of all the necessary facts. They are like gods. *But unfortunately all else is not equal.* We live in a world that changes all the time, in which the changes cannot be predicted.

In an attempt to introduce greater realism to our methods of description, let us now ask the following two questions about the methods of accounting:

1. Is it possible to describe the system known as "the financial position of a business enterprise" in scientifically viable and thus meaningful fashion by using linear mathematics, and thereby to assume a deterministic and proportional relationship between cause and effect?
2. Is it possible in the real world—in theory and practice—to find examples of such a method of description being used as the primary method?

The answer to the first question is "No, science indicates that there is no reason to believe that this is possible. On the contrary, everything points to the fact that the prediction of an enterprise's financial situation is still an unsolved problem belonging to the difficult category of nonlinear problems." And the answer to the second question is "Yes. The accounting theory used in practice boldly claims the possibility of using predictions based on the principle of linearity."

People know that linearity does not exist in the financial statements of the real world, so accounting theory is taught in peculiar fashion by first describing and explaining the methods based on linearity, and then making all sorts of reservations about these methods.

Skepticism is absolutely vital here, and can best be expressed by quoting my good colleague Dennis Clausen: "Financial ratios have a built-in potential for over-interpretation." This phrase is witty, accurate and certainly no exaggeration.

In a Danish textbook, the first sentences explain that the postulate of inertia is the main element in accounting theory, and that students should therefore believe in predictability as a basic principle. It is claimed that analysis of financial statements is a feature of the financial control of enterprises, and shows the way in which the financial situation of enterprises has changed in recent years, thereby providing an indication of the way this financial situation will change in the years ahead.

Danish students are thus taught to believe that studying old financial statements enables analysts to predict the financial situation for no less than the next few years. But there is also clear uncertainty. Predictability for several years into the future is mentioned and regarded as possible, but the claim is then weakened by the use of the words "an indication."

Let us now demonstrate that traditional accounting analysis consists of a set of procedures based on linearity as a basic principle. It is well known that the equation defining a straight line can be written as follows:

$$y = \alpha \times x + \beta$$

where α is the coefficient of inclination of the straight line, and β is the point at which the line intersects the y axis. For instance, if we write

$$y = 0.25 \times x + 3$$

we have described the straight line shown in figure 8.1.

Naturally, the equation for a straight line is always soluble. For instance, if you ask "What is the value of y when x is 12?" the answer is easy; $y = 6$ because:

$$y = 0.25 \times 12 + 3$$

If the financial situation is shown on the y axis and time on the x axis, a marvelous prediction model becomes available that is always capable of providing answers about the future. If you wish to know the financial sit-

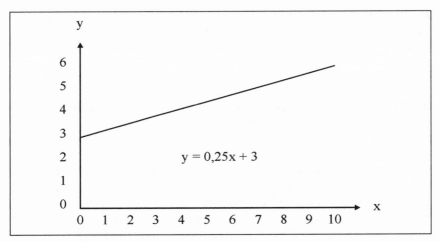

Figure 8.1. The straight line and its equation.

uation of a given business enterprise at any point in the future, a simple calculation is all you need. The problem of predictability is solved, providing that the postulate of inertia is assumed.

In our textbook we also find that an accounting analysis based on a comparison of time should describe the following factors:

1. The financial level of the enterprise
2. The direction of financial development of the enterprise
3. The speed of financial development of the enterprise

These are the necessary and sufficient conditions required to describe the financial situation using linear mathematics. The "financial level" is the value of the variable x (i.e., the intersection with the y axis). The "direction of development" is the sign in front of the variable x, which may be positive or negative. And the "speed of development" is the value of x (i.e., the coefficient of inclination).

Figure 8.1 shows that an attempt can be made to describe the financial situation using the familiar concept of *return on investment*. This figure is supposed to show how well or how poorly invested capital produces a return. The point of view used is clearly that of the investor asking "If I buy shares in this enterprise, how good will the return on my capital be in relation to the other investment opportunities available to me at the same time?"

The basic data needed for the analysis and attempt at prediction is taken from traditional financial statements. The linear philosophy, the possibility of predictability, and the vague reservations concerning the postulate of inertia are all quite clear in the textbook. It says that the main purpose of analysis of financial statements is to form the basis of an evaluation of the future financial development of business enterprises. This can be achieved by ensuring that the analysis contains an examination of financial level, direction of development and development speed, which requires the incorporation of the financial statements of several years for the enterprises concerned.

Let us now pause for a minute in order to draw the following subconclusion:

Traditional accounting theory rests on the postulate of inertia—on the condition that the basic financial laws are deterministic and linear. If we abandon the postulate of inertia, we shall be forced to abandon traditional accounting theory, too.

Readers now have the chance to choose whether they wish to be active participants in or passive observers of the development of accounting theory as a science. Readers who think independently will only heed the advice that they feel inclined to heed, and the rest of this chapter will thus be addressed to such independent-thinking readers. Let us now apply Occam's Razor and say "Never assume the existence of more objects than necessary." We do not necessarily have to accept the postulate of inertia in accounting theory.

Wiin Nielsen writes that at any event it is desirable to mention the following to "all producers of predictions":

1. The method of prediction
2. The accuracy of prediction
3. The a priori factor of trust

None of these well-founded scientific requirements can be met by traditional accounting theory. Scientific requirements regarding a given *method* are generally expressed in the demand for repeatability. In other words, the method in question and its application should be described so clearly that they always produce the same result in identical conditions, even though the method is used by two or more different people. But, apart from the logically incomplete method of double entry bookkeeping, traditional accounting theory contains no repeatable methods for predicting the financial situation of business enterprises.

Nor can traditional accounting theory meet the requirement concerning *the accuracy of prediction*, a claim that is borne out by the frequent incidence of suspension of payments and bankruptcy. Accounting specialists who claim to be able to derive "valuable signals" about the future by studying old financial statements have still not demonstrated the value of these signals in a convincing fashion. Perhaps they will succeed one day—who knows?

Finally, traditional accounting theory contains no *a priori factor of trust*. The key figure used (return on investment) is calculated by using two concepts (profit and assets). Despite a great number of well-meaning attempts, no scientifically viable definition of these two concepts has been found (see chapter 3).

No one takes seriously weather forecasts based on the weather last New Year's Eve. So surely we shall have to stop regarding predictions of the financial future based on similarly frail foundations as reliable.

Such predictions of the financial future are really little more than *superstitions* that have tragic consequences if they are used for any purpose. Scientifically viable hypotheses must be levelheaded, and for reasons of strict logic the financial situation of business enterprises simply cannot be described and predicted using linear mathematics.

Consequently, the conclusion concerning the predictability of financial situations is the same as the conclusion concerning a prediction of the weather next New Year's Eve based on data that is a year old: *such a prediction is impossible*. Period.

Readers who tremble at the thought of abandoning traditional accounting theory should simply stop reading on. The wish to continue using familiar theory and practice is understandable. It is always comforting to have traditions. But if the ideas presented here are accepted, traditional accounting theory must be abandoned.

Expressing the same thing more diplomatically, we might describe the continuation of determinism and linearity applied to financial situations as being "optimistic." Let us quote again from Wiin Nielsen:

> Nonlinearity is present everywhere, and linearity is the exception rather than the rule. Flags normally behave in nonlinear fashion in the Danish wind, and can be seen and heard as they flap violently and irregularly. Flags only move in almost linear fashion when there is a slight breeze ruffling the surface of the flag in regular patterns. . . . Similarly, waves in the atmosphere and sea are nonlinear, as are the curves of a garden hose or artery. Even the classical pendulum, which was examined both theoretically and experimentally by Galileo, is nonlinear if its movements from resting position are large. The fact that Galileo failed to find the equation capable of determining the periodic movements of a pendulum and failed to confirm his results was due to the fact that his experiments confined themselves to small movements because his pendulum was a chandelier in the Cathedral of Pisa. . . . Ever since Galileo and Newton, a great number of physicists and mathematicians have spent a good deal of time trying to find the simplification needed to transfer a nonlinear system into a linear system. The advantage of straightforward linear systems is not only that they can be solved, but also that two solutions can be combined to produce one solution. This does not apply to nonlinear systems. Separate solutions to linear problems can be combined to produce complicated solutions. But the simplification of nonlinear systems into linear systems will always be an unsatisfactory way of solving real, nonlinear problems.[8]

Once again it is apparent that theorists are interested in *soluble* problems, whereas practitioners are interested in *serious* problems. But not all soluble problems are serious, and not all serious problems are soluble.

Applying the term "optimistic" to traditional accounting theory is diplomatic. But people who lose their jobs or money owing to financial catastrophes may be forgiven for abandoning such diplomacy. Terms such as "careless," "irresponsible," "incompetent," "crazy" or other such tactless and emotional descriptions may be applied to accounting specialists who say that the financial situation of business enterprises can be predicted and who are subsequently forced to admit in tragic (or tragi-comic) fashion that their earlier predictions proved completely false, confessing "Oops, another unpleasant surprise."

We have seen how acceptance of the postulate of inertia enables people to believe that they can look into the future. But practical managers who have tried applying accounting theory to the real world will surely be forced either to despair, or to change their views. They must either continue to make mistakes, or abandon the beliefs held until now.

The consequence of abandoning traditional accounting theory may seem to be leading us into chaos. But, there is order in chaos: randomness has an underlying geometric form. Chaos imposes fundamental limits on prediction, but it also suggests causal relationships where none were previously suspected.

The problem of cause and effect is an ancient one, but new knowledge makes it highly interesting. We already know that the problem is difficult. The Scottish philosopher David Hume demonstrated way back in the early 1700s that our belief in the connection between cause and effect could be viewed as a kind of psychological automatic programming. If B follows A a great number of times, we start to feel we "know" that there is a connection between A and B. But the reason for this belief is only the logically sterile argument about repetition. I cannot conclude anything general about cause and effect by referring to observations alone, even if the number of these observations is great and there are no exceptions.

It becomes apparent that the principles of determinism and linearity have been part of the working hypothesis in accounting theory, which regards business enterprises as systems that are, in principle, deterministic, or predictable. If you simply collect the right information in sufficient amounts and treat it in the right way, business enterprises become systems that can be controlled. We may have believed ourselves capable in principle of predicting and controlling the financial situation of enterprises for long periods chosen at random. For many years, this form of "management accounting" seemed to succeed. The boom lasting from the 1950s to the middle of the 1970s was a happy time for the vast majority of business enterprises, but it may also have had another effect. It may have led many managers to believe that the boom experienced by their enterprises was solely due to their own efforts. But do we control the world, or does the world control us?

We return to the article about chaos. Once again the foundations of traditional accounting theory are swept away, leaving us with the conclusion that *even deterministic systems can develop in completely unplanned fashion*. The problem has been regarded as one of information. But:

Such a viewpoint has been altered by a striking discovery: Simple deterministic systems with only a few elements can generate random behavior. The randomness is fundamental; gathering more information does not make it go away. Randomness generated in this way has come to be called chaos. . . . A seeming paradox is that chaos is deterministic; generated by fixed rules that do not themselves involve any elements of chance. In principle the future is completely determined by the past but in practice small uncertainties are amplified, so that even though the behavior is predictable in the short term, it is unpredictable in the long term.[9]

Fundamental scientific theory is based on a surprisingly small number of general ideas about predictability. Once again, the decisive element is determinism. We say that things that happen are the results of previous events, so we refer to cause and effect and believe that we can predict the effect next time we see the cause. But can we? It is not as simple as many people think.

The most convinced disciple of determinism in the history of scientific theory was the French mathematician Pierre Simon Laplace. He was so impressed by Newton's results with laws formulated in linear fashion that in 1776 he claimed that the state of the universe could be predicted in detail for the rest of eternity if only the position and speed of each individual particle were known in advance. We quote his views from the article by Crutchfield et al. entitled *Chaos*: "The present state of the system of nature is evidently a consequence of what it was in the preceding moment, and if we conceive of an intelligence which at a given instant comprehends all the relations of the entities of this universe, it could state the respective positions, motions and general affects of all these entities at any time in the past or future."

Wiin Nielsen describes this as "the most optimistic, deterministic view ever stated." Nor was it allowed to pass without contradiction. The linear philosophy with its assumption of complete predictability in principle and proportional relationship between "cause" and "effect" was attacked as early as 1903 by the French mathematician Henri Poincaré, who is regarded as the founder of the theory of dynamic systems. Poincaré claimed that there is not a natural linear and proportional relationship between cause and effect. A small cause sometimes has a large effect, and vice versa. Or as the proverb puts it, "Little strokes fell great oaks."

A very small cause which escapes our notice determines a considerable effect that we cannot fail to see, and then we say that the effect is due to chance. If we knew exactly the laws of nature and the situation of the universe at the initial moment, we could predict exactly the situation of that same universe at a succeeding moment. But even if it were the case that the natural laws had no longer any secret for us, we could still only know the initial situation *approximately*. If that enabled us to predict the succeeding situation with the same approximation, that is all we require, and we should say, that the phenomenon has been predicted, that it is governed by laws. But it is not always so; it may happen that small differences in the initial conditions produce very great ones in the final phenomena. A small error in the former will produce an enormous error in the latter. Prediction becomes impossible, and we have the fortuitous phenomenon.[10]

Wiin Nielsen notes that this is very alarming, because in principle it means that tiny changes can have huge effects. Another meteorologist says that he hardly dares to sneeze for fear of changing the climate. One American scientist has described this as the "butterfly effect." The idea of a small cause having a huge effect might in principle mean that a butterfly in China flying towards a flower could cause a hurricane in America.

The new chaos theories are the result of experiments that are basically very simple. You ask the computer to calculate the value of a given mathematical expression. The result of the calculation is then inserted as a variable in the expression, the calculation is repeated, the new results inserted, and so on. The computer carries out the calculation a couple of thousand or million times, and the development over time can then be studied.

Such an experiment will certainly give a picture of a deterministic but unpredictable system. The result of the previous calculation is the "cause" of the result of the next calculation, which is the "effect." But even simple conditions at the outset can lead to chaos. A given system is regarded as chaotic if

1. the butterfly effect can be observed
2. the system fails to generate repetition

Using a computer as a tool makes it possible to produce a picture of a system that is definitely *deterministic* and undoubtedly *unpredictable*. It can only be described as a series of calculations.

The American Edward Lorenz has expressed the new basic tenet of the chaos theory, which is a shock to the world of accounting theory and perhaps for economics as a subject in general: "I realized that any physical system that behaved nonperiodically would be unpredictable."

Readers may now be asking "What does this have to do with the world of accounting?" or "Has this anything to do with reality?"

Not necessarily. The question we must now ask is whether the model and the real world are *isomorphic* (i.e., whether there are any structural similarities between the model and real life). If I operate with a picture of a financial situation that is not structurally in accordance with a financial situation in the real world, I will constantly be confused, surprised or disappointed.

The only readers to be unaffected by this will be those who believe that the physical system known as "the financial situation of a business enterprise" is periodic. Is the financial situation of an enterprise like a pendulum swinging on the end of a string, or a planet moving in its orbit? Or is it better defined as the exchange of goods, services, information and money in a dynamic and varying interaction between the enterprise and the world around it? Readers who believe the latter to be true are forced to the shocking but unavoidable conclusion that

The long-term financial position of business enterprises is basically unpredictable. Period.

This is always true. It is a basic tenet of science. And attempts to carry out impossible tasks will always fail.

Let us now conclude this chapter about the predictability of financial situations with a brief summary. Basically, we have considered three different versions of predictability based on determinism.

All events can be regarded as being caused by previous events, so we do not need to assume that gods or demons are at work. Nor do we need to assume that the particular demon called Inertia is at work. Determinism can be maintained while considering the following explanations, all of which are based on science:

1. The simple and familiar idea that causes always have an effect. If A then B. So B can be predicted with certainty.
2. The stochastic explanation. A causes B, but not with certainty, only as one of several possibilities. So B can be predicted with a certain amount of certainty.
3. The chaos explanation. A caused B, but this could not have been predicted. So B is unpredictable.

These scientific results can now be combined in the logical diagram given as figure 8.2.

Lawyers might use this figure as a contribution to the discussion about intent and negligence. Naturally, it should not be regarded as a postulate about the truth. But the basic concepts of intent are already clearly and adequately defined, so it must be possible to ask whether progress might be made if lawyers and behavioral psychologists joined forces to study the logical foundations of the concept of intent in greater detail. A foundation based on scientific behavioral psychology might be preferable.

Let us conclude this chapter on the predictability of financial situations by quoting the conclusion to the article about chaos:

Even the process of intellectual progress relies on the injection of new ideas and on new ways of connecting old ideas. Innate creativity may have an underlying chaotic process that selectively amplifies small fluctuations and molds them into macroscopic coherent mental states that are experienced as thoughts. In some cases the thoughts may be decisions, or what is perceived as the exercise of free will. In this light, chaos provides a mechanism that allows for free will within a world governed by deterministic laws.[11]

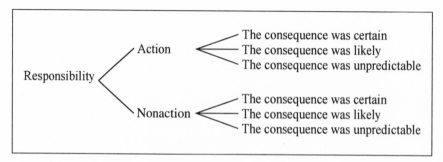

Figure 8.2. Responsibility and predictability.

Deterministic explanations of predictability are presented as closed systems, as language and theory not necessarily connected to reality. What would happen if these closed systems were opened?

NOTES

1. Vagn Greve, "*Er tiden moden til en ny straffelov?*" 1984.
2. A. Wiin Nielsen, *Predictability*, p. 7.
3. Ibid., p. 8.
4. Ibid., p. 12.
5. Ibid., p. 26.
6. H. A. Simon, *The Shape of Automation*, p. 75.
7. Wiin Nielsen, *Predictability*, p. 27.
8. Ibid., p. 28.
9. James P. Crutchfield et al., "Chaos," p. 38.
10. Ibid., p. 40.
11. Ibid., p. 49.

9 LIKE WORKING FOR AN UNDERTAKER

Advice after damage is like medicine after death.

—*Danish proverb*

Anyone attempting to deal systematically with an unpredictable system as if it were predictable will be constantly prone to surprise, disappointment and frustration. Managers who seek to stick to the same financial course when exterior circumstances change often steer blindfolded into the arms of catastrophe. In this chapter we seek to disprove the claim that traditional financial statements are beset by the problem of invisibility. But our attempt fails. Once a business enterprise is in financial difficulties, it is often far too late to save it. The approach of catastrophe is not seen in time. The exterior circumstances facing enterprises change fast, which is why time is of the essence to business managers. Experienced lawyers point to a conflict between two laws—the law of life, and the law of bookkeeping. Business enterprises in financial distress often fail to keep financial statements altogether, and even if they do, the financial statements they keep are generally described as disorderly, distorted and hazy instead of giving a true and fair picture. They can be used as the instrument of opportunism, providing a misleading picture that is supposed to indicate the financial situation, but that fails to do so. As long as people continue to believe in the myth of the information value of traditional financial statements, no one will succeed in reducing or preventing the large financial and human losses so often incurred in business life.

The somewhat morbid title of this chapter has been chosen in order to describe and emphasize the irrevocable and generally highly tragic consequences in the form of great human and financial losses that arise when a formalized system of dealing with insolvency is used. Once words like "composition," "compulsory composition" or "bankruptcy" start being used about business enterprises, such enterprises are generally in such deep financial water that there is no longer any realistic hope of survival. And it is highly likely that someone will suffer considerable losses in such circumstances. The point at which such losses could have been limited or even avoided altogether has been passed some time previously.

Danish Law Professor Niels Ørgaard describes this lost hope of survival in an article on the Danish Bankruptcy Act of 1977, and it is the following quotation from this article that provides the inspiration for the title of this chapter:

Business enterprises that experience financial difficulties so serious that they are prepared to allow themselves to be processed by the formalized system for dealing with bankruptcy are generally so weak both financially and managerially that they cannot be saved. . . . The logical and merciless system used to deal with bankruptcy has the same function as an undertaker.[1]

This use of the word "undertaker" may well seem gloomy and almost frightening to practical business managers and accountants, most of whom tend to feel that things only go wrong for others, not for themselves, in the belief that their own enterprise and clients will continue to prosper. But perhaps many of the managers and accountants who experience that things do sometimes go wrong also said the same thing once upon a time. The problems inherent in business enterprises are often invisible. Perhaps people *cannot* see them in time. Or perhaps they *refuse to* see them in time.

In chapter 4 we saw that incipient insolvency is often invisible to the management and creditors alike. In this chapter we shall describe and comment upon this situation, and on the problems arising when insolvency has finally become visible and concrete, so that no one can ignore it or deny its existence any longer.

Niels Ørgaard writes that the aim of the rules relating to what is known as the "suspension of payments institute" in the Danish Bankruptcy Act is to limit the number of bankruptcies occurring—that is, to seek to save as much as possible. But he remarks that it has not yet been possible to achieve this aim:

The recommendations of the Danish Ministry of Justice . . . state that the proposed Act primarily (seeks) to restrict the number of bankruptcies and insolvent liquidations by improving opportunities for reaching amicable agreement with the creditors of business enterprises that are threatened by bankruptcy. The fact that the suspension of payments system was unable to live up to this ambitious goal was undoubtedly due to a certain extent (but only to a certain extent) to the fact that the system was designed by the committee dealing with the Bankruptcy Act for use with small enterprises. In general it is doubtful whether the Bankruptcy Act is a suitable instrument for meeting the overall requirement concerning the survival of business enterprises.[2]

The only comment required here is that in a social/liberal economy like that of Denmark (or western Europe) it is highly likely that the only instrument capable of ensuring "the survival of business enterprises" in the long term is the proven will and capacity of such business enterprises (personified by their managers) to survive financially. Business enterprises in the private sector must be managed in such a way that they are able in the long term to earn at least as much money as they spend, otherwise the managers responsible are writing the death sentence of such enterprises. And if this happens, the only question is how long it will be before things fall apart, and what the manner of collapse will be, including the losses to be suffered and the people to suffer them. In the long term, no bankruptcy act in the world can ever make up for the failures of business managers.

The following four realistic subconclusions can be drawn up concerning the chances of saving business enterprises in financial distress and the chances of avoiding final suspension of payments:

1. It is vital to take action as early as possible, so early warnings about incipient insolvency are also vital.
2. During attempts to reconstruct business enterprises, it is vital to be able to obtain a reliable idea of the assets and liabilities of such enterprises. In other words, reliable and up-to-date accounting material is essential.
3. In practice, financially distressed enterprises rarely keep reliable accounts. Experienced accountants often say that the total absence of financial statements is typical of such enterprises.
4. A good proportion of failed attempts made to reconstruct business enterprises are due to the lack of up-to-date and reliable accounting material.

When the best attempts to reconstruct business enterprises fail, the result, as mentioned is that the "undertaker" goes into action. So let us now consider the system described by Niels Ørgaard as the system for dealing with insolvency in greater detail. This is the system that goes into operation when suspension of payments is no longer invisible or kept secret, but is announced to all interested parties in the fatal and always depressing statement "Company X has suspended its payments."

In order to consider this system, we need to imagine that we are in court, where the issue of bankruptcy and the resulting legal effects are decided. Naturally, there are major changes in management and responsibility at enterprises that suspend their payments. The management is taken out of the hands of the person or people in charge, and transferred to the creditors and trustees involved in the estate. In addition, there are a number of drastic changes in the way claims and debts are paid.

The result may be a compulsory composition offering the chance of survival to enterprises believed capable of surviving. But the result may also be bankruptcy—the total winding-up of the enterprise concerned. In both cases, it is almost certain that the creditors concerned will incur losses that are often considerable. So the issuing of a bankruptcy statement by the court is a very weighty matter for all parties involved. Consequently, it is also important to ask what kind of information is used as the basis for the decision of the court.

The material for the following discussion is derived from Danish Supreme Court Judge Mogens Munch's comments on the Danish Bankruptcy Act, and in the following we shall pursue our interest in the two key concepts of *financial statements* and *time*.

When a court decides whether or not a given enterprise should be declared bankrupt, there is no formal doubt about the conditions that must be met. Section 17 of the Danish Bankruptcy Act states that the criterion used to decide whether a debtor can be claimed bankrupt by a creditor (or by himself) is *insolvency*: "If a debtor is insolvent his estate shall be subject to bankruptcy proceedings when so required by the debtor concerned or any creditor."

The definition of insolvency is contained in section 17 subsection 2. This definition has already been mentioned and dealt with in chapter 4, but we should like to repeat it here all the same: "A debtor is insolvent when he is incapable of meeting his obligations as they fall due, unless his inability to pay can be regarded merely as a temporary phenomenon."

But how shall we decide whether insolvency has occurred? This question is not easy to answer satisfactorily. Mogens Munch comments on the concept of insolvency as follows: "According to section 17 subsection 2, the concept of insolvency has two aspects: the debtor is incapable of meeting his obligations as they fall due, and this state of affairs is not temporary. In other words, insolvency means inability to pay."

We note that there is no contradiction between this comment and the definitions of basic concepts and the appurtenant comments contained in chapter 4. Managers and their advisors often try to hide the difficulties facing enterprises from their creditors, to keep incipient suspension of payments quiet while they try to remedy the situation. But if creditors become aware of the situation nonetheless, they may take action themselves, and it is hardly likely that the creditors will regard the attempt to conceal what was going on as comforting:

If a creditor proves the existence of worrying factors whose importance cannot immediately be refuted by the debtor, the debtor must present financial statements, budgets and other information concerning these factors. If the debtor fails to pay his debts on time, even though he has not yet suspended his payments . . . he must explain the reasons for this failure, e.g. disputes about such debts or their size. If he is forced to admit that the reason is the lack of funds, he must explain how he intends to acquire the funds required.[3]

Naturally, this explanation by the debtor about how he intends to acquire funds needs to be convincing if the court is to be persuaded of its genuineness. Financial statements and budgets will be required, but in many cases this kind of information is not available in enterprises that are in financial distress. The very attempt to suppress incipient suspension of payments is often enough of a "worrying factor" to result in official suspension of payments. This underlines the fact that attempts to keep incipient suspension of payments quiet while solutions are found should be avoided altogether, or should be very brief. Once again, the importance of time and financial statements can be appreciated.

Creditors may believe that "worrying factors" are present without the presence of any obvious symptoms in the form of problems making payment. Creditors only need to have a reasonable doubt about the future ability of enterprises to fulfill their obligations. If they have such doubts, creditors may approach the court on their own initiative and require that the debtor is be declared bankrupt. But in such cases common symptoms in the form of illiquidity may be entirely absent, and if so the creditor may be the one faced with the problem of convincing the court that the debtor should be declared bankrupt. This is sometimes difficult:

The debtor may be insolvent even though he is capable of paying his due debts, if he is incapable of paying his other debts as they fall due. In such a prediction . . . future income and expected future items of debt must be taken into consideration. The more distant the moment at which the debtor will be unable to pay his debts, the more convincing the proof of insolvency needs to be before bankruptcy can be declared.[4]

In practice, the "prediction" referred to here will generally comprise a list of all the debtor's rights, assets and liabilities, as well as the flow of payments associated with them. But it is often difficult or even impossible to obtain this information. Reliable, up-to-date financial statements are rare in such situations. Even debtors themselves find it hard to make such predictions because enterprises in financial distress rarely keep reliable financial statements. And if the debtors find it hard to make the prediction, how will the creditors ever succeed?

As we shall see, bankruptcy courts generally have difficulty in regarding the available financial information as reliable. Neither budgets nor financial statements can be depended on in such circumstances, and Mogens Munch's reasons for the skepticism of the court are quite clear. We recall our sharply worded working hypothesis to the effect that traditional financial statements are worthless for evaluating the solvency of business enterprises. Is this hypothesis in danger of being contradicted, or is it about to be confirmed?:

When the reason for bankruptcy is the (not merely temporary) lack of ability to pay, the debtor's *budgets* come into focus. However, the bankruptcy court may find it hard to evaluate the reliability of these budgets, given the fact that the court only has superficial knowledge of the enterprise concerned, and the fact that the court may not always have the necessary insight into business affairs. Naturally, the most recent *financial statement* issued by the enterprise may give an indication of the situation, and of course an increasing deficit may be a grave threat. However, the importance of such financial statements is often limited. . . . The situation may have changed since the end of the last accounting year, often for the worse. Very often the most recent financial statements will simply be in disarray. . . . The future does not always correspond to the past, and in particular the picture given by financial statements is often distorted. Sometimes financial statements may be hazy without being incorrect, perhaps to conceal a deficit. Income or expenses may be included in the wrong period. To gain a true and fair picture, it may be necessary to supplement financial statements with internal accounting material from the enterprise concerned, and even though the accountant is expected to consider any significant events that occur between the expiry of the accounting year and the issuing of the auditor's report . . . he may never have been informed of any such events.[5]

These views are surely discomforting for accounting specialists who swear by tradition and traditional financial statements. Financial statements and budgets are certainly not regarded as being informative, and thus as being valuable sources of knowledge. Their form and content are both open to doubt. The court often has "only superficial knowledge of the enterprise concerned," and is in general hampered by "the fact that it may not always have the necessary insight into business affairs." Financial statements may give no more than "an indication of the situation," and only contain a clear message if they reveal several years of "increasing deficit." But accounting specialists are all aware that concepts such as "profit" and "deficit" are *unclear* and *imprecise*. And even allowing for this reservation, the importance of financial statements is often "limited" because the circumstances of the enterprise concerned have changed, making the previous financial statement out-of-date. They also have "limited" importance because they may be "in disarray," "distorted" or "hazy," or they may include items concerning a "wrong" period. Nor is it certain that the auditor's report can be attributed much reliability. The traditional, so-called "unqualified" auditor's report is a stereotype, worded in meaningless fashion, and even when the auditors have done their work well they may easily be overtaken by events occurring after the most recent completion date.

Let us put it diplomatically. The working hypothesis to the effect that traditional financial statements are worthless with a view to evaluating the solvency of business enterprises has not yet been clearly refuted.

The balance sheet intended by accounting legislation to be a vital aspect of the "true and fair picture" is actually described by Munch as an almost completely unrealistic, vague and random collection of information that no sensible person could possibly take seriously. We are very far from having a "true and fair picture." In fact, what we have is a healthy suspicion founded on bitter experience that financial statements are unclear, opportunistic, hazy, outdated and therefore systematically *misleading* pictures:

The *balance sheet* may vary, since it may be drawn up in various ways to suit the management, the tax authorities, or lenders. Even the most conscientious of accountants is allowed considerable leeway when summarizing assets. . . . The fact that auditing and counter-auditing processes arrive at completely different figures is well-known in criminal cases. The value of stock depends on the potential for selling it, the fixed assets are only of any value if they are sold, and the purchase price of second-hand equipment is rarely the same as that stated in the financial statement. The meaning of the item known as "depreciation" is debatable. . . . The financial statements of production companies often fail to give a clear picture of the way work in progress has been recorded.[6]

An opportunist is someone who allows his or her actions to be determined by whatever seems most advantageous in the current situation. In other words, opportunism involves utilizing a given situation for your own immediate advantage, if necessary by ignoring other considerations, or by giving them low priority.

Anyone reading the quotation by Mogens Munch again will find that financial statements are described as varying according to the immediate objectives of users. This is the same as calling financial statements opportunistic. Their content and form vary, depending on their usefulness in taking advantage of specific situations for the benefit of the person presenting them.

Some people may not like the use of the term "opportunistic" to describe financial statements. On their behalf, let us pose the following questions: "If the purpose of financial statements is not to describe the current situation within the terms of the law and without damaging the interests of the enterprise concerned, what is their purpose? What is wrong with managers seeking to protect their own financial interests, and thereby the interests of the owners of the enterprise concerned? Why should this be called opportunism?"

The answer is that of course there is nothing wrong with managers seeking to fulfill the goals they have set themselves, as long as they keep within the bounds of the law. And of course there is nothing wrong in using financial statements to this end. *But financial statements should really be an expression of the same picture of reality in all the situations in which they are used.* The fact is that the information contained in financial statements, which should always be the same "true and fair" information, is molded pragmatically to suit the problem currently requiring a solution. As a result, it is perfectly legitimate to claim that financial statements, which are already unclear in terms of the concepts they use, and which can also be suspected of being "in disorder," "distorted" and "hazy," are opportunistic.

The task of advisors in case of incipient bankruptcy is to determine whether reconstruction of the enterprise concerned is possible, and whether a strengthening of its financial foundations would be a better idea than the alternative, which is suspending payments and processing by the "system for dealing with insolvency." What does this problem look like after payments have been suspended or bankruptcy filed for? How do the bankruptcy courts approach the task previously facing the advisors?

Actually, the bankruptcy courts face exactly the same problem as the advisors, although their chances of solving it may be somewhat poorer. Once payments have been suspended, enterprises and their managers have already lost the regard of the world around them. Mogens Munch describes the task and problems facing the bankruptcy courts as follows:

> In brief, the bankruptcy court must decide whether the difficulties of making payment are so great that there is no reasonable chance of the enterprise concerned continuing business. If the enterprise is involved in projects stretching a long time into the future, e.g. major contracting projects, prediction becomes more uncertain. If the enterprise is running at a loss, and if this situation cannot be expected to change in the near future, continuation will normally be pointless. However, often the difficulties are actually due to excessively tight liquidity, owing perhaps to excessive expansion in the good years followed by a downturn in the economy. If capital injection and credit expansion are impossible, the difficulties will often accelerate owing to enforced realization resulting in poor prices, refusal of or neglect of profitable but capital-intensive contracts, and purchasing in small quantities without the discount allowed for large-scale purchases.[7]

Mogens Munch then mentions the factors involved in the assessment by the court, and once again we see that the world of accounting at its current stage of development cannot be used to provide information about the decisive factors. The information provided by traditional financial statements (assuming that they have been kept) is encumbered by a number of uncertainties that are all too obvious to accounting specialists. Booked values cannot be used to determine whether an enterprise in suspension of payments is able to continue business. Traditional financial statements are presented as being rather helpless:

> In assessing the future chances of enterprises, a number of factors must be considered (competition, available skills, chances of the State stepping in, etc.) that can certainly not be converted into dollars and cents using current accounting techniques. . . . The value of work in progress depends entirely on whether this work can be expected to be completed or not, i.e., on a prediction. The value of machinery depends on whether the enterprise is expected to be sold as a going concern, or whether the machinery is to be sold piecemeal. The evaluation of future potential is also of decisive importance for goods that are prone to major price variations.[8]

We note the phrase "using current accounting techniques," indicating that the author has a quiet but clear hope that future accounting techniques may be better than current ones.

The preceding quotations show clearly that *bankruptcy courts are interested in predictions in the key areas,* and that financial statements are regarded as worthless for the simple reason that even if they are both present and in order, they *can only be regarded as descriptions of the consequences of past events.*

As far as the information needed is concerned, the situation described here is little different from the situation in which the management discusses the allowance of potentially risky operating credit with its bank. However, the loss of patience by a bank or creditor may mean that all attempts to save enterprises in distress founder immediately:

The decision made by the bankruptcy court is very similar to the decision made by a bank as to whether it should continue to offer credit to an enterprise in distress. . . . There may be certain slight differences. The bankruptcy court may be slower than the bank to decide that insolvency exists in the current situation, but may make greater demands with regard to documentation of expectations for future improvement, and will probably be less willing to base its decision on the character of the debtor or management concerned. Sometimes there may be a more direct connection between the decisions of the bank and bankruptcy court respectively. If the bank decides to stop all credit and demand termination of its arrangement, the fate of the enterprise concerned will be more or less sealed. In this situation the debtor will rarely find it possible to take out a loan in another bank, . . . and the bankruptcy court will undoubtedly be skeptical with regard to claims of nonutilized credit opportunities elsewhere. The demands of the main suppliers or tax authorities may also have the same effect.[9]

Let us now conclude these quotations by Mogens Munch concerning the Danish Bankruptcy Act with a few comments to show that the difference between insolvency and illiquidity dealt with in chapter 4 actually has a decisive practical role to play. The existence of insolvency must be certain before declaring an enterprise bankrupt, and if there is any doubt it is the debtor's responsibility to prove that the enterprise's assets are greater than its liabilities, and thus that the means of payment required can be obtained in the near future.

The basic concepts dealt with so far are clearly of great importance, and the information that the debtor must present in order to save his enterprise is related to *future payments.* The future is actually the only thing that matters:

Even if the debtor is unable to pay the debt fallen due, it is not certain that he is insolvent in the eyes of the law. Bankruptcy cannot be declared if the inability to pay is merely *temporary.* The debtor may demonstrate that his inability to pay is temporary. . . . The law has not set a specific deadline. The more likely it seems that a debtor will one day be able to pay, the further the deadline may be extended. The basic deadline is probably "a few months." . . . If the debtor is able to pay assuming he is allowed a reasonable period to sell his assets, bankruptcy should not be declared.[10]

Let us now conclude this brief description and evaluation of the world of the law with a suitable quotation taken from Niels Ørgaard's *Konkursret* (Bankruptcy Law). We have just seen Mogens Munch claim that the data contained in financial statements is designed to suit specific situations, that it is distorted and hazy and that it is in general difficult to use such data to shed light on the problems at stake. We have described this difficulty as reflecting opportunism, and Niels Ørgaard describes it as follows:

> Naturally, balance sheets drawn up by the debtor cannot necessarily be used as evidence. In a balance sheet written for tax purposes the assets will often be written down to less than their actual value, whereas they may be overvalued in a balance sheet drawn up with a different end in view. Some assets (e.g., real estate) can be valued with great accuracy, but the evaluation of other assets must be based on prophecy regarding the future development of the enterprise concerned. So the value of the intangible assets of an enterprise, such as goodwill, know-how and patents, depends on a prediction of the enterprise's future viability. Evaluation of the debtor's production plant and stock also depends on a prediction of future developments. There may be big differences between evaluating the debtor's production plant and stock as part of a going concern, and evaluating it in terms of its scrap value. The choice of evaluation method often decides whether the debtor is insolvent or not. . . . The difficulty of using the criterion of illiquidity resides in the fact that when deciding whether a debtor is capable of paying his debts as they fall due, the expected income of the debtor in the intervening period must also be taken into consideration.[11]

There is a striking similarity between the comments of Munch and Ørgaard. We also note that the "opportunistic financial statement," in which all the data is arranged to suit the situation in question, is described clearly by both authors.

We have now outlined a number of characteristic and authoritative examples of the serious problems that arise in connection with enterprises in distress. It is clearly advisable to conclude that the absence of financial statements that have been drawn up correctly may be regarded as part of the explanation why enterprises find themselves in distress in the first place, since financial control is impossible without accounting data. We have also seen that attempts to save such enterprises must be made in earnest if they are to succeed, and that they therefore depend on the availability of reliable and up-to-date information. But unfortunately, we have also seen that such information is almost always absent.

We cannot avoid the conclusion that as far as the presence, relevance and reliability of financial statements are concerned, this chapter shows that there is *a very serious and unsolved problem.*

This serious problem is linked to the fact that, in practice, accounting lacks a scientific foundation. The "theory" of accounting has been far too retrospective, authoritarian and traditional. The lack of a scientific basis for accounting has already been described in chapter 3. The great number of defects indicated by lawyers in chapter 9 have a practical, clear and direct connection with the fact that the world of accounting has lacked a scientifically viable frame of reference. If we had such a frame of reference, accounting legislation would be far clearer and more precise than it is, and accountants would have drawn up clear minimum requirements for the ongoing bookkeeping carried out by their clients. But there are no such requirements, and this is undoubtedly a significant part of the reason why orderly and careful bookkeeping is such a rare thing.

But it should be possible to escape from uncertainty and opportunism by presenting accounting information as a single *general system of registration* whose purpose is *to provide full coverage of all the details needed*, instead of continuing to put our faith in traditional financial statements, which merely provide information to suit specific situations (i.e., are opportunistic).

In this chapter we have seen that lawyers experience difficulties in finding financial statements at all, and in trusting the information they contain even if they are to be found. We shall now try to solve the problem of the invisibility of insolvency by solving the problem of the lack of accounting theory. The result will be a description of the logical contours of a system of *accounting for management*. If it is applied systematically, accounting for management may well be an important means of solving the problems that the quotations contained in chapter 9 have demonstrated with undeniable clarity.

NOTES

1. Niels Ørgaard, *Artikler om Konkurs og Tvangsakkord*, p. 11.
2. Ibid., p. 10.
3. Mogens Munch, *Konkursloven*, p. 123 ff.
4. Ibid., p. 125.
5. Ibid., p. 126.
6. Ibid., p. 128.
7. Ibid., p. 129.
8. Ibid., p. 129.
9. Ibid., p. 131.
10. Ibid., p. 132.
11. Niels Ørgaard, *Konkursret*, p. 32 ff.

10 IMPRUDENT PRUDENCE

Doing nothing is the first step towards doing wrong.

—Danish proverb

The so-called principle of prudence is probably the best-known of all accounting dogma, and it is no exaggeration to say that it is also the most dangerous of the seven groundless accounting principles to which people still cling. It requires accounting specialists to exhibit a pattern of behavior that is in direct contradiction to everything else required of them. What people *really* want accounting specialists to do is to accept the uncertainty and risk involved in running business enterprises, and to calculate the extent and possible consequences of this risk both clearly and at an early stage. Effective financial control can only be exercised if problems are discovered as early as possible. But the principle of prudence results in the systematic delay of financial statements owing to the rule that income must never be registered until it is certain. It also results in systematic distortion owing to the rule that expenses must be shown as soon as they "threaten." The principle of prudence is in direct contradiction to all reason and common sense, and its use is a good part of the reason why accounting patients die despite careful attention by accounting doctors. The principle of prudence does not prevent financial catastrophe, a fact that is apparent every day. But some people are unwilling to accept that this is the case. Is that what they call prudence?

In a later chapter we shall seek to demonstrate that the theory and new ideas about accounting presented here can be used in practice. We shall present the reader with an entirely new view of accounting that is radically different from the traditional view in several vital respects. The new method of accounting proposed here is capable of showing *future payments*.

Our intention is not to persuade readers of the truth of our remarks, since theorists generally find it difficult or even impossible to persuade others of their theories. Instead, we hope to enable readers to discover the truth of our remarks for themselves. Researchers who draw up new theories are never the best judges of whether these theories are better than the old ones, since they may not be impartial. The best judges of new theories are interested, qualified readers. The only theories worthy of acceptance are those that are drawn up, tested, presented and described in such a way that they seem useful from the point of view of interested, qualified readers. Researchers must subject themselves to the judgment of their contemporaries, and theorists must allow practitioners to determine the usefulness of their ideas.

But the people given such powers also have a responsibility. And anyone seriously interested in the world of accounting who reads on now must be prepared to consider the new theory carefully. Because if the new theory is accepted, the old one must be rejected—and this will of course have a huge impact on the future role of accounting specialists.

The new theory says that financial statements should contain a prediction of future payments, whereas the old theory says the opposite—that is, that financial statements represent financial history. So the new theory clearly contradicts the old one. Naturally, modern society cannot accept two contradictory theories about something as important as accounting, so a choice between the theories must be made. And no one claiming to think independently and logically will be able to sit on the fence. Serious readers will not be able to pretend that the new theory does not exist. Readers considering the new theory may find themselves forced to abandon the comfortable habits of years of accounting practice. But readers failing to consider the new theory at all will find themselves in the role of passive spectators as their profession develops.

The main difficulty in reading and considering this chapter is that readers are asked to abandon traditional assumptions, skepticism and prejudice without abandoning their alertness and common sense. In other words, readers are asked to relax their guard without putting their weapons aside. We shall require that the old theory of accounting is abandoned, but first we shall seek to demonstrate in this chapter and the following chapters that the old theory is both unclear and impotent. We shall then introduce the new theory with the necessary evidence in support, and consider the way it takes effect. A new view of accounting will then be presented, which readers are invited to attack if they wish.

We shall now attempt to topple one of the best-known and most highly regarded idols of financial statements. This idol is known as *The Principle of Prudence.* All accountants know the rule stating that incomes should never be shown in financial statements until they are certain, but that expenses should be shown as soon as they threaten. We shall attempt to prove that this rule is muddled and dogmatic, and that its application has precisely the opposite effect from that intended. There is always a certain amount of risk attached to the running of business enterprises, and financial statements should reflect this risk. No one who believes that prudence is the most important virtue should ever be involved in the world of accounting. In the future, the accounting profession promises to be a highly risky business. The world of accounting will no longer be a haven of prudence from which the pandemonium of the world can be observed at a safe distance.

We shall not erect a new theory to replace the toppled idol of prudence, but instead we suggest that accounting specialists use their own common sense and a concept that has already been familiar for some time. Let us regard the financial statements of the future as an expression of *calculated risk.*

Let us now consider the hopeless position of an accountant working for a business enterprise threatened by bankruptcy, a position that demonstrates the paradox of "imprudent prudence."

The position of an accountant when the client's enterprise is under financial threat has been described and discussed many times, but we have chosen to quote here from an article written in 1984 by Poul Erik Gruning, entitled "Revisors position i konkurstruede virksomheder" ("The position of accountants in enterprises threatened by bankruptcy"). We have already considered the problem of invisibility in traditional financial statements in an earlier chapter, and we shall now seek to describe, discuss and then suggest a solution to this problem. And finally we shall demonstrate that the factors that are invisible in traditional financial statements become visible when our new theory is applied.

The management becomes aware of the existence of financial problems in business enterprises far too late. That was the conclusion of chapter 4. That chapter focused on the opinion of lawyers, and accountants apparently agree: "The characteristic feature of enterprises that do not practice sensible financial control using interim accounts, budgets and so on is that the presence of negative tendencies is often realized too late to take any preventive action. . . ."[1]

Accountants are also familiar with the problem of *pressure of time* described by one lawyer when incipient suspension of payments threatens. It is striking how much lawyers and accountants agree on this point. The problem is discovered far too late, and once it has been discovered there is hectic activity to save the situation. There is often a lack of adequate accounting material in such circumstances, and one of the most important tasks of the accountant is to help draw up financial statements and budgets as fast as possible:

Experience teaches us that when a crisis is finally discovered, it is vital to take action quickly to prevent the risk of total collapse. In such circumstances, accountants are expected to help draw up accounting material and budgets under considerable pressure of time so that negotiations can take place without delay with capital investors, banks and creditors with a view to helping the enterprise survive the crisis that has arisen.[2]

The definition of insolvency contained in the Danish Bankruptcy Act, the distinction between temporary and permanent inability to pay one's debts, is the most important factor in such circumstances, and Gruning goes on to describe the impotence of traditional financial statements when a crisis occurs. The unclear and thus difficult-to-interpret concept of "owners' equity" is mentioned, and Gruning points out that the substance of this unclear concept often varies considerably, depending on the "accounting principle" used:

In other words, the Act declares that the first criterion of insolvency is the lack of liquidity . . . and the second is whether or not the illiquidity that has arisen can be regarded as permanent. . . . Naturally, the owner's equity will be much smaller in such circumstances if its balance sheet is calculated according to the principle of realization value instead of the going concern principle.[3]

Here is a point that the layman may find very difficult to understand. The fact is that the figures contained in financial statements vary, depending on the "accounting principle" used in drawing them up. This means that the information contained in financial statements cannot be regarded as constant. Financial statements are drawn up in opportunistic fashion, to suit the requirements of the situation at hand. If you want to wind up the enterprise concerned you use the "realization principle," and if you wish the enterprise to continue you use the "going concern principle." The only problem is that no one knows which of the two principles will be required. No one is aware of negative financial trends until it is too late, so everyone is surprised by the events that then occur.

But if the problem of invisibility could be solved, the discussion about which opportunistic "accounting principle" should be used would presumably become superfluous.

In scientific theory the word "principle" can be explained by the following axiom: "A principle is a basic concept on which thought or action is based; a principle is a guiding light." But in scientific theory all principles are well-founded, and this does not apply to the "principles" used in accounting theory. The "principles" of accounting theory are regarded as both instructions and excuses for practical behavior that is best described as "uncritical observance of a priori principles that have no rational foundation" (this is what the adjective "dogmatic" implies according to one dictionary published recently).

Until such time as the principles of thought and action in the world of accounting are expressed in a way that can be relied on, we should really be honest and use the word "dogmatic" to describe the "principles" on which current accounting is based. Consequently, we should call the "realization principle" the "realization dogma," and the "going concern principle" the "going concern dogma" until the use of the term "principle" is sufficiently justified. And the principles of accounting will never be sufficiently justified until accounting practice is based on a theory that cannot be refuted.

The article quoted in this chapter emphasizes "the problem of invisibility" in financial statements, as well as the pressure of time to which accountants are exposed. It also claims that the lack of reliable accounting theory releases accounting specialists from all responsibility. And if the absence of a reliable accounting theory means that even accounting specialists are unable to see the problem that everyone else expects them to solve, then surely most people will admit that Robert N. Anthony is right when he says that we are in desperate need of a new theory of accounting.

Gruning's article clearly indicates who is responsible for financial statements, and makes it clear that accountants are *not* to blame. He points out that accountants are often no more than passive spectators to the actions and decisions of managers. But if this is so, what is the good of the accountant's signature on financial statements? Such signatures are supposed to indicate that the accountant is a *witness to the reliability of the management*:

The management is responsible for drawing up financial statements, as well as for the decision to present financial statements according to the going concern principle. The optimism retained by the management in a crisis may place the accountant in a difficult position, since he may not share the management's view of the future potential of the enterprise concerned.[4]

The position of the accountant in such circumstances is very difficult. Accountants wishing to do their job properly and conscientiously may experience great qualms. Conscientious accountants, who are widely regarded as accounting specialists, audit and evaluate financial statements on a regular basis. They keep a close eye on the financial situation of the enterprises with which they are associated, and so they really cannot claim ignorance when things start to go wrong:

As mentioned earlier, an acute crisis in liquidity often follows on the heels of negative operational trends that may have been evident for several years without ever becoming apparent in the financial statements published.[5]

But if negative trends are not apparent in the financial statements that are *published*, are they apparent in the financial accounts that are *kept* on a regular basis? Readers who are not accounting specialists may be wondering why the financial statements published fail to reflect the actual financial trend, if this trend has been evident to managers and accountants for several years. Surely the law requires the presentation of a "true and fair picture." Are business enterprises really entitled to decide themselves whether they wish to conceal or distort information about their financial situation? Are financial statements really distorted deliberately, and are accountants really aware of the fact? Do they even help to conceal information?

Accountants would never present the problem in this fashion, and Gruning tries to lay the facts on the table openly. He says that there is a serious problem, and the problem is defined, described and discussed. But the remarkable thing is that it is also regarded as an unsolved cognitive problem. It is described as a paradox, as an example of "imprudent prudence." Figure 10.1 illustrates the paradox in graphical form. What we describe here as a paradox is described in the traditional, unclear language of accounting as "the loss of reserves during the decline of the enterprise."

The dotted line in figure 10.1 indicates the "accounting profit," whereas the solid line shows the "actual profit." The figure was presented at a conference of accountants in 1975 by Tage Andersen, a respected certified public accountant in Denmark.

Apart from being an illustration of the paradoxical problem, figure 10.1 also illustrates a number of remarkable details, which we shall now identify

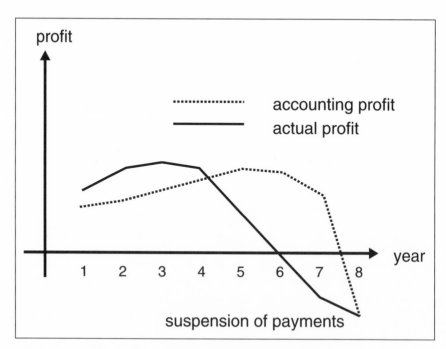

Figure 10.1. The paradoxical problem: imprudent prudence.

and discuss. The very existence of the paradox may contain the key to new understanding. Logical paradoxes have often been the launch pads leading to entirely new ways of thinking. When phenomena appear to be self-contradictory, there is always a chance that they may be understood in a new way. It may be possible to remove the contradiction by thought.

It is noteworthy that figure 10.1 contains a distinction between two different expressions of profit, one of which is described as "accounting profit," and one as "actual profit." In other words, there is a clear difference between the accounting profit and the actual profit, and the accounting profit is obviously *not* the same as the actual profit.

In Denmark people have long been aware of the fact that financial statements do not show the "actual" or "true" profit. And yet figure 10.1 still contains a line supposedly illustrating the "actual" profit. Why is this?

This particular issue has been dealt with by Professor Palle Hansen in a short book entitled *The Accounting Concept of Profit.* The interesting thing about this book is that it is based on data illustrating the progress of an enterprise over the course of several years leading to its collapse. After the collapse a total calculation can be carried out to compare with the "profit" or "deficit" mentioned year by year. As far as accounting theory is concerned, the importance of the book is that it proves that the financial result of the operations of any enterprise can only be determined with certainty after enterprises have been wound up, which means that figures stated as the profit or deficit each year will always be uncertain.

But the acceptance of a degree of uncertainty does not mean that we simply have to stand on one side and passively watch accounting degenerate into the instrument of opportunism. We have tools to describe the uncertainty, and thereby to calculate the risk involved. And the fact that it is logically impossible to say anything precise about profit in *only a single figure* does not necessarily mean that it is impossible to say anything precise about profit when using *more than a single indicator*. If it is not possible to describe financial results using a single figure, perhaps two, three or four figures will suffice.

Let us return to figure 10.1. Even though everyone agrees that no "true" interim profit ever exists, the figure still contains something called the "actual profit." The man responsible for figure 10.1 is an accounting specialist who is thoroughly familiar with the theory on which his profession is based. And this is where the paradox becomes apparent. No "actual" profit exists, and yet it apparently exists nonetheless.

This paradox becomes even more evident when we mention the dogma about prudence and the rule that income must not be included in financial statements until it is certain, but that expenses must be included as soon as they threaten. There is always an element of uncertainty when evaluating stock, and many managers/owners of business enterprises want to avoid paying too much in tax and dividend to shareholders. So the dogma of prudence in practice means that in "good years" it is permitted and even advisable to publish an accounting profit lower than the profit actually believed to apply. This is justified by saying that it involves *consolidation*. The term "reserves" is often used in accounting, and it sounds extremely sensible and logical. In the fat years it is wise to lay a little aside to cover the lean years. *But paradoxically enough, the money laid aside as "reserves" always seems to have disappeared mysteriously by the time it is needed.*

The paradox of imprudent prudence can be expressed as follows: If you are "prudent" and lay money aside as "provisions" in the fat years, and yet subsequently are forced to suspend your payments to everyone's surprise and disappointment because there are no funds left, then the "lack of prudence" displayed between the fat years and the suspension of payments must have been greater than the "prudence" shown in the same period.

Gruning's comment on the paradox that is evident in his article clearly shows what the paradox looks like to an accounting specialist. He says that figure 10.1 shows:

that an enterprise has managed to spread its profit over the course of several years in such a way that the financial statements issued every year have failed to show the seriousness of the actual situation. Readers of the enterprise's financial statements are only able to evaluate its financial situation in the last year of its life, when catastrophe is unavoidable. . . . The financial statements presented in the intervening years were probably drawn up according to the requirements of the law, and the profit or deficit was probably distributed more evenly by changing accounting principles, tightening existing principles, releasing secret reserves, and so on. It is true that the Danish Company Accounts Act of 1981 prohibits the use of secret reserves, but there is still so much elasticity in the general principles used for evaluation that situations such as that outlined in the figure may well continue to occur in future.[6]

This is worth noting. The author clearly states that unexpected suspension of payments leading to major losses is a well-known phenomenon, since otherwise it would not be possible to write about it. He also says that accounting practice is powerless to deal with this problem, and that such catastrophes may well continue to occur in the future. The law attempts to prevent such situations from arising, but the dogma on which accounting practice is based means that the profit shown in financial statements is a flexible figure, which can be adapted to suit the requirements of specific situations. The current model of accounting is unclear, so in practice financial statements often become the tool of opportunism despite the best intentions of preventing this from happening.

It is hard to believe that this is the case, but the fact is that such occurrences are inevitable because we lack a theory on which accounting practice can be based.

What action should accountants take if they have reason to believe that financial developments are starting to threaten the existence of the enterprises for which they work? At the moment, accountants find this question very hard to answer, and the problem impossible to solve. In such circumstances accountants are faced with a serious moral dilemma. It would be wrong to take action, but it may also be wrong to refrain from taking action:

The situation of an accountant in auditing the financial statement of an enterprise in decline is extremely difficult. He/she must ensure that the financial statement has been drawn up in such a way that it meets the requirements of current accounting law. If the financial statement has been drawn up with a view to ensuring the continuation of the enterprise concerned, and if there is any doubt about the feasibility of this aim, then he/she must ensure that this uncertainty is expressed sufficiently clearly in the annual report, notes, and so on to leave readers of the financial statement in no doubt about the problems facing the enterprise.[7]

This is wishful thinking. Financial statements never give readers any idea that the enterprises in which they have invested or to which they have given credit may be in serious difficulty. And even if such readers are in doubt about the financial situation of such enterprises, these doubts will only be reinforced when they consult a financial statement, because there are no real standards for the "notes" and "annual report" mentioned earlier. The information contained in financial statements is always unclear and impossible to interpret. And this is why the problem of invisibility arises.

Some accountants obviously feel convinced that financial statements can actually be understood by their users. But there is irrefutable evidence to prove that this is not the case, and very little evidence to indicate that such understanding is possible. If financial statements could be understood by nonspecialists, they would be used for some purpose. And as a rule financial statements are not used for any purpose at all.

The uncomfortable dilemma in which accountants find themselves when the suspicion of serious financial problems is confirmed has been mentioned already. But the reader is asked to note the remote, distant manner in which this dilemma is described in the following. The reader may also notice that *accountants apparently have absolutely no responsibility.* The worst thing that can happen to accountants is that they "may be criticized":

However, if the management does not wish to inform the public of the problems facing an enterprise by making these problems sufficiently evident in the financial statement, the accountant must decide whether the situation is serious enough to warrant a reservation being made when signing the statement. . . . The accountant is now in a dilemma in which he may be criticized if the enterprise experiences financial collapse shortly after publication of an unreserved financial statement. On the other hand, he may also be criticized if a reservation is made that causes unwished-for drama, which at worst may cause the final nail to be driven into the coffin of the enterprise concerned.[8]

There are grounds for serious concern here. We have just seen that Gruning believes that "when a crisis is finally discovered, it is vital to take action quickly to prevent the risk of total collapse." And yet here is the opposite— the view that hesitation may be necessary because accountants "may also be criticized if a reservation is made that causes unwished-for drama, which at worst may cause the final nail to be driven into the coffin of the enterprise concerned." What does he mean? Which of the two statements should we believe?

Are accountants responsible for financial statements, or are they not? Is the worst thing that could happen that accountants might be criticized mildly for remaining passive and silent instead of issuing a warning against a trend that could cause serious losses for interested parties and society in general? Are accountants responsible for financial statements? Yes or no? If they are, what is their responsibility? And if they are not, what is the point of having accountants?

The question of the responsibility of accountants will simply not go away. And of course it is nonsense to try and turn the question aside by referring to the "vow of silence" taken by accountants. Most people would probably love to see accountants fulfilling the role of authoritative witnesses in all accounting issues. But even a child can see that a silent witness is a worthless witness.

Anyone who regards these lines as an attack on accounting as a profession is making a grave mistake. An attack on accounting would only be justified if an attempt were being made to ignore the problems. And Poul Erik Gruning does not make any such attempt. He leaves us in no doubt that accountants have the opportunity and responsibility to keep an eye on the financial development of the enterprises with which they are associated. They must never remain silent when they can see that enterprises are in trouble. They can and should push the button and sound the alarm:

Active accountants are normally among the first people to sense a negative trend. Based on the principle that the sooner action is taken, the greater the chance of finding a cure, accountants should inform the management of their observations and views as soon as possible. . . . It may be vital for the survival of the enterprise that accountants react with no undue delay once they have ascertained a negative trend. [9]

There is no lack of clarity here. The author has two clear messages. It is vital to act as soon as possible, and it is also the responsibility of active accountants *to act, not to remain silent*.

The dogma of prudence states that income must not be shown in financial statements until it is certain. This causes a systematic delay, of course. And yet we are told by Gruning that the management must be informed as soon as possible. The paradox can thus be expressed as follows: A dogma that demands systematic delay in giving information that accountants regard as vital to informing the management as soon as possible could also be described with some justification as *the dogma of imprudence*. It is extremely imprudent to wait before giving people information that might be vital to the survival of an enterprise.

The conclusion is that the so-called principle of prudence could also be called the "principle of imprudence." The dogma is self-contradictory, and should be abandoned forthwith.

Double entry bookkeeping is not a complete system. When something is not complete, it is fair to say that it is incomplete. The proof of the logical incompleteness of double entry bookkeeping is as follows.

The first premise is that we assume that the task of accounting is to describe the financial consequences of the actions of enterprises, and that agreements are actions that have financial consequences.

The second premise is that double entry bookkeeping can be regarded as a formal system of expression that only contains the payment criterion (concerning payments of money) and the realization criterion (concerning the creation of claims) as systematic financial points of measurement.

The conclusion is that *double entry bookkeeping is a system of information that only describes the financial consequences of the actions of enterprises incompletely and unsystematically.*

Accounting theory controls our thinking about and understanding of accounting. If the theory is unclear, then during attempts to apply it rules will be made that may seem sound enough, but that in fact are incoherent and self-contradictory. In such circumstances mental short circuits occur far too often, and are dangerous for the profession as a whole.

The imprudent but nonetheless vital questions are "When will we accounting specialists realize that readers of financial statements care absolutely nothing for the figure stated as owners' equity?" and "When will accounts managers and accountants realize that the only thing that readers of financial statements really want to know is the extent to which the enterprise concerned risks bankruptcy?" Solvency and the risk of bankruptcy are two complementary expressions of exactly the same phenomenon. Solvent enterprises run no risk of bankruptcy, and enterprises threatened by bankruptcy are insolvent.

Niels Bohr once said that opposites are complementary. Opposites that are complementary form a single whole, and this can be seen with extreme clarity here. The presence of solvency implies the absence of the risk of bankruptcy, and the presence of the risk of bankruptcy implies the absence of solvency.

Financial statements that describe solvency on a regular basis also regularly describe the risk of bankruptcy. Financial statements that regularly contain a calculation of solvency are exactly the same as financial statements that constantly show the calculated risk of bankruptcy.

The concept of owners' equity means nothing. The risk of bankruptcy means everything. Owners' equity means nothing because it is a logically empty concept without meaning. The risk of bankruptcy means everything because we can see that it is present. It may be invisible in *financial statements*, but it is evidently not invisible in *the real world*. If the "true and fair picture" required by law means that financial statements should give readers a realistic impression of the financial position of enterprises, then the accounting practice currently applied is quite simply illegal.

Why is it that people who call themselves accounting specialists fail to appreciate this point? Why does prudence, apart from being the name of one particular form of accounting dogma, also apparently result in blindness or fear of a change that everyone else sees as being vital? Why do people apparently ignore reality, regard proposals for improvements as threats and cling obstinately to the empty rules and dogma of the past? Why do people try to patch up the holes in the old picture by applying even more rules and dogma?

One of the sharpest and most acute critics of the current lack of scientific approach in accounting theory is Richard Mattessich. In his book *Die Wissenschaftlichen Grundlagen des Rechnungswesens* he says that scientifically anchored accounting theory and practice would regard current accounting theory and practice more or less *like modern chemistry regards the alchemists of the past*. He also believes that in terms of development, current accounting theory belongs to the scholastic and dogmatic world of the Middle Ages.

But is this true? Are we accounting specialists really unrealistic, ignorant and blindly controlled by regulations? Can this really be true? Let us consider briefly another profession in a different era. Let us consider the world of medical science in the Middle Ages.

In the scholastic and teleological universe of the Middle Ages, the nature of illness was explained using a beautiful and purely deductive theory about "the four body fluids, or humors." The balance between these four humors determined the temperament of men and women, and a distinction was drawn between the sanguine, the choleric, the melancholic and the phlegmatic personality. Illness was also categorized using a complex set of regulations based on the four humors. This alluring theory was based on dogma concerning the purposes of the Almighty, and thus on the purposes of Nature. This belief in the purpose of God was the foundation that allowed people *to work everything out*. Everything could be worked out by applying reason, and the logical tenability of the reasoning could be tested by debate.

Perhaps the reader senses an awkward similarity between this way of looking at things and the theory and practice of accounting today. The truth about medieval medicine was stated in *the rules*, everything was explained in advance, and doctors never needed to doubt their diagnoses of patient complaints. The reasons and cures for all illness were also stated in the rules. Everything was logical and complete, so medieval doctors never needed to doubt their efficacy or use the evidence of their eyes.

For instance, in the Middle Ages doctors *knew* from their studies of medical theory that when patients were suffering from stomach pains and fever, the *cause* of the stomach pains was that food had rotted in the intestines, and the *cause* of the fever was that the rotten food had poisoned the bloodstream. So the cure was logical. The rotten food and poisoned blood simply had to be removed from the body of the patient.

Naturally, appendicitis also existed in the Middle Ages, and its characteristic symptoms were also fever and stomach pains. But the cure for such symptoms was always to remove rotten food and poisoned blood, so patients suffering from appendicitis were given enemas and blood-lettings.

Such patients died like flies, of course. These deaths were unexpected and often regarded as highly regrettable, but doctors learned to regard them as "exceptions to the rule." No one could ever blame the doctor for such deaths. Doctors did what they could, and everyone could see that the patients concerned had been given the best possible treatment. The doctor only experienced problems if he had made mistakes by *breaking the rules* and failing to prescribe enemas and blood-letting. There is no doubt that medieval doctors regretted inexplicable deaths and consulted apothecaries with a view to improving the quality of the enemas administered. Moliere's comedy *Le Malade Imaginaire* gives a good impression of the kind of interesting but totally futile research carried out in this field.

Current medical science shows that the cures administered in the Middle Ages were not as good as they might have been, and the treatment of illness has been altered accordingly. Appendicitis is now cured by surgery, and the results are clearly better. The majority of patients survive the treatment, so modern doctors tend to regard surgery as a better way of treating appendicitis than enemas and blood-letting.

Accounting specialists are also doctors. Their patients are not individuals, but groups of individuals known as companies in the private sector, and organizations in the public sector. The illnesses in question are financial by nature.

Recently there have been a number of sudden, tragic and inexplicable financial deaths. We react by describing such incidents as "exceptions to the rule"; we require financial statements to be issued more frequently, and we discuss whether notes and annual reports could be expressed differently. In the Middle Ages doctors reacted in precisely the same fashion. Inexplicable events were described as exceptions to the rule, and doctors then discussed whether blood-letting should be more frequent, or enemas more effective.

The incautious, unavoidable question now is "Does anyone really claim that we fully understand the connection between reality and pictures, between finances and financial statements? In other words, *do we fully understand financial statements as a concept?* We regard financial statements as a limited amount of data accumulated according to a specific set of rules. But this does not really answer the question. *Do we understand and appreciate the reasons for the rules?*

Is it possible that the progress urgently needed in the world of accounting has been hampered by our lack of understanding? Can we find new, improved methods by starting from scratch and considering accounting in an entirely new light? Could a new appreciation of financial statements as a concept be used as a launching pad for improvements in our profession?

A very large proportion of the serious theoretical research carried out in recent years concludes that the vital focus of interest for the world of accounting should be *future payments*. These days accountants are expected not to be surprised by events. Instead, we are asked to predict future payments, and thus any possible future suspension of payments. If we are to meet these new demands, we must learn that from an accounting point of view the past is not actually very important. This means that we must abandon the belief that "historical accounting" has any information value. Armed with philosophical weapons supplied by Karl Popper, we must now take courage and declare openly that the dogma concerning the information value of historical accounts is nothing but *superstition and nonsense*. Old financial statements are worthless and irrelevant, because there is no scientifically viable way of predicting the future by considering the past. Plenty of people make the attempt, but such people lack a scientific foundation for their actions, and can only achieve credibility if they are able to refute Karl Popper's philosophy and replace it with something better. And that will be no easy task.

What we need to do is admit the complete impotency of the accounting profession of today. And of course this will be difficult for some of the guardians of the traditions of our profession to accept.

But an admission of the impotency of accounting is necessary to open new doors and find new paths to progress. J. Witt-Hansen, Danish Professor of Philosophy, believes that "the admission of impotency is the first step towards scientific revolution," and points out that the interaction between philosophical and scientific research in the twentieth century has produced some of the most important advances in the history of research:

Paradoxically enough, disappointment and deep resignation have often been the launch pads of new advances and the scientific revolutions that follow in their wake. The *impotency* resulting from unfulfilled expectations has led time after time to the realization that it is *impossible* within a certain given framework to solve certain fundamental theoretical or existential problems that *had to be solved* to ensure the survival of the current world picture, unequivocal communication, or the welfare of human beings. . . . It is only during the twentieth century that researchers have become aware of such situations of impotency, and started to examine their cognitive status and the role they play in philosophical and scientific methodology. In particular, attention has focused on the fact that there are many examples in the history of philosophy and science of situations in which such impotency has been "conquered," leading to epoch-making discoveries in the history of research. In their attempts to gain understanding of the subject of impotency, philosophical researchers have described a number of situations of impotency occurring in mathematics, logic, physics, the theory of cognition and social science, drawing up their descriptions in the form of postulates, which they have called *postulates of impotency.*[10]

Postulates can only be proposed by people who have achieved realization. The only people capable of postulating the impotency of their profession are people who acknowledge the impotency of their profession. And *no breakthrough can ever be made without such acknowledgement.* The breakdown of the old is the breakthrough of the new.

When we claim that the accounting model that we are currently forced to accept is unreliable because it is incomprehensible, we are making a *postulate of impotency.* And it is also a *postulate of impotency* to say that current financial statements are no more than financial horoscopes in which only confirmed believers could possibly trust.

Readers who are outraged by such statements must seek to prove that they are false. And perhaps some readers will be convinced of the value of the arguments laid out here, and be prepared to admit that prudence may not be the best answer any longer. Anyone wishing to retain credibility as an accounting specialist must be prepared to acknowledge the existence of the opposite of financial prudence, which is the willingness of those in business to take risks. We calculate the financial consequences of our actions *before* and *while* we carry them out. If the calculation of consequences reveals too great a risk, we refrain from carrying out the actions concerned, and *this can in truth be regarded as exercising prudence.*

And perhaps the pain caused to some accounting specialists when acknowledging the truth of the postulates of impotency about their profession will pass. In a few years' time, perhaps it will be possible to compare this pain with the pain of giving birth. It may hurt while it lasts, but it passes, and is generally replaced by great joy.

Let us conclude that accountants, like everyone else, must accept that it is dangerous to live because there is a great risk that we shall die. As we have seen, in the world of accounting, *it is actually very imprudent to be prudent.* The acceptance of this fact leads us to the question *What do imprudent financial statements look like?* What do financial statements look like that reflect the calculated risk facing enterprises?

In the following chapters we shall present a number of possible contributions towards answering this question. But naturally, in the last resort the answer must be provided by readers themselves, so in practice new systems of management accounting will vary considerably. Some people might feel that the good answers are easy enough to find if the right questions are asked. And others might even claim that the good answers cannot be found *without* asking the right questions.

Ultimately, the main issue must be what is more important for practicing accountants—to do things right, or to do the right things?

NOTES

1. P. E. Gruning, "Revisors Position," p. 33.
2. Ibid., p. 34.
3. Ibid., p. 35.
4. Ibid., p. 35.
5. Ibid., p. 35.
6. Ibid., p. 36.
7. Ibid., p. 36.
8. Ibid., p. 36.
9. Ibid., p. 36.
10. J. Witt-Hansen, *Filosofi,* p. 321.

11 THE OBJECTIVE OF FINANCIAL STATEMENTS

> Far too many theoretical presentations concentrate on answering the question "how?" instead of the question "why?" or on saying what we "should" be doing. This is not only a Danish phenomenon.
>
> —H. Hjerno Jeppesen, Danish CPA

It may now be possible to solve the basic cognitive problem facing the world of accounting. We should refrain from discussing *how* to keep accounts until we have decided exactly *why* we keep accounts. The American Institute of Certified Public Accountants (AICPA) regards accounting as an open, social system that is subject to constant development and change. An unfounded claim is made that an a priori assertion of the objectives of financial statements is needed. And this reasoning forces us into a cul-de-sac. Philosophers are afraid of claims based on a priori assumptions, because there is no way of being certain about the validity of such assumptions. Acceptance of the postulate of objectives in accounting means that any situation that does not contain a "rational" or "optimum" decision is regarded as unimportant. This is surely a dangerous and myopic stand to take. Instead, an attempt should be made to satisfy Karl Popper's demand for empirical openness and falsification. The basic concepts of accounting should be formulated in such a way that it is possible to contradict them. Statements that have to be assumed a priori cannot meet this requirement. So traditional financial statements are more religious than scientific in their concept of reality. They are based on belief, not on knowledge.

In 1971 the AICPA asked a group of nine accounting experts to draw up a report concerning *the objectives of financial statements*, with a view to answering the question posed as the title of this chapter, a question naturally asked by users of financial statements all over the world.

After about two years' work the report was completed in October 1973. It was entitled *Objectives of Financial Statements*, but is better known as The Trueblood Report, since one of the leading members of the group was Robert M. Trueblood, a certified public accountant.

We should like to discuss some of the points of view expressed in The Trueblood Report in this chapter. In chapter 1 of the report, in an attempt to establish a platform or overview of the objectives of accounting, it is striking that accounting is basically regarded as a *social phenomenon*, a stage on which people are the most important elements. Accounting is also regarded as *a living system*, which interacts with its environment and adapts when there are any changes in this environment:

Accounting is a social system much like language and law. As such, it tends to evolve by adapting to its environment; but evolutionary changes may occur which are incompatible or even in conflict with current notions of what the objectives of this system ought to be. An explicit statement of objectives, therefore, is essential to its rational development.[1]

The final sentence in this quotation seems different from the first two. First the report draws a picture of a living, changing, organic system that adapts to its surroundings, and then the authors claim confidently (but without a shred of evidence) that it is vital to make an explicit statement of objectives in order to promote the rational development of accounting.

The second paragraph of the report apparently contradicts this postulate concerning the necessity of stating objectives:

The Study Group sees the defining of objectives mainly as a means for evaluating desirable goals and helping to achieve them. The Study Group recognizes that the development of objectives is ongoing. Its conclusions are in no sense unalterable or unchanging.[2]

This seems a little strange. First the group states that it is absolutely essential to be aware of the objectives of accounting, and then it concedes that these vital objectives are changeable and unstable. The next paragraph does nothing to quell our mounting concern. Despite the uncertainty, and despite its acceptance that the objectives formulated are changeable, the group apparently abandons any attempt to use logical argument, and instead claims a priori that there *are* one or more precise objectives of accounting. As always when logical arguments are abandoned, it is necessary to make such claims with great force in order to banish any doubt. And that is what happens here. The Trueblood Report is thus based entirely on a single basic axiom, a claim made in the form of an unfounded postulate, about which even the group itself clearly realizes there may be some doubt:

The fundamental function of financial accounting has been unchanged almost from its inception. Its purpose is to provide users of financial statements with information that will help them make decisions. Of course, there have been substantial changes in the types of users and the kinds of information they have sought. Nonetheless, this function of financial statements is fundamental and pervasive: *The basic objective of financial statements is to provide information useful for making economic decisions.*[3]

The term "an axiom" is used in philosophy to describe a fundamental assertion that, without itself ever being proven, is used as the logical basis of other statements. Naturally, axioms must be valid—otherwise the systems based on them can never be valid, either.

Is the basic axiom of The Trueblood Report valid, or does it have evident defects? This question is of the utmost importance, because the report represents the foundation of the entire logical structure of accounting today, and if defects in the foundations of buildings are discovered and repaired, it may be possible to reconstruct the buildings concerned in a new and far better way.

This analogy to buildings is taken from *Objectives of Financial Statements for Business Enterprises*. Here we find absolute surrender, and admission of the fact that the accounting model we know today is no more than a logical mess. The revealing words are written in italics:

The body of today's accounting rules, therefore, is not a neatly designed, tightly constructed whole. The rules are sometimes inconsistent, not being parts of a clear plan that logically leads users to similar conclusions when presented with comparable facts. *The result is not unlike a house that successive generetions have lived in and added to, without a master plan or any goal other than to satisfy current need or desire.*[4]

Is there a connection between these two observations? Is it possible to trace the lack of clarity in and dissatisfaction with the traditional accounting model back to The Trueblood Report? Anthony claimed that a lack of accounting concepts was the reason why financial statements were so useless in practice. It may therefore be worth examining the axiom concerning the objectives of financial statements a little more closely.

The Greek word "telos" means objective. When philosophers find an explanation that refers to an objective, they describe such an explanation as *teleological*. In other words, teleological explanations are explanations that refer to the fact that a given phenomenon has an objective or purpose. Nonteleological explanations are generally referred to as "causal" or "mechanistic."

We are now dealing with an ancient and fundamental cognitive issue. We all wonder about things every now and then, and ask ourselves the question "why?" But not everyone realizes that there are two entirely different answers to the question "why?"

One answer is teleological, and indicates an *objective*. The other is causal, and indicates a *consequence*. One answer leads us into the vague, confused blind alley of dogma, whereas the other may lead us along the path towards scientific discovery:

When we ask "why?" concerning an event, we may mean either of two things. We may mean: "What purpose did this event serve?" or we may mean: "What earlier circumstances caused this event?" The answer to the former question is a teleological explanation, or an explanation by final causes; the answer to the latter question is a mechanistic explanation. I do not see how it could have been known in advance which of the two questions science ought to ask, or whether it ought to ask both. But experience has shown that the mechanistic question leads to scientific knowledge, while the teleological question does not. The atomists asked the mechanistic question, and gave a mechanistic answer. Their successors, until the Renaissance, were more interested in the teleological question, and thus lead science up a blind alley.[5]

The remarkable thing about this quotation is that it seeks to explain the fact that scientific development stood still for about 1,800 years, from about 400 B.C. until the start of the Renaissance in the fifteenth century. The "Dark Ages" are regarded as being dark because all attempts to explain the world and its phenomena (i.e., all answers to the question "why?") ended in a single teleological system of explanation based on religious dogma administered by what were known as "scholars."

The preceding quotation is taken from *A History of Western Philosophy* written by Bertrand Russell, one of the most important philosophers in the twentieth century. All economists and particularly accounting specialists have good reason to take note of Russell's views concerning the dangers of teleological explanations. All microeconomic textbooks contain the axiom that the *objective* of all business managers is to maximize the profit made by their enterprises.

Microeconomics is teleological, so accounting theory is to a large extent teleological, too. Readers are welcome to test the truth of these claims by examining the literature on the subject, paying special attention to teleological axioms such as the following: "The objective is to maximize profit, so activities are aimed at optimization," "The objective of users of financial statements is to cover their information requirements," "The objective of users of financial statements is to make rational decisions"and so on.

When we teach students of economics that the objective of managers is to earn as much money as possible, and that their behavior is therefore directed towards finding optimum solutions to problems, in other words solutions ensuring the maximum possible profit, are we programming such students only to look for problems for which they already have solutions? Have we taught such students to ignore the evidence of their own eyes, unless such evidence confirms the preprogrammed teleological answers we have given them? Perhaps we accounting theorists have done serious damage by assuming the existence of a teleological theory and then indoctrinating students with this scientifically barren theory, the main function of which seems to be that it acts as a filter between us and the real world. These are disturbing questions. But they must be asked.

Albert Einstein once said that the only way to decide what is observable and what is nonobservable is to use a theory. In other words, in order to observe the world around me I need a theory to tell me what I am observing. A theory of observation is the foundation of what I observe, and of my attempt to explain what I observe. *A theory or idea of what I am observing is the axiom or foundation of my system of explanation.* And it is not particularly comforting to know that the basic axiom in my own field, which is accounting, can be regarded as teleological, that teleological explanations can be regarded as scientifically barren, and thus that as a researcher I may be walking up a cul-de-sac with no prospect of ever discovering anything at all. This thought makes me feel impotent and confused. The carpet is pulled from underneath my feet. And such carpets should ideally remain where they are.

What is the nature of the axiom or axioms of accounting? What are the basic postulates on which the system of accounting is based? A number of researchers have already attempted to answer these questions, among them Maurice Moonitz and Richard Mattessich. But their results stem from the 1960s and 1970s; these results are well known. And so Kaplan, Anthony and Staubus must have been familiar with them when they claimed at the end of the 1980s that the problems of definition were still unsolved despite all attempts to solve them.

What are the principles on which accounting is based?

This cognitive nut may prove extremely hard to crack, unless one is satisfied with a teleological answer, in which case all you need is to be satisfied with a plausible objective that can be stated a priori, after which the problem disappears of its own accord. Belief in the objective directs the believer into a cul-de-sac. The end justifies the means.

People convinced of the fact that *objectives exist* are automatically assured of a theory on which they can base their observations, after which they can view their world through a window shaped by conviction about such objectives. Psychologists call this phenomenon "selective perception." You experience what you expect to experience, what you are programmed to experience.

Teleological explanations often consist of several different elements. It is quite possible to have more than one objective, and in such cases the objectives in question need organizing. This is how so-called "hierarchies of objectives" arise. The development of such multiobjective decision models is based on the following reasoning: "Some objectives must be more important than others, so they are called general objectives." In the theory of business economics a number of learned books have been written about the decisions that can and should be made whenever several objectives apply. Such multiteleological theories, composed of axioms that in Bertrand Russell's view are scientifically barren, may well seem relatively complicated, and may fool people into believing in them for this reason alone. Most students humbly accept the theory of the subjects they are studying, as well as the teaching methods employed by their teachers. They often fail to learn the theory concerned, but they only blame themselves if this happens ("If I can't understand the theory, there must be something wrong with me. The others look as if they understand it.")

There is, of course, often something wrong with the students. Life is wonderfully exciting, and accounting theory is dull by comparison. But perhaps it is not *always* the students with whom there is something wrong. It may be possible to improve the theory somewhat.

Is there a general objective in teleological objective/means hierarchies? How can we answer this existential question? How can we determine the general objectives involved in running an enterprise or being a manager? Let us see how Bertrand Russell deals with the problem. The following quotation contains an example of British understatement. The issue is what happens when you continue to ask the question "why?" of people who continue to give you a teleological answer. Climbing up the ladder of objective hierarchy, you end up in a position in which everyone realizes that it would be tactless to continue to ask the question. Russell has the following to say about the two types of question:

In regard to both questions alike, there is a limitation which is often ignored, both in popular thought and in philosophy. Neither question can be asked intelligibly about reality as a whole (including God), but only about parts of it. As regards the teleological explanation, it usually arrives, before long, at a Creator, or at least an Artificer, whose purposes are realized in the course of nature. But if a man is so obstinately teleological as to continue to ask what purpose is served by the Creator, it becomes obvious that his question is impious. It is, moreover, unmeaning, since, to make it significant, we should have to suppose the Creator created by some super-Creator whose purpose He served. The conception of purpose, therefore, is only applicable within reality, not to reality as a whole.[6]

But it is not simply a question of rejecting the concept of objectives and accepting the other type of answer, because here, too, there may be certain cognitive problems:

A not dissimilar argument applies to mechanistic explanations. One event is caused by another, the other by a third, and so on. But if we ask for a cause of the whole, we are driven again to the Creator, who Himself must be uncaused. All causal explanations, therefore, must have an arbitrary beginning.[7]

Are Russell's explanations and views of any use to us here? Is there any visible similarity between the practice of accounting in the second half of the twentieth century, and the description of the closed, teleological systems of explanation used in the Middle Ages, which were based on religious dogma, and which were also usually expressed in such complicated language that it was only possible for so-called "scholars" to understand and interpret them?

The German physicist and Nobel Prize winner Werner Heisenberg achieved results that were epoch-making in the history of nuclear physics. Even in the world of physics, where communication between researchers is widely regarded as being easier than in the humanities, Werner Heisenberg believes that there are great problems in introducing new ideas. In the following quotation the fact that conflicts arise when new basic viewpoints are presented is regarded as being perfectly normal but nonetheless painful. There are always problems when new groups of phenomena force changes to be made in the philosophy on which an entire branch of science is based:

Even the greatest of physicists encounter difficulties at this point, since the need to change thought patterns often makes people feel that the ground is being swept from beneath their feet. Researchers who have worked hard for many years to achieve . . . results in their own particular fields using patterns of thought acquired in their youth cannot simply change these patterns because a number of new experiments have been carried out. At best . . . and after years of philosophical struggle and debate about the new situation, a change of awareness may occur that opens the door leading to new ways of thinking.[8]

Werner Heisenberg's experiences are typical examples of what happens when new ideas challenge traditional ideas. Louis Pasteur was criticized harshly for many years for proving that microorganisms were the explanation of all fermentation and decomposition processes, and that life did not appear of its own accord, as people had claimed previously. The Italian scientist Galileo was in danger of losing his life when he discovered the moons of the planet Jupiter, and what these moons meant for the picture of the universe in which people believed at the time. Galileo's "crime" was that his observations in a telescope and the results of his research proved that the geocentric picture of the universe with a stationary Earth at its center was false. He was accused of heresy, and only escaped with his life by denying the truth of his own claims. Galileo invited his accusers to look at the moons of Jupiter through his telescope, but they refused in horror. They preferred to deny the existence of the moons using classical Aristotelian logic. In their view, the truth had already been established in the literature on the subject. Current theory and force of habit were the main thing, which meant that anything you could observe using your own senses and reason was necessarily false. The history of science is checkered with examples of new ideas encountering stiff resistance because they were regarded as threats, leading to violent battles that latter and wiser generations regard with amazement. The German physicist Max Planck, who has also carried out epoch-making research, admits the futility of such battles and simply says that new ideas only achieve recognition as their opponents die of old age.

Let us now take the next step in our search for the basic principles of accounting, and consider a problem that can be expressed in the paradox *the future is the past*. A paradox is an assertion that appears to be self-contradictory. And our paradox about the future and the past is given substance when we consider the cognitive basis for claiming anything at all based on the information contained in financial statements. If we wish to discuss and solve a specific problem, we must first be able to identify it exactly.

Karl Popper, a prominent modern philosopher, has achieved startling results in methodology, logic and the theory of cognition. The name of Popper is associated with logic and modern rules for research and the testing of hypotheses. Anyone asking the question "How can we decide whether a given theory, explanation or method is scientifically viable?" can find the answer in the works of Karl Popper. And the answer provided by Popper to this question is now regarded as the best answer on the subject yet provided by philosophy.

In *The Poverty of Historicism* Popper says that it is *pure and simple superstition* for anyone to claim that future events can be predicted by referring to past events. In an article published in 1950, Popper claims to have demonstrated that owing to strictly logical reasons it is impossible to predict future events. Readers will note the year 1950. Long before chaos theories finally demonstrated that unpredictability was a basic scientific principle, Popper had proven by clear and simple logic that it is superstition to claim that any signals about the future ever exist. The reasons are clear and precise, and cannot be denied:

1. The course of human history is strongly influenced by the growth of human knowledge. (The truth of this premise must be admitted even by those who see in our ideas, including our scientific ideas, merely the by-products of material developments of some kind or other.)
2. We cannot predict, by rational or scientific methods, the future growth of our scientific knowledge.
3. We cannot, therefore, predict the future course of human history.
4. This means that we must reject the possibility of a *theoretical history*; that is to say, of a historical social science that would correspond to *theoretical physics*. There can be no scientific theory of historical development serving as a basis for historical prediction.
5. The fundamental aim of historicist methods is therefore misconceived, and historicism collapses.

Economics is a branch of the social sciences, and accounting is an economic discipline. So these logical judgments must also apply to financial accounting. J. Witt-Hansen has the following to add about the fall of dogma:

Popper warns us against interpreting these theses to mean that he rejects all possibility of prediction in the social sciences. On the contrary, . . . Popper is thus in tune with modern research into the future, which flatly denies the possibility of predicting "the future" or the future progress of history because neither scientific discoveries nor technological inventions can ever be predicted.[9]

Popper leaves little doubt. He clearly denies all forms of scientific prediction using the clear, precise arguments outlined. He does not reject predictions as such, but if predictions are to be taken seriously they must be precisely specified statements to the effect that certain processes of development are assumed to take place in certain specified and controllable conditions. This is the type of hypothesis testing that the world of medicine calls "the controlled experiment," or "controlled testing." Anything else is merely superstition in Popper's view.

Our paradox about the past and the future now has substance, and readers are invited to consider two entirely different basic explanations, both of which concern financial statements, and each of which rests on its own set of reasons.

The first explanation is *scientifically based.* It tells us that for clear and logical reasons it is impossible to predict future events. You cannot predict the future by referring to the past. There are no scientific theories about historical developments that can be used as the basis of prediction.

The second explanation is based on *reference to tradition.* It tells us that practice and experience show that there is an extremely close connection between the past, present and future, that it is possible to forecast historic financial development mathematically, and that such data can be called predictions about the future. However, this explanation is expressed somewhat vaguely, with a reference to the fact that old financial statements only have "a certain predictive value." In addition, the second explanation requires that only experts can produce predictions of the future. *The two explanations quite clearly contradict each other.* The scientific explanation is nontraditional, and the traditional explanation is nonscientific.

Logic is described by J. Witt-Hansen as "the strongest intellectual weapon possessed by Modern Man," and he adds that it is worth being concerned with cognitive theory because cognitive theory, despite its apparently remote nature, can teach us something about the strength of logic. The logical "not" is a statement as sharp as a surgeon's knife used to cut away bad tissue so the healthy part of an organism can survive. The word "not" in logical judgments means "not under any circumstances." Readers familiar with logic can never be in any doubt. Night is not day, and day is not night.

The use of logic and cognitive theory means that readers are now able to choose between the two different explanations, to choose whether they should accept the scientific or the traditional explanation about the information contained in financial statements. Readers will by now realize that a choice must be made, and that no one is telling them what their choice should be. They can choose what they wish. The only duty researchers have is to make their results available to those interested in using them. But the decision to accept and use the results of research is never the researcher's decision. Researchers are the toolmakers of their trade. They make the tools, test them, and hand them to users. But this does not necessarily mean that the tools will be used. Old habits die hard, and there is always a certain amount of resistance to new ideas.

Readers looking for scientific foundations will say that the financial statements with which we are currently familiar are documents showing past purchases and sales, and past payments received and made. So the data contained in financial statements can, of course, be used as evidence if anyone needs such evidence in other connections (for instance in a legal case). Otherwise, financial statements are worthless documents that cannot be used to make predictions of the future. And yet predictions of future cash flows are vital, so the main aim must be to find the logical contours of a new system of accounting that has scientific foundations and that meets the needs of users. Such a system will contain statements that are logically clear and comprehensible to anyone, so there will be no need to summon the assistance of so-called "scholars" to help interpret their meaning.

This Herculean task has still not been accomplished, and readers looking for an accounting system with scientific foundations still have considerable problems to overcome. But readers who have respect for modern science will say that "specialists" who continue to look for "valuable signals" about the future by analyzing old financial statements are like modern mechanics who continue to search for *perpetuum mobile*, a perpetual motion machine. Such people are engaged in tasks that are logically impossible, so they can only be certain of one thing—they will be kept busy for the rest of their lives.

Authoritative psychologists claim that we all seem to be born with a *strong desire to believe in things simply because we are told that they are true*. The truth of this point is evident in our daily lives—people will believe anything, as long as the information given is sufficiently convincing. Horoscopes, slimming diets, flying saucers, auras, quack doctors—we are prepared to believe in them all. The main thing in many cases is not to know anything about such things, but to cling to a certain belief that is shared by others. And since we all have this fear and desire to believe in things, it is hardly surprising that people continue to believe that the odd and incomprehensible information contained in old financial statements can be used as the basis of predictions about the future, and that such predictions can be made as long as you know enough about such matters. Of course it is always easiest to stick to tradition, to run with the crowd. It is always hardest to paddle against the current, and easiest to flow with the stream. It is even possible to make a virtue out of necessity and claim that you are simply being democratic when you abandon all pretense of independent thought and common sense, and simply accept what the majority accepts. But anyone considering such matters carefully will surely reach the conclusion that the very nature of democracy actually demands the use of independent thought and common sense from every single citizen.

Using science and logic as our weapons, we have now succeeded in gaining two different pictures of accounting experts. Either we must regard such experts as modern gods capable of the most amazing feats, or we must regard them as medieval alchemists conscientiously working to make gold from nonprecious matter, convinced that their attempts will succeed if only they can find *the right process*. Which of these two pictures should we now adopt as the most realistic? Or to use one of the many strange expressions of traditional financial statements, which of the two seems to be the most "true and fair picture"? Readers must answer for themselves. But to indicate a couple of good potential answers, let us now return to Bertrand Russell, who said that teleological answers led us into blind alleys. Which answer would lead to a scientific conclusion in Russell's opinion?

The answer to the question "why?" that is not teleological is called "mechanistic" by Russell, but we prefer to use the expression "causal" or "consequence-oriented." Let us repeat the types of question mentioned earlier in the quotation from Russell.

The teleological question was "What was the objective of this event?" And the causal or mechanistic question was "Which previous events caused this event to occur?" This is the same as asking "Of which previous events is this event a consequence?"

J. Witt-Hansen emphasizes that our idea of *time as a concept* is regarded as the central problem in twentieth century philosophy: "time as a scientific problem has also appeared in a discipline that is as apparently timeless as logic."[10] The question now is whether Bertrand Russell's view, that the teleological explanation is barren, is related to the observation that time as a concept does not form part of objective-oriented answers.

Readers can probably predict the next highly relevant question for themselves. "Should we demand that scientifically viable axioms and systems of explanation specifically take time into account, and thus answer the question 'why?' in such a way that *phenomenon B should always be regarded as a possible consequence of a previous phenomenon known as A*?"

This is a question that cannot be dismissed easily, and if readers accept that it can be answered in the affirmative, this affirmative answer will have a colossal impact on the development of accounting theory, since it will mean that a scientifically viable axiom is then available, on which a logical system can be based. We will then have, as demanded by Einstein, a theory that will tell us what we are observing in accounting theory.

In order to illustrate this point, let us now briefly discuss the aspect of Karl Popper's scientific theory that deals with scientific criteria.

Popper's main view is that it is impossible in a strictly scientific and logical sense to *prove* that a given theory or explanation is "true" or "correct." So when statement A is offered as an explanation of phenomenon B, A should be expressed as a hypothesis capable of being tested. Popper's formal requirement is that the hypothesis should be expressed in such a way that *it is logically possible to falsify it*. This possibility is clearly absent in teleological explanations, where the objective is to achieve a priori belief. Popper also says that hypotheses should be tested by attacking them with every possible weapon with a view to falsifying them. Such hypotheses can only be regarded as scientifically viable *until further notice* if these attacks can be resisted.

The obvious advantages of Popper's philosophy are his demands for openness and falsification. Explanations and theories that cannot be falsified today may be proved completely incorrect tomorrow. All human knowledge is provisional, and entirely new forms of scientific discovery can be expected to appear in the future, even though they cannot, of course, be predicted accurately. Current scientific knowledge and insight should be regarded not as being encased in armor, but as being an open system capable of change and movement as new advances are made.

So we conclude this chapter by returning to the question "What is the purpose of financial statements?" We are skeptical about the axiom on which The Trueblood Report is based, and the reasons for this skepticism have already been mentioned. If the only thing I know is that I am searching for scientific knowledge, and I then see a blind alley with a sign saying "Only believe in objectives and all your doubts will be banished!" then I am forced to seek another path instead of entering the cul-de-sac, because for me doubt is a valuable scientific instrument that I never intend to lose.

Instead of accepting the teleological axiom about accounting, we prefer to listen to Albert Einstein's advice about building a system on a foundation resting on a theory about our observations. We also intend to meet Karl Poppers' demand for falsification.

We should now like to propose a new logical foundation for accounting theory. We suggest that the logic on which accounting is based should be founded on the *axiom* contained in the following *new definition of accounting*:

Accounting is theories and methods for description, explanation and prediction of the financial consequences of the actions of organizations.

This definition is discussed in greater detail in chapter 13. This is the definition at which all supporters of traditional financial statements should direct their attacks. Readers who regard the demand for new ideas as a threat, and who believe that old financial statements contain information relevant for the future, should now (if they wish to retain their professional credibility) seek to refute this definition. And if they fail in this task, they should start to revise their views.

The target is now out in the open, and the debate can begin. Can this definition be refuted by the supporters of tradition? Can it be contradicted logically, or can it withstand attack and thus be adopted as a complete, consistent, necessary and sufficient definition of accounting? The gauntlet has been thrown down, and it is up to readers to pick it up. There is no authoritarian demand about being right or wrong. Readers must be the judges in this important matter. On their own terms, they are invited to think the matter through, discuss it with others and then decide where the line between clear information and meaningless nonsense should be drawn in financial accounting. For there is no doubt that this line needs to be drawn.

Bertrand Russell's view about the scientific barrenness of teleological explanations must surely make an impression on most people, and readers who accept Russell's view will probably approach the concept of *objectives* with more caution in the future. One objection might be that philosophizing on this issue is a waste of time, and that the proposal for a new basic principle of accounting could just as easily be drawn up teleologically: "The objective of accounting and thus of financial statements is to describe the financial consequences of the actions of organizations." What is wrong with this? Is the word "objective" to be banished from the English language altogether?

Readers must decide for themselves. But one possible answer may be found in Russell's comment that nothing in the two questions makes any sense if they are asked about life as a whole, but only if they are asked about certain aspects of life. For instance, it is quite legitimate to say that a contractor's *objective* in tendering a quotation is to win an order, and that my *objective* in writing this book is to contribute to the theory of accounting. But both cases lie within the boundaries of real life, and in both cases an element of time is involved even though time is not stated directly. The contractor's quotation must be handed in by a given deadline, and I must work hard if I want to finish my book this year. The statements have meaning because they can be made and interpreted in clear connection with actions that can be carried out. The methodologist Russell L. Ackoff emphasizes that a scientifically viable definition must contain *a description of an operation (i.e., an action) that can be carried out*. Ackoff uses the term *operational definitions*.[11]

Let us make one final comment in support of the proposals made in this chapter. We have pointed out that teleological explanations make people blind to phenomena that are not covered by the objective whose existence they assumed a priori, thereby encouraging people to believe that any aspects of reality not covered by their theory are simply unreal.

But occasionally we are surprised by real events that *do not* behave in the way we expect them to behave. And then we have to ask whether there is something wrong with the real world, or something wrong with us. What should we think of a runner who gets lost during an orienteering race, looks at his map and then claims angrily that something is wrong with the terrain?

Accounting specialists are also surprised by events sometimes. Enterprises regarded as going concerns sometimes suspend their payments, and in such circumstances everyone asks the accounting specialist for an explanation. The customary answer is that the events were not covered by the financial statements of the enterprise concerned. The events were not deliberate, so the accounting specialist could not have known that they would occur, and so no criticism should be directed at him. *But it is the task of accounting specialists to calculate financial consequences in good time, and the task of the management to be aware of these consequences in good time.*

So the *concept of accountability* will acquire new and highly relevant meaning in future systems of accounting for management. And herein lies both an opportunity and a challenge.

NOTES

1. AICPA, *Objectives of Financial Statements*, p. 17.
2. Ibid., p. 17.
3. Ibid., p. 13.
4. Andersen, Arthur and Co., *Objectives of Financial Statements*, p. 7.
5. Bertrand Russell, *A History of Western Philosophy*, p. 67.
6. Ibid., p. 67.
7. Ibid., p. 67.
8. J. Witt-Hansen, *Filosofi*, p. 229.
9. Ibid., p. 273.
10. Ibid., p. 11.
11. Russell L. Ackoff, Scientific Method, p. 151.

12 TIME AND MONEY IN FINANCIAL STATEMENTS

Time is money.

—American proverb

The concept of time has been a stepchild of traditional accounting theory. In practice it is impossible to make meaningful statements about payments of money without mentioning the specific time at which such payments are made, so the lack of clarity in financial statements is also evident with regard to time. Time is considered to be a vital element in modern scientific theory. There have always been two different views about what time actually is, but perhaps one is sufficient. As far as economists are concerned, it is of great interest that in all branches of science from astronomy to biology there seems to be general agreement that *the progress of time is irreversible*, and that any attempt to treat time as a reversible concept is an escape from reality. As far as accounting theory is concerned, the great advantage of accepting that time is irreversible would be that we would then no longer need to accept the myths claiming that goods or services can be valued by finding out the original cost of their acquisition or production. Everyone must realize that the concept of value can never be based on past events, but only on current or future usefulness. Many efforts to achieve change result in nothing worthwhile, but even modest efforts coming at the right time often produce considerable gain. The effort required to change course is only slight; but once their tracks have been changed, trains tend to thunder on in new directions, and the change achieved cannot be reversed. Once performed, actions cannot be recalled.

Readers may be surprised to see that we now intend to spend an entire chapter dealing with two concepts as familiar as *time* and *money*. But there are three good reasons for discussing time and money in greater detail.

First, this book is not written for accounting experts alone, and non-specialists may be entirely unaware of the way accountants deal with time and money in financial statements. Second, even accountants might feel that a closer look at two such central concepts may well be worthwhile. And third and most important, the concept of time in particular has caused modern scientific theory considerable difficulties. Time can be regarded in at least two entirely different ways. And the problems arising due to the existence of two different concepts of time do not yet seem to have been dealt with by accounting theory, even though the concept of time is of such huge practical importance.

All financial statements contain information about time in the sense that they are *dated* in relation to the calendar. The *balance sheet* describes the assets and liabilities of organizations at a given *time*, whereas the *profit and loss account* describes what has happened during the *period* between the previous balance sheet and the current one. The balance sheet and profit and loss account are coordinated, and time is an extremely familiar but also almost banal phenomenon in accounting practice.

The concept of time applied in traditional financial statements is not the only one possible, nor is it necessarily the most appropriate. There are two possible concepts of time, a fact that has not attracted sufficient attention in the past.

As mentioned earlier, the concept of time has caused modern scientific theory a number of problems. These problems are so difficult to solve that the Danish philosopher J. Witt-Hansen regards them as the central issue of twentieth century philosophy. In his book *Filosofi. Videnskabernes historie i vort århundrede (Philosophy. The History of Science in Our Century)*, we find the following descriptions and considerations of the problem of time. The issues raised have great and very direct significance for accounting theory, where the concept of time and its associated issues have either been ignored completely or dealt with insufficiently and indirectly until now. If time really can and should be seen as a common and central philosophical problem, then time must also be a problem for accounting theory, and thus for the accounting practice based on this theory.

In the introductory chapter to Witt-Hansen's book we find the following description, which shows us that the concept of time can be regarded in two completely different fashions. The interesting key word for economists lies in the distinction between *reversibility* and *irreversibility*. And for accounting theorists in particular, it is noteworthy that Witt-Hansen does not merely distinguish between *the past* and *the future* (ex post, ex ante). *The present* is also very important:

Analysis by cognitive theory is always being supplemented by historical reviews and historical-philological analyses that tend to provide new answers to old questions. But scientific research is not content to provide new solutions to old problems. It is oriented towards both the present and the future. Entirely new problems appear, after which they are identified and subjected to analysis.[1]

We note the reference to *the present* and *the future*. The past is clearly defined, a definition that is completely in accordance with Karl Popper's view that it is logically impossible to make predictions about the future by analyzing the past. The consequence of this view as far as accounting theory is concerned is that financial statements covering periods in the past must be regarded as having no relevance for the financial future. We have already seen in a previous chapter that there are still some accounting specialists who believe that the figures contained in old financial statements "can be attributed a certain value as the basis of prediction," and we have also seen that such claims were regarded by Karl Popper as "pure and simple superstition." Let us now continue Witt-Hansen's description of the concept of time:

When scientific research makes future events the subject of its inquiries, it assumes a distinctive form whose nature is far from clear. However, the perspective of time that has left its mark on modern scientific research indicates that *time* has now become *a central problem of scientific theory*. This becomes particularly clear in the debate about future-oriented scientific research, which is associated with *research into the future*. But time as a problem for scientific theory has also appeared in a discipline as apparently timeless as logic. In this field, time appears under the name of temporal logic. People have started to talk about "the re-discovery of time," a slogan which takes on special meaning in the light of the following. . . . In an attempt to account for some of the main problems in the development of physics and chemistry during the last century, the French . . . philosopher Emile Meyerson (1859–1933) emphasizes the attempts of researchers to make what was changeable static again, and to reduce what was different to what was identical. He does this in a book entitled *Identité et Réalité*, published in 1908. . . . In these laws or principles of which the causal laws of classical dynamics . . . contain examples . . . Meyerson sees the attempts of reason to introduce strict rationalism to our concept and description of Nature. What interests Meyerson is that the principles, identities and equations in question lead to the "elimination of time," to a kind of cancellation of the boundaries between the past, present and future. This view is based on a reference to the fact that time in classical dynamics can be reversed at random, that all processes are *reversible*, that using the equations of classical dynamics makes it possible to move forwards and backwards in time. This means that the speeds in a mechanistic system (e.g., the speed of heavenly bodies in our planetary system) can be reversed, and that we can calculate the state of the earth and moon and eclipses of the sun and moon both in the future and in the past. In principle, it would then be possible to say that the eclipse of the sun that Herodotus (c. 484–420 B.C.) claimed occurred during a battle between the Lydians and Persians, actually occurred on May 28th, 585 B.C. instead.[2]

It is very easy to find examples of time used as a reversible concept in economic theory. The most straightforward and clearest example is the way interest is calculated. If we wish to know the future value of an investment that we intend to make now, all we need is information about

1. the value of the present investment (PV)
2. the number of periods in question (p)
3. the interest rate in each period (i)

after which we can calculate the future value of the investment (FV) as follows:

$$FV = PV \times (1 + i)^p$$

This equation enables us to calculate the future based on the present. But the process can be reversed, and time can easily be regarded as moving in the opposite direction, too. If we can calculate the future value of a present sum of money, we can also work the other way. The equation enables us to work out the value of a present or future sum of money at any previous moment chosen at random:

$$PV = \frac{FV}{(1 + i)^p}$$

However, anyone familiar with the use of such methods of calculation also knows that at some point they become meaningless. The fact is that the future value of a given investment increases exponentially as a function of time. This makes it possible to perform strange imaginative experiments. For instance, it is possible to imagine a pile of coins growing as the interest (and interest on the interest) accrues. The height of the pile of coins grows at *increasing speed*, so it is possible to calculate the time at which the pile will overtake a beam of light emitted at the same time as the experiment starts, because although the speed of light is very high, *it is constant.*

Experiments of this nature and similar mathematical games are often entertaining, but they have little else to recommend them. Einstein once said that "Whenever the principles of mathematics are applied to reality, they are uncertain. And whenever they are certain, they bear no relation to reality." The moment we visualize the pile of coins growing faster than the beam of light is the moment at which we have departed from reality.

The calculation of interest is an example taken from the world of economics in which the concept of time can be reversed at random, enabling us to calculate from the present into the future and from the future back to the present or the past. We quote from Witt-Hansen again:

Any such "elimination of time" indicates that the concept of time in classical dynamics is quite different from the concept of time used by the biological and historical sciences. In biological and historical theories of development, involving birth, flowering and death, in which old structures die and are replaced by new ones, a major distinction between the present, past and future has clear meaning. It is meaningful to say that certain natural processes are *irreversible*, that time has a specific direction.[3]

So the idea of *irreversibility* and the direction of time as a basic component of the processes of change has a major role to play in the so-called "biological and historical sciences," to which economics and thus accounting also belong. But irreversibility is also apparent in the modern so-called exact sciences. Witt-Hansen goes on to say that the development of the discipline now known as classical thermodynamics started as long ago as the 1800s. Here, too, the idea of processes of change being reversible is denied:

The new theory not only resulted in a basic departure from classical Newtonian dynamics, it also indicated a development in our universe that is the direct opposite of the tendency towards greater order and more complex structures that we find in biology and human history. According to classical thermodynamics, developments in our universe, regarded as an isolated system, are moving towards increasing lack of order, towards a lack of structure that will end in chaos. As in biology and history, the process involved in the thermodynamic universe is irreversible. Here, too, time moves in a specific direction. The distinctions between the past, present and future that classical dynamics had abandoned are reestablished within physics itself. In *The Nature of the Physical World* (1928) the British mathematician, physicist and astronomer Sir Arthur Stanley Eddington (1882–1944) introduced the expression "the arrow of time" to emphasize the directional nature of time, which had no analogy in space. And he added that our entire world would become meaningless if the "arrow of time" changed direction or turned around. According to Eddington, this would result in the dead returning from the grave, and adults returning to their mothers' wombs.[4]

Our conclusion must be that modern scientific theory regards time as having a direction, and that "the arrow of time" is a meaningful expression of this fact. The processes of change that occur in Nature are irreversible. This view is shared, as we can see, by theorists from the sciences of both biology and history (to which economics belongs), and from the so-called exact natural sciences such as astronomy and physics.

Let us now consider in greater detail the philosophical assumption that time has a direction, and that no natural processes of change are reversible. Let us also recall that enterprises can be seen as living organisms, which like other organisms *constantly exchange energy and information with their environment*. According to modern scientific theory, the development to be expected in such an open, interactive system moves in one specific direction. Time has an arrow, and this arrow cannot be reversed.

More specifically, economists would describe this exchange of energy and information between enterprises and their environments as an ongoing "flow" or "cycle." Models that show such flows or cycles are familiar in economic theory, the logical components of these models being *information, goods, services* and *money*.

The concept of money is the second of the two key concepts that are the subject of this chapter. The aim of our new theory of accounting is to enable readers to view familiar concepts in a new light. And the most familiar concepts are the prime objects of financial statements, that is, *money* and *payments of money*. We have already stated that financial statements describe the financial consequences of the actions of organizations. We shall consider such financial consequences to be payments of money and nothing else.

But we cannot be certain that the basic concept of money is interpreted in the same way by all our readers. So let us briefly describe the general meaning of money. The concept of money can be regarded as a *means* by which we express prices, pay debts, pay for goods and services and keep reserves in the bank. The concept is created by humans. It is a *tool* for communication and the exchange of energy and information; it is part of our language. Money has three specific uses or *functions*, which can be briefly described as:

1. *a means of exchange* for goods and services
2. an accepted *scale of measuring cost and benefit*
3. a *reserve* for use if rapid action is needed

No one spends much time thinking about the basic, time-honored function of money as a means of exchange in everyday life. This function is taken for granted. We are used to asking for goods and services and then paying for them with money. The history of the invention and development of the concept of money is itself both extensive and fascinating, but we shall refrain from going into it here. We know that money can be regarded as a "symbol of wealth" or "purchasing power." People in possession of money thus have a claim on the society in which they live.

It is also apparent that our description of money assumes that payments of money can be made *at a different time* than the actual exchange of goods and services. When you buy something you can either pay in cash or incur a debt. Payment can be made either immediately or when the debt is settled.

The second function of money is as a scale of assessing cost and benefit. Cost and benefit are reflected in claims concerning the value of goods and services. In other words, the concept of money can be used as a common denominator for various types of information about expense and revenue, making it possible to consider cost and benefit in the same information system without fear of contradiction. Money is the unit of calculation used to keep accounts, calculate costs and compare expressions of value. Money is a means of stating the prices of goods and services, and of expressing debts, wage and salary contracts, rental, insurance commitments and countless other agreements.

At this point it is worth emphasizing a banal but very important detail. *Information about value must always contain information about time if it is to have any meaning.*

It is not sufficient to mention the currency in question and then state a figure. If I claim that Mr. M. Schwarz is the owner of a sum of money of 1,000, of course I need to say whether this is 1,000 dollars, marks, pounds, kroner, lire, and so on. But I also have to include a statement of time to ensure complete understanding. Exchange rates and purchasing power change over time, so I have to say that Mr. M. Schwarz owns U.S. $1,000 at time T to give my statement any real meaning. The statement can then be tested if necessary.

The third function of money is directly connected to the concept of "financial preparedness" or "preparedness to make payments." In this sense, money is seen as a reserve that is ready for use if necessary. Money is the only asset that is entirely liquid. Owning a sum in cash in the form of currency or a current account makes it possible to take rapid action if circumstances require.

Let us now direct our attention to the distinction between reversibility and irreversibility, a distinction that is absolutely vital for the world of economics and thereby of financial accounting.

No one finds it difficult to accept the basic assumption concerning the "arrow of time," and thereby the absolute irreversibility of the flow of goods and services. Business economics is full of analogies to Eddington's comment that our world would become meaningless if the "arrow of time" were suddenly capable of changing direction. The effect would be the same as that of a film shown backwards. It might be amusing, but it would hardly contribute to a realistic description of the world as we know it. Furniture factories cannot turn their stocks of chairs and tables back into trees in the forest, and slaughterhouses cannot turn their ham and bacon back into pigs. Retailers who sell coats cannot send unsold autumn fashions back to the manufacturer. The flow of goods and services has a specific direction *that cannot be reversed.*

We also saw in a previous chapter that modern scientific theory regards it as logically impossible to predict the future using data describing the past. Flows of goods, services and money cannot be reversed or predicted by using data from the past. *There is a vital distinction between the past, present and future.*

Let us now consider the assertion that both accounting theory and the practice based on it could be made much more clear, credible and useful if they encompassed the basic view of modern scientific theory about time. Because the fact is that the current frame of reference used by the world of accounting (if it is even fair to talk of such a thing) is based on a fundamental assumption concerning

1. the reversibility of time
2. a certain amount of order and stability
3. a certain amount of predictability

And yet we have just seen that the basic beliefs of the new philosophy are that time is irreversible, that the world is characterized by flux and change, and that the future cannot be predicted by considering the past. Our conclusion must be that current accounting theory lacks a scientific foundation, which means that the reality, procedures and methods of modern financial accounting resemble those of the world of medicine 200 years ago. Accounting has a large number of apparently rational procedures that are simply not explained properly and systematically in relation to the tasks they are supposed to perform. The procedures used are therefore always difficult to understand, because users lack the most important thing of all, a reason for using the methods in question.

What would an accounting theory based on modern cognitive theory look like? Naturally, this is a very wide ranging question requiring a very wide ranging answer, so for individual researchers the question is difficult or impossible to answer exhaustively. But contributions to an exhaustive answer should probably always be based on the following:

1. realization of the existence of the problem
2. an analytical/critical description of current methods
3. scientifically based suggestions for future methods

Let us now outline an example of the nature and extent of the task facing us if the current norms of financial accounting are to be examined critically and replaced by a scientifically based set of accounting guidelines.

Consider the traditional procedure used to establish the value of stock, an example that experts and nonprofessionals alike should be able to understand. In traditional financial statements companies try to fix a figure in the profit and loss account that is known as the "contribution margin," "gross profit" or similar terms. This figure represents the difference between "income from sales" and "consumption of goods."

It is relatively easy to calculate the sales income of such a company in a given period. The sales income is simply the sum of the registered sales during the period both in cash and on credit. "Consumption of goods" is traditionally calculated as follows:

	Opening stock	120
+	*Stock purchased during the period*	650
–	*Closing stock*	200
=	*Consumption of goods during the period*	570

If we imagine that the sales income for the period is 1190, the gross profit will then be 1190 – 570 = 620.

The calculation of *sales* and *purchases* during the period can be regarded as a precise and thus scientifically viable description because the figures are sums of a limited amount of verifiable individual transactions between buyers and sellers. Each figure in the calculation can be traced to an individual transaction (assuming that the accounts have been kept properly), and all the data can be revised.

But the same does not apply to consumption of goods. To calculate consumption of goods you need to decide *the value of your current stock*. Traditionally, the value of a given product is calculated on the basis of its original cost. This basically unrealistic idea is the foundation of the apparently rational "theory" about "stock evaluation principles."

In a world of calm stability, predictability and reversibility, the claim that a product has a value of ten because it originally cost ten would be perfectly acceptable. Price increases and inflation do not matter, either, since if such increases amount to ten percent, a product with a value of ten last year will have a value of eleven now. In a simple world the problems are simple.

Let us now prove that this oversimplified assumption about stability and reversibility *is the basic philosophy in the financial accounting practiced all over the world.* Our source is *International Accounting Standard No. 2* from 1975, which has the following awe-inspiring title: *Valuation and Presentation of Inventories in the Context of the Historical Cost System.*

The title reveals immediately that data from the past is regarded as having great importance for financial statements, and the following so-called explanation expands on this assumption:

Inventories comprise a significant portion of the assets of many enterprises. The valuation and presentation of inventories therefore have a significant effect in determining and presenting the financial position and results of those enterprises.

We shall now consider various concepts (first-in, first-out (FIFO); last-in, last-out (LIFO); and so on) that are familiar to accountants, but that may require a brief explanation for others. The abbreviations stand for specific, traditional procedures used to calculate the value of stock. The FIFO principle means that the stock purchased first is used first, whereas the reverse is true of the LIFO principle. For instance, on conclusion of an accounting year you have a stock of eight units of product X. You purchased 20 units during the year, six of these in January at a price of 40, nine in May at a price of 45, and five in November at a price of 48. How can you "evaluate" the closing stock of eight units?

Using the FIFO principle, our example would result in a stock value of 375. The closing stock is assumed to consist of the goods purchased last $((5 \times 48) + (3 \times 45))$. But according to the LIFO principle the stock value will be 330. The closing stock is assumed to consist of the goods purchased first $((6 \times 40) + (2 \times 45))$.

There is no need to carry out any additional calculations. The procedures used date back to the 1920s and 1930s, and are already described at length in the literature on accounting. Let us now return to the International Accounting Standard concerning stock evaluation and what is known as *historical cost price*.

Apparently precise and meaningful definitions are given. The concepts of "stock" and "historical cost price" are both mentioned and described. But readers will notice that the focus is on the past, that past events are given great importance. Stock undoubtedly has the same "value" as its cost after bringing it to its current location:

Inventories are tangible property, (a) held for sale in the ordinary course of business, (b) in the process of production for such sale, or (c) to be consumed in the production of goods or services for sale. . . . *Historical cost* of inventories is the aggregate of costs of purchase, costs of conversion, and other costs incurred in bringing the inventories to their present location and condition.

This seems credible enough at first glance. But there is absolutely no reason or explanation for the assertion made. The introduction merely refers to the fact that this is the common procedure to adopt. The only reason given for the so-called "historical cost price system" is a variation on a familiar tune, "We do this because it is generally accepted."

The following description of the methods of calculating the "cost price" is a precise, literal repetition of the current international accounting standard. Readers will notice that a great number of subtle methods are mentioned and described, that the use of the methods may result in great differences, that no criteria are given for which method to choose, and that the only thing of any apparent interest is the effect on the "profit." Under the heading "Cost Formula Used," we find the following:

a. First-in, first-out (FIFO)
b. Weighted average cost
c. Last-in, first-out (LIFO)
d. Base stock
e. Specific identification
f. Next-in, first out (NIFO)
g. Latest purchase price

The FIFO, weighted average cost, LIFO, base stock, and specific identification formulas use costs that have been incurred by the enterprise at one time or another. The NIFO and latest purchase price methods use costs that have not all been incurred and are therefore not based on historical cost. . . . Specific identification is a formula that attributes specific costs to identified items of inventory. This is an appropriate treatment for goods that have been bought or manufactured and are segregated for a specific project. If it is used, however, in respect of items of inventory that are ordinarily interchangeable, the selection of items could be made in such a way as to obtain a predetermined effect on profit.

Readers who are not accountants may be surprised to learn that this inadequate, unclear, and even incomprehensible text is seriously regarded as providing *guidelines when evaluating stock in financial statements,* and that it has been accepted as such by accounting organizations in Australia, Canada, France, Germany, Great Britain, Japan and the United States! It seems incredible that sensible professionals can believe in the validity of such vague statements, but this is in fact the case. An air of tragic collective illusion hangs over the world of financial accounting.

Accounts managers and accountants have no idea what they are doing when they evaluate stock using these guidelines, and no one knows the effect of using one "principle" instead of another. The principles are incomprehensible, and *accounting theory offers absolutely no assistance.* For many years inquisitive and conscientious accounting theorists have been carrying out computer simulations using various stock evaluation principles and comparing the results they have obtained. All these efforts have produced nothing more than a discussion of the relative merits of the systems used, which can only be of interest to overoptimistic theorists still looking for the "best," "optimum" or perhaps merely "most appropriate" principle. The reason why the search for the "best stock evaluation principle" has been in vain despite years of devoted effort may well be *that it has proved impossible to define the criteria needed to choose such a principle.* And the reason for the lack of criteria may well be that *accounting theory* is based on an excessively simplified frame of reference concerning reversibility, stability and predictability, whereas *accounting practice* has often shown (with painful results) that the world around us changes constantly, that time passes and never returns and that it is meaningless to claim that the value of stock at any time is the same as its value when purchased.

These considerations result in two points. First, there is a chronic lack of clarity in the world of accounting. No one understands traditional accounting standards, because they do not actually contain guidelines (guidelines should contain descriptions of well-documented procedures). And yet everyone continues to observe the rules owing simply to tradition. Accountants have to act blindfolded, just like the doctors of the past who often helped to kill their patients instead of curing the ailments from which they suffered. The analogy may be hard to swallow, but it is nonetheless accurate, which is the most important thing. Practicing accountants have not yet been able to explain in clear, well-founded and unequivocal fashion how stock should be evaluated.

The second point is related to the confusion and lack of clarity in financial accounting. Responsibility cannot be established and allocated, so we cannot prevent unfortunate events from occurring again. In practice, we are paralyzed spectators witnessing one financial catastrophe after another in business life, but we do not yet know where to place the responsibility for such events. We simply lack the terminology needed. So when the next suspension of payments and bankruptcy occurs, no one can blame the managers or accountants involved, because they only followed the rules. The unclear and ineffective rules act as a shield against the slings and arrows of the world.

It is easy to demonstrate that traditional stock evaluation principles are without content. All we have to do is imagine a manager whose enterprise has the following "current assets" a couple of days before the accounting year expires:

Cash and bank deposits	90
Stock	10
Debtors	0
Total current assets	100

Let us now imagine that our manager receives a tempting offer asking her to buy a large consignment of fashionable goods at a price of 80, which she regards as being an extremely low price. The fact that the goods concerned are fashionable at the moment naturally makes it risky to use almost all her liquid capital on the purchase, but our manager decides to run the risk anyway. She buys the products. The question is "What will the new financial statement say about this high-risk decision?"

The answer is that the financial statement says nothing at all about it. Following the risky purchase, the balance sheet looks like this:

Cash and bank deposits	10
Stock	90
Debtors	0
Total current assets	100

The only thing that has happened is that two items in what are traditionally regarded as "current assets" have swapped figures. External analysts trying to discover something about the financial position of the enterprise concerned will be none the wiser, because the "total current assets" remains unchanged. This example shows the inherent assumption of reversibility, stability and order in the world of accounting. The financial statement shows that there has only been a "temporary" adjustment of items traditionally used to describe liquidity. But observations of what has really happened give the impression that the risk involved in buying the new products was far too great, since the future of the enterprise will be threatened if the fashions change unexpectedly and the goods cannot be sold on the expected terms and at the expected sales prices.

It is hardly necessary to twist the knife in the wound. We do not need to continue our demonstration of the impotence of traditional accounting. The theorists, practitioners and observers of accounting are already familiar with the problem, and some are even prepared to admit their impotence and open the door to new points of view.

What would practical methods of evaluation look like if they were based on modern scientific theory's basic assumptions about:

1. the irreversibility of time
2. the lack of a priori order and stability
3. the lack of a priori predictability?

The conclusion is simple: *In general, in all connections, we must abandon the idea that the value of goods and services is logically connected with their original cost price.* All talk of "historical cost price" in accounting practice must be rejected as vague and out of touch with reality.

A viable definition of "the value of goods" must reflect the three basic assumptions outlined. The acknowledgement of *uncertainty* and the acknowledgement of *time* as phenomena must be apparent in any such definition.

Indeed, the very expression "the value of goods" is too narrow. Economists generally use the term "goods and services" to underline that as far as economics and its methods of description are concerned, it does not really matter whether payment is for a physical object (for example, a pair of shoes) or a service (for example, a play performed at the theater).

In a previous chapter we quoted the well-founded view of Russell L. Ackhoff that scientifically viable definitions are *operational.* They must be based on descriptions of operations (actions) that can be performed in real life.

We should like to round off this chapter with a proposed new definition of the concept "the value of goods and services." This new definition which should meet the requirements outlined earlier, looks like this:

The value of goods or services is the amount of money transferred from buyer to seller when and if an agreement regarding purchase is reached, when and if the seller delivers as agreed, and when and if the buyer pays as agreed.

It is evident that time plays an important role in our new definition. The logical condition "when" means that registration of relevant times is necessary, enabling us systematically to identify the financial consequences when financial statements are either delayed or altogether out of date.

It is also evident that uncertainty is part of the new definition. The logical condition "if" indicates uncertainty, enabling us systematically to identify the reliability or credibility of various statements and various individuals.

The requirement that our new definition should be based on a description of actions that can be performed in real life is also met. The definition rests on a hypothesis, an expectation that we can observe managers in the real world performing the following four actions as a feature of the "financial life" of their enterprises, that is, as part of the exchange of energy and information between these enterprises and their environments:

1. the expression of expectations of payments
2. the signing of agreements about payments
3. the declaration that claims have arisen
4. the sending and receipt of payments

For the sake of readers who are already familiar with accounting and tradition, it is worth pointing out that these new definitions contain a number of clearly realistic features, so the new definitions may well appear to be nothing but common sense. Readers may well feel that the definitions are in no way surprising, and certainly not new.

The answer to this point is that perhaps some readers did know all about these definitions already, but if this is so, then such readers have not been aware of the fact, and have not considered all the consequences of their knowledge.

It takes very little time to understand the theory involved, but readers may find it takes longer to consider all the extensive consequences that follow if the theory is accepted. Let us merely indicate a couple of these consequences.

One of the significant consequences of accepting the new ideas is that the item currently known as "fixed assets" in its current form will disappear completely from financial statements. The randomly evaluated item known as "book value," which has a vital influence on the size of the inexplicable concept known as "owners' equity," can no longer be applied either if the new definition of value is accepted.

Everyone knows that "fixed assets," which often make up a considerable proportion of the total "assets" in traditional balance sheets, are evaluated by registering the historical cost price and then carrying out various forms of depreciation, revaluation, write-down, and so on. Everyone knows that these strange procedures are nothing but mental arithmetic with no connection to the real world. Virtually all the textbooks on the subject say that "book value" is not the same as "real value." And yet the strange ritual of adding and subtracting unrealistic figures continues in accounting practice.

Why is this so? If we know that "book value" is not the same as "real value," why do we not ask the sharpest of questions and demand clear answers on this subject?

As mentioned earlier, the new definition of value comprises "goods and services," and this term should be understood in its widest sense. It does not matter whether the price is high or low, or whether the object being sold is a chair, a factory building or an airline. The "goods" or "services" may be an investment in a new factory building or in an entire enterprise. In all cases, the question of the value of the goods, factory building or enterprise must be answered using the new definition, if we want an answer with a scientific base. We have already pointed out that economists or managers who consider the concept of historical cost price in financial statements to be meaningful have a world picture that has long been abandoned by modern scientific theory. If a ticket for a train that left yesterday cannot be refunded or exchanged, it has no value other than its educational value for the person suffering the loss concerned.

In conclusion, we emphasize that our new definition of value is logically formed as *a prediction of payments*, that is, as an identified set of typical hypotheses about the future. The only question that Venetian investors needed to ask about their trade journeys to India was "Is the prognosis good?"

And this is still the only important question that modern managers must ask and answer, using accounting specialists as their assistants when they wish to know something about the financial position of their enterprises. Modern managers seldom refer to camels journeying through the Persian desert, since transport has developed somewhat since the days of the Venetian traders. Nor are modern managers forced to trust in guesswork and prayers for the safe return of their caravans, since communications have developed greatly, too.

But the indicators of good and bad financial results remain the same as always. It is always *the quality of the management* that is the decisive factor. But it is by no means certain that quality can or should be described using figures on a piece of paper. There are other means of communication.

In the next chapter we intend to describe the basic concepts of our new accounting theory, which is based on these hypotheses.

NOTES

1. J. Witt-Hansen, *Filosofi*, p. 11.
2. Ibid., p. 11.
3. Ibid., p. 12.
4. Ibid., p. 13.

13 NEW BASIC CONCEPTS OF ACCOUNTING THEORY

> It is wrong to believe that the task of physics is to discover what Nature is. Physics is concerned with what we can say about Nature.
>
> —*Niels Bohr*

It is wrong to believe that the task of accounting is to find out what the financial position is. Accounting is concerned with what we can say about the financial position. The things we say about the financial position will make other people act or refrain from acting, and the things other people say about the financial position will have the same effect on us. If we wish to inspire actions that can be understood, we must use a language that can be understood. Our new basic concepts should enable interested readers to understand the substance of financial statements. In addition to the demand for empirical openness and the possibility of falsification, a new definition should meet the following four demands. It should be *complete, consistent, necessary* and *sufficient*. In a previous chapter we said that the problem facing accounting is that no one has yet been able to define *assets* and *liabilities* in a way that could defy all contradiction. The information presented using our new theory of accounting is information about payments that are to be made in the immediate future. Predictions of payments all have a logical connection with actions that can be performed. This makes it possible to falsify them, and financial statements then become as reliable as managers themselves. But if managers are not reliable, the financial statements of their enterprises will not be reliable either.

In this chapter and those that follow we shall present and describe the use of a set of new accounting concepts. In purely quantitative terms this task is perfectly straightforward. After all, there are relatively few fundamental questions in accounting, questions that the Financial Accounting Standards Board (FASB) (despite all its hard work) failed to answer, owing to what the FASB itself described as the still unsolved issue of the problem of recognition.

The new basic definitions that we shall propose here should be seen by readers as suggestions for a new professional language that is so clear, well-founded and comprehensible that in the long term it should help resolve the all-too-familiar conflict between relevance and tradition in accounting practice.

Some of the traditions of accounting are irrelevant. But on the other hand, some of the new and relevant practical accounting procedures have not yet become part of tradition. Some of the new methods that would actually be extremely effective problem solving tools, meeting the requirements of users, have not yet been accepted as part of accounting tradition. The task facing us can thus be described by the logical diagram shown in figure 13.1.

As figure 13.1 shows, we have no intention of storming the gates of *all* the traditions of accounting. A good deal of traditional accounting is perfectly acceptable as it is. Nor does our task involve the continuation of familiar, one-sided criticism, which may be both necessary and important, but which is basically barren unless constructive alternatives are also indicated.

No, our task is rather to solve two subtasks that must be *solved simultaneously* and *seen in relation to each other*. The first subtask is to define precisely the irrelevant aspects of familiar accounting practice. The second and far more important subtask is to outline and justify the use of the relevant new methods that should in fact already be traditional. In other words, *some traditions must be abandoned*, and *some new relevant methods must be introduced*. We shall try to perform both tasks, with the main emphasis on the latter.

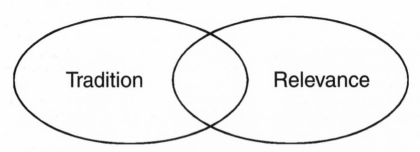

Figure 13.1. Tradition and relevance in accounting.

However, if we are to perform both tasks it is not enough to make marginal adjustments to each task separately. Readers must still be able to appreciate the *wholeness* of accounting. The requirement that an overall view must be maintained is indispensable, so we must go back to basics, returning to the starting point of accounting and then establishing and justifying a new basic, all-encompassing and general set of concepts.

In what follows we shall regard the special language used by the accounting profession as a *formally logical system of information*, in other words as a so-called system of postulates. Certain demands must be made on such a system with a view to ensuring that it is scientifically reliable. Thus it should be

1. complete (generally applicable)
2. consistent (without contradictions)
3. necessary
4. sufficient

Let us start by defining the profession of accounting and the object with which it is concerned.

Accounting is theories and methods for description, explanation and prediction of the financial consequences of the actions of organizations.

Let us now briefly comment on the individual elements of this new definition. Instead of the terms "theories and methods" the definition could have said "ideas and procedures," which would have the same meaning. The main point is that the definition includes two elements, making possible the creation of the previously almost entirely absent connection between research ("theories," "ideas") and the requirements of practical life ("methods," "procedures"). In other words, it must be possible to use theories in practice, and practical procedures must be well-founded, instead of resembling a random and messy collection of rough rules of thumb. People who justify their actions by saying "that is what we have always done" act unadvisedly, and are unable to make others understand the reasons for their actions.

Our definition of accounting states that the only objects described by accounting are the "financial consequences" of "the actions of organizations." In order to be of interest for accounting, it is *necessary* that actions have financial consequences. In other words, *actions with no financial consequences are not objects of interest for accounting.*

It is also a *sufficient* criterion for study by accounting that actions have financial consequences for the organizations concerned. In other words, *all actions that have financial consequences should be objects of interest for accounting.*

Readers with insight into the world of accounting will immediately realize that there is a clear, incontrovertible contradiction between the new definition and the accounting practice observed all over the world today. This clear contradiction is apparent in two different areas.

First, in practice, traditional accounting fails to provide a systematic and thus complete registration of the financial consequences of certain actions. *Agreements* concerning purchases, sales, employment or loans are undoubtedly actions that have financial consequences, but such agreements are not included systematically in traditional financial statements. This failure to ensure systematic registration of agreements results in a very serious consequence with regard to accounting methods. As systems of information, traditional financial statements are *incomplete*.

Second, traditional financial statements contain information that does not reflect the financial consequences of actions. *Depreciation* is a term reflecting the "loss of value" of investments over one or more periods, investments entered as "fixed assets" when they are originally made. But no one can logically justify the use of one particular rate of depreciation in preference to any other. The rate of depreciation is an issue that could be debated ad infinitum. The concept of depreciation is always an *arbitrary* estimate of loss of value. Information about depreciation is based on *assumption*, not on *observation*. And this is the fundamental difference between depreciation and the categories of information contained in financial statements that can be regarded as scientific. We are asked simply to accept the rate of depreciation given, but actions that have financial consequences can be observed and measured in the real world.

We also note that our definition uses the term "organizations" instead of "enterprises." One of the points of criticism raised by Robert N. Anthony against the FASB's attempt to establish basic accounting principles was that useless distinctions had been made between public and private enterprises. The use of the term "organizations" should ensure that the new theory is generally applicable, since this term can be applied to any form of common enterprise. In other words, the principles outlined here should be equally applicable to both private and public organizations.

To summarize, we believe the most important thing about our new definition of accounting is that it should not be based on assumptions, belief or speculation, but on direct observation of the actions or behavior of organizations. The simple but powerful reason for choosing our definition, and thus for rejecting all other definitions, is that actions (behavior) can be observed and measured, making it possible to convert them into information that is meaningful in given contexts even for people other than the observers themselves.

We said in a previous chapter that scientifically viable concepts are concepts that are fixed in relation to actions that can be performed. In recent years, in many subjects other than economics and many disciplines other than accounting, great research progress has been made, progress that has almost always been due to the clear definition of the object being studied and the linkage of this object with observations and the measurement of actions. For instance, modern behavioral psychology, as its name implies, is based on observation of the particular *behavior* of special groups or individuals, not on speculation concerning particular qualities or other explanations that cannot be measured.

Having defined the concept of accounting itself, let us now take the next step and define the concept of financial statements.

Financial statements are descriptions of the financial consequences of the actions of organizations.

This definition is also new. It is derived from the definition of accounting outlined in the preceding paragraphs, and has a close linguistic link with this definition, and thus a close link in terms of content. The points raised earlier concerning completeness, consistency, necessity and sufficiency that we applied to our basic definition of accounting can also be applied without alteration to our definition of the products of accounting, that is to financial statements. We can then proceed to consider the four logical categories of "descriptions of financial consequences" that are involved.

We must emphasize that we use the term "descriptions of financial consequences" to indicate that the descriptions provided by accounting are always made using the concepts of *money* and *payments of money*. This, too, can be expressed precisely. The objects of the measurements carried out by accounting are payments and nothing but payments. The next step in our establishment of basic concepts is to classify the descriptions in question. The financial consequences of the actions of organizations can be described completely and consistently using a system of information about payments made and received in four and only four logical categories:

1. expected payments (e.g., plans, budgets)
2. agreed payments (e.g., orders, contracts)
3. claims (e.g., invoices, bills, deposits at banks)
4. payments that have been made (e.g., cash holdings)

The basic concept of payments can be classified according to two signs placed in front of it. We talk of payments received (+) and payments made (−). So we shall now regard the formal system of information as consisting of a total of eight (4 × 2) logical categories.

We have already pointed out that our system of information consists of *predictions of payments*. In order to persuade readers to accept this viewpoint, let us now consider the four categories of payments in the order in which they have been named. Clearly, category 1 (*expected payments*) must be regarded as involving prediction. But readers will quickly realize that categories 2 and 3 must also be regarded as predictions in order to be meaningful. Neither agreed payments nor claims are normally paid at the same time as they are contracted. Finally, category 4 (*payments that have been made*) must logically be regarded as providing confirmations of the predictions made by the first three categories.

The financial consequences of actions can now be illustrated in terms of *financial points of measurement covering a chain of transactions.* Measurement involves controlled consideration of all four logical states. First we regard a given payment as "expected," then as "agreed." Once delivery has been completed and the claim can thus be justified, payments can be regarded as "realized" (invoiced), and finally predictions of payment become confirmed as "paid."

Let us illustrate this idea by using a simple example, considering the financial consequences of the same action at four different points in time designated $t(1)$, $t(2)$, $t(3)$ and $t(4)$ respectively.

We shall consider a straightforward purchase from the point of view of the seller. At time $t(1)$ the seller has been asked to make an offer for delivery of goods, which the buyer wants to have delivered at time $t(3)$. Following negotiations with the buyer, the seller sends an offer stating that he can deliver the goods at a price of 100 on condition that an order is received no later than time $t(2)$, and assuming that payment is made no later than time $t(4)$.

The time axis in figure 13.2 shows the names of the four financial points of measurement in abbreviated form. E = "expected," A = "agreed," R = "realized" and P = "paid." Above the axis we state the name of the document concerned.

At time $t(1)$ the offer can be regarded as documentation of an *expected payment*. At time $t(1)$ the seller can say, "I expect to receive a payment of 100 at time $t(4)$. This prediction is based on the fact that I have sent the buyer an offer. Payment is thus *expected*, and must be regarded as such. The money will not be in the box until the buyer has said "yes," until I have delivered, and until the buyer pays."

Let us now assume that the buyer accepts the offer and the seller receives the order by time $t(2)$. Once the seller has registered the order, it can be regarded (see figure 13.3) as documentation of an *agreed* payment received.

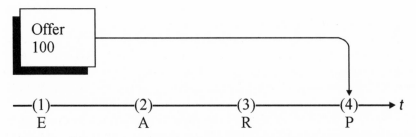

Figure 13.2.   Expected payment received according to documentation.

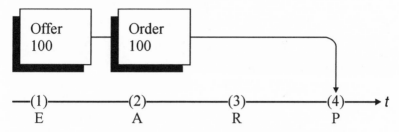

Figure 13.3. Agreed payment received and documentation.

At time $t(2)$ the seller can say, "I expect to receive a payment of 100 at time $t(4)$. This prediction is based on the fact that I have received the buyer's order. Payment is thus *agreed*, and must be regarded as such. The money will not be in the box until I have delivered, and until the buyer pays."

Let us now assume that the goods are delivered and that the invoice is sent to the buyer at time t(3). Once the seller has issued the invoice, it appears in figure 13.4 as documentation of a *claim*. The agreement has been fulfilled (realized) by the seller.

At time $t(3)$ the seller can say, "I expect to receive a payment of 100 at time $t(4)$. This prediction is based on the fact that I have delivered in accordance with the buyer's order, which means that I now have a claim. The claim is thus *realized*, but must still be regarded as a claim. The money will not be in the box until the buyer pays."

Finally, let us assume that the buyer pays by check, and that payment takes place by time $t(4)$. Once the seller has received and registered the buyer's check, it appears in figure 13.5 as documentation of a *payment that has been made*.

At time $t(4)$ the seller can finally say, "My previous predictions of payment received have now been confirmed. As expected, I have received payment today, and I can explain this payment by stating that at time $t(1)$ I sent the buyer an offer, that at time $t(2)$ the buyer accepted this offer, that

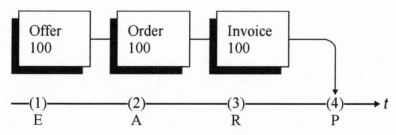

Figure 13.4. Realized claim and documentation.

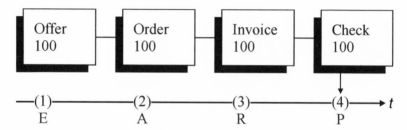

Figure 13.5. Payment and documentation.

at time *t*(3) I delivered and invoiced the goods, and that I received the buyer's payment today. The money is now in the box, and I can dispose of it unless any guarantee commitments or other commitments fall due. I regard this as unlikely, because if I had expected such commitments to be claimed by the buyer I would have acted differently from the outset."

This small and simple example shows us the logic of an individual sales transaction in terms of a chain of transactions and their associated payments. In this example the sign in front of the payment is positive—payment is received because we regard the transaction from the point of view of the seller. But if we regard the chain of transactions from the point of view of the buyer, the sign in front of the payment will of course be negative.

The example can be used by readers as a basis of the general logic applying to *purchases* in analogy with the logic applying to *sales*.

The logic behind the way information is handled here is very simple and clear. There are two interested parties involved in all actions with financial consequences—a buyer and a seller. The payment of money cancels a claim that has arisen previously. A claim arises because an agreement reached previously is fulfilled, and finally an agreement is reached based on expectations expressed previously.

This logic is general, and thus covers *all* selling and buying transactions, whether a cash purchase of a pencil or a contract costing billions is involved. The concrete description of the transactions involved is straightforward when you buy a pencil, whereas many different elements are involved in projects costing billions, which are of course far more complex. But if the descriptions of the two transactions are analyzed, it will be discovered that they consist of four and only four types of logical statement about predictions of payment. And it is in this new but basically very simple and obvious viewpoint that the decisive shift in cognitive theory can be found. Traditionally, financial statements are never regarded as *containing predictions*. In fact, the reverse is true. In both traditional accounting literature and current accounting practice, financial statements are without exception regarded as *descriptions of the past*, as financial history. Budgets alone are regarded as a type of prediction.

Our new viewpoint leads us to the following new definition of the key concepts of assets and liabilities:

An asset is a well-founded prediction of payment received.
A liability is a well-founded prediction of payment made.

These definitions express both the necessary and sufficient conditions on which descriptions of assets and liabilities can be based.

If I claim that an item in a financial statement is an asset, then it is *necessary* that I state whether its existence can be equated with a future payment received. And if I can identify a future payment received, this is *sufficient* to enable me to call this future payment an asset.

Logically, it follows that items in financial statements that do not describe future payments received cannot be regarded as assets.

If I claim that an item in a financial statement is a liability, then it is *necessary* that I state whether its existence can be equated with a future payment made. And if I can identify a future payment made, this is *sufficient* to enable me to call this future payment a liability.

Logically, it follows that items in financial statements that do not describe future payments made cannot be regarded as liabilities.

Once the concepts of assets and liabilities have been defined, financial statements themselves have been defined. The items in the profit and loss account reflect the items in the balance sheet. The "result" of any period is of course logically identical with the "change in the balance sheet" for the same period. Anyone who is familiar with the formal itemization rules of double entry bookkeeping knows that an item of income is logically identical with and balanced by a corresponding item of growth in the registered holdings of the balance sheet (either claims or cash holdings increase). And an item of expense is logically identical with and set off by either a reduction in the registered holdings of the balance sheet, or an increase in the registered debt (cash holdings = "assets" decrease, or debt = "liabilities" increase).

This logic is straightforward enough, and yet it has proved difficult for many people to understand. So let us illustrate the logic of itemization with a simple example of traditional registration of the financial consequences of a sale on credit and subsequent payment on the date due for payment.

We shall reuse the example given in the preceding paragraphs, using the method of registration applied at present. It is still regarded as "generally accepted" accounting practice to delay the systematic registration of the financial consequences of any transaction until the realization time. So if we examine the procedures used in practice, we can only be certain of finding the double entry registration shown in figures 13.6 and 13.7.

We recall from the preceding example that once the buyer has received the goods and invoice at time $t(3)$, we have reached the point of measurement known as R. The chain of transactions has been "realized," but not yet "paid." In the itemization logic of double entry bookkeeping this can

Balance Sheet Account		Profit and Loss Account	
Buyer's Account		Loss And Profit	
Debit (+)	Credit (−)	Debit (+)	Credit (−)
t(3) 100			t(3) 100

Figure 13.6. Measurement of "realized" by double entry bookkeeping.

be shown as in figure 13.6. The sales account is "credited" and the buyer's account is "debited." But let us now consider the logical content of what has happened, instead of wondering about the use of these strange words.

When the buyer sends payment the second of the two logically linked registrations, which have given this special system of registration its more than 500 year old name, ensues. The buyer's account is "credited" and the bank account is "debited." The description of the financial consequences of the chain of transactions can now be described as paid at time $t(4)$.

This example shows that the profit and loss account is affected by the first but not by the second of the two itemizations that make up the system of double entry bookkeeping. The logical content of the income itemization is precisely the same as that of the example of the chain of transactions given earlier. The seller makes a prediction of payment received, and defends the reliability of this prediction by saying that delivery has taken place, and that a claim has thus been realized. This shows us that the familiar concept of "an income" can be regarded as identical with "a new claim" or "a prediction of payment received based on the fact that delivery has occurred." Similarly, we must say that "an expense" can be regarded as identical with "a new debt" or "a prediction of payment made based on the fact that delivery has occurred." Once payment has been made, it is regarded as confirmation of a prediction, but *it does not affect the profit and loss account*. The registration of payment in our example is entered in the balance sheet only.

We have already seen that the rules of double entry bookkeeping are used for the systematic registration of claims and debts, and for the cancellation of such items by making payments. The use of the logic of double entry bookkeeping makes it possible chronologically, systematically and with a very high degree of data reliability (i.e., formal reliability) to describe the financial consequences of actions by using the familiar pairs of

Balance Sheet Account		Profit and Loss Account	
Buyer's Account		**Loss and Profit**	
Debit (+)	Credit (−)	Debit (+)	Credit (−)
t(3) 100			*t*(3) 100
	t(4) 100		
Bank Account			
Debit (+)	Credit (−)		
t(4) 100			

Figure 13.7. Measurement of "paid" by double entry bookkeeping.

concepts known as income/payment received and expense/payment made. The first term in each pair of concepts (income, expense) describes the consequences at the point of financial measurement known as "realized," and the second term (payment made, payment received) describes the financial point of measurement known as "paid." There is nothing new in this, of course. It has been well known for more than 500 years.

But how do the rules work if we also wish to register predictions of payment that are based on the fact that an agreement has been contracted but delivery not yet made? How do we systematically register the financial consequences of an action occurring at the financial point of measurement known as "agreed?"

It is immediately apparent that agreements have binding financial consequences that are not expected to become evident until after agreements have been reached. And it is also immediately apparent that a logical category of information is involved that is different from the two categories already mentioned. The special prototype of an agreement seen as a well-founded prediction of payment received (and thus as an asset) has already been shown in figure 13.3.

We cannot use the term "an income" about this measurement without producing an inconsistent logical system of information. The concept of "an income" already has a well-defined content—it describes a realized claim.

But the agreement is contracted *before* the income itself can be measured, so we can use the term "income calculated in advance." We add an account for the order concerned to the balance sheet, and we set off the amount in the balance account so the profit is not affected. We can now register the order as early as time $t(2)$, and can thus expand our itemization example to encompass three types of asset as follows: 1) *liquid holdings* (payments that have been made), 2) *debtors* (realized claims), and 3) *orders* (agreed but not realized payments received). Let us now try to itemize this in our accounts. The measurement of financial consequences is traditionally delayed until time $t(3)$, but in figure 13.8 we shall seek to *enter such consequences as early as the time of agreement $t(2)$*.

Auditors would never protest against registration at such an early stage. On the contrary—early registration ensures a clearer view. The order is registered in the order account, and we have observed the principle of prudence, calling the item set off against the order "income calculated in advance." But how shall we then carry out registration at time $t(3)$, at the financial point of measurement known as "realized?"

A banal but nonetheless extremely important and striking difficulty arises at this point in the traditional registration system. We can now see that we need what could be called "double-double-itemization." Once delivery has been completed, we need to reitemize our prediction of payment received by changing "volume of orders" into "debtors," but we must also *simultaneously* change "income calculated in advance" in the balance sheet into "income" in the profit and loss account. This is shown in figure 13.9.

Balance Sheet Account		**Profit and Loss Account**	
Volume of Orders		Income Calculated in Advance	
Debit (+)	Credit (−)	Debit (+)	Credit (−)
$t(2)$ 100			$t(2)$ 100

Figure 13.8.   Order registration with no impact on result.

Balance Sheet Account		Balance Sheet Account	
Volume of Orders		Income Calculated in Advance	
Debit (+)	Credit (−)	Debit (+)	Credit (−)
t(2) 100			*t*(2) 100
	t(3) 100	*t*(3) 100	

Balance Sheet Account		Profit and Loss Account	
Buyer's Account		Losses and Gains	
Debit (+)	Credit (−)	Debit (+)	Credit (−)
t(3) 100			*t*(3) 100

Figure 13.9. Clumsy double-double-itemization.

This may be a banal problem, but it is nonetheless extremely important in practice. We now realize that although the rules of double entry book-keeping worked with admirable simplicity, clarity and data reliability in their original form, where systematic description was necessary at two and only two financial points of measurement, the same set of rules certainly does not have the same simplicity, clarity and data reliability when managers wish to know the financial consequences of all the agreements they reach in a single picture describing all agreed future payments simply, clearly and with good data reliability.

Wishing for such a total picture of payments is like wishing for a system of registration that systematically deals with all three points of measurement. This wish is shared by virtually all managers of modern organizations, for the simple reason that there is almost always a considerable lapse of time, in all chains of transactions in the real world, between the points of measurement known as "agreed" and "realized" with regard to both purchases and sales.

In order to complete the picture of this very serious conflict between the registration system used and the information required by managers, let us now combine the booking of the accounts items derived from all three financial points of measurement in figure 13.10. We recall that the three points of measurement were "agreed" $t(2)$, "realized" $t(3)$ and "paid" $t(4)$.

The terminology has been altered slightly in figure 13.10 with a view to ensuring greater clarity and general applicability. The holdings of the balance sheet are now described as "volume of orders" at the financial point of measurement known as "agreed," "volume of claims" at the financial point of measurement known as "realized" and "cash holdings" at the financial point of measurement known as "paid." The predictions of pay-

Balance Sheet Account Volume of Orders		**Balance Sheet Account** Income Calculated in Advance	
Debit (+)	Credit (−)	Debit (+)	Credit (−)
$t(2)$ 100			$t(2)$ 100
	$t(3)$ 100	$t(3)$ 100	

Balance Sheet Account Buyer's Account		**Profit and Loss Account** Losses and Gains	
Debit (+)	Credit (−)	Debit (+)	Credit (−)
$t(3)$ 100			$t(3)$ 100
	$t(4)$ 100		

Balance Sheet Account Cash Holding	
Debit (+)	Credit (−)
$t(4)$ 100	

Figure 13.10. Itemization involving all three financial points of measurement.

ments received (assets) are thus described in three logical categories, but the predictions of payments made are also described indirectly. All we need to do is change our point of view from that of the seller to that of the buyer. Predictions of payments received (assets) for the one will always be predictions of payments made (liabilities) for the other.

We can now extend our new basic concepts of accounting, and supplement our three logical categories of assets with the three corresponding categories of liabilities. Figure 13.11 shows these new pairs of concepts in connection with their respective financial points of measurement, and thus explains the content of the concepts in the real world. We recall that both assets and liabilities should be regarded basically as well-founded predictions of payment.

These new definitions of the basic concepts of assets and liabilities, which we have already put forward and given reasons for, now allow us to present the following new definition of the concept of the balance sheet:

A balance sheet is an information system consisting of well-founded predictions of payments received and made, and of nothing else.

Readers who are generally familiar with current accounting practice, and who notice that figure 13.11 has a few empty blocks, may feel that something is missing, and that certain unexpected elements are present. Let us therefore first discuss the content of figure 13.11, and try to fill in the empty blocks if possible.

The first obvious question is that although the item "cash" is included as an asset at the financial point of measurement known as "paid" in figure 13.11, there is no corresponding item on the liabilities side. Why not? Surely something is missing here. The answer is that the block is logically empty, and it must therefore be physically empty, too. It is impossible to conceive of a "negative payment." Enterprises that can no longer make payments suspend their payments. In the real world payments can only be made in two ways. Either you use your own means of payment, or you use other people's (that is, you borrow). There are no other possibilities if the information in this system is to be meaningful.

Point of Measurement	Assets	Liabilities
Expected		
Agreed	Volume of Orders	Agreed Purchases
Realized	Debtors	Creditors
Paid	Cash	

Figure 13.11.   Assets and liabilities seen as predictions of payment.

The next question that arises about figure 13.11 must naturally concern the financial point of measurement known as "expected." What do the assets and liabilities corresponding to this point look like?

Asking this question is the same as "What do predictions of payment made and received that are based on expectations but not yet on agreement look like *in the real world*?"

It is certainly not easy to give an entirely satisfactory answer to this simple question. The chance of finding an answer that is meaningful depends on two things. First, we must ask whether the management of the enterprise in question concern themselves with strategy, that is, do they adopt active and specific attitudes to their future options? And second, we must ask whether any such strategy is presented and documented in the form of well-founded and thus reliable budgets. If the concept known as "expected payments" cannot be justified by agreements that have been reached or claims that have arisen, but only by expectations, then such expected payments cannot be regarded as reliable unless the *content* of the plans is realistic, and unless the plans have an appropriate *form*, that is, unless their content can be communicated in such a way that the plans appear reliable to others besides the management concerned.

For now we shall content ourselves with calling these items "budgets of payments received" and "budgets of payments made" respectively. Figure 13.11 can then be altered to show us the entire system of information viewed as the complete balance sheet model in figure 13.12.

We shall now try to put ourselves in the place of readers for whom the concepts presented here seem new and strange. On behalf of such readers we should like to ask the following pertinent questions:

1. Is it really possible to include expected payments in financial statements? Surely this is a very uncertain practice.
2. What does "well-founded predictions of payment" mean in the new definition?

Point of Measurement	Assets	Liabilities
Expected	Budget of Payments Received	Budget of Payments Made
Agreed	Volume of Orders	Agreed Purchases
Realized	Debtors	Creditors
Paid	Cash	

Figure 13.12. The new balance sheet model.

3. What is the effect of indicating the conflict between the information requirements of management and the registration traditions of accounting?
4. Why have fixed assets disappeared?
5. What about owner's equity?

The first question can be answered by simply referring to our new definition of assets and liabilities. But the question can also be answered by saying that when the logic of double entry bookkeeping was formulated more than 500 years ago, the system was able to cope with "expected payments." It is true that the expectations involved were "certain," that is, they involved claims and debts. It was possible in each case to justify such expectations by referring to the fact that an agreement had been contracted and delivery made. But the main thing is that a claim must logically be regarded as an expected payment received, and an item of debt as an expected payment made. So it is certainly not illogical to claim *that the most important (and perhaps the only) justification of accounting is that accounting deals with information about expected payments.*

Readers will now realize that the new theory merely supplements the original balance sheet model of double entry bookkeeping, which only contained claims and debts, with other meaningful information about expected payments. This enables us to achieve logical completeness and consistency. All the information in the system belongs to the same universe (expected payments), but there are clear and well-defined differences between the four different types of information.

The differences between these four logical categories lead us on to question 2. What does "well-founded predictions of payment" mean in our new definition? The answer is that an expectation of payment can naturally be more or less well founded, but the various reasons that we can see enable us to combine information in a straightforward system of well-defined logical categories, that is, into a classification of descriptions of financial consequences.

As figure 13.13 shows, "agreed" is regarded as a subcategory of "expected," and "realized/paid" as a sub-category of "agreed." Readers who study the various categories of information in the diagram will discover that they can all be seen as a reflection of practical situations. Buyers sometimes pay for goods before they are delivered, but not before agreement has been reached. Agreements are never reached unless they have been discussed first by the parties concerned, and in practice such discussions or negotiations can be documented as precalculations, estimates, offers, project budgets and so on. The names may vary, but the phenomenon involved does not.

The classification of predictions of payment tells us something very important about the situation of the buyer and seller in two areas. First, we can say whether the information is *up-to-date*, thereby answering the

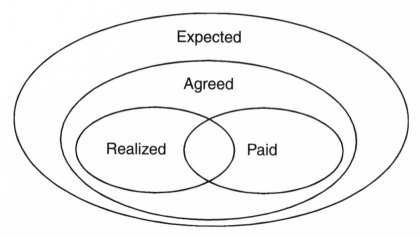

Figure 13.13. Classification of predictions of payment.

question "When is the information needed?" And second, we can also describe the *reliability* of the information, and thereby the credibility of the prediction of payment, answering the question "How reliable is this information about financial consequences?" Our example concerning the chain of transactions in figures 13.2 through 13.5 showed that predictions of payment that are only based on expectations are always less reliable than predictions based on agreements that have been reached. Payments that have been agreed are in turn less reliable than claims that have been realized. And finally, documented payment received (money in the box) provides complete confirmation of a previous prediction of payment about the transaction concerned. Our example about the chain of transactions shows us that the information in such cases becomes *less and less uncertain* as the points of measurement proceed. Everyone will surely accept the truth of the postulate that the latest information about the financial consequences of a given transaction is always the most reliable.

People who require absolute certainty in the information they are given must wait until all payments have been received, and actually until no further guarantee commitments or other forms of commitment can possibly arise.

Managers, of course, are unable to wait this long. In practice, they have to make decisions and then take action based on these decisions. And one should never act without knowing the financial consequences of one's actions. So it is hardly surprising that the American organizational theorist Henry Mintzberg has concluded, following a study of the behavior of American managers, that in practice managers consistently prefer information that is *up-to-date*—information that is available and relevant for the actions currently under consideration.

This conflict between the reliability of accounting information and the extent to which it is up-to-date can be described as *the information dilemma of accounting*:

Real-time information is not certain, but information that is certain is not real-time.

This information dilemma is illustrated in figure 13.14, where three types of time span have been added between the four now-familiar financial points of measurement.

We assume in figure 13.14 that a certain amount of time elapses between "expected" and "agreed" (time for sale), and that this time is taken up by discussion of terms of delivery and payment. A certain amount of time also elapses between "agreed" and "realized" (time for production), time used by the seller to perform his side of the bargain. Finally, a certain amount of time elapses between "realized" and "paid," time that is identical with the period of credit allowed to the buyer.

Let us now assume that the likelihood of a prediction of payment being correct in a given case is regarded as "low" at the point of measurement known as "expected," but "high" at the point of measurement known as "paid." The question is at which point does the important shift from "low" to "high" occur?

Practitioners will surely agree that the shift from low to high probability occurs *when agreements are reached*. At this point both buyer and seller conclude their nonbinding negotiations and undertake commitments that we must assume they both take seriously. The importance of the time at which agreement is reached helps greatly to explain why managers demand information that is up-to-date, and that is therefore a relevant and useful tool when making the decisions they have to make and implementing decisions that have already been made. But we have just seen that information that is reliable is not up-to-date. In other words, information that is certain is available too late in relation to situations in which decisions have to be made. Is there any way out of this dilemma?

Let us now briefly distinguish between *keeping* financial statements and *using* financial statements, and let us distinguish between the people whose

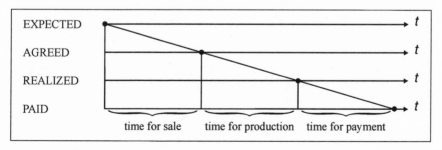

Figure 13.14. The chain of transactions and the time spans involved.

job is to keep and use financial statements. Managers rarely keep financial statements for their enterprises. In the vast majority of cases this task is entrusted to specially trained individuals. Even in small enterprises accounting is left to the specialists (often to accountants), and large enterprises generally have their own accounts and finance department with specially trained managers.

Let us now consider figure 13.14 and ask the questions "Who administers the four financial points of measurement in practice? Who expresses expectations, who reaches agreements, who controls claims and debts, and who sends and receives payments?"

These questions are very easy to answer. We know that managers make the decisions, so we know that it is generally managers who administer the first two financial points of measurement known as "expected" and "agreed." And we also know that accounting specialists deal with the last two points "realized" and "paid." These two last points of measurement are identical with the two logical registration dimensions of double entry bookkeeping.

We have now answered the third question posed ("What is the effect of indicating the conflict between the information requirements of management and the registration traditions of accounting?"). Let us imagine a manager who has drawn up a budget of sales for the next period (orders received). The budget shows an *expected* volume of orders received of 100. Immediately after the expiry of the period we can see an *agreed* volume of orders received of 92. Owing to various circumstances (inability to deliver, cancellation by a customer) only 90 are delivered and invoiced, which can be regarded as a *realized* holding of claims of 90. Finally, the inability of a customer to pay means that an amount of 89 is actually *paid*.

Four different accounting results are involved, and three different types of error in prediction. The four accounting results are:

1. Expected result (100)
2. Agreed result (92)
3. Realization result (90)
4. Payment result (89)

Each of the four interim results has its own distinctive characteristics, and each result can be defined in terms of a financial point of measurement in the chain of transactions. The expected result may be available at an early stage. And the absolutely certain result (the payment result) must wait until all possible errors in prediction are known.

The three types of error in prediction can be defined as the errors that can be measured by shifting from one financial point of measurement to a later point of measurement:

1. type 1: E-A: Error between "expected" and "agreed" (8)
2. type 2: A-R: error between "agreed" and "realized" (2)
3. type 3: R-P: error between "realized" and "paid" (1)

The reason why the expected result (the budget) is often regarded as uncertain is that all the errors in prediction at this stage have to estimated. During the planning stage no one knows exactly how many orders will be received, exactly how easy delivery will be or exactly what the customer's ability to pay will be like. But if you wait until the payment result is available there is no longer any uncertainty. All three possible errors in prediction are known.

The connection and transition between the four interim results and the errors in prediction are shown in figure 13.15. As we have mentioned, the payment result is the best financial result for people requiring certainty above all else, people who are prepared to manage with information that is not up-to-date. But more than 500 years ago managers discovered that waiting until the payment result was known was not a particularly good idea. It was accepted that the uncertainty between "realized" and "paid" would have to be estimated. This is how the interim result achieved by using the logic of double entry bookkeeping (*the realization result*) arose. Whereas the payment result is defined as the payments received during a given period minus the payments made during the same period, the realization result can be defined as registered income during a given period minus registered expenses during the same period.

These two interim result concepts are a tried and tested part of the tools used by accounting specialists. Thanks to the inherent logic of the registration system, the great advantage of these two concepts is that they can be calculated with a high degree of formal reliability. But the two interim result concepts of double entry bookkeeping also have two disadvantages, which have grown increasingly evident as managers experience more frequent and drastic changes in circumstances both inside and outside their enterprises.

Accounting specialists who believe that double entry bookkeeping is a necessary and sufficient model of accounting registration must also accept that critics of traditional financial statements will find it easy to identify the two crucial defects of this old system. The information contained in financial statements is both *out-of-date* and *incomplete*.

Practical managers are all familiar with the problems that arise when they wish to know the financial consequences of actions performed in a given period, when they ask for a financial statement for the period concerned.

Interim Result	Error E-A	Error A-R	Error R-P
Expected Result	Unknown	Unknown	Unknown
Agreed Result	Known	Unknown	Unknown
Realization Result	Known	Known	Unknown
Payment Result	Known	Known	Known

Figure 13.15. Interim results and errors in prediction.

They have to wait. It always takes time to produce financial statements. Even using modern computer technology there is always a delay. First of all the period concerned has to be completed, then you have to be certain that all the relevant documents have been received. This often takes time, because the speed at which suppliers send invoices for the goods they supply varies.

Consequently, it is not surprising that managers regard financial statements as financial history. Even after financial statements have finally been presented, the information they contain is out-of-date in relation to the new and perhaps entirely different options for action under consideration. And information that is out-of-date is also irrelevant. So even if financial statements are accurate, the information they contain is irrelevant.

The other and equally serious disadvantage is that financial statements are incomplete. If we want a complete financial statement we must insist that it contains *the financial consequences of all our actions*, as well as describing *all the financial consequences of our actions*. Agreements, of course, have financial consequences. So if agreements are not registered systematically, the result is an incomplete financial statement.

The effect of the conflict between the registration traditions of accounting and the information requirements of management is undoubtedly that the concern of accounting specialists for balance, accuracy and formal reliability has been regarded as so vital that other considerations have had to be either abandoned altogether or regarded as being of secondary importance. But the price of balance, accuracy and formal reliability has been extremely high, since the relevance and completeness of financial statements have both been lost. Accounting specialists provide managers with out-of-date and therefore irrelevant data, data that cannot be understood in connection with the actions managers wish to perform, actions that they are already performing.

The conflict between the registration traditions of accounting and the information requirements of management is a very serious one. The conclusion must be that the traditional accounting model provides an unreliable description of the financial consequences of the actions of organizations. Nonetheless, in the following chapters we shall try to indicate a way out of the terrible information dilemma facing accounting.

We shall conclude this chapter by trying to answer the last two unanswered questions concerning fixed assets and owners' equity. Fixed assets are always included in traditional financial statements at their so-called "book value." This means the "historical cost price," which often includes specified additions and deductions resulting from all the many types of depreciation, revaluation, write-down and so on used in traditional accounting.

This type of information, however, is not the same as a *prediction of payments*, so the inclusion of fixed assets would make our new accounting model inconsistent.

The distinction made between fixed assets and current assets is a false one. It does not actually matter whether the "asset" you buy is an office chair whose cost price you regard as reasonable, or a factory costing millions. There are three and only three reasons for buying anything. Let us apply these reasons to the purchase of an office chair, bearing the factory in mind as we do so.

The first reason is "I buy this office chair because I have received an order from a customer of which the office chair is part. I buy to order, I agree to make a down payment, and I justify this action by the fact that I shall receive an agreed payment that is greater than the down payment I have made."

The second reason is "I buy this office chair because I expect to be able to sell it later at a price that gives me a profit. I buy for my stock, I agree to make a down payment and I justify this action by the fact that I expect to receive a payment that is greater than the down payment I have made."

The third reason is "I buy this office chair because it is needed in my office. Once it has been bought the price I paid is irrelevant. But it might be a good idea to ask what I could sell it for if necessary, and how long it would take to sell it. Reliable answers to these questions can be used to describe my ability to make any other necessary payments."

There are no other reasons apart from these three.

There is only one question left. Traditionally the difference between "assets" and "liabilities" has always been known as "owners' equity." We have already given reasons why this concept should be regarded with skepticism.

So we shall refrain from using the term "owners' equity" altogether. The term is unclear and misleading, and has therefore been directly damaging on several occasions in the past. Financial statements have often given the impression that enterprises were perfectly sound, only for the same enterprises to suspend their payments and be declared bankrupt shortly afterwards, resulting in the loss of millions.

The concept of "owners' equity" belongs to the same category as astrology and other pseudoscientific practices, so it should be abandoned in accounting theory and practice as soon as possible. Indeed, we believe that its use should be forbidden by law.

We have now redefined the familiar concepts, and thereby redefined the concept of the balance sheet as a whole. From now on we shall describe the difference between assets and liabilities in the most obvious of ways; as "the difference between assets and liabilities," or merely "difference." But later on we shall try to find and justify a new and more revealing concept to use about this difference.

If readers are now prepared to consider the information contained in financial statements as a prediction of payments, and to reject all information that is not a prediction of payments, then the objective of this chapter of definitions will have been achieved.

It is not our intention to convince readers of the truth of our claims. But it is our intention to enable readers to convince themselves. We may not succeed, because it is always difficult for people to abandon the convictions they have held for many years. But we hope readers think "This looks interesting, at least. Let us assume as a working hypothesis that financial statements describe the financial consequences of the actions of organizations, and that this description, both in detail and in general, has the logical form of a prediction of payments. And then let our reading and consideration of what follows be a critical test of this hypothesis."

14 THE NEW MEASUREMENT SYSTEM—JUSTIFICATION AND BASIC FORM

> Measure everything that can be measured, and make things that cannot be measured measurable.
>
> —*Galileo Galilei*

Accounting theorists have long been aware that it is an advantage to carry out registration in such a way that all the different calculation and reporting tasks involved in accounting can be supported by data describing the real world. The problem of the fatal logical incompleteness of double entry bookkeeping can be solved by using modern technology. For 500 years we have accepted the idea that two financial points of measurement were necessary and sufficient in chronological and systematic accounting. But this is no longer acceptable. We now need a basic form of accounting that permits and supports the use of four logical situations—"expected," "agreed," "realized" and "paid." This means that the T-shaped account with its debit-credit itemization and principle of accruals must now make way for databases and communication. "Accounting for management" is the name of a new information system on which a description of the financial consequences of the actions of organizations can be based. But we now have the chance to make financial statements describe reality, too. The financial statements of the future can be made logically complete and therefore clear and easy to understand. They can also be made up-to-date, and be used to show the financial situation right now. And this is what will make them reliable.

In a previous chapter we pointed out that double entry bookkeeping can be seen as an information system, a set of concepts and algorithms used for measurement and data processing in support of a description of financial consequences. However, we have also indicated that there has been serious criticism of accounting practice in recent years, leading us to the conclusion that double entry bookkeeping is logically incomplete as a tool for describing the financial consequences of the actions of organizations. And naturally, if the accounts on which we keep using double entry bookkeeping are logically incomplete, the financial statements presented on the basis of these accounts will be incomplete, too. It is not possible to present a financial statement that is any better than the accounts on which it is based. If you wish to communicate data to others, you need to have data available.

Double entry bookkeeping has existed for more than 500 years. Its logic as an information system is still regarded all over the world as the incontrovertible foundation of accounting registration, so the discovery of the logical incompleteness of this system will inevitably have a great impact on the world of accounting. Many people will find it difficult to accept that the old familiar information system, with its T-shaped account and all its items of debit and credit followed by a conclusion, balancing and all the rituals of accruals, *is no longer sufficient.* Accounting specialists must get used to using computers in a new way if we hope to recover the lost credibility of our profession.

Recognition of the existence of problems is always necessary before progress can be achieved. If we are interested in clear information leading to action instead of endless talk without action, we must accept the postulate of impotence, an acceptance of which will make all new ideas and professional progress possible. The new recognition gives us a very realistic and practical opportunity to solve the terrible problem of logical incompleteness in traditional financial statements. The financial statements of the future can be designed as information systems based on a viable cognitive foundation and can be themselves logically complete. The introduction of such financial statements could be a considerable achievement for the profession of accounting.

Humans always want to find natural explanations of life and its phenomena instead of explaining life as the result of the actions of gods, spirits and demons. Humans are naturally inquisitive, and love to experiment and learn. We like to replace belief and speculation with recognition and knowledge. And that is why we constantly seek to distinguish between the objective and the subjective.

How can we tell the difference between the objective and the subjective? When we say that information is objective, we mean that it describes reality independently of the consciousness of the individual. If I say "Peter is 6 feet tall" I am making an observation, and giving you the opportunity of contradicting it. I have observed a phenomenon, and say something about it using the language at my disposal. My statement mentions a scale of measurement, and enables you to check the statement and contradict it if it does not match your own observations. If you make a counterclaim we must both check the measurement, after which one of us will admit making an error, and we shall agree on the truth of the matter.

But if I say "Peter is rather tall" there is a considerable risk that I will not be understood, and there is no easy way of checking the truth and agreeing with you if you contradict me. We both end up sticking to our own imprecise statements.

The opposite of objectivity, of course, is subjectivity. The distinguishing feature of subjective statements is that they are influenced or affected by the beliefs or evaluations of the individual. Naturally, I make all my statements myself, so they will all be influenced or affected to some extent by my beliefs and evaluations. This means that I can never decide when my statements are "objective" and when they are "subjective." I may well feel that I am being objective, but my subjectivity is revealed by the simple fact that I have chosen the topic about which I am talking. Why am I writing a somewhat aggressive book about accounting theory instead of refraining from doing so?

There are people who can be recognized primarily by their use of intuition, and others who are largely dominated by their intellect. To some extent it is fair to claim that artists are subjective and scientists objective. Artists are often regarded as independent individuals who are not bound by norms, who intuitively transcend all barriers and experience and describe reality in new and often surprising ways. On the other hand, most people regard scientists as inquisitive people who carry out experiments critically and coolly, and test their results carefully. The language of science can be used by other people to a far greater extent than the language of art. But each person seems to contain a mixture of subjective and objective elements. We are apparently equipped from birth with a certain amount of imagination and intellect. The fact is, of course, that art is not entirely subjective, and science is not entirely objective:

A theory may be tested by experience, but there is no path leading from experience to the creation of a theory. This means that the world of concepts is not logical, nor can it be derived from experience in any other way. To a certain extent it is a product of the creative human spirit[1]

Was this said by a scientist or an artist? It does not seem to be very precise. It says that the world of concepts is not logical, and disappointingly it also says that there is no path leading from experience to theory. Finally, it claims that basic concepts, which we are desperately seeking in the world of accounting, are "products of the creative human spirit." In other words, the statement can be seen as a demand for creativity when drawing up theories, which is also a demand for creativity when drawing up accounting theory. Perhaps the word "demand" is too strong, but there is no doubt that the quotation deals with the phenomenon of creativity. Reality must be renewed, and it can be renewed if we use "the creative human spirit" and adopt new basic attitudes.

Readers must decide whether the term "artist" or "scientist" best suits the man who made this quotation. The decision will of course be subjective, and is best left to readers themselves. But there is no doubt that the name of the person was Albert Einstein. The basic cognitive evaluation contained in the quotation comes from a summary of his work on the problems facing modern theoretical physics.

Our new basic attitude with regard to accounting theory is founded on the axiom concluded in chapter 11, and justified and discussed in chapter 13. This axiom states that accounting consists of theories and methods used to describe the financial consequences of the actions of organizations.

Following Galileo's advice about measuring everything that can be measured and making things that cannot be measured measurable results in what is regarded as progress not only in accounting theory but also in scientific theory as a whole. Measurements always give specific terminology greater impact and clarity, enabling us to abandon dubious, vague interpretations in favor of clear, precise and objective statements that everyone can challenge and check, thereby enabling us to reach agreement.

So it would be an advantage if future accounting practice could be based on granting readers of financial statements access to objectively measured and clearly defined information describing the financial consequences of the actions of organizations. Information distinguished by its qualitative nature may well be far more important than the actual figures presented, and it should definitely be included. But it should also always be seen in its true light—as the object of interpretation and evaluation.

Let us now derive more inspiration from Galileo. This time we shall describe how he used a simple hypothesis to deny the truth of a law that had been accepted for more than 1,500 years, albeit in metaphorical form. The law concerned the mass and gravity of fixed bodies, and was propounded by the Greek philosopher Aristotle (384–322 B.C.): "If a given weight passes through a given distance in a given time, then a greater weight will pass through the same distance in a shorter time, and the times will be inversely proportionate to the weight."[2] In other words, an iron ball weighing eight pounds falls faster than an iron ball weighing two pounds.

This was accepted for more than 1,500 years. After all, the books said it was true. No one thought of denying it until Galileo produced the following completely simple and logical counterevidence: "Tie the two balls together and let them fall as one. The faster ball will now be slowed down by the slower one, and the slower one will move faster because of the faster one. If this is true, the body weighing ten pounds falls more slowly than the body weighing eight pounds on its own. So the heavier body falls more slowly than the lighter one. So the law cannot be true."

This was all that was needed to reveal that the accepted views of the experts were nonsense. Galileo's simple logic could not be refuted, so researchers were immediately aware that the great Aristotle had been mistaken, that his law of gravity was self-contradictory. And yet it had been regarded as "the truth" for more than 1,500 years.

Let us now try to make a hypothesis characterizing current accounting traditions. Consider the following two postulates:

1. agreements contain information that describes reality
2. depreciation consists of information that does not describe reality

The reason for making these postulates is that agreements are phenomena that can be observed objectively in the real world, whereas depreciation is an abstract concept based on subjective assumptions, belief and speculation.

Agreements have financial consequences, and agreements can be made the subject of measurement. We can say that agreement X has been reached, and prove the truth of this claim. If anyone doubts the existence of the agreement, the claim can be tested and the statement about the existence of the agreement can be confirmed or denied. An agreement is a concept with which all businesspeople and lawyers are familiar, with which they can operate. As a result, there are practical laws and customs related to agreements, and people have confidence in them.

Depreciation, on the other hand, has no financial consequences, and depreciation cannot be measured. We cannot say that depreciation X exists, and prove the truth of this claim. If anyone doubts the existence of depreciation, the claim cannot be tested, and endless discussion will ensue. Depreciation is a concept that businessmen and lawyers cannot understand, so they are constantly surprised by events when they seek to use it in practice. There are no well-founded customs related to depreciation, only a number of rules with no content. This may be one reason why people who are not accounting specialists are skeptical, dubious and even directly suspicious of the concept of depreciation.

The general model of accounting that is still used all over the world as we approach the end of the twentieth century systematically ignores agreements and systematically includes depreciation. *A scientifically viable model of accounting, on the other hand, would systematically include agreements and systematically ignore depreciation.*

Let us now consider the basic structure of the new form of notation that we believe should replace the old T-shaped account. We recall that the word "account" originally meant "calculation."

In the chapter concerned with traditional accounting registration we pointed out that even medieval merchants were able to calculate future payments, and thereby to make a reliable prediction of any incipient suspension of payments. If they wished to calculate both solvency and liquidity at a given moment, all they needed to do was organize their data and use it to calculate several possible logical consequences. We recall that the logical elements of the calculation were quite simple and therefore easy to understand. The following three concepts were involved:

1. claims (debtors)
2. debts (creditors)
3. cash (cash holdings)

The only things, therefore, that medieval merchants needed in order to review their future payments were the two pairs of concepts income/expenses (bills/acceptances) and payments received/payments made. We pointed out that the use of the algorithms of double entry bookkeeping resulted in a number of enormous advantages with regard to the description of profitability, but also in the significant disadvantage that the information was systematically "locked" into one and only one system, that is, the system that was most appropriate for the control of payments. The fixed account was thus not unlike a prison.

Modern information technology gives us the key to open the door of this prison. Thanks to database technology, with its new data communication potential and not least the vastly improved ratio between the price and usefulness of hardware, the situation nowadays is far better than that that faced medieval merchants. We now have a financially accessible and extremely powerful general tool for the processing of information, a tool that accounting specialists can and should start to use.

The most important advantages provided by the new technology are time and flexibility. In the precomputer age *registers* (ledgers, files) were used to record and store data produced by measurements, and the term "register" is still more commonly used than the relatively new term "database." But databases are far better than registers.

What are the differences between registers and databases seen from the point of view of the nonspecialist? What are the consequences of these differences for accounting?

There are two very important general differences between the old form of registration and the new, both of which will have a major impact on the way in which we develop and use the accounting systems of the future. But let us consider the exact definitions of the basic concepts of registers and databases before discussing the differences between them.

1. A *register* (or a file) is a complete collection of data organized for use in a given task.
2. A *database* is the sum of registers in a system, stored and organized in such a way that the data can also be used for tasks that could not be identified when the system was originally constructed.

Registers are also known as files, archives and so forth. The word "file" really means a *systematic register*, and we are accustomed to seeing the word "register" used to refer to the physical location in which data can be found. Naturally, data carriers cannot necessarily be read by machines, although this is often the case. Registers may be kept manually, consisting of ordinary notes written on a sheet of paper.

The unfortunate thing about registers is that they always *tie information down to the form that has been chosen*. The data contained by registers is organized in advance for use in a given task, which naturally means that it is not organized for use in any other task. We use the expression *dedicated registers* to illustrate this close tie with the task in question, for which the register concerned was constructed. As a result, even when registers contain data that can be read by machines it is often difficult and therefore time consuming to arrange such data for use in different tasks. And if the data contained by a register cannot be read by machine, its application to different tasks becomes so time consuming that in practice it is impossible to use such data for any other task than the task for which it was intended.

In other words, registers are traditionally used *to consider and perform individual tasks for individual users*, neglecting or ignoring (without meaning to do so) any connection to other users or other tasks. As long as our technology is limited, our imagination is also often limited.

But databases consist of *all the registers in a system*, and are therefore the location of *all the systematically registered data of organizations*. Using refined data addressing technology, information is now stored in electronic data carriers in such a way that double storage, or the copying of registers, is no longer necessary. Computer scientists regard the double storage of data as being *redundant*.

In traditional registration techniques, the double storage of data is highly necessary but also very inconvenient. In order to process a given case using the same basic data in more than one place, copying from the original register has always been necessary, followed by distribution of the copies to the users concerned. Problems arise whenever any of the register copies are updated with new information, because when this happens all the other copies immediately become out-of-date. Users can no longer be certain that their copies contain up-to-date information describing the current situation, and this uncertainty is a major problem in practice. Users cannot be certain that the data at their disposal is 100 percent valid. Naturally, attempts are made to update the original register frequently, and to distribute new, updated register copies on a regular basis. But this only makes the problem less acute by reducing the probability that users are working with out-of-date data. It does not solve the problem of redundancy.

Everyone agrees that quick, competent and reliable processing of data is a vital aspect of all administration, so it is clear that the double storage of data presents a very serious practical problem. It has always been extremely difficult to use a system containing redundancy, but in the past it has been impossible to solve the problem.

The basic idea of databases is that *any given data should only be stored in one physical location*, and the same basic data is used and updated at the same time in all the situations in which it is required. Data is not *copied* in databases, it is *structured*.

We can now clearly see the apparent strength and latent weakness of traditional registers. Registers are often regarded as efficient tools to solve primary tasks, but unfortunately as being difficult or even impossible to use in solving any other tasks. Registers are dedicated to the solution of specific tasks, and will thus remain closed and inaccessible to anyone apart from their own primary users.

We have now mentioned two important differences between registers and databases, and can proceed to describe these differences and discuss the consequences for the world of accounting.

The first important difference is the number of tasks that can be solved using the data registered. *Registers* permit and justify the solution of only *a single primary task*, whereas *databases* also permit and justify the solution of *several coordinated tasks*. The second important difference is the number of users able to use the information available at the same time. Traditional technology is typically designed for one user at a time, whereas modern information and communication technology allows in principle any number of users access to the same data at the same time.

What does all this mean for the world of accounting?

It is immediately apparent that financial statements drawn up on the basis of double entry bookkeeping have the same form as that of dedicated registers. In the chapter on traditional accounting registration, we pointed out that double entry bookkeeping provided registers of customers and suppliers that were highly suitable for the control of payments because the current balance of individual customers and suppliers was evident at any time. Bookkeepers whose job it is to control claims, debts and payments naturally feel that this system works perfectly. Double entry bookkeeping, with its dedicated registers and good data reliability, is regarded as a strong and useful tool by all its primary users.

But the fact is that this method of organizing data has significant weaknesses whenever data has to be used for tasks other than the control of payments. Everyone is aware of these weaknesses in practice, but it seems as if an invisible wall has been erected between bookkeepers and managers.

Bookkeepers have never been able to give managers a clear impression of the financial facts. Dedicated registers make it possible to keep the balance up-to-date, and to make predictions of payment precisely for individual customers or suppliers, but they do not permit overall predictions of payments for all customers and suppliers to be made.

Over the years, many business managers have asked the following question, and wondered why it was impossible to obtain an immediate answer: "How much do our customers owe us at the moment, and how much do we owe to others?" Another way of posing this question is "What is our overall financial position *right now?*"

When managers say "right now" they mean that there is a situation, a risk or a chance that makes it necessary *right now* to ask questions and get the answers, to discuss and consider, *to calculate financial consequences* and *to act.* It is not easy for managers to wait for an answer until some time next month.

Using double entry bookkeeping as a system of registration and traditional technology as a tool, it is impossible to obtain an immediate answer to the question about the current financial situation. This answer has to wait until the presentation of a financial statement. And when the answer is finally available at the end of the period concerned, it is no longer relevant because the question is no longer relevant. If managers forget that they ever asked the question, it is hardly surprising that they are startled when the answer is finally presented. Reading financial reports that are out-of-date is like reading newspapers that are several weeks or months old. The news they contain is no longer important. Bookkeepers only succeed in irritating managers, and all their carefully drawn up, precise financial reports are regarded as containing nothing but irrelevant information.

The closed and dedicated nature of double entry bookkeeping may well be the basic reason why bookkeepers, accounts managers and accountants all over the world have always found themselves in the unfortunate situation that whenever managers ask them financial questions they are unable to answer, and when they finally believe themselves capable of supplying an answer, managers are no longer interested in asking them the questions concerned.

Technological developments and an improvement in the ratio between price and hardware capability now give us the tools needed to solve this problem. Whereas registers are *dedicated,* databases are *general.* In other words, databases are intended to perform several tasks simultaneously. Registers contain financial statements that are *closed systems,* but databases and modern communication technology enable us to consider the financial statements of the future as *open systems.* In databases specific information intended for specific tasks, as well as more general information, will always be accessible simultaneously for both producers and users of financial statements.

Previously, we pointed out that general information about the current financial situation was relatively uncomplicated in terms of its form. It simply consists of totals and balances based on individual accounting items. The only requirement in order to present this general information, which is so important for managers, is that basic data must always be available, and that rapid and reliable calculations can always be carried out. And naturally, computers are excellent at performing this task.

The development of computers means that an answer to the question "What is our overall financial position *right now?*" is no longer delayed due to technical reasons. And we shall now demonstrate that there are no theoretical reasons for delaying this vital answer, either, thanks to the new basic concept known as *the dynamic account*. The definition of this concept is as follows:

The dynamic account is a description of an individual project divided into stages, with associated logical rules covering the successive contributions of individual stages to the financial statements of enterprises.

In other words, the dynamic account is the measuring tool with algorithms needed *to describe and calculate the financial consequences of the actions of organizations at any time.*

The basic philosophy on which the dynamic account is based is illustrated in figure 14.1, where the financial consequences of a single action are shown as a summary of four and only four logical situations. The left-hand side of the figure shows the names of these logical states *in general*, and the right-hand side shows them *specifically* as examples of the kind of tangible documentation that is evident in the real world. Naturally, other specific names are possible, but it is important to note *that the new theory is equally applicable in both public and private sectors.*

Figure 14.1 classifies the four payment situations that make up the new system of accounting for management. Classifications must always meet three different requirements in order to be of scientific value, and these three requirements also apply here:

1. *Classifications must be exhaustive.* In other words, there must be no information about payments outside the categories given. All

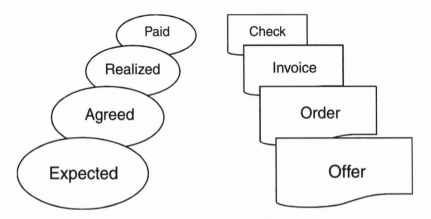

Figure 14.1. The dynamic account, general and specific.

information about payments as the consequences of actions must be contained in the expressions "expected," "agreed," "realized" (i.e., claimed) and "paid" (i.e., effected). There must be no information about payments other than this.

2. *The categories must be disjunctive.* In other words, it must *not* be possible to place information about specific payments and combinations of such information in more than one category.

3. *Classification must be based on measurable properties.* The concepts of *time* and *money* are expressed as scales of measurement. Information about payments must be specified in terms of both time and money in order to meet this requirement.

We remind readers of figure 13.3 in chapter 13. "Agreed" is always regarded as a subcategory of "expected," and "realized" and "paid" as subcategories of "agreed." Readers may find it advantageous to consider the possible combinations of meaningful statements once again. Some people may object that customer orders are occasionally received without being expected, and that agreements are thus not always expected. But the counterargument to this is that from the moment the agreement is reached neither of the parties concerned can claim that the financial consequences of the agreement are unexpected.

Readers will observe that figure 14.1 incorporates the concept of time. If we regard the figure as a description of the financial consequences of a specific action, we can see that time separates the four financial points of measurement from each other. A sense of perspective is used in the figure to emphasize that time is included. Both accounting specialists and nonspecialists should consider this point carefully. The ability to include time when systematically describing the financial consequences of our actions may well prove to be of decisive importance.

Let us imagine that figure 14.1 describes the processing of a typical sales order in a medium-sized company in which the various administrative functions (purchasing, production, sales, and so on) are divided into separate departments. In such companies, different individuals deal with different financial points of measurement.

The manager deals with the points of measurement known as "expected" and "agreed," because it is the manager who negotiates terms with customers and makes offers. It is also the manager who enters into agreements, thereby binding the seller and buyer to their mutual obligation to fulfill the agreement and pay for the goods or services received respectively. The term "manager" simply means the person who has responsibility.

But of course it is not the manager but *the bookkeeper* who generally deals with the financial point of measurement known as "realized," and it is *the treasurer* who deals with the financial point of measurement known as "paid." It is now apparent that different people become aware of the financial consequences of the same action at different times. Although the order being considered is the same, the successive descriptions of various financial consequences have different names, as shown in figure 14.1.

The manager must work out an offer before an agreement can be reached, and the bookkeeper and treasurer are naturally forced to wait until an agreement has been reached before the rules of traditional double entry bookkeeping can be applied in the form of registration of an invoice, and in due course a check.

Our new theory of accounting is based on this fundamentally simple series of events. Of course there are differences between offers, orders, invoices and payments. Of course different employees have different tasks to perform, and of course these employees become aware of the financial consequences at different times. But they will all agree that the same action is involved, even though the financial consequences of this action are being considered from different points of view and at different times. This is the kind of insight that can help us towards a new understanding of financial statements as a logically complete system of information. The essence of the new system is that we should *book decisions*. We should describe the financial consequences in a financial statement at the time at which decisions become binding or irreversible. And this occurs when the decision is no longer expected but agreed—and therefore binding.

The dynamic account is a general descriptive tool, a tool with no exceptions. With regard to *all* actions with financial consequences, it is true to say that these consequences can be described as a summary of four and only four financial points of measurement. Readers can test the truth of this assertion by applying their own insight into the ways in which expectations, agreements, deliveries and payments are documented in practice for the actions known as sales, purchases and employment of staff. Is it true to say that information about financial consequences is always available within an organization, and that this information is virtually always available in dedicated subsystems?

Are readers familiar with the term "personal" or "individual" accounts? This term can be applied to the kind of informal information systems that bright, inventive managers in both private and public sectors invent and keep out of sheer desperation. Readers who are aware of the existence of such individual systems kept on spreadsheets or on a piece of paper in the drawer will be able to argue convincingly in favor of the claim that traditional financial statements do not meet the requirements of managers in the real world. The important information is not formalized, and the formalized information is often not at all important.

In practice of course, descriptions of financial consequences will always be more complex and thus harder to understand than the simple picture shown in figure 14.1. When an agreement is reached it is generally necessary to consider several different financial factors, so calculations are made to describe these factors.

We have used the expression "manager" several times in this chapter, explaining that we regard managers simply as people who have responsibility. In other words, managers are not gods. They are not able to gaze into a crystal ball and predict future events with any accuracy.

On the contrary, we shall seek to regard management as a process, and to regard this process as being connected with personal responsibility. People who perform specific actions with financial consequences for organizations, or who commit others to perform such actions, are managers in the sense that we intend to use here. For us, managers are *project leaders* or *people with responsibility*, not mythical figures with mythical powers. Let us repeat the following definition: "Responsible managers are managers who know or who should know the consequences of their actions. Financially responsible managers are managers who know or who should know the financial consequences of their actions."

Financial consequences, of course, become binding on the parties concerned at the moment an agreement is reached. The seller undertakes to deliver, and the buyer undertakes to pay. The point of measurement known as "agreed" should thus be included systematically in basic registration, alongside the two other points of measurement known as "realized" and "paid."

Readers may recall that in chapter 5 we pointed out that the basic registration carried out by merchants, that is, the actual *measurement* of financial consequences, took place *chronologically* in a journal, whereas the transition to a *systematic* description of financial consequences was achieved using debit-credit bookkeeping and the familiar T-shaped account. It is important to note that the data describing the financial consequences of actions is already available when chronological measurement is carried out. Bookkeeping gives rise to information but no new basic data, and the functions performed by double entry bookkeeping can thus be regarded simply as a type of data processing. Familiar, traditional bookkeeping can simply be regarded as program-controlled copying and organization of information that is already available in a register. So it is the chronological measurement of financial consequences that is important, since this is what makes up the database. The rest simply consists of data processing and data communication.

The problem of chronological descriptions is that they are not always easy to understand, and that they make an overall picture hard to achieve. Registers contain several different logical types of information, which makes it difficult for readers to retain an overall picture of the connection between profitability and liquidity. Let us now try to solve this problem by recalling a figure contained in chapter 5. Figure 14.2 shows us once again the basic notation used in double entry bookkeeping, with the two systematic financial points of measurement known as "realized" and "paid."

R-Day	T-No.	Description of Transaction	P-Day	$
1	1	Buy on credit from merchant A	11	− 10
1	2	Cash sale	1	20
1	3	Cash purchase	1	− 10
2	4	Buy on credit from merchant B	12	− 25
4	5	Sale on credit to customer C	15	40
4	6	Sale on credit to customer D	20	30

Figure 14.2.   A register with two financial points of measurement.

Readers may recall that this was the register containing the chronological transactions of a business trip that we used in chapter 5 to describe the pure itemization technique of double entry bookkeeping and the achievement of a realized result of 45. Double entry bookkeeping showed us the financial *result* of an individual business trip or of several business trips within a specific period in the form of the difference between income and expenses. But *the general picture of liquidity was lost* owing to adherence to what we call "the prison of the fixed account." The primary and reasonable requirement for the precise control of each individual debtor and creditor makes a dedicated system inevitable, keeping information at a level of detail that suits bookkeepers and treasurers, but that does not please managers because the use of the fixed account makes it impossible to obtain an overall picture of the current situation.

Let us now try to regard our register in figure 14.2 as a database in order to demonstrate that all the basic data necessary and sufficient to describe liquidity is already present in the register. We need no additional registration in order to gain a simultaneous, coordinated general picture of the result and liquidity. All we need is the ability to organize the same basic data in several different ways at the same time. This has not been possible in the past because data processing techniques have been too simple.

The register in figure 14.3 is a subregister of figure 14.2 in which certain unnecessary information has been removed to allow sufficient space. We shall now use the term "P-Day" (agreed day of payment) as the new key to our information about payments. This will enable us to draw up the list shown in figure 14.4, which shows us the liquidity contribution or financing requirements of a business trip over time. We recall that the actual register has day four as its closing date.

The two concepts *liquidity contribution* (LC) and *financing requirement* (FR) have not been mentioned until now, and so a brief comment about them is necessary. The two concepts basically express the same thing, although each has its own plus or minus sign. If we say that at a given time a certain situation will produce a liquidity contribution, we mean that the situation results in an increase of liquidity in the enterprise concerned. On

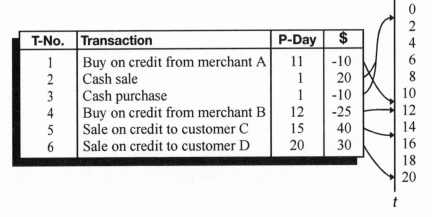

Figure 14.3. The structure of the register as a prediction of payments.

the other hand, if payments are required at a certain time due to the situation in question, we say that the situation has a financing requirement.

The two concepts of liquidity contribution (LC) and financing requirement (FR) are calculated and shown in figure 14.4. A positive liquidity contribution at any time is the same as a negative financing requirement, and vice versa.

It is worth noting that the two expressions "liquidity contribution" and "financing requirement" are both *dynamic*. They only have meaning if time is incorporated. The liquidity contribution or financing requirement of a given situation can only be described using a string of data containing a chronological number of statements about payments.

Let us briefly consider figure 14.4, which contains a prediction of payments and thus also the possibility of predicting the suspension of payments. We recall that the business trip that we have used to produce our data finished on day four, so it is clear that the register enables us to make a reliable prediction of payments lasting until the final agreed payment

P-Day	T-No.	Transaction	$	LC	FR
1	2	Cash sale	20	20	– 20
1	3	Cash purchase	– 10	10	– 10
11	1	Buy on credit	– 10	00	00
12	4	Buy on credit	– 25	– 25	25
15	5	Sale on credit	40	15	– 15
20	6	Sale on credit	30	45	– 45

Figure 14.4. Prediction of liquidity contribution and financing requirement.

date, which in our example is day 20. The example also shows that our merchant can predict that he will have a financing requirement of 25 on day twelve, a requirement he must cover in good time to avoid disappointing his creditors and losing credibility in the eyes of these creditors.

Figure 14.4 also shows us that the business trip will produce a total liquidity contribution of 45 once all payments have been made, and we note that the size of the liquidity contribution is identical with the realization result that double entry bookkeeping produced.

Once again we can confirm the truth of the statement "Information about profitability and information about changes in liquidity is information about the same thing."

We have already seen that the two pairs of concepts in double entry bookkeeping have a logical connection with our two systematic financial points of measurement. At the point of measurement known as "paid" we use the concepts of payments received (I_p) and payments made (U_p) to describe the *payment result* of any period:

$$R_p\,(T) = \sum_{t\,=\,0}^{T} (I_p(t) - U_p(t))$$

And at the point of measurement known as "realized" we use the concepts of income/expenses to describe the *realization result* of the same period:

$$R_r\,(T) = \sum_{t\,=\,0}^{T} (I_r(t) - U_r(t)) - d(r,p)$$

The reason why the realization result is regarded as reliable is (as already mentioned) that an income can be regarded as a reliable prediction of payment received, and an expense as a reliable prediction of payment made.

So the realization result for any period is a reliable contribution helping to predict the payment result of any future period.

But even the agreement provides reliable information about future payments. An agreement about a deal is a reliable prediction of payment, too.

So a third concept can be added to the two periodic result concepts of double entry bookkeeping, describing the same period. This third concept is known as the *decision result*:

$$R_a\,(T) = \sum_{t\,=\,0}^{T} (I_a(t) - U_a(t)) - d(r,p) - d(a,r)$$

The decision result, which is based on the agreed payments received for a period (I_a) minus the agreed payments made for the same period (U_a), contains the following two types of prediction error:

1. $d(r,p)$: prediction error in the interval "realized"-"paid"
2. $d(a,r)$: prediction error in the interval "agreed"-"realized"

The realization result only contains the prediction error $d(r,p)$, and the payment result contains no prediction errors at all.

Readers may remember our example of a medieval merchant being able to predict his future payments by using a loose-leaf system consisting of bills and acceptances, allowing time consuming changes to be made in the system whenever there were changes in basic data. We have already mentioned that this simple calculation logic, the object of which was predictions of payments, and which was regarded at the time as a logically complete information system, was considered to represent an enormous progressive step.

The organization of data and calculations and recalculations when there were changes or errors used to be so time consuming that in practice people refrained from performing these tasks. But modern information technology now enables us to carry out this organization and calculation swiftly and reliably using computers, and the programs used to control the computers can be designed in advance.

The logical incompleteness of the old information system can also be remedied using the new accounting theory. If we include agreements as a systematic financial point of measurement, we can add a third periodic result concept to the two concepts already in existence in double entry bookkeeping, a third result that is necessary in order to make an early, reliable and logically complete prediction of future payments, thereby enabling us to predict any incipient suspension of these payments.

Figure 14.5 contains a list of six purchase and sale agreements. In addition to the three financial points of measurement known as "agreed," "realized" and "paid," the list contains an ongoing list of transaction numbers, a verbal transaction description, and finally the figure that must be paid as a consequence of the agreement about the transaction concerned. It is worth noting that certain highly inconvenient but previously obligatory limitations in the description (coincidence in time between agreement and realization, cash payment) have now been removed. We note that transaction no. 4

A-Day	T-No.	Transaction	R-Day	P-Day	$
1	1	Sale to customer A	10	14	40
1	2	Buy from supplier B	7	9	-40
2	3	Buy from supplier C	6	10	-25
4	4	Buy from supplier D	4	18	-30
4	5	Sale to customer E	7	15	50
5	6	Sale to customer F	12	12	60

Figure 14.5. Chronological and systematic measurement of agreements, basic form.

describes a situation in which goods are delivered in connection with and simultaneously with the agreement, since the agreement and realization dates are identical. We can also see that transaction no. 6 describes a sale in return for payment in cash. The realization and payment dates are identical—delivery and payment must both take place on day twelve.

If we now consider this list at a time immediately after it has been completed (i.e., on day five), it is easy to see that the data structure shown in figure 14.5 contains the necessary and sufficient data to allow us to make predictions of both delivery and payment. This applies to individual transactions, to several connected transactions (business trips, projects, and so on) and *thus also in general to all transactions in any given period*. The chronological and systematic registration of agreements enables us at any time to obtain a general picture of future actions, since predictions of both delivery of and payment for goods and services can be made. In addition, it will be possible to make an early and clear prediction of payments. Modern technology enables managers to demand constant access to an updated overall picture of payments showing the patterns of cash flows in the immediate future. This picture will enable managers to consider both individual situations and the overall situation, and to predict whether extra liquidity is present in the form of reliable predictions of payment received, or whether predictions of payment made are present, such as a financing requirement that must be covered in good time.

Let us briefly comment upon what we shall call *the control of actions*, which is also known as production control, distribution, logistics and other names. Figure 14.5 gives us immediate access to the data needed to form the following two types of prediction of actions. *The receipt of goods* can be expected on days six and seven, and *the dispatch of goods* can be expected on days seven, ten and twelve. These predictions can be made reliably already in the evening of day five.

Hopefully, this small example will have convinced readers that the basic registration form of our new accounting theory can be related easily to previous theories and methods used to control the physical resources of organizations. But *financial* control is the focus of our attention here, so we shall now abandon logistics and turn our attention once more to predictions of payments.

Figure 14.3 showed that the register can contain a prediction of payments, and that this prediction can be made by using a database and a calculation program. However, we also saw that the prediction of payments in figure 14.3 was logically incomplete. We can now present an agreement-based prediction of payments using the data shown in figure 14.5. Our starting point is the financial point of measurement known as "agreed," but otherwise we shall adopt the same procedure as in figure 14.3 and 14.4. Readers may like to carry out the calculation for themselves, and then compare their results with figure 14.6.

P-Day	T-No.	Transaction	$	LC	FR
9	2	Buy from supplier B	−20	−20	20
10	3	Buy from supplier C	−25	−45	45
12	6	Sale to customer F	60	15	−15
14	1	Sale to customer A	40	55	−55
15	5	Sale to customer E	50	105	−105
18	4	Buy from supplier D	−30	75	−75

Figure 14.6. Agreement-based prediction of payments.

Once again, figure 14.6 confirms the theory that information about financial results and information about changes in liquidity is information about the same thing. The result of the business trip involving six sale and purchase transactions is 75, and this 75 is seen as a liquidity contribution at the end of the period in question. The end of the period is the last day, day 18.

But a prediction of payments can be made as early as the evening of day five. And the *decision result* (75 in our example) of a project or period is an entirely new accounting concept, to which readers may need time to grow accustomed. The two other result concepts, however, are as familiar as double entry bookkeeping itself, since they are inextricably linked to the logic of this system.

In order to assist the reader's understanding of this new concept, let us now imagine three key figures—a treasurer, a bookkeeper and a manager. The treasurer looks after the cash holdings and thus fulfills the role of supervisor at the financial point of measurement known as "paid." The bookkeeper keeps an eye on outstanding claims and debts, fulfilling the role of supervisor at the point of measurement known as "realized." Finally, the manager reaches agreements with customers and suppliers, and can be regarded as fulfilling the role of supervisor at the point of measurement known as "agreed."

Let us now ask the decisive question with regard to financial control. "*When* do the three people involved know anything about the financial consequences of the actions shown in figure 14.5?" The question can be made more specific by asking "How much do the treasurer and bookkeeper know about the financial consequences of the actions in figure 14.5 in the evening of day five?"

The answer is simple. *The treasurer knows nothing*, since her information system has not yet registered any trace of the six purchase and sale transactions. The payment associated with transaction no. 2 will not be visible in the payment account until day nine, as the first of six payments. So the treasurer is entirely ignorant of the financial situation in the evening of day five.

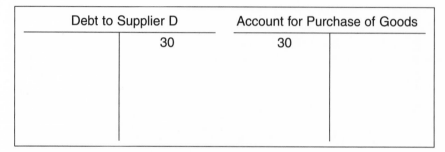

Figure 14.7. The bookkeeper's limited knowledge

So how much does the bookkeeper know? He is not as ignorant as the treasurer, but *his knowledge is incomplete.* The answer to the question about the bookkeeper's knowledge of the financial situation is that in the evening of day five he can only have registered the items shown in figure 14.7.

The only transaction shown in figure 14.6 that has been realized and that can thus be invoiced on day five is transaction no. 4, which shows a purchase of 30. So the only information about the business trip that is apparent in traditional double entry bookkeeping concerns the consequences of this action. The other five transactions at the time in question are still invisible to the bookkeeper, since they have not yet been realized.

This gives a clear and very realistic impression of the effect of the logical incompleteness of double entry bookkeeping. If the bookkeeper is asked on day five to give a general picture of the financial situation of the enterprise, he simply cannot do so.

But *the manager* is not ignorant. *He has been party to all six agreements, so he also knows the financial consequences of each agreement, and he can document this by using his register of agreements.* His only problem is that after registering the six individual transactions he has entirely lost any overall picture of payments, so he needs data processing and a system of logic capable of controlling this data processing to provide the overall picture he needs. Decision and control accounts have the logic he needs. With the new theory as a tool, and with the chronological and systematic registration of agreements as his basic data, *the manager possesses the necessary and sufficient information to draw a picture showing both the result and the financial situation* in the form of a summary of future payments, thereby providing an up-to-date and reliable impression of his company's finances. This picture can be drawn for a single "business trip" or for several such trips or projects, so a general picture of the financial position and future payments is available at any time. And if this is possible for the manager in our example, it is possible for all managers. Some people may claim that our examples are simplistic and therefore misleadingly straightforward, and that in practice accounting systems are far more complex. But as we have already pointed out, the presence of large amounts of data and complex systems does not in itself mean that the new theory cannot be applied in general. Even large amounts of data consist of items, and individual items are never more complex in principle than the examples shown here.

The aim of this chapter has been to show readers that the new logic of registration can help accounting specialists to gain something without losing anything. The basic registration and data processing techniques of double entry bookkeeping have not been abandoned. They have simply been expanded to produce a new and better basic system of accounting.

NOTES

1. J. Witt-Hansen, *Filosofi*, p. 109.
2. Ibid., p. 104.

15 THE LOGIC AND ELEMENTS OF SOLVENCY

Understand the reasons, and you can do without the experience.

—*Leonardo da Vinci*

At any given time or within any given period, enterprises are either solvent or insolvent. This means that the pair of concepts solvency/insolvency expresses a logical whole consisting of two complementary parts. Until now, solvency—and in particular insolvency—have been invisible in financial statements. But they are certainly not invisible in real life. The terrible problem of invisibility can now be solved, and in the future solvency and insolvency can be described systematically in financial statements, making it possible to produce a reliable picture of an enterprise's solvency at any given time. Naturally, solvency changes constantly. This means that it can only be shown by using a system of management accounting that also changes constantly, producing a picture that changes constantly from item to item. Any description of solvency is based on a few familiar basic concepts, but these concepts are placed in a new context in this chapter.

In chapter 14 we described *the prediction of payments based on agreements*. We saw that such predictions are logically simple and easy to understand, and that they can be made both for individual projects and for organizations as a whole. The overall picture can be formed using an algorithm—with the computer carrying out a program-controlled combination of predictions of payments for all agreements reached. Each purchase or sale has financial consequences that are binding as soon as agreements are reached. This is the same as *predicting a financing requirement* if the consequence of the event concerned turns out to be payments that have to be made, and the same as *predicting a contribution to liquidity* if the consequence of the event concerned turns out to be payments that will be received. This makes it possible *to systematically predict the suspension of payments*. Payments are suspended if and when an enterprise's financing requirement at any time is greater than its ability to pay, which the management can demonstrate by using the enterprise's liquidity reserves and agreed drawing options on various credits and loans.

Readers may notice that the following two expressions are different, but that in reality they mean the same. "Financing requirements" and "capital requirements" are synonyms, as are "financing" and "capital employed." Let us try to express this more precisely. We talk about a financing requirement or capital requirement that can be predicted when the payments needed to cover purchases of production resources, goods and services at any given time are greater than the payments received following an enterprise's sale of production resources, goods and services. To prevent the suspension of payments, sufficient financing or capital employed must be acquired in the form of the enterprise's own savings, loans or risk capital injected by investors.

A *negative financing requirement* at any time or in any period reflects the fact that an enterprise is earning money. The enterprise creates a liquidity contribution, generates net liquidity, and thus finds it possible to repay loans, pay dividend to stockholders, finance future purchases, or increase its payment capability by refraining from tying up money in new purchases, and by keeping liquid reserves available for use in current accounts or securities that are easily negotiable instead.

We shall not attempt an in-depth analysis of all the many different ways of practical financing, since that would be beyond the scope of this book. We shall merely point out that there is a comprehensive theory of financing and risk, which can be used alongside the new theory of accounting outlined here. We also know that there is a well-organized and dynamic capital market that offers many different forms of practical financing. We shall not deal with the way capital is employed in detail. Our aim is to find *a reliable and dynamic description of solvency*, so we shall focus on the prediction of capital requirements.

Figure 15.1 is a simple but precise model showing the ongoing interaction between an enterprise and its environment. The financial consequences of this interaction can be described accurately as a finite number of observable (and thus measurable) payment transactions. In fact there are only six different types of payment.

We distinguish between payments made and payments received, and then between payments that concern the following aspects of an enterprise's operation:

1. plant and operations (capital requirement)
2. financing (capital employed)
3. taxes, duties and subsidies

Naturally, *payments received for plant and operations* primarily involve payments by customers arising from sales of the enterprise's normal products and services. But the distinction between plant and operations that is traditionally made in financial statements is in fact artificial. No one can provide logically convincing criteria for the distinction. So we shall abandon the attempt to distinguish between fixed assets and current assets, because no resources last forever, and all resources will be either used or converted eventually. The sale of machines and other parts of an enterprise's development and production resources is identical with the sale of "normal" products and services. Any purchases made by customers using the enterprise concerned as a supplier are sales. *All sales are identical with liquidity contributions*, and in this connection it does not matter whether the object or service being sold is an office chair, the repair of a machine, or an entire subsidiary.

All sales are identical with new predictions of payments received. New predictions of payments received increase the assets of an enterprise. So *all sales affect solvency positively*.

Similarly, *payments made for plant and operations* comprise the entire acquisition of goods, services and development and production capacity. Employees thus become suppliers of services that it would otherwise be necessary to buy from other enterprises, and investments are identical with ordinary purchases of goods. *All purchases are identical with financial requirements*, no matter whether the object or service being bought is an

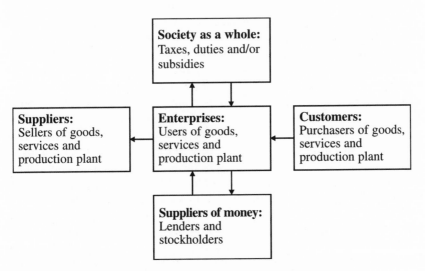

Figure 15.1.   The exchange of energy seen as a flow of payments.

office chair, the repair of a machine, or an entire subsidiary. All purchases are identical with new predictions of payments that will have to be made. New predictions of payments made increase the liabilities of an enterprise or reduce its assets. So *all purchases affect solvency negatively.*

Payments received in the form of financing are either loans or injections of so-called risk capital. Lenders pay an agreed sum of money to the enterprise concerned, which thus increases its assets in the form of its payment capability. But lenders require the payment of interest in return for making the money available, and not surprisingly they also expect the loan itself to be repaid at the agreed time. So loans are naturally identical with an agreement about future payments that have to be made by the enterprise; in other words, they increase the enterprise's debts. *Loans affect solvency both positively and negatively.*

Subordinated loan capital (generally consisting of stock and share capital plus retained earnings) is placed at the disposal of an enterprise in the form of risk capital, which means that investors buy the right to receive future dividend and to help make decisions about the enterprise's development. Should future profits in the form of net liquidity be paid as dividend to stockholders, or should they be used for the future development of the enterprise? Retained earnings, which are known under the misleading names of "owners' equity" or "stockholders' equity," run a great risk of being lost in the event of poor financial results, but running this risk also produces the best possible interest in the event of good financial results. Agreements concerning the injection of risk capital do *not* normally imply that the regular repayment of specific sums has been agreed. Repayments depend on the earnings made by the enterprise in future. Subordinated loan capital is like payments received that do not imply any agreed liability to make payments in the future. So *all retained earnings affect solvency positively.*

Payments related to financing comprise interest and installments paid to lenders, and dividend paid to investors of subordinated loan capital. Interest and installments are agreed in advance, so these payments affect solvency in two ways—*both debts (liabilities) and liquid holdings (assets) are reduced.*

Payments of dividend to stockholders affect solvency negatively. Such payments can be compared to "rewards" made in return for the involvement of other interested parties in the enterprise. The "calculated risk" now becomes evident in practice. If things go well the stockholders earn a lot of money, and if they go badly they lose their money. Some people regard active investments in projects as an opportunity, others see them as a risk. The same phenomenon is involved, but it can be evaluated differently.

Payments made by the enterprise to society in the form of taxes and duties, and *payments received by the enterprise from society* in the form of various sales, production and training subsidies are only included here for the sake of completeness. These flows of payment exist, of course, but we shall refrain from considering them here, even though our new accounting model enables us to calculate the tax due simply, accurately and without fear of any conflicts arising. The issue of taxation is extremely complex, and is best dealt with in collaboration with tax experts.

Figure 15.2 summarizes the six types of payment, after which we shall proceed with our systematic prediction of financing requirements and liquidity contributions, two concepts that are absolutely identical, apart from the fact that they have contrasting plus/minus signs in front of them. As we shall see in the rest of this chapter, these two concepts are very closely linked to the concept of solvency.

We have already emphasized that the new theory of accounting makes no distinction between "plant" and "operations," or between "ordinary" and "extraordinary" items. There is no valid reason for distinguishing between "current assets" and "fixed assets," nor is there any logical reason why some items should be defined as "extraordinary" and others as "ordinary." Readers will no doubt notice that the very word "ordinary" clearly reveals that the world described by traditional financial statements is regarded as being *orderly*, developing in stable and thus predictable fashion, in which most of the items in financial statements are "ordinary," and very few are "extraordinary." This attitude arises because traditional accounting theory regards enterprises as going concerns distinguished by their continuity, which is clearly a linear way of approaching accounting.

The new theory of accounting, on the other hand, is based on the expectation that *the world is not orderly and stable*. It is meaningless to talk of "ordinary" accounting items when constant and regular changes in internal and external circumstances are expected, and when predictability is not expected. The most important thing is the ability to monitor developments, to maneuver and survive in a changing world order, and this means that we need to be able to predict the financial consequences of our actions, even when we do not expect any order or predictability.

Types of Payment	Payments Received	Payments Made
Plant and operations = capital requirement	Sale and rental of resources, goods and services	Purchase and rental of resources, goods and services
Financing = capital employed	Interest, installments on loans, share dividend etc.	Interest, installments on loans, share dividend etc.
Payments to and from the public sector	Subsidies for production, training etc.	Tax and duty

Figure 15.2. Six types of payments received and made by enterprises.

In the new accounting theory all accounting items are "extraordinary." We no longer believe that enterprises are necessarily going concerns distinguished by their continuity. The only thing of which we can be sure is our terminology and the precise concepts we use. An expense is an expense, and an income is an income, irrespective of the source, size or reason connected with the amount concerned. Basically, all incomes and expenses are "extraordinary," because basically we must always be prepared for the lack of order.

But perhaps we should have faith in each other and the terminology we employ, and start to regard agreements as a reliable starting point for all predictions of payments. Even though we expect a lack of order and predictability in the world around us, it is still possible to predict the consequences of our actions, calculate the overall financial picture in the form of "total" predictions of payments and thus create an entirely new order out of the chaos.

As mentioned previously, the organization and combination of data containing information about payments produces *a dynamic picture of an enterprise's total agreed future financing requirements or liquidity contribution*. We also mentioned that in principle the basic data of this new picture can be registered at the time agreements are reached. The necessary calculations are carried out by computer, so they can be repeated quickly if there are any changes or additions. In other words, the overall financial picture can be kept up-to-date dynamically and constantly, so the management is no longer forced to wait for the financial information it needs. The agreed cash flow patterns of the future can be visible at any time.

The question now is "Have we solved the problem?" If we base predictions of payments on agreements, have we solved the problem of the logical incompleteness of double entry bookkeeping? Do agreement-based predictions of payments provide us with a logically complete description of the financial consequences of the actions of enterprises? Predictions of payments based on agreements contain all the information of double entry bookkeeping in the form of the points of measurement known as "realized" and "paid," as well as systematically including the new point of measurement known as "agreed." Have we solved the problem?

The answer is "No, not yet." We still lack a logical category of information concerning future payments. Readers may remember that we dealt with four logical categories in chapter 13. The last remaining category is that of *expected* payments. In practice the arrangement of future payments made and received always involves *dealing with individual transactions*, and the special circumstances involved in most transactions mean that we cannot simply consider them to be straightforward. In practice, such transactions generally consist of a number of different types of information about payments.

Each transaction is a separate subsystem, which consists in practice of a number of related items of information concerning payments made and received. For instance, when a man with a retail clothing business buys clothes he agrees to make a payment when he places his order with the supplier. But he justifies this *agreed payment made* in terms of a number of *expected payments he will receive* when the goods are sold subsequently. His calculations have also convinced him that the expected payments received will be a good deal larger than the payment he agrees to make himself, because otherwise he would be a poor businessman. However, despite all the care in the world his calculation can never be entirely accurate, and in due course our businessman will discover the errors in prediction by comparing the *expected* and now *agreed* payments made with the *claims* and *payments received* as stated in his double entry bookkeeping. There are four different items of information about the payments in question.

So in practice there will always be four different types of information about payments. The use of agreement-based predictions of payments described in the previous chapter does not entirely solve our problem. We need to build up an information system that enables us to consider the financial consequences of each individual transaction in the form of related information about payments in the situations defined as "expected," "agreed," "realized" and "paid." But once this new, logical system of information has been established, the task we are trying to perform will have been completed. The accounting system that results will provide *a logically complete picture of the financial consequences of the actions of enterprises.*

Let us now repeat some of the basic concepts and subconclusions drawn in previous chapters, after which we shall continue the construction of our new system of concepts. The following definition was included in chapter 4:

Enterprises are solvent at a given time or within a given period when their assets are greater than or equal to their liabilities at the time concerned or at any time within the period concerned. And enterprises are insolvent when their liabilities exceed their assets.

We recall the comment that this definition is only valuable if the basic concepts of assets and liabilities have been defined clearly. In chapter 13 we stated that *a balance sheet is a system of information consisting of well-founded predictions of payments received and made, and of nothing else.* We can also repeat the definitions of assets and liabilities: *assets are well-founded predictions of payments received, and liabilities are well-founded predictions of payments made.*

When we incorporate these new basic definitions, the following new definition of solvency/insolvency can be reached:

Enterprises are solvent at a given time or within a given period when their predictions of payments received are greater than or equal to their predictions of payments made at the time concerned or at any time within the period concerned. And enterprises are insolvent when their predictions of payments made exceed their predictions of payments received.

We can now claim to have reached a scientifically reliable description of the key concepts of solvency/insolvency in the form of a logically *complete, consistent, necessary and sufficient* definition. This definition is made with a view to meeting requirements for empirical openness and falsification. In other words, anyone is welcome to try and refute the new definition, and it will have no value for any readers who succeed.

On behalf of the skeptics, let us now ask the following basic questions: In what way do the old and new theories differ from each other? How can anyone claim that we can now make rapid and convincing progress in accounting practice? What is the decisive factor that enables accounting specialists to construct a new, reliable and dynamic accounting model, and thereby recover the lost connection between their profession and the real world?

The conclusive answer to these questions is that the basic, previously poorly defined accounting concepts of assets and liabilities can now be defined precisely as well-founded predictions of payments received and well-founded predictions of payments made, and as nothing else. We have already pointed out that in order to define anything as an asset or liability, information about future payments received or made must be involved. We also pointed out that if fulfilled, this condition was sufficient.

Readers probably recall that in chapter 13 we described the problem using two logical factors that only coincided partially. We viewed the problem as a conflict between relevance and tradition. Some of the procedures of traditional accounting are irrelevant, and many relevant procedures are not yet traditional. Progress lies in the possibility of combining these two logical factors in the near future. Future accounting traditions can be made to consist of relevant procedures, and all new relevant procedures can be made interesting to accounting specialists. In the future, accountancy can be made into an open, dynamic and unbiased profession. This, regrettably, is not the case at the moment.

The new balance sheet model brings all managers face to face with a simple, general and easily understood *demand for responsibility* whenever they buy anything, thereby committing their enterprise to make future payments and affecting solvency negatively. All investments, lease contracts, staff appointments and purchases must be justified using one of the following three arguments. There are no others.

1. I buy these goods or services because they have already been ordered by a customer. The purchase is registered as an agreed purchase, which forms part of the calculation of what we shall earn on order X. This order is registered as an agreed sale. The reason for the purchase is our wish to supply what the customer has ordered and thus realize the liquidity contribution that the order will result in when and if we deliver, and when and if the customer pays.

2. I buy these goods or services because I expect to be able to sell them at a profit by time *t* at the latest. The purchase is registered as an agreed purchase, and an expected future sale is registered at the same time, which forms part of the calculation of what we shall earn on purchase order X, and is thus part of the reason why we are buying these goods or services now. The reason for the purchase is to obtain a prediction of the liquidity contribution that will appear when and if the customer places an order, when and if we deliver and when and if the customer pays.

3. I buy these goods and services because I expect them to be used by my own enterprise. The purchase is registered as an agreed purchase, and no corresponding source of income or other assets is registered. If the goods, services or machine are expected to produce a profit when sold, this expected sales value can be entered in a special register along with information regarding the time the sale is expected to take. The information about the expected sales price and sales deadline should be revised frequently. However, the reason for the purchase is not subsequent sale, but the wish to develop new products, new ways of meeting customer requirements. We wish to plan for the future. Our enterprise can only survive and grow if we can create the liquidity contributions of the future. This will happen when and if we can offer our customer a new and up-to-date product, when and if the customer places an order, when and if we deliver and when and if the customer pays.

Readers will note that the three basic reasons for purchasing goods and services are expressed in colloquial language. No special terms are needed, apart from "financing requirement" and "liquidity contribution," terms with which readers should be familiar by now. All three reasons are expressed in the form of predictions. The future and the uncertainty are both visible. The reasons are viewed as descriptions of future actions that can be performed, not as the results of speculation and rituals involving figures. One of the criteria for the scientific validity of definitions is that they describe the concepts in question in terms of actions that can be performed.

The immediate advantage of this new accounting terminology is its clarity and simplicity. The accounting picture, which previously seemed to comprise "complicated" and "strange" special terminology, and which was thus impossible to understand, is now simple, clear and easy to understand for everyone.

So here is our new acid test: *Financial statements or partial financial statements have real information value when and if they describe the financial consequences of actions that can be performed.*

This is also the necessary and sufficient condition for auditing financial statements. The auditing of financial statements is the same as testing both their formal and real reliability. Such tests are only possible if a description of the financial consequences of actions is involved. Without a scientific foundation, it is not possible to discuss responsibility for financial statements and financial issues meaningfully.

The condition just named, which has to be fulfilled if financial statements are to be reliable, is rarely met in practice. Many so-called plans, budgets, projects and prospectuses contain descriptions of the future that are essentially forecasts based on more or less sophisticated processing of old accounting data. In other cases pure guesswork or estimation is used, often involving wishful thinking. Such figures are rarely worth the paper they are written on because they have no real information value. This applies irrespective of the nature and size of the financial statements involved, irrespective of the size of the investments in question, and naturally irrespective of the number of signatures attached. Unless the material is carefully worked out, and unless it describes both actions and payments, it will be unreliable as a description of financial consequences.

The third reason for purchasing goods and services includes future payments made, but not future payments received to set off against purchases. The two first reasons for purchasing goods and services are clearly connected with future payments received, which may not actually occur simultaneously, but which will be greater than the payments made in both cases. In other words, the two first reasons for purchasing goods and services are based on a straightforward expectation of *profitability*: "This purchase will undoubtedly be a good transaction for us, because the income involved is greater than the expense, and this income will soon appear in the form of payment."

This third reason only contains a statement about the expense involved. Accounting specialists may feel that something is missing, and may ask where is the corresponding and simultaneous statement about future payments received that makes it possible to view the third reason as concerned with profitability, too. The answer is that there is no such statement, but that in many cases a statement is invented in such circumstances owing simply to wishful thinking and force of habit.

In chapter 11 we described how easy it is to lose one's way when making categorial a priori statements concerning the purpose of doing business. Readers may recall the view that the purpose of anything (teleological statements) only gives clear meaning if it, in the words of Bertrand Russell, is "within the bounds of the real world." We should now like to mention another attempt to define the purpose of doing business. The statement in question is extremely concrete, so it certainly lies within the bounds of the real world. It is derived from the well-known and hotly disputed "profit maximization objective." It is the postulate that the only purpose of doing business is to earn as much money as possible. This postulate has already been dealt with, and its limitations revealed.

Peter F. Drucker is a well-known and highly respected American theorist and management consultant. In *The Practice of Management* (1954) he describes the profit maximization objective as both *wrong* and *irrelevant*. And he continues as follows:

If we want to know what a business is we have to start with its purpose. And its purpose must lie outside of the business itself. In fact, it must lie in society since a business enterprise is an organ of society. There is only one valid definition of business purpose: *to create a customer.*[1]

The noticeable thing about Drucker's definition is that it is based on a description of an action that can be performed. But it is also noteworthy that the definition is clear and easy to understand, and that it is impossible to contradict. Managements that fail to ensure in the long term that income from sales is greater than expenses for purchases have undoubtedly demonstrated their inability (or the inability of their enterprises) to survive in the changeable world of today.

Virtually all enterprises experience *temporary positive capital requirements*. New enterprises and enterprises that are growing quickly are especially prone to experience positive capital requirements. The management must try to calculate these requirements and decide how to cover them by using money from outside sources. They may choose to borrow money from the bank or find sources of subordinated loan risk capital. But there is always an agreement or expectation that such payments made to enterprises will have to be paid back at a later date. This repayment will require the enterprise to make payments that in the long term will, of course, be larger than the original payments received. Naturally, people whose business is to lend money to others only do so in the expectation that they will receive interest on top of the original amount. Basically, stockholders have the same attitude. People who buy stock instead of lending their money to others have exactly the same expectation concerning the acquisition of interest, although naturally stock carries a greater risk of loss or opportunity for gain than loans.

In other words, managers are naturally expected to manage their enterprises in such a way that positive capital requirements are only temporary, and that at some point in the future they will become negative again. When capital is made available, enterprises are expected to make liquidity contributions that are sufficient to cover the claims of the people making the original investment. *There is only one source of money that never has to be paid back by enterprises—satisfied customers.* We have already pointed out that the value of goods and services cannot be based on their original cost in any circumstances, but that their value can only be estimated based on their value for the enterprise that has purchased them, or on future payments received when sold. We can now see the extremely clear conflict that exists between the purely formal reliability of accounting data, and its relevance.

Historical cost prices are always available in old accounting data. Data about old prices is formally reliable because the original receipts can be found to prove what was paid. But the exercise is quite simply a waste of time for managers, since data about prices and conditions yesterday has no information value as far as prices and conditions tomorrow are concerned.

The two key questions that the accounting specialists of the future will ask and require answers for are as follows: *What payments can we expect to receive from satisfied customers now and in the future? And when can we expect these payments to be received?* The answers to these questions can be obtained from the managers whose job is to keep an eye on the market and develop and sell the enterprise's products and services.

But this may not meet with the approval of traditional accounting specialists. They may feel that such information about future payments received is far too *uncertain* to enter in financial statements, which normally describe the past only; they may feel that information describing the future should be called a budget, and be regarded as guesswork. Such specialists may feel that they can already produce a liquidity budget containing the payments of the future. The answer to such points is that double entry bookkeeping was and still is a system of making predictions of payments, so there is no doubt that traditional financial statements contain information about future payments in the form of the items known as debtors and creditors. Quite simply, it is *not true* to claim that future payments are described in traditional budgets, and past payments in traditional financial statements.

Relevant information is information that contains an up-to-date description of the future, and naturally, such information is not necessarily 100 percent certain. In chapter 13 we pointed out that errors could be made in predictions. But uncertainty is a phenomenon with which we must learn to live. The world around us changes in ways we cannot predict. So-called *certain* information reflects a *dangerous assumption* and gives a *false sense of security* because it describes the world of yesterday, when what we are interested in is the payments of tomorrow. We recall the information dilemma of accounting described in the same chapter. Let us now repeat the figure first mentioned in that chapter, showing the connection between the four different accounting result concepts for periods of random length, and the three types of error in prediction that connect these result concepts logically. See Figure 15.3.

We can then repeat and complete the description of the necessary and sufficient measurements from chapter 14, whose sums over time are identical with the four interim result concepts, and which are also necessary and sufficient to describe solvency.

Let us briefly repeat the logic of itemization. We recall from chapter 5 that all items of income are accompanied by simultaneous and corresponding items that increase assets. *All itemization of income represents an*

Interim Result	Error E-A	Error A-R	Error R-P
Expected Result	Unknown	Unknown	Unknown
Agreed Result	Known	Unknown	Unknown
Realization Result	Known	Known	Unknown
Payment Result	Known	Known	Known

Figure 15.3. Interim results and errors in prediction.

improvement in solvency. And similarly, all expenses in double entry bookkeeping are identical with a simultaneous marginal reduction in assets or increase in liabilities. *All itemization of expenses represents a reduction in solvency*.

We should also like to repeat a question asked by managers in a previous chapter: "What should we do if we wish to live up to our financial responsibilities, and therefore wish to know what the financial consequences of our actions will be, both in terms of individual transactions, and as a whole? What should we do if we wish to have a system of *management accounting* that is clear, up-to-date and logically complete?" We have already seen that there are four clearly different answers to the question about the financial result for any given period. And these different answers show us the connection between the various concepts: There is an *insurmountable conflict between the uncertainty and possibilities for action in traditional financial statements*. This means that a vital choice must be made with regard to the future. Accounting specialists who refuse to accept the uncertainty of the new ideas will become passive spectators to the type of management practiced in the future.

Managers who wish to gain *certain* knowledge about the financial consequences of the actions of their organizations are by definition unable to take any action. And managers who wish to act must accept the uncertainty of any description of financial consequences on which their actions are based.

Accounts managers and accountants who are not content to be passive spectators to future financial developments must now start to think and act in completely new ways.

People who wish to be regarded as reliable managers must realize that any description of financial consequences is—and always has been—a *description of risk*. The management accounting of the future contains a description of calculated risk, and accounts managers and accountants must accept some of the responsibility for this description. Accounting specialists do not have to take responsibility for the risk itself, since this responsibility is the manager's alone. But they must undoubtedly take responsibility for both the language and content used to describe the risk.

There are only three ways of organizing basic accounting information, and until now only the first two of these have been used:

1. *Simple payment accounting* (cash flow accounting), using an information system with only one financial point of measurement: "paid."
2. *Claim and debt accounting plus payment accounting* (double entry bookkeeping), using an information system with two financial points of measurement: "realized" and "paid."
3. *Management accounting* (integrated expectation, agreement, claim/debt and payment accounting), using an information system containing four financial points of measurement: "expected," "agreed," "realized" and "paid."

Let us consider *payment accounting* (cash flow accounting) first. This is the simplest and thus easiest of the three. Financial statements based on this system cannot be presented until the final payment has been made, that is, until the description of financial consequences is certain. This system produces a payment result that consists of precise financial history containing known prediction errors. People who use this system are incapable of taking any action because they know nothing about the solvency of the organizations concerned until it is too late to take any action. We stated in a previous chapter that this was primarily the point of view of the *treasurer*.

We use the financial point of measurement known as "paid" to describe the payment result of a period chosen at random: "This is the payment result for the period. The money is in the box":

$$R_p\,(T) = \sum_{t\,=\,0}^{T} (I_p(t) - U_p(t))$$

where I_p stands for payments received, and U_p for payments made. But if the expected and agreed capital requirement has been positive for some time, the treasurer, bookkeeper, management and accountants will discover to their great surprise that the money that should be in the box has disappeared. Payments have been suspended. No one had any idea that this might happen because no one kept any financial statements capable of describing the capital requirement —and thus incipient insolvency—in good time.

Let us now consider *claim and debt accounting* (double entry bookkeeping), which can be regarded as a prediction of the payment accounting described earlier. Financial statements based on this system can be kept systematically at an early point when claims and debts arise (are realized) following the fulfillment of agreements. This is the accounting system normally used in the public and private sectors today. Financial statements all over the world are drawn up according to the rules of double entry bookkeeping, which could be justifiably regarded 500 years ago as a complete, consistent, necessary and sufficient method to describe the financial consequences of actions. Claim and debt accounting commences at an earlier stage than payment accounting, usually as soon as claims or debts have arisen. In its day this method was regarded as epoch-making, and people believed that double entry bookkeeping made it possible to make a reliable prediction of future payments.

But these days we need to draw up financial statements even earlier, because the financial consequences of actions are binding as soon as agreements are made, agreements that normally take a certain amount of time to fulfill. As a result, double entry bookkeeping has lost its original authority, and is now regarded as only capable of providing delayed information. At the moment people *wait* to draw up financial statements until agreements have been fulfilled when delivery is made, and when the description of financial consequences is certain apart from the uncertainty that claims and debts might not be paid as agreed.

The realization result for any given period can be calculated, and the payments arising from the items known as debtors and creditors in the balance sheet can be monitored and controlled on a regular basis.

But managers are unable to take action because they lack an overall picture of the situation. They have a certain amount of information, but no clear idea of the situation with regard to solvency until it is too late. In general, this is the point of view of *the bookkeeper*.

Starting with the realization result, it is possible to draw up a reliable prediction of payments on this basis—but the prediction will only comprise claims and debts. The monitoring and control of claims and debts only occurs when payments are made.

This makes it possible to predict and remedy any lack of liquidity concerning these payments, but nothing systematic is known about total future cash flows. The financial point of measurement known as "realized" is used to form the realization result for any given period: "This is the realization result. The money will be in the box when and if claims and debts have been paid as agreed":

$$R_r(T) = \sum_{t=0}^{T} (I_r(t) - U_r(t))$$

where I_r stands for realized payments received, and U_r for realized payments made. But if the expected and agreed capital requirement has been positive for some time, the bookkeeper, management and accountants will discover to their great surprise that their enterprise's debts are greater than its claims. It can be predicted (far too late) that the money will soon no longer be in the box, and payments will have to be suspended. No one knew for certain that this would happen because no one kept any financial statements capable of describing the total capital requirement—and thus incipient insolvency—in good time.

Finally, let us consider *management accounting*. Financial statements based on this system contain all the payments expected, agreed, realized and made, based on the statements and language used by the management in communicating with its agreement partners. This language could be the basis of the standard financial statements of the future in the private and public sectors. Modern technology means that in a few years' time it will be possible to regard financial statements as complete, consistent, necessary and sufficient descriptions of the financial consequences of the actions of organizations. Financial statements are kept at the same time as expectations are expressed in the form of predictions of the consequences of future payments, and at the same time as agreements are reached. Management accounting is thus up-to-date and realistic, as well as reflecting the uncertainty of the real world in the form of the calculated risk. This uncertainty simply has to be accepted. We expect that some of the expectations will not become agreements, that some agreements will not be kept and that some claims will never be paid. The same action is seen first as expected, then as agreed, completed and finally paid, and this makes it possible to calculate the expected result for any period, and to monitor and control all the transactions and payments concerned.

An overall picture can be obtained and kept up-to-date on a regular basis. So managers can have constant awareness of the solvency of their organizations. They are able to discover any negative financial developments at an early stage, and to take action, limit losses and perhaps save the situation before it is too late. In general, this is the point of view of *the manager*. The expected result can be calculated as the most comprehensive interim result, and reliable predictions of payments based on this result can be made and updated to include all the financial consequences, and can thus be regarded as complete. Overall financial control becomes possible because each individual prediction of payment is included within the same information system. Any lack of future liquidity will be immediately visible in management accounting, because all future payments are systematically included. Four financial points of measurement are used ("expected," "agreed," "realized" and "paid") as the basis of the expected result, calculated risk and known errors in prediction for any given period; this is the expected financial result for the period. The money will be in the box when and if the expectations become agreements, when and if the agreements are kept, and when and if claims and debts are paid:

$$R_e\,(T) = \sum_{t\,=\,0}^{T} (I_e(t) - U_e(t))$$

Where I_e stands for expected payments received, and U_e for expected payments made. There is only one way of discovering whether the expected and agreed capital requirement is too small—by carrying out an overall calculation including the capital requirement or liquidity contribution of each individual transaction. Managers can never say anything definite about the capital requirements or liquidity contributions of their enterprises until these amounts have been calculated. *Information about the solvency of an organization at a given time without realistic, consistent, complete and up-to-date measurement of the financial consequences of individual transactions and rapid and precise calculation of the overall picture is information about solvency that has no reliability.*

The next sentence may seem obvious to readers: A negative expected result for a given period is a prediction of a capital requirement for a future period, and thus provides an *early warning about any future insolvency*.

These sentences reveal the weakness of traditional financial statements and all the futile attempts that have been made to describe solvency and predict insolvency at a sufficiently early stage. Traditional financial statements, despite all the well-meaning attempts to make them look formally correct and "true and fair," are no more than a collection of unrealistic, logically incomplete, self-contradictory and out-of-date statements that cannot be used in any meaningful way to form a reliable all-round picture of the financial situation.

We can now draw two conclusions. The first is that a logically complete system of management accounting is not yet used in practice. And the second is that the solvency of any organization can now be expressed in scientifically reliable fashion, and thus meaningfully and comprehensibly, as the difference between assets and liabilities. We recall the new definition of these basic concepts, and repeat that any information concerning value must contain information about time to give any meaning. The new description of solvency is as follows:

$$\text{Solvency}_t = \text{Assets}_t - \text{Liabilities}_t$$

or, using our new definitions:

$$\text{Solvency}_t = \text{Predictions of payments received}_t - \frac{\text{Predictions of}}{\text{payments made}_t}$$

Our expression of solvency should be regarded as an accounting balance sheet, which should ideally be a *report on demand, produced in real-time by computers*. The new concept of solvency demonstrates the logical content of our new system of management accounting. It shows us solvency *here and now*. The basic data should ideally be registered at the same time as transactions occur. The overall picture of solvency can be calculated and recalculated constantly by a computer, which can process huge amounts of data very rapidly, and which never becomes tired of performing such a task.

The result is that *the picture of solvency is ready for use whenever any-one asks for it.* Information is available here and now. Managers can now consider, discuss and assume real responsibility, based on the fact that they always know the financial consequences of their own actions and the actions of others. This has not previously been the case.

Traditional financial statements are composed of formally certain but irrelevant and thus (for managers) unrealistic data. But the picture provided by the new system of management accounting is composed of uncertain but up-to-date and realistic data. The new term "dynamic management accounting" is more than just a name.

Accounting specialists are being asked to accept something of which they are actually already aware. Descriptions of financial consequences are always uncertain, but this uncertainty can be reduced if managers are given access to up-to-date and relevant financial information *before* making decisions, and *while* their decisions are being carried out. Let us now try to identify this uncertainty in the three types of accounting discussed.

We have just stated that *the treasurer's cash flow accounting* is the latest but also the most certain system of accounting possible. Once the money is in the box, it is surely easy to assume that the information in question is true. But actually it is easy to indicate uncertainty even in these circumstances. First, subsequent demands for guarantee commitments or product liability may be made by dissatisfied customers. And second, the value of any cash sums always depends on the purchasing power of their currency. Money is something that human beings have invented, and there is no natural law stating that cash always retains its purchasing power in any circumstances. We are familiar with concepts such as inflation and devaluation, and we know that a great deal of attention is focused on financial tools (futures, options and so on), which enable us to buy our way out of the uncertainty that will always be associated with money as a concept.

The second systematic form of accounting is *the bookkeeper's claim and debt accounting.* For more than 500 years, this has been the standard, general language used to describe financial consequences. The language of double entry bookkeeping consists of income and expenses, and produces a picture that is somewhat less certain than the payment accounting mentioned earlier. In general, a logical prediction is made that claims and debts will be paid as agreed, and that they will thus soon be apparent in the information system of the treasurer. In addition to the uncertainty about currency that applies to payment accounting, another uncertainty is apparent here. Claims and debts, of course, are items that may contain surprises. The concept of "bad debts" has been familiar ever since the system of double entry bookkeeping was invented more than 500 years ago. Everyone knows that customers may not actually pay despite all the agreements reached, and that this may mean that creditors are unable to make their payments at the due date, as well. These risks concerning debts and claims are familiar, and tools are available to *reduce* the uncertainty. But it is not possible to *remove* it altogether.

The accounting specialists of the future will draw up *management accounting, which includes agreements*. In addition to the uncertainties mentioned above, management accounting also contains the risk that agreements will not be kept as expected. But here, too, there are suitable tools to reduce the uncertainty.

We stated earlier that in addition to the categories of information contained in double entry bookkeeping, our new concept of insolvency also contained agreed and expected payments. Does this mean that four accounting systems exist in fact? Is it possible to draw up an accounting model that fits each of the four types of payment? So far, we have only mentioned three.

To answer these questions we shall now try to combine the new categories. The combination of agreed and expected payments made and received produces the following:

1. Information about agreed payments received without simultaneous information about agreed or expected payments made (e.g., when customers make written orders for goods that are in stock).
2. Information about agreed payments made without simultaneous information about agreed or expected payments received (e.g., a new employee is hired).
3. Information about agreed payments received and simultaneous information about agreed or expected payments made that are due to this agreed payment received (e.g., a contractor's quotation is accepted).
4. Information about agreed payments made and simultaneous information about agreed or expected payments received that are due to this agreed payment made (e.g., a retailer places an order for a consignment that is expected to be sold during the coming season).
5. Information about combinations of payments received and made that are not agreed, and that are thus composed purely of expected payments (e.g., calculations of investment, nonbinding offers, budgets and other predictions of consequences).

We note that *only the last category has no binding financial consequences*. It comprises the so-called "what happens if . . . calculations," which can be made in advance, and which support a description of the financial consequences of planned actions before such actions are agreed and thereby result in irreversible consequences. In accounting theory this point of view has been designated *ex ante*. Let us emphasize the most important fact: *ex ante* calculations of consequences describe and support decisions, but they are not binding. As long as no agreement has been reached, there can be no binding consequences.

Categories three and four give us reason to claim that information about payments may appear to be reliable even though "nothing more than" expected payments are involved. When an accountant asks a retailer about the reasons for the expected payments received during the next six months, and the answer is "Have a look in the shop and count up the stock at sales prices. Use the price tag codes to check that 80 percent of the stock consists of new and therefore probably saleable goods. Your sum will amount to $2.6 million. I expect that 60 percent of this stock will be sold at its full price, and that 20 percent more will have to be sold at a reduced price, perhaps a 50 percent reduction. Waste of 5 percent and 15 percent unsold remaining stock are also included. That is the reason for my expectation that I will receive $1.82 million during the next six months." Accountants who know their clients, and who check this information, will probably find it easy enough to regard the budget as reliable.

Similarly, contractors will be able to lay their new orders on the table and explain the expected payments made resulting from them. Accountants will be able to check the information, and will end up regarding the budget as reliable.

The decisive criterion for reliability is that the information in question is scientifically viable. It is presented in the form of statements about the consequences of actions that can be performed, not as forecasts with no content using figures from last year, and not using wishful thinking with no basis in reality. *Information about expected payments can never be certain. But it can form a reliable basis for management.*

Naturally, solvency can be described in other ways, too. Depreciation can be included, as well as "historical cost prices." The so-called principle of prudence can be exercised, and the presentation of financial statements can be delayed until the payment result is known. *Such information may be certain. But it can never form a reliable basis for management.*

As we have seen, in practice people often operate with complex information about cash flows. Management accounting will only be meaningful when and if all four categories of information can be monitored in the same information system. This means that we must be able to describe each individual component of the management accounting system as a transaction or a limited number of transactions with financial consequences. This problem will be dealt with in the next chapter.

NOTES

1. P. F. Drucker, *The Practice of Management*, p. 37.

16 A REAL-TIME DESCRIPTION OF SOLVENCY

Savoir pour prévoir.
We seek knowledge to predict.

—*Auguste Comte*

This chapter shows how the new system of dynamic management accounting works. A single project is traced from the moment it arises until the moment it is completed. We demonstrate that it is possible at any time to monitor the financial consequences of the project in question, because the relevant data is updated constantly. A previously ignored but very important connection between the concepts of *contribution margin* and *financing requirement* is demonstrated. The connection is surprisingly simple—if the two concepts are regarded dynamically, they are *identical* apart from the fact that there are opposite plus/minus signs in front of them. Profitability and liquidity images now can both be included in the same information system. Many traditional budgeting procedures wither and die as a result, but very few people will miss them. Instead, we shall concentrate on keeping individual financial statements for individual projects only. If each project is kept up-to-date the overall account will also be up-to-date, since the overall picture consists of no more than a number of automatically combined individual pictures. It then becomes possible to warn about incipient insolvency at a very early stage, and in principle a negative balance of any size will be visible, no matter how small. Responsibility can now be discussed and allocated in meaningful fashion.

In the preceding chapter we described and gave reasons for the content and logical components of our new, dynamic concept of solvency. We demonstrated that solvency is a concept that is only meaningful if it is regarded as consisting of dated information about all the future payments of an organization.

What are the factors that decide whether an enterprise is solvent and will remain solvent? In the previous chapter we demonstrated that accounting descriptions have always been (and will always be) vitiated by a degree of uncertainty, and that consequently new accounting theories cannot be rejected merely on the grounds that they are based on "uncertain" data. *Uncertainty is the only certain distinguishing feature of financial statements.* The only difference in the reliability of figures lies in the degree of uncertainty in the four logical categories with which we are now familiar (expected, agreed, realized and paid).

The solvency of an enterprise can only be explained in terms of a *hypothesis,* which may be supported more or less convincingly. Any hypothesis about solvency and the factors that determine solvency must be expressed *so that it can be tested and refuted (if possible).* We recall once again the basic and irrefutable requirement for scientifically useful definitions—such definitions must be based on actions that can be carried out, and that can thus be observed in the real world. And the day the information contained in financial statements is based on descriptions of actions that can be carried out in the real world may well be the day on which accounting recovers its lost credibility.

Let us now imagine two enterprises (A and B), which are identical, and which have identical balance sheets at time t_1. See figure 16.1.

We note that the new system enables us to show future payments. The figures stated as the difference between assets (well-founded predictions of payments received) and liabilities (well-founded predictions of payments made) represent the information available to the management concerning future net payments received and made by enterprises A and B. So these figures can be used to describe solvency. We have already demonstrated that this information is obtained by summarizing chronological data strings containing information about future cash flows. We have also demonstrated that it is possible at an early stage to discover temporary future liquidity problems by merging these data strings. This problem will be dealt with in this chapter, where we shall also demonstrate the way management

	Assets	Liabilities	Difference
Enterprise A	352	330	22
Enterprise B	352	330	22

Figure 16.1. Identical enterprises, same payment capability.

accounting can solve it. Let us once again consider our example of the two identical enterprises A and B. We shall simplify reality and imagine that the only events that take place are as follows.

In competition with each other, the two enterprises give quotations for the same project. Enterprise A is asked to supply the order, and at time t_2, when it is agreed with the customer, the order consists of the following individual items, whose logical state (S) at the now-familiar points (E = expected, A = agreed, R = realized and P = paid) is indicated in the left-hand column. See figure 16.2.

The figure shows that only the income is *agreed*. The expenses are still only *expected*, because at time t_2 no agreement has yet been reached with the workers, nor have any materials been ordered from the subsuppliers. None of the necessary deliveries have yet been made, and no payments have been made or received. Consequently, there are no invoices or money transfers at the moment the order is placed. Nothing has been booked yet.

So *in traditional financial statements this order would be quite invisible at the time the order is placed,* since double entry bookkeeping does not register descriptions of financial consequences until claims have arisen. In practice, this system of acting blindfolded has been turned into a "principle" called "the principle of prudence." But it is not easy to explain in convincing fashion why omitting the description of binding financial consequences should be regarded as prudent in an information system whose task is to describe the financial consequences of the actions of organizations.

Traditional financial statements do not reveal that the solvency of enterprise A changes at time t_2. The financial picture for both enterprises will still be identical. But if *management accounting* is used, a difference in solvency will become apparent. The management of enterprise A has performed an action that is clear and visible to everyone, and that Peter F. Drucker emphasizes is the only purpose of doing business. A created a customer, and B *did not* create a customer. Consequently, A's financial statement is different from B's once the order has been agreed. *A's solvency is better than B's.* See figure 16.3.

It is apparent that A is now in a stronger position than B. A's holding of "well-founded future net cash flows" has grown from 22 to 52, and it

S	Item	Amount
A	Income	100
E	Wages	– 40
E	Materials	– 30
	Liquidity contribution	30

Figure 16.2. New order, enterprise A.

	Asset	Liabilities	Difference
Enterprise A	452	400	52
Enterprise B	352	330	22

Figure 16.3. A reliable real-time signal of a change in solvency, provided by management accounting.

is easy to explain this improvement. The difference between the balance sheets of A and B is quite simply identical with the liquidity contribution of the new order. Readers will notice the simplicity of the new accounting concepts. Assets are future payments received, and liabilities are future payments made. If the difference is positive we can regard the enterprises concerned as being solvent. But even though the difference is positive, there may still be liquidity problems, although these problems will be predictable and solvable. As we demonstrated in chapter 4, solvent enterprises can always solve their liquidity problems as long as these problems are discovered in good time. And as we saw in chapter 5, even medieval merchants could predict future liquidity crises as long as they regarded their financial statements as systematic predictions of payments, and arranged their data accordingly.

The realization that the new system of accounting is a composite system of four well-defined logical categories of information about future cash flows means that the reliability of financial statements can be doubted and tested. And this is the task of the auditor. Each individual item of information in management accounting can be traced back to the *manager responsible*. So it is hardly an exaggeration to claim that the new system can also be called *responsibility accounting*. In this chapter and the final two chapters, we shall try to show that the designation "responsibility accounting" is more than just an empty phrase.

Let us now consider a small example whose purpose is to illustrate and emphasize the *dynamic interpretation of accounts*. The word "dynamic" generally means something that moves. And concepts involving movement can only be described and understood if time is included in the description. Movement and change always take a certain amount of time. In theory, pictures of reality are often called "models," and a distinction is drawn between static models (pictures of something not moving) and dynamic models (pictures of something moving).

Economists would say that models are static when their variables coincide in time, and dynamic when their variables do not coincide in time. Traditional financial statements are dated, and are thus *static models*, pictures of something that stands still. But does the financial position of enterprises ever stand still?

Let us now consider the following chain of events, which has been described as realistically as possible, although a certain amount of simplification is inevitable:

1. On December 10, 1996, seller A receives a request from buyer B to give a binding quotation for delivery of a specified sales object in early February 1997.
2. It takes a week to prepare the quotation, which is concluded, checked and approved by the seller on December 17, 1996, after which it is sent to buyer B. Seller A offers to deliver as required in early February. The price is $1,000, and 30 days' credit are allowed from the invoice date.
3. The order is placed by buyer B on December 28, 1996, and the buyer stipulates that delivery must be made no earlier than February 2 and no later than February 5, 1997.
4. Owing to accidents during production, the goods are not delivered until February 8. Despite the delay, the buyer agrees to accept the goods. The invoice is dated February 10.
5. Payment is made on March 20, 1997.

This example enables us to illustrate the nature of dynamic accounting: *Information about the financial consequences is a function of time.* We now suggest that readers draw a time axis on a piece of paper, and then mark the times stated in our example on this axis. Having done this the various time intervals (periods) can be considered, and it will then become apparent that different people will interpret the same information entirely differently, depending on the period in which they are placed. Readers can slide their pens along the axis to indicate the passage of time, which brings our model alive. This is the new dynamic system of accounting. The same information is present in the system at all times, so it is also visible at all times. But its value for the recipient varies depending entirely on the period in question. It is clear that time is the decisive variable in this model of dynamic accounting.

During the period December 10–17 the information system is *formally erroneous.* Seller A is the only one who knows about the new asset arising if the order goes through, and his knowledge is not yet certain. But if the seller had been able to produce his quotation immediately, the system would know that an expected payment received had been registered.

During the period December 17–28 the system shows a prediction of payment received that can clearly be connected with a concrete action in the real world. *The reason* for this prediction of payment received is also clear—an expected order and subsequent delivery of specific sales objects to customer B. However, the prediction of payment received is still very uncertain, since it can only be designated *expected.* We recall the three conditions of payment received: The money will not be in the box until 1) when and if we obtain the order, 2) when and if we deliver and 3) when and if the customer pays.

During the period December 28–February 5 the certainty of the prediction of payment increases significantly. It has now been *agreed*. Seller A obtained the order. The information concerning future payment now only depends on two *conditions*: The seller must deliver, and the buyer must pay.

But during the period February 6–8 the prediction of payment is *threatened*. The first of the two conditions has not been met because the seller has not delivered on time. If the system has been constructed correctly, it should now be possible to reveal this fact and inform all interested parties using an exceptional report describing the "threatened orders," that is, the agreed deliveries that have not yet taken place.

During the period February 8–10 the information system is once again *formally erroneous* because it is not up-to-date. The invoice should be written at the same time as delivery is made. The agreement has been fulfilled by the seller, and the prediction of payment received is now a claim. But this claim is not yet visible in the system owing to a lack of correct data.

During the period February 10–March 10 the prediction of payment received is only dependent on *one condition*: The money will be in the box when and if the buyer pays.

During the period March 11–20 the prediction of payment is again *threatened*, since the buyer has not yet paid as agreed.

On March 20 the prediction of payment is *finally confirmed*. It will only lose reliability if the buyer subsequently brings guarantee or product liability commitments to bear.

Readers will notice that observers of this system experience and learn as they go along. The rule is simple: *The latest information at any time is the valid information.* New information replaces old information, but old information should not be discarded. It must be kept for reasons of explanation and auditing at a later date.

This simple example demonstrates the completeness and dynamism of management accounting. There are no longer any technical hurdles preventing the practical implementation of complete and dynamic accounting systems. Such systems are available now, and their use is only prevented by force of habit and resistance to change. But the development of such systems in practice has two wide ranging requirements. The first is that *modern information technology* must be employed, and the second is that users of the new system must have *the necessary discipline when working with data*. Brief comments will now be made about these two requirements, since they are wide ranging and may therefore give rise to objections to the applicability of the new dynamic accounting system. Those who resist change may say that these new ideas are too expensive and difficult to implement in practice, and that users will not be capable of exhibiting the necessary data discipline.

The first objection can be met by referring to a previous chapter in which we described the register and the database—the two basic concepts of information recording. Readers may remember the description of the new technology as the carrier of an information system capable of meeting the needs of several users and several tasks at the same time. The example just outlined can also be used to illustrate this point. If seller A is employed at a sales department that is part of a large corporation, then the order processing information contained in our example can in principle be made just as accessible to all relevant employees in the corporation as it is to seller A. In addition, the overall picture provided by the system can be updated constantly, and the latest variant of the financial consequences of the project can be incorporated in the dynamic financial statements, which can be updated constantly for ready use by the management.

Readers who are familiar with information processing in practice will immediately be aware that this new system requires decisions to be made about a number of important questions concerning the frequency of updating, access control, data security, back-up copies and so on. The task might be daunting, but it is not impossible. The strongest argument against the guardians of traditional accounting techniques must surely be the constant improvement in the ratio between the price and capacity of modern computers. User-friendly and relatively inexpensive information technology, which was only a dream yesterday, will be available to everyone tomorrow.

The second objection is based on a pessimistic fear that users might not be capable of the required data discipline. This claim, too, is easy to refute, because the fact is that double entry bookkeeping, which has been the essential tool of accounting specialists for more than 500 years, also requires data discipline. Most people know that double entry bookkeeping can be abused, and examples of embezzlement, fraud and other abuses abound. The claim that a tool might be abused can never be a valid argument against its use. Of course any formalized information system will only work if it is used with care. The familiar view about the structure of systems is that "Anything that can go wrong will go wrong sooner or later. And even when nothing can go wrong, it may go wrong all the same." Systems are never 100 percent reliable, and systems that are easy to use are often easy to abuse, too. So there is often a conflict between making a system easy to use and ensuring data security. But of course this does not mean that the task of constructing such a system is impossible. It simply means that the task involved is comprehensive and often daunting, and that the size of this task should never be underestimated. But it is a task, not a problem.

Let us now recall our new definitions of assets and liabilities, and then ask the questions "What do we mean by well-founded predictions of cash flows? How can predictions of payments made and received be regarded as well-founded or not?

The answer is that in order to be well founded, predictions need to consist of specific individual projects. We are currently considering an *information system* that we call *dynamic management accounting*. This system consists purely of items, or information about the financial consequences of actions, which can be regarded as subsystems. Each subsystem is always regarded as a *project*. We recall our definition that each project consists of an action or set of actions with financial consequences. Each project is described using *the dynamic account*. This means that any information about future payments—any item in financial statements—can be traced to a specific action or pattern of actions in the real world. Consequently, the component parts and overall picture of this information system can be revised systematically. Each individual item or group of items can be doubted and tested in terms of reliability both formally and in reality. Accountants can ask a number of questions.

The question *what?* is a general logical key to each individual project. The limits of each project can be defined and tested critically by accountants. Each project can be recognized by its identification code, designation and specific situation-oriented composition in the form of sales orders, purchase orders, development projects, advertising campaigns, building projects and so on. The question *who?* is a general key to the type of accounting we call responsibility accounting. The manager or group of managers and project managers who have made decisions can be identified, and special reports can be drawn up to define the patterns of responsibility involved. In general, these descriptions of responsibility answer the question "Who knew what, and when?" Consequently, they can make good supporting structures for the calculation, control and explanation of individual projects. Regular monitoring and management, rapid action and change to meet the requirements of the situation and final calculation of the financial results can now be carried out based on exactly the same data. This data is available at any time, providing a new opportunity unknown in traditional accounting calculations, which are drawn up either before or after the event. And as the name implies, calculation after the event is nothing more than history. There is no chance of taking any relevant action by the time the results of such calculations are available.

The question *where?* is a general key to a description of place in accounting. Reports can be drawn up according to the location of profit centers, cost centers and so on.

The question *when?* is the new general key to a description of time and the interval between the logical and financial points of measurement of various actions and patterns of actions. The fact that time is now included systematically in the description of financial consequences means that we can now obtain a system of dynamic management accounting, comprising a constantly revised and therefore constantly up-to-date, all-round picture of the financial situation.

The question *how?* is a general key to the categories into which income and expenses can be divided, categories that are already well-known in theory. Income (the financial consequences of an organization's services) is traditionally divided according to sales market segments (customer groups, districts). Expenses (the financial consequences of an organization's consumption) are traditionally divided according to purchase market segments (wages, materials, rent). These divisions are important, because the data generated can be used in various forms of analysis and cost calculation that are important tools for use in adapting an organization to suit its external circumstances. However, they will not be dealt with here, since they are already familiar concepts in traditional accounting theory (for example, investments, transfer pricing, cost calculations, make or buy decisions and so on)

Finally, the question *why?* is a general key for use in describing the objective of individual projects, and thus the reason for the action taken. All such descriptions of objectives occur within the "limits of existence," as Bertrand Russell puts it. Information about objectives is always *situation oriented*, and can thus be understood in direct connection with concrete, individual projects.

We shall now consider the way dynamic accounting works by observing the contribution of an individual project to an all-round description in management accounting. We recall that an overall description of financial consequences can be carried out using two concepts that we now consider to be identical, apart from the plus/minus sign in front of them—*the liquidity contribution* (contribution margin) and *the financing requirement*. A positive liquidity contribution is exactly the same as a negative financing requirement, and vice versa. We also now know that these key concepts are not static. They are dynamic, and consequently they can only be described meaningfully as data strings containing chronological information about payments, divided into various logical categories.

From the point of view of the project manager, let us now consider the way individual projects arise and are carried out. The manager informs the system that the project exists as soon as it becomes real to her. The data of the project is then updated constantly to ensure that it reflects the latest (i.e., the current) situation.

This gives rise to the rule that the latest information is the only valid information. The information system thus becomes *a model of an organism that is constantly able to experience and learn*.

The various data operations that can be performed in connection with the processing of each project are as follows. These operations are necessary in order to systematically update the available information about the project in question. It should be possible for managers and relevant employees to carry out the following steps in relation to the data describing each project:

set up (declare as existing)
change (maintain, update)
check (monitor, control)
retrieve (produce in new connections)
send (copy in full or in part)
forget (delete, declare to be nonexistent)

It is worth noting that these operations are *logical* operations using data. They are not physical operations. They describe what people do, not what computers do. This means that users can delete any given project logically without losing the actual data involved. Physical deletion would involve the actual destruction of data—that is, the irreversible loss of documentary evidence—and this should never be contemplated until after the expiry of the legal time limit.

We shall now focus on the dynamic description of solvency by observing the actions of enterprise A, which was given an order whose liquidity contribution (contribution margin) at the time the quotation was given can be calculated as shown in figure 16.4.

The following details can now be added. The quotation is given on March 10 in year N. The customer will decide who is to supply the order on March 28. The work concerned is to start on April 2 and last 28 days. The customer asks for 15 days' credit after the invoice date, so payment cannot be expected earlier than about 40 days after the work starts.

The materials have to be bought from a subsupplier, for delivery on the fifth day after commencement of the work. From the invoice date, 20 days' credit must be allowed, and it is assumed that the subsupplier invoices the materials two days after they have been delivered.

Wages have to be paid in two equal portions 14 and 28 days after the start of work. The dates of R (realization) and P (paid) are identical as far as the wages are concerned. At the time the quotation is made there are no agreements with the supplier of materials or the employees whose wages are mentioned in the calculation.

We shall now follow the progress of this project, demonstrating that the contribution of such individual projects to the solvency of enterprises can be made visible to the management at any time.

S	Item	Amount
E	Income	100
E	Wages	− 40
E	Materials	− 30
	Liquidity contribution	30

Figure 16.4. The new quotation.

We return to the aforementioned situation, in which enterprise A has not yet been given the order, which is thus no more than an *expected* liquidity contribution at this stage. On March 10 the basic data in our example is as shown in figure 16.4.

The picture of profitability shows us the connection between actions and their financial consequences *systematically*, but although the picture of payments is composed of exactly the same data, it is considered *chronologically*, as a description of the financial consequences of actions using time as a variable. The description of the *financing requirement* of the order, which is formed using exactly the same data, is shown in figure 16.5.

The advantage of the dynamic account as a descriptive tool is now apparent. In traditional accounting *profitability* and *liquidity* have always been regarded as two different concepts, requiring different systems (for example, advance calculations/financing calculations, profit and loss budgets/liquidity budgets). But we can now see that all the logical dimensions of management accounting can be contained in a single information system. There are two different pictures, but they are formed using exactly the same data. We have calculated the order's expected liquidity contribution (also known as the contribution margin), and the expected financing requirement. We have also demonstrated that the two concepts of liquidity contribution and financing requirement are identical, apart from the use of different plus/minus signs in front of them. Readers now have one final chance to try and disprove the claim that information about financial results and information about changes in liquidity is information about the same thing.

Readers will no doubt also notice that the calculations in our example are logically constructed in the form of *predictions*. The calculations are made on March 10, and the payments are predicted systematically.

Let us now move forward in time, and assume that we reach March 28. We now know that the quotation given was accepted, and that a contract has been signed with the customer. We also assume that the quotation has been given on the basis of an income/cost estimate, and that there are certain changes in the organization of the project. On the same day an agreement is reached with the employees for a total wage payment of 42 in two installments of 21. This means that a prediction error of 2 was made in the advance calculation.

Date	S	Payment	Amount	Σ FR
April 16	E	Wages (1/2)	−20	20
April 29	E	Materials	−30	50
April 30	E	Wages (2/2)	−20	70
May 12	E	Income	100	−30

Figure 16.5. The financing requirement.

We can now update our management account, producing the picture in figure 16.6. The profitability has decreased owing to the wage agreement, and the contribution margin is now only 28.

The financing requirement has increased accordingly, as is shown in figure 16.7.

We can now assume that more time passes, bringing us to April 1. The cost of materials does not turn out as expected, either. A special offer of 27 made by the subsupplier is accepted on March 30, thus saving 3. Yet again, a prediction error in relation to the expected figure becomes evident, but this time the error is to enterprise A's advantage. However, the subsupplier will only offer the special price if payment is made quickly, and allows only five days' credit instead of 20.

The updated account of the project now shows an improved liquidity contribution, as shown in figure 16.8. Naturally, the financing requirement is also reduced, but it is also changed owing to the requirement for rapid payment for the materials supplied by the subsupplier. So the financing requirement profile must also be recomputed and redrawn again, as shown in figure 16.9.

Time passes once again, and we reach April 15. The materials were delivered on April 7, and the invoice was received on April 9 and paid on April 14. Once again, we can calculate and comment upon the updated picture of the situation. The liquidity contribution is unchanged, but the financing requirement on April 15 is shown in figure 16.10.

S	Item	Amount
A	Income	100
A	Wages	−42
E	Materials	−30
	Liquidity contribution	28

Figure 16.6. Profitability of the project on March 28.

Date	S	Payment	Amount	Σ FR
April 16	A	Wages (1/2)	−21	21
April 29	E	Materials	−30	51
April 30	A	Wages (2/2)	−21	72
May 12	A	Income	100	−28

Figure 16.7. Financing requirement on March 28.

The only change is that the code reflecting the cost of materials has changed from A (agreed) to P (paid). This item has now passed two financial points of measurement. The materials have been delivered (realized) and paid as agreed. This is how dynamic management accounting works. *The same information is under consideration all the time, but it changes its relevance as a function of time.*

We now move even further forward in time, reaching April 18, when another unexpected event occurs. The customer visits the site, has a good idea and an extra task is added to the original order. Following negotiation with the employees and the customer, it is agreed on April 19 that the employees should perform this additional task and receive an extra payment of 8 in return. The customer agrees to pay 12 for the extra service. The order can then be concluded as agreed.

S	Item	Amount
A	Income	100
A	Wages	−42
A	Materials	−27
	Liquidity contribution	31

Figure 16.8. Profitability of the project on April 1.

Date	S	Payment	Amount	Σ FR
April 14	A	Materials	−27	27
April 16	A	Wages (1/2)	−21	48
April 30	A	Wages (1/2)	−21	69
May 12	A	Income	100	−31

Figure 16.9. Financing requirement on April 1.

Date	S	Payment	Amount	Σ FR
April 14	P	Materials	−27	27
April 16	A	Wages (1/2)	−21	48
April 30	A	Wages (2/2)	−21	69
May 12	A	Income	100	−31

Figure 16.10. Financing requirement on April 15.

Calculating the liquidity contribution and financing requirement is now straightforward, due to this change at the time the agreement was reached, that is, on April 19. We have omitted this calculation here, in the hope that readers may wish to carry it out themselves to see how dynamic management accounting can be practiced. The attempt may be worthwhile.

The final picture we shall consider occurs on May 15, by which time all the delivery and payment transactions have been completed, and all prediction errors revealed. The final calculation is shown in figure 16.11.

The financing requirement profile can also be demonstrated precisely at this time, producing a final picture (figure 16.12), which is the same as the familiar ex post documentation carried out by traditional accounting.

The reliability of this description of the financial consequences of the project can only be challenged if the customer unexpectedly brings guarantee or product liability commitments to bear. The final calculation clearly shows the impotence of the traditional accounting model. Traditional accounting might provide a precise description, but this description cannot be used as the basis for action for the simple but vital reason that it arrives too late. In management accounting the final picture is only interesting because it provides formal documentary evidence that can be used if anyone subsequently decides to contest the accounting information that has been used. This is not, of course, unknown. But as a tool for management, the traditional accounting model has the same value as last week's newspaper. You might be lucky enough to find a useful story or two, but otherwise it is a waste of time to read *news that is out of date*. Everyone knows

S	Item	Amount
P	Income	112
P	Wages	−50
P	Materials	−27
	Liquidity contribution	35

Figure 16.11.   Profitability of the project on May 15.

Date	S	Payment	Amount	Σ FR
April 14	P	Materials	−27	27
April 16	P	Wages (1/2)	−21	48
April 30	P	Wages (2/2)	−29	77
May 12	P	Income	112	−35

Figure 16.12.   Financing requirement on May 15.

this to be true, but some accounting specialists have not yet admitted to themselves that they know.

In figure 16.3 we showed the immediate effect on the new accounting balance when enterprise A obtained the order used in our example. Figure 16.13 shows that it is also possible to keep the assets and liabilities of the all-round account up-to-date at all times.

Let us take this opportunity of abandoning the misleading and there-fore damaging concept of "owners' equity" in the balance sheet. Using our new accounting model the management is always able to obtain a reliable picture of all future cash flows. The difference between assets and liabili-ties is known as *the financial capability*, or simply *the payment capability*. There are two important reasons for suggesting the term "payment capa-bility" in the new, future oriented system of management accounting instead of the traditional, hazy and misleading term "owner's equity." These two reasons are related to the two logical components of the new concept—the term "payment capability" being composed of the two terms "payment" and "capability."

The first reason is that the concept is based on a new definition of the basic concepts of assets and liabilities, and that the payment capability has been calculated and can be recalculated at any time as the difference between well-founded predictions of total payments received and well-founded predictions of total payments made. The concept is derived from the action "to pay," and thus provides an extremely direct and comprehensible expression of solvency. If the difference between assets and liabilities is greater than zero, and if all the information is reliable, the enterprise *is solvent* at the time in question. And time is not restricted to any particular date. *It could be any time,* because the situation can change at any moment.

The second reason is that we no longer regard enterprises as mechanisms, but as living organisms of which managements are part. Instead of regarding financial statements (i.e., descriptions of financial consequences) as figures on a sheet of paper or data in a computer, we now regard financial statements as

Date	Action	Assets	Liabilities	Payment Capability
March 10	Quotation given	352	−330	22
March 28	Order received	452	−400	52
March 28	Wages agreed	452	−402	50
April 1	Materials ordered	452	−399	53
April 18	Extra work agreed	464	−407	57

Figure 16.13. The dynamic description of solvency, all-round view.

information used as the basis of actions. Financial statements contain insight into financial consequences that is available to the management, that can be updated constantly and that can therefore be used in various relevant situations. The word "capability" indicates a state of preparedness, of being ready to face unexpected situations. Consequently, it can be associated closely with the concept of responsibility, with which we have already dealt. A responsible manager can be regarded as *a manager who knows or should know*. In other words, the job of the responsible manager is to take responsibility for something or someone, and to take the blame if anything goes wrong. Obviously, managers must remain alert and the situation must be reviewed constantly. The words *responsibility* and *capability* are clearly meaningful when seen in this light. There are at least two clear messages.

The first message is that *responsibility implies the duty to describe consequences and monitor solvency*. And this duty is inextricably linked with the role of the manager. Anyone assuming the task of manager should also take the initiative in acquiring information about the financial consequences of the actions of their organizations, when and if this information is needed. Responsible managers can never claim that the blame should be attached to others if things go wrong. But in this respect the situation of managers in the real world is not enviable at the moment, as we have seen.

The other message leads to yet another revelation of the impotence and worthlessness of traditional, static financial statements. The state of preparedness that is possible using management accounting means that action B can be performed if situation A arises. Management accounting thus provides *an early warning system*, and the situation that sounds the alarm is *incipient insolvency*, which may occur at any time.

Consequently, it is quite meaningless to continue spending time and serious consideration on static financial statements that are logically tied to fixed periods or moments, when what we need are dynamic financial statements reflecting the financial life of enterprises and thus the consequences of changeable situations.

Readers who study figure 16.13 more closely will probably draw the following two conclusions:

1. Modern technology makes it possible to produce reliable management accounts, and thus a dynamic description of solvency, too.
2. However, it is difficult to relate the payment capability figure to payment capability in the real world.

Regarding the first conclusion: The registration and calculation logic demonstrated here is composed of familiar, simple elements. The fact is that all the information contained in the example is known by the manager, which means that additional data registration is not required. We simply need to register the data we already know in a slightly different fashion. It is also difficult to maintain that the calculations involved are impossible in practice. Even large amounts of data and different registration locations should present little problem. It is true that the task of calculation and recalculation is large. But the algorithm (i.e., the program) that controls the calculation is so logically simple that it verges on the trivial. Anyone familiar with modern technology will surely agree that the task is possible. After all, we have computers at our disposal that are excellent at registering, organizing, calculating and communicating even large amounts of data.

Regarding the second conclusion: It is true that figure 16.13 shows that the payment capability changes constantly. It increases by 30 on March 28, which is the time the new order is registered. It is also easy to see that 30 is identical to the liquidity contribution of the new order. But it is not entirely easy to derive concrete meaning from the new concept of payment capability by simply looking at figure 16.3, which represents the difference between assets and liabilities. This is not surprising, because figure 16.3 is incomprehensible, as is shown in figure 16.13. The concept of *payment capability* has the same distinguishing feature as the symmetrical concepts of *liquidity contribution* and *financing requirement*. The model is dynamic, so time must be a visible part of the description. The concepts of payment capability and its synonym solvency cannot be understood as single figures or as the difference between two figures. Pictures of payment capability (i.e., of solvency) can only be understood if they have the form of data strings containing chronological information about payments, divided into four logical categories.

The difference between assets and liabilities may well be an expression of solvency or insolvency, but these expressions must always be considered dynamically if they are to be meaningful. We can only understand assets and liabilities if we view the figures in connection with time and human actions. In order to make understanding easier, we must therefore express the data in figure 16.3 differently. Instead of describing sums, we shall try to describe the distribution in time of the component parts of these sums, and consider them in connection with the individual items of information contained in the project calculation.

Let us start by specifying the figures in the balance sheet when the order has not yet been received. Our new balance sheet is taken from chapter 13. We shall first reset the balance sheet model (see figure 16.14), and then consider the way our example's contribution to the accounts becomes apparent *as time progresses*.

We can compress this model, and then consider it in connection with the descriptions we have already used in this chapter. The figures used contain reliable information about future payments, the sums of which can be seen at all times in our picture of solvency.

The first time our project becomes evident in management accounting is March 10, when all the items are "expected." Figure 16.15 shows the connection between the quotation and its contribution to the balance sheet.

We recall that the project as a whole is still only expected on March 10, so it has no binding financial consequences at that time. Projects at this stage are known as quotations, estimates, budgets, advance calculations and so on. It is easy to distinguish them from other projects, making it possible to see which items are *only* expected.

Readers familiar with traditional accounting will not be accustomed to seeing expected projects appearing in financial statements. But there are the following reasons for this break with tradition:

- Even expected projects (with a certain degree of likelihood) give rise to future payments, so management accounts would be incomplete if expected projects were omitted. The probability in question may be low, but it exists. After all, the customer has asked for the quotation.
- It is impossible to decide whether a project can finance itself without comparing the financing requirement and the overall picture of liquidity in good time.

But the most important reason is probably as follows:

- Unless all the financial consequences of all the management's actions are included in the calculation, the picture will be incomplete, and it will not be possible to predict insolvency and the suspension of payments in scientifically reliable fashion.

State	Assets	Liabilities
Expected	Expected Payments Received	Expected Payments Made
Agreed	Volume of Orders	Agreed Purchases
Realized	Debtors	Creditors
Paid	Cash	

Figure 16.14.   The new balance sheet model. Basic form.

S	Item	Amount
E	Income	100
E	Wages	−40
E	Materials	−30
	Liq. cont.	30

State	Assets	Liabilities
Expected	100	−70
Agreed		
Realized		
Paid		

Figure 16.15.   The contribution of the quotation to the balance sheet.

We recall that the financing requirement of the project has already been described precisely in the information system as a series of individual payments over time. Figure 16.16 shows the project on March 28, immediately after the receipt of the order.

It is worth noticing in figure 16.16 that only the income is shown as being "agreed." The two items of expenditure (wages and materials) are still only "expected." However, it is also worth pointing out that if you ask the manager himself at this stage whether these two items are only "expected," he will undoubtedly reply "I have already decided that the expenditure will be realized." But this is not yet apparent in the management account.

Nor should it be. The concept of a decision cannot withstand scientific criticism. It can be interpreted in many ways, and it is not until the management makes its "decisions" visible in the form of agreements that we return to linguistically safe ground again. Managers may regard their decisions as reliable descriptions of consequences, but they may easily be proved wrong if there are any surprises in the future.

Our example contains just such a surprise. The management immediately realizes that the employees were not entirely in agreement about a price of 40 for their wages. The result of this surprise is that the management's "decision" becomes an agreement, and the balance sheet changes its appearance the very same day. See figure 16.17.

S	Item	Amount		State	Assets	Liabilities
A	Income	100		"Expected"		−70
E	Wages	−40		"Agreed"	100	
E	Materials	−30		"Realized"		
	Liq. cont.	30		"Paid		

Figure 16.16. The contribution of the accepted order to the balance sheet.

S	Item	Amount		State	Assets	Liabilities
A	Income	100		"Expected"		−30
A	Wages	−42		"Agreed"	100	−42
E	Materials	−30		"Realized"		
	Liq. cont.	28		"Paid"		

Figure 16.17. The contribution of the order to the balance sheet after the wage agreement.

As discussed, our imaginary management was fortunate enough to reach a favorable agreement for the purchase of materials from the subsupplier, and as a result the balance sheet changes once again. See figure 16.18.

Figure 16.18 shows us the liquidity contribution and financing requirement of the order at the moment when binding agreements have been signed with regard to both income and expenses. Managers would all agree that we now have a very reliable prediction of financial consequences. Of course it is not 100 percent certain that the order will have exactly the consequences expected, but the description has the best possible form and substance at this stage. The management of enterprise A certainly has no difficulty in regarding this calculation as comprehensible and thus reliable. After all, they have drawn it up, negotiated and checked it themselves.

Figure 16.19 shows the situation on April 10. The materials have been delivered and invoiced, but not yet paid for. Nor has either of the two wage installments been paid. Readers comparing figure 16.19 with current accounting practice will realize that *it is only at this stage that the project becomes partially visible in double entry bookkeeping.* The invoice for materials is the first visible contribution to the realization account.

Readers will notice that the project is constantly updated in the system of management accounting. The picture always shows the financial situation right now, and only the most recent information is valid. If there are any changes, it will be possible to show them.

S	Item	Amount
A	Income	100
A	Wages	−42
A	Materials	−27
	Liq. cont.	31

State	Assets	Liabilities
"Expected"		
"Agreed"	100	−69
"Realized"		
"Paid		

Figure 16.18. The contribution of the order to the balance sheet after the material purchasing agreement.

S	Item	Amount
A	Income	100
A	Wages	−42
R	Materials	−27
	Liq. cont.	31

State	Assets	Liabilities
"Expected"		
"Agreed"	100	−42
"Realized"		−27
"Paid"		

Figure 16.19. The first balance sheet contribution to double entry bookkeeping.

We end our description of the project by proceeding to its conclusion. After the customer's check is received, the contribution of the project to the accounts is as shown in figure 16.20.

If an auditor pays an unannounced visit to enterprise A at this stage, a check will be visible in the cash holdings. But in the future, inspections of cash holdings will lose their importance as a feature of auditing procedure. Payments in cash are already a rare occurrence, and checks will probably disappear soon, too. In the future, money transactions will primarily consist of electronic transfers directly from one account to another. In order to illustrate this point, let us assume that the check is paid into enterprise A's account. The final picture of the project now appears in figure 16.21.

The liquidity contribution of the project is now present in the accounts as *a claim not on the customer, but on the bank.* Clearly, if enterprise A leaves the money in the bank it can be used as part of enterprise A's future payment capability, that is, as its ability to finance future activities. But if enterprise A spends the money on purchases, to reduce its debt, or to distribute as dividend, then it will be forced to borrow money next time a financing requirement needs to be covered.

We have now seen how the dynamic account works, and demonstrated that the individual contribution of a project to the overall financial statement is visible as part of the new dynamic balance sheet produced by management accounting. Readers may be wondering what the rest of the management account looks like. Figure 16.3 illustrated that enterprise A's

S	Item	Amount	State	Assets	Liabilities
P	Income	112	"Expected"		
P	Wages	−50	"Agreed"		
P	Materials	−27	"Realized"		
	Liq. cont.	35	"Paid"	35	

Figure 16.20.   The project after receipt of payment by check.

S	Item	Amount	State	Assets	Liabilities
P	Income	112	"Expected"		
P	Wages	−50	"Agreed"		
P	Materials	−27	"Realized"	35	
	Liq. cont.	35	"Paid"		

Figure 16.21.   The project after electronic transfer of payment.

account showed assets of 352 and liabilities of 330 at the time the new order appeared. We have seen that the dynamic account can be used to update constantly the picture of the financial consequences of individual projects. But what about the rest of the management account? What does the overall picture look like?

The answer is that the rest of the management account also consists of individual projects, and that projects never contain more logical elements than the ones indicated here. In other words, the overall picture of management accounting is nothing more than a summary of the future payments of each individual project.

Let us try to illustrate this by changing the perspective of the new balance sheet model. Our starting point is the now-familiar basic form of the balance sheet shown in figure 16.14. We simply rotate the table to produce the diagram shown in figure 16.22.

The next step is to include time in our diagram, and this is shown in figure 16.23.

We shall now complete the shift in perspective so the balance sheet formerly viewed "from the front" is now viewed "from the side." The sums apparent in the individual fields can now be explained simply as the sums of the information about future payments contained in each individual project, incorporating time. Figure 16.24 shows both the time dimension of the payment information and the contribution of each item of information

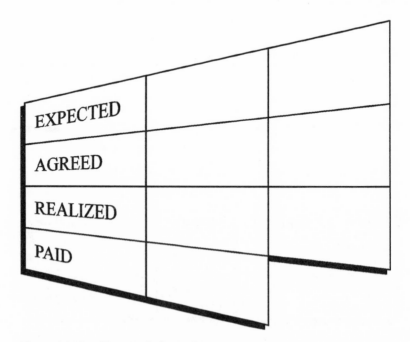

Figure 16.22. The new balance sheet perspective.

to the overall account. If you place your hand, a pen or a sheet of paper on the left-hand side of figure 16.24 and move it to the right, the passage of time will become apparent.

The dynamism of this model is now visible. Anything to the right of your hand, pen or paper is still in "the future," whereas anything to the left is in "the past." The right-hand limit of your hand, pen or paper is a vertical line representing "the present." The vertical arrows in figure 16.24 now show the times by which the logical state of the information about payments stated in advance *must change*—otherwise these payments will become "threatened" or "unreliable." An expected payment (i.e., a quotation) must have become an agreement by the time your hand, pen or paper reaches the limit of the prediction in question. An agreement must have been fulfilled and become a claim, and a claim must finally have been met by payment.

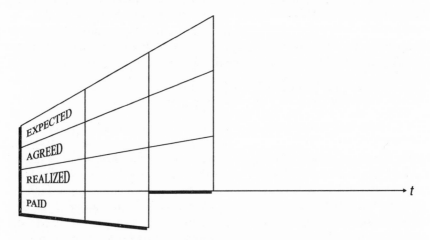

Figure 16.23. Time incorporated in the new perspective.

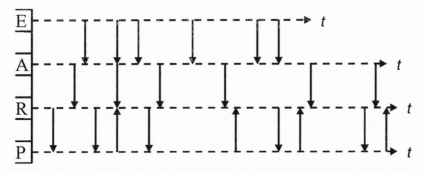

Figure 16.24. The connection between the sums and individual payments of the balance sheet.

If all these events actually take place, each individual piece of information about payments must have been reliable. And if this is the project, the conclusion must be that the management account as a whole is also reliable.

If the events do not take place, it is possible to determine which information about future payments was not reliable. This kind of "threatened information" can be traced at any time (and without wasting much time) to the manager who provided it, and the reliability of this manager can then be tested. He may explain that his predictions were good, but that their fulfillment was somewhat delayed. Or perhaps he may be forced to admit that his predictions were unrealistic, in which case they can no longer be regarded as reliable. If this happens too often with the same manager, *the specific manager will be regarded as unreliable*. And this is the logical conclusion of responsibility accounting.

We note that the arrows between the states of "realized" and "paid" in figure 16.24 point in both directions. This shows that claims become cash when they are met. This cash does not stay where it is. It can be used to set off against debt, or to deposit in deposit accounts. We are now able to distinguish between the two main logical components of the concept of payment capability. The concept can be divided into:

1. *an agreed* payment capability (liquidity reserve)
2. *an expected* payment capability (negotiation reserve)

The payment capability found in the logical state "agreed" consists of liquid assets, deposits in bank accounts, nonutilized cash credits and so on. But it also consists of all the payments agreed in connection with the enterprise's plant and operations, payments that have been invisible in financial statements until now because double entry bookkeeping simply fails to measure agreed payments unless they have already been realized or made.

Predictions of payment that are "agreed" but not yet "realized" or "paid" are actually always invisible to managers who are content to use double entry bookkeeping. But using the dynamic account these payments become visible, thereby making dynamic management accounting a logically complete accounting system.

We use the term "logically complete accounting system" to mean an accounting system that shows us the financial consequences of *all* an organization's actions and also *all* the financial consequences of these actions.

The commitments omitted systematically from traditional financial statements are by no means imaginary. The kind of commitments omitted include leasing contracts, wages to employees entitled to long periods of notice and so on. Readers will undoubtedly be able to find their own examples of predicted payments received and made that are agreed at a given time but not yet realized or paid.

The payment capability to be found in the logical state "expected" consists of funds that are not immediately accessible, but that can be converted from "expected" to "agreed" following negotiation with banks, stockholders or other investors. In practice, this involves various types of loan and injections of new subordinated loan capital. We must assume that it always takes a certain amount of time (calculation, preparation, negotiation) to change an expected payment capability into an agreed financial capability. If this assumption about the time required holds water, it is a very potent argument in favor of providing the kind of early warnings that dynamic management accounting offers.

The agreed and expected financial capability now form *the overall financial capability*. So this concept only contains two logical categories.

The expression "capability" underlines the fact that enterprises are regarded as organisms. Accounting information no longer consists of figures on a sheet of paper, but is now part of the information available to (and ready for use by) the management. We have imagined a future situation, and prepared one or more actions to carry out when and if this situation arises. Managements who establish a financial capability will always be able to act and make payments rapidly. Enterprises are now seen as organisms, not as mechanisms.

Let us conclude this chapter by giving an example of an all-round management account. Once again, we shall use our example of enterprise A. We choose the date March 28, and ask to see the account immediately after wage agreement X has been finalized. Readers probably remember that the wages were changed from 40 to 42. Figure 16.13 showed that the assets at the time in question were 452, and the liabilities -402. It must be possible to describe the payment capability (or solvency) as the difference between assets and liabilities. But the difference cannot be understood simply as one amount of money. Solvency and payment capability are expressions of the same thing, but the concepts can only be understood if they are described dynamically. Time must be incorporated. We shall now demonstrate *the dynamic all-round description of solvency*.

In our picture there are two other projects, designated X-1 and X-2. The other expenses are only indicated as a single payment of rent and two payments of wages. But it would not be difficult for readers to draw up a more realistic example. In practice, none of the many types of income and expenses in the real world are more complicated than the ones we have chosen to include.

Projects X-1 and X-2 are both *in progress* on March 28, which is the time chosen for our description of solvency. Let us now describe both these projects in the same way as project X. On March 28 projects X-1 and X-2 are as shown in Figure 16.25 with regard to *profitability*.

The *financing requirements* for projects X-1 and X-2 are shown in figures 16.26 and 16.27, respectively. Readers will not be surprised at the identical content of the two symmetrical concepts of contribution margin and financing requirement.

Two wage payments have been agreed, a simplified situation that may be instructive nonetheless, resulting in the financing requirement shown in figure 16.28.

Finally, on February 19 a contract is signed for the purchase of a machine that is to be delivered and paid for on May 20, as shown in figure 16.29.

We have already observed the full progress of project X. Let us now place ourselves in the position of the manager of our imaginary enterprise on March 28, at the moment when she has just negotiated and finalized the contract for project X. We recall that the expected wage amount was 40, but the agreed wage amount was 42.

The manager now asks the questions *"Is my enterprise solvent at the moment?"* and *"What about liquidity?"* Figure 16.30 enables her to answer these important questions herself in convincing fashion. The list can be produced by the computer any time the manager needs it.

We can now view all the items in the dynamic management account in context. As mentioned before, we have assumed that there are no items other than those included here. Naturally, this is a simplified and thus unrealistic assumption to make. But a truly realistic picture would be highly complex and thus difficult to reproduce here, so readers will perhaps forgive the simplification. The reliable description of solvency

	Project X-1	Project X-2
Income	200	80
Wages	−105	−35
Materials	−70	−35
Contribution margin	25	10

Figure 16.25. Projects X-1 and X-2, profitability.

Date	S	Payment	Amount	Σ FR
March 30	R	Income (1/2)	100	−100
March 30	A	Materials (1/2)	−45	−55
March 30	A	Wages (1/3)	−45	−10
April 3	E	Materials (2/2)	−25	15
April 6	A	Wages (2/3)	−45	60
April 10	A	Income (2/2)	100	−40
April 16	E	Wages (3/3)	−15	−25

Figure 16.26. Financing requirement, project X-1.

in figure 16.30 can now be compared with the dynamic balance sheet in figure 16.31.

Adding the figures contained in figure 16.30 together results in total assets of 452 and total liabilities of 402. The difference between the two amounts is 50, and 50 reflects the solvency of the enterprise as a whole on March 28, at the time the wage agreement of 42 in project X is finalized, but before the manager is aware of the saving in terms of material costs. Readers can now compare figures 16.3, 16.30 and 16.31, and will realize that the account balances. The same figures occur throughout, although they are arranged differently.

Figure 16.3 reflects the solvency, but it is nonetheless illogical to try and describe something that is constantly changing using one amount only. Figure 16.30 is the only one that contains an up-to-date and comprehensible description of solvency. Solvency changes all the time, so it needs to be measured and recalculated all the time, too.

The questions asked by our manager about solvency and liquidity on March 28 can be answered as follows: "Yes. When and if the current projects are completed as expected and agreed, and as long as no new agreements are made, we shall be liquid all the time, and on May 30 there will be 50 in our account. So no creditors will lose any money by

Date	S	Payment	Amount	Σ FR
March 29	R	Materials (1/1)	−35	35
March 31	R	Income (1/2)	40	−5
April 3	A	Wages (1/1)	−35	30
April 5	R	Income (2/2)	40	−10

Figure 16.27.   Financing requirement, project X-2.

Date	S	Payment	Amount	Σ FR
March 31	A	Wages (1/1)	−15	15
May 30	A	Wages (2/2)	−15	30

Figure 16.28.   Wage agreements.

Date	S	Payment	Amount	Σ FR
May 20	A	Machine purchase	−55	55

Figure 16.29.   Investment in new machine.

doing business with us. We can meet all our obligations." This answer has the same general form as *logical calculations of the future*. The payments of the immediate future are visible all the time, at both the transaction and all-round level. There are no more problems of comprehension, because each line in figure 16.30 can be traced back to the manager whose actions it describes, and there are no other elements of description in our picture of solvency.

As we have seen, there is always a degree of unavoidable uncertainty in describing solvency. Things never remain the same for long. The outside world is not static; it changes constantly. And these changes cannot be predicted precisely.

Readers are now invited to consult figure 16.30 and answer the following questions on the evening of March 28:

Project	Date	State	Payment	Amount	Liquidity
	March 28	R	Cash at bank	72	72
X-2	March 29	R	Materials (1/1)	−35	37
X-1	March 30	R	Income (1/2)	100	137
X-1	March 30	A	Materials (1/2)	−45	92
X-1	March 30	A	Wages (1/3)	−45	47
X-2	March 31	R	Income (1/2)	40	87
Wages	March 31	A	Wages (1/1)	−15	72
X-1	April 3	E	Materials (2/2)	−25	47
X-2	April 3	A	Wages (1/1)	−35	12
X-1	April 5	R	Income (2/2)	40	52
X-1	April 6	A	Wages (2/3)	−45	7
X-1	April 10	A	Income (2/2)	100	107
X	April 16	A	Wages (1/2)	−21	86
X-1	April 16	E	Wages (3/3)	−15	71
X	April 29	E	Materials (1/1)	−30	41
X	April 30	A	Wages (2/2)	−21	20
X	May 12	A	Income (1/1)	100	120
Invest.	May 20	A	Mach. purchase (1/1)	−55	65
Wages	May 30	A	Wages (2/2)	−15	50

Figure 16.30. The reliable real-time description of solvency.

State	Assets	Liabilities
"Expected"		−70
"Agreed"	200	−297
"Realized"	252	−35
"Paid"		

Figure 16.31. The dynamic balance sheet.

- What happens if the second payment installment for project X-2 is made seven days later than agreed?
- What happens if the machine supplier offers us a price reduction of 2 if we pay on April 20 instead of May 20?
- What happens if we are asked about an order that has the same terms as project X, but that is to be started and completed exactly five days later than project X?

The new management accounting system does not contain the concepts of depreciation, profit or owners' equity, because these concepts are scientifically inexplicable, and should therefore be discarded. But the new system *does* show us the financial position and the enterprise's solvency or insolvency at all times. And that, after all, is the object of the exercise.

The next chapter describes the logical database in detail.

17   THE FINANCIAL DATABASE—
THE NEW AUDIT TRAIL

> We shall make no progress by thinking about individual
> situations in isolation. Thought must always result in
> reflection, reflection in careful consideration, and careful
> consideration in knowledge about connections.
>
> —*Johann Wolfgang von Goethe*

No one wishes to lose the excellent, inspiring form of data security that has
made accounting specialists adhere to double entry bookkeeping for the
past 500 years. Many people may feel insecure at the thought of abandoning the measurement and data processing rules of double entry bookkeeping. But it is actually possible to transfer the idea of data security to modern
times, and modern technology actually offers a better chance of guarantee-
ing data security than the technology available in the past. Double entry
bookkeeping's basic idea about the connection between chronological basic
registration and systematic processing of the data registered is also the
backbone of dynamic management accounting. Computer scientists are
ready to perform the tasks accountants require of them, using modern technology. The only problem until now has been that they have found it hard
to understand the terminology used by accounting specialists. We might be
able to improve in certain respects. We could obtain better, more up-to-date
information using far less data, if only we thought a little more carefully
about what we were doing.

In the previous chapter we demonstrated how our new accounting
model works, pointing out that the new dynamic balance sheet still

describes the solvency of enterprises in terms of their permanent payment capability. Managements need to be able to demonstrate the payment capability of their enterprises at any time in terms of the difference between assets (well-founded predictions of payments received) and liabilities (well-founded predictions of payments made). So we can now claim to have identified the logic on which management accounting is based.

But of course management accounts are only reliable if each of their component parts is reliable. So in this chapter we shall describe and discuss the degree to which systematic testing of the reliability of management accounting is possible. The reason for doing this is that we claim the following statement as our postulate:

The task of the auditor is to systematically test the overall picture provided by financial statements—as well as the individual components that make up the whole. Testing should comprise both formal and real reliability.

The distinction between *formal* and *real* is familiar in accounting theory and practice. But accounting specialists would be the first to admit that formalism has dominated the accounting scene until now.

The first questions are "Does the new theory of management accounting provide a reproducible method of describing the financial consequences of the actions of organizations? Can we claim that students will have no difficulty in systematically learning the difference between documents expressing *expected* payments (quotations, calculations, estimates, budgets), *agreed* payments (contracts), *claims* and *debts* (invoices, bills, bank accounts), and *cash* (Danish Kroner, Italian Lire, U.S. Dollars)? Can students also learn to control modern accounting tools, enabling them to draw up sums of the figures contained in such documents in any organization, at any time and in any situation? Will others reach the same conclusions if we check?" If readers believe that the answers to these questions may be "Yes," then there is hope ahead. Because this might mean that in future we shall be able to draw up scientifically reliable procedures for accounting registration, auditing and accounting reports.

The accounting measurements and calculations that can take place using reproducible methods have already been identified—they are scientifically reliable if they can be seen as the consequences of actions that can be performed, not in terms of mere belief and speculation. It will always be possible to determine whether documentation for such measurements and calculations is available. And it will also be possible to test systematically whether the documents concerned are reliable, that is, whether they reflect reality. If they do, it will then be possible to regard accounting specialists and accountants as the expert, critical and competent partners of management.

Basing our description of financial consequences on the familiar legal concept of "an agreement" has the following advantages:

1. The essential need for reproducibility can be met, owing to the fact that the buyer and seller can both describe the same agreement. They give the elements of the agreement different names, with the buyer talking about expenses and the seller talking about income, but they are undoubtedly describing the same phenomena.
2. The fact that such a description is objective or intersubjective is also demonstrated by the fact that the parties agree about the description. And if they subsequently disagree, negotiations, mediation, legislation and judicial practice will all help to re-establish agreement.
3. Systematic testing will always enable accountants to decide whether a given document is formally reliable or viable, or whether the document concerned is false.
4. Systematic testing will always enable accountants to decide whether a given document is really reliable (i.e., whether it actually describes reality) or whether the document represents an agreement that has already been broken or delayed.
5. Management accounts consist of nothing but the cash account and the sum of assets and liabilities, that is, well-founded predictions of payments received and made. So the logical completeness of management accounts can be audited systematically by accountants.

The final point is probably the most important. Management accounts only consist of predictions made by managers themselves, so there may be disagreement between managers and accountants about the information being audited. All the entries in such accounts consist of information provided by managers, with whom the issues concerned can be discussed. There will be fewer conflicts of interest between managers and accountants, and opportunism will be more difficult. Everyone concerned will be interested in describing the financial position of the enterprise concerned in a realistic way. It is quite impossible to find any group of interested parties with *bonus pater familias* characteristics who will *not* be interested in obtaining precise, up-to-date information about the financial situation. Consequently, the following subconclusion can be drawn about the auditing method of the future:

The description of an enterprise's solvency can always be monitored and confirmed systematically by accountants. This enables us to get very close to solving the problem of the reliability of accounting. The solution is really quite easy to understand, as long as we distinguish between registration and reporting. Financial accounts *kept* for any given period traditionally consist of no more than a chart of accounts and a finite number of entries. There are no other components of basic registration, so there are no other components in the object being audited. All the financial statements *presented* in various situations are, of course, reports, which are based without exception on copies or part-copies of a systematically maintained financial database.

The definition of the concept of an accounting entry is as follows:

An accounting entry is a logical statement about the financial consequences of an action or a set of actions.

The connection between an entire financial statement and its component parts can be expressed simply as follows: The concept of an "accounting entry" is the name given to the only subsystem present in the information system known as "management accounting." There are no other components. Consequently:

An organization's financial statement consists of a finite and thus countable number of chronologically measured entries and the systematic organization of these entries, and of nothing else.

We can now proceed by considering management accounting as an information system that is ready for use, but that has not yet been given any content—that is, as an opportunity that has not yet been taken. The system does not start to work until entries are actually made, reflecting the financial consequences of actions that can be performed. In chapter 13 we outlined an example of the basic logical requirements made of any system of information. Such systems must be *complete, consistent, necessary* and *sufficient*. Let us apply these requirements to our definition of the subsystem known as "an accounting entry."

We shall take the term "logically *complete* accounting entry" to mean an accounting entry that comprehensively describes all the financial consequences of a given action.

We shall take the term "logically *consistent* accounting entry" to mean an accounting entry that describes the financial consequences of a given action in a coherent, consistent way. In other words, each accounting entry can only be in one logical state at any time.

It is *necessary* for accounting entries that they contain descriptions of financial consequences, which means that all descriptions of actions that do not have financial consequences must be rejected. They are not the objects of accounting, so they should not be used as the basis of accounting entries.

Finally, it is *sufficient* for accounting entries that they contain descriptions of financial consequences, which means that all actions that have financial consequences are the objects of accounting.

Agreements have financial consequences, so they should be measured reliably in order to produce reliable accounting entries. Another subconclusion can be drawn at this stage, showing that it is vital for the reliability of financial statements that the system of registration used always works quickly and precisely. *Delays in basic registration result in logical incompleteness.*

In practice there are entries that do not meet the definition and methodical requirements mentioned here. We shall call these entries *pseudoentries*.

In general, such entries comprise deferred charges and income, which are used to try and solve the logically impossible task of describing the dynamic financial situation of enterprises using a picture that is static. But there are also other pseudoentries, such as so-called "supplementary entries" (calculated interest, internal debiting and so on) Our new definition of accounting entries and methodical requirements should make it easy for readers to distinguish between accounting entries and such pseudoentries.

The logical content of accounting entries has now been described, and we can consider the form of accounting entries in greater detail. What is the best *method of* describing the financial consequences of any given actions or chain of actions?

In chapter 5 we considered the old, time-honored but no longer entirely tenable system of double entry bookkeeping, with its T-shaped account and entries and "supplementary entries" of both debit and credit. But we now realize the unfortunate and fatal logical incompleteness of this system, which is used all over the world today. The information system that was regarded 500 years ago as a brilliant new way of describing the current financial situation now seems more like a paralyzing straitjacket that is a direct barrier to progress. It can no longer be regarded as an adequate tool for use in financial descriptions. The most significant effects of double entry bookkeeping are 1) the management lose their overview of the financial situation, 2) financial statements lose credibility as pictures of the financial situation and 3) auditors lose their role as the witnesses of reliability.

Do modern technology and the new ideas about its use offer us the chance to recover these serious losses? In an attempt to answer this question, let us now consider another familiar and key concept in auditing theory—*the audit trail.*

The concept of the audit trail, like many other key accounting concepts, is defined differently (and not always precisely) by different people. We should like to suggest the following new definition:

An audit trail is a data structure that describes the logical connections between (1) an action or a set of actions with financial consequences, (2) measurement of the financial consequences and (3) the use of these measurements in accounting reports.

The audit trail contains three elements, which can be described briefly as *actions, measurement* and *reporting.* A brief comment is required on these three elements.

Actions are the actions of the management of any given enterprise. These actions can be described unambiguously, so it will also be possible to refer precisely to any failure to perform them, thus making it possible to attribute responsibility to individual members of the management. As mentioned earlier, financial statements consist of entries that are organized systematically, and of nothing else. The requirement made in management accounting is that in order to be scientifically reliable, each entry must reflect an action that can be performed. The designations of such actions are purchases and sales, contracts of employment, agreements, loans, leasing contracts, agreements about the injection of capital and (in all cases) the payments arising from these actions.

Traditional financial statements with their debit and credit sides very rarely provide a complete description of the financial consequences of actions. Consequently, we need a concept that allows us to demonstrate the logical completeness of accounting entries. The concept we need is *a project*, and the person responsible is known as *a project manager*. We shall use the following definition of a project: A project is an action or a set of actions that have financial consequences.

In practice projects may comprise many different things, such as contracts, sales campaigns, and agreements. The concept of the agreement is always the logical heart of any project, which means that projects are the true objects of accounting. That is, projects are what accounting should observe and measure.

The audit trail retains its vital importance for the practice of accounting. It should enable us to count and identify all current projects, to delimit each individual project and to carry out critical testing of the quality of project predictions and thereby of the reliability of the management concerned. This is the true purpose of auditing financial statements, asking these questions: Which projects and payments are described? Why has the management expressed the data in this particular way? and Why are the predictions of payment in this particular project regarded as reliable?

Measurement involves the formal side of description: How does the registration system work? What is the origin of the basic accounting data? How is this data fixed? Who is the project manager responsible? When will the data that has been measured be ready to use? How is the data protected against misuse? These questions represent the auditing of the formal content of financial statements. Do we now have all the necessary and sufficient data? Or is basic registration delayed, defective or in any other way incomplete? Can we be certain that redundant registration cannot occur, making our basic data inconsistent?

Finally, *the use* of information in the database ensures the logical completeness, relevance and reliability of management accounting. Assuming that project descriptions and basic registration are reliable, and that data discipline has been good, it should be possible in the future to describe the insolvency or incipient insolvency of enterprises using simple, programmed addition, which can take place automatically at any time.

This also ensures the availability of *an early warning system for insolvency*. If the management is no longer able to convince itself and/or the enterprise's accountant of the reliability of its predictions of payments received, and if the assets (including cash holdings) can no longer cover the liabilities, the enterprise is insolvent. In principle, it does not matter how small the negative balance is. The main point is that it can be revealed using dynamic management accounting.

Our new insight and clearly formulated requirements concerning substance and form mean that we can now describe, explain, measure and delimit accounting data precisely and without exception. We can distinguish between accounting data and all other data. We can still produce all the traditional reports and financial statements. Improved basic registration does not restrict our capacity in this respect. But readers will now be able to see the difference in individual entries in any given accounting report. The entries can be clearly distinguished from the pseudoentries.

Traditional tools used for measurement and calculation are now obsolete, and the registers and debit-credit entries of double entry bookkeeping are now insufficient. We need much more powerful data registration and data processing tools. Let us now recall the example quoted in chapter 5, involving the medieval merchant and the task he managed to solve. We still face the same task. The tools used 500 years ago were pen and paper. Nowadays we have electronic technology at our disposal, and paper is fast disappearing as a data carrier. In the future, information about the current financial situation will be measured, processed and transmitted electronically, and users will be able to call it onto their monitors or other information carriers.

At first sight, the new technology may seem problematic. For instance, we stand to lose the traditional original documents used to verify individual transactions. People cannot read electronic data carriers as easily as paper. It may be difficult to prevent accounting entries being deleted either intentionally or by accident. In many cases, the system will draw up accounting entries itself (for example, the accrual of interest) that are also needed in the description required. So there are many reasons for treating the new technology with respect. But the same task has to be performed now as 500 years ago. The questions we must ask are identical: How can we set up and ensure chronological basic data registration? How can we ensure the data security and logical completeness and consistency of the new electronic register?

Even though this task is both large and awe-inspiring, it can still be performed. All we have to do is acknowledge that the task of accounting registration has been achieved as soon as chronological measurements have been performed. This is clearly the case, because traditional bookkeeping in T-shaped accounts does not actually involve registration. It involves data processing, and copying and organizing information that is already available. In the past chronological information and systematically organized copies of information were kept in the register and ledger. The bookkeepers of the past could always reproduce a reliable financial statement even if the ledger was lost, simply by referring to the register. But if the ledger and register were both lost, it was no longer possible to prove that financial statements were complete.

Once chronological data registration has been assured, we can ask the next question: How can we systematically transform chronological measurements of the financial consequences of projects into pictures that help to describe the financial situation of enterprises with regard to both individual projects and the overall situation? If basic registration is updated constantly, then each accounting report becomes a current report, not an interim account. The distinguishing feature of current reports is that they answer questions that the management asks in specific situations, here and now. They are never out-of-date, in contrast with traditional reports, which are tied to specific periods of the past.

Naturally, it will still be possible to produce all the traditional types of accounting report. Interim reports are always current reports. But current reports are very rarely related to fixed periods of the calendar.

Consequently, we now need to consider the details of chronological basic registration—the basis of our register. To meet the requirements of data security and user-friendliness, the fundamental demand must be that the register's data must be physically available in a *data carrier that is transportable and readable by machine, as well as being impossible to delete*. The reasons for these demands are as follows:

1. It must not be possible to delete basic accounting data by accident, and such data must also be protected against deliberate deletion.
2. It must be possible to form back-up copies automatically, and to keep them in places where they will not be lost if the original material is lost.
3. It must be possible to reproduce financial statements quickly if there are any accidents or infringements of security.

It is relevant at this point to draw attention to a conflict that practical constructors of information systems always have to face—the conflict between user-friendliness and data security.

Unfortunately, systems that are extremely user-friendly also tend to be easy to misuse. Naturally, bookkeepers and treasurers are not all able to stick to the narrow path of righteousness, so when constructing information systems the risk of misuse must always be borne in mind. We shall not deal with this point in depth here, but simply mention that it is possible to a large extent either to prevent deliberate misuse altogether, or to make it very difficult. In the past people used to say that the bookkeeper and treasurer should never be one and the same person, since this might tempt the person concerned to abuse the trust placed in him or her. In addition, the people participating in accounting should always be trusted individuals.

In the future the division between the roles of the bookkeeper and treasurer respectively will be reflected in the division between *the responsible manager* and *the financial controller*. The people *agreeing to an expense* on behalf of an enterprise should never be the ones to *make payments* as well. The people agreeing to an income with a customer or provider of subsidies should never be the ones to register payments received. This division, which has been acknowledged practice in the world of practical accounting for many years, will always prevent misuse (or make misuse difficult) to a certain extent. But probably no system is 100 percent perfect.

User authorization, of course, requires knowledge of certain predetermined codes in order to gain access to the system. But in this respect, too, it is very difficult or even impossible in practice to prevent misuse without making the system difficult or impossible to use. Having made this point, let us now return to our task, which involves describing the fields required in our financial database.

The tool used to describe individual projects, and thereby to describe the all-round situation, is (as mentioned previously) the dynamic account. Figure 17.1 shows that it is possible to describe simultaneous and parallel *profitability* and *liquidity* in an extremely simple way. Project X, which we used as an example in chapter 16, is easily recognized, but this time it is seen as a logical relational database.

We remind readers that this picture is dynamic. It changes constantly because it is updated as soon as the management takes any action that has financial consequences. So a new version is already available on March 30 (see figure 17.2).

Both the data and the structure of project X should be easily recognized, as are the profitability (contribution margin, or liquidity contribution) and

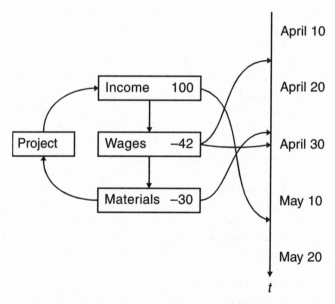

Figure 17.1. The dynamic account as a logical relational database. Project X on March 28.

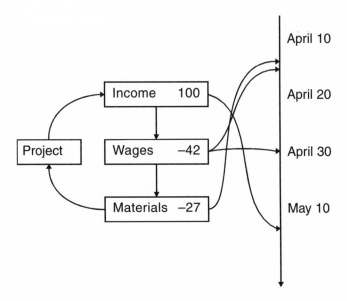

Figure 17.2. The dynamic account as a logical relational database. Project X on March 30.

the liquidity (financing requirement). In the past these concepts were always dealt with separately, but we now consider them simultaneously and parallel to each other, in the same picture. The two traditional concepts of *profitability* and *liquidity* can now be seen as *two sides of the same coin.*

The fact that we now distinguish clearly between the task of registration and all the many situation-related reporting tasks enables us to see that users considering accounting reports are always considering an organized copy of chronologically measured basic data. Let us therefore consider a report and demonstrate that all the data it contains is present in basic registration. If this is the case, financial statements will always be available for use here and now. The only possible delay is the delay that might be caused by defective or obsolete technology. And this problem can be surmounted.

A certain amount of information concerning future payments can now be associated with each project. Each entry of information can and should be updated as soon as events or actions occur to affect the logical validity of the current information. Updating means that previous information about payments is declared to be logically invalid. *The latest information is always the valid information.*

As mentioned previously, each accounting entry is a logical statement concerning the financial consequences of individual actions, and thus it always contains information about future payments. Each entry of information about payments is composed of project-specific data.

The necessary and sufficient data required to describe individual projects is as follows:

1. *Project identification.* A unique number or name used to refer to the project and distinguish it from all other projects.
2. *Project description.* The distinguishing characteristics of each project in the form of the familiar, traditional categories based on specific agreements such as sales orders, wage agreements, leasing contracts, loans, rent contracts and so on
3. *Document reference(s).* Specification of the physical location in which documents are kept and where they can be found.
4. *Original date.* The time at which agreement is reached.
5. *The manager responsible.* Specification of the person or persons entering into the agreement on behalf of the organization.
6. *The other party to the agreement.* Specification of the person or persons outside the organization with whom the agreement has been made, for example, customers, suppliers, employees, telephone companies or banks. The description should contain extra classification opportunities to provide complex statistics, such as sales statistics for particular market segments (customer groups, districts and so on)
7. *Place of registration.* The physical location at which registration takes place.
8. *Time of registration.* The time at which the information is obtained.
9. *Transaction number.* Ongoing and unbroken numbers should be used for reasons of data security. This ensures the consistency of basic data: Financial statements can be checked to ensure completeness, and data redundancy can be avoided. In addition, the use of transaction numbers provides an emergency capability—any financial statement can always be reproduced from any given point in time up until the present day.
10. *The manager responsible.* Specification of the person making statements about the project, who should ideally carry out updating himself or herself. The manager responsible is regarded as being synonymous with the project manager, that is, the person who has concrete knowledge of the other party involved in the agreement, and who can thus provide reliable information about payments.
11. *Logical state code.* The information about payments specifies the current state of the entry, whether a given payment is *expected, agreed, realized* as a claim, and/or *confirmed* in the form of completed payment. These logical combinations are the only possible ones.
12. *Realization date.* The date on which the sales object or service must be supplied or carried out, and thus the date on which the sum concerned can change logical state and become a claim or debt.
13. *Document reference.* A reference to the document for each claim/debt (normally a copy of the invoice).

14. *Payment date.* The date on which actual payment is expected/agreed. In special circumstances, specific claims or debts can be described as a series of payments, that is, a number of dated entries of information, each containing an expected payment, with the total representing the total claim or debt concerned.

15. *Document reference.* A reference to the document for the payment transaction, such as check number, receipt or number of bank transaction.

16. *Name of currency.* Specification of the currency in which payment is made.

17. *The amount concerned.* A figure reflecting the size of the payment.

This is the necessary and sufficient basic data for the description of each individual project. And management accounting involves nothing but a finite and therefore countable number of combined individual projects, so this data is also necessary and sufficient for the formation of the overall picture.

Each individual field is straightforward, containing information that is always available in any organization. Once again we must add that the new theory of dynamic management accounting is constructed as a form of logic, architecture or prototype that will only ensure good results if users are *bonus pater familias,* that is, knowledgeable and conscientious people. But it may be worth practicing this new form of accounting nonetheless. The inexpensive and powerful computer technology now available will enable us to do so, and the new system only involves processing information that is already available in a slightly different way.

Let us now conclude this chapter by asking two questions on behalf of readers who are interested but still skeptical:

1. What is the connection between the old and new accounting systems? I can see the advantages of the new system, but I want to be sure I am not losing anything valuable if I abandon the old system. Traditional methods cannot simply be abandoned from one day to the next. In other words, we need to retain the traditional trial balance. The question can also be phrased as follows: Where are the account numbers used by traditional bookkeeping?

2. What will happen to data security if we start regarding the latest information as the only valid information, and therefore discard the old information? I admit that up-to-date information is more important for the management than highly precise information. But in practice will it not become too easy to misuse this rule?

The answer to the first question must start by underlining the vital importance of retaining the connection between the old and new accounting systems. Accounting specialists who are familiar with the demands and responsibilities of the real world would never dream of accepting a new system of basic data registration if this meant that the old, well-tried system disappeared as a result.

But the old accounting system is still present, although it is now merely part of the new and logically complete picture. Figure 17.3 shows an example of a suitable computer representation of a project.

Readers will recognize the entries of data in figure 17.3 from the previous chapter. Figure 17.3 reflects material supplies in project X on April 7, immediately after the supplier's invoice has been registered in the system. Clearly, it is still easy to determine the trial balance. All we need to do is ensure that the traditional, familiar account numbers are used for the time being in two and only two situations:

1. When new claims or debts arise, that is, when the system can be informed of an income or expense.
2. When money is received or paid either to set off against existing claims or debts, or to give rise to new claims or debts in the form of loans.

A single account number is all that is needed. Counterentries can be entered automatically, and the explanation of this is easy for readers who recall the chapter about the logic of double entry bookkeeping. Each entry affects the balance sheet, so each description of financial consequences can always be found in one and only one disjunctive logical category. Whether we are dealing with income or expenses, there are only two possibilities. Either payment is made at the same time as services are provided, in which case the counterentry is a money account. Or payment is not made at the same time as services are provided, in which case the counterentry is a debtor or creditor account.

Nor is the answer to the second question very difficult. In the old days bookkeepers were never allowed to make corrections in registers or ledgers by deleting previous entries that had become invalid. Correction always had to be carried out by adding a counterentry to enable the accountant to trace what had happened.

Exactly the same principle is now used on the computer. Any given entry accompanied by the identity of the project manager can of course be replaced by a new entry at any time, and thus declared as being no longer

State	Date	True	Amount	Account No.
Expected	10.3	yes	−30	
Agreed	30.3	yes	−27	
Realized	7.4	yes	−27	1250
Paid	14.4	no	−27	2250

Figure 17.3. Retention of the account numbers used in double entry bookkeeping.

logically valid. But it must be stored *physically*, making it possible to draw up and print a complete chronological *project explanation*.

There is one particular detail that is important in order to help readers understand the dynamic nature of this new system of accounting. The times stated in the chronological register reflect financial points of measurement. Accountants might also choose to call them financial points of control, since points in time can also be used for the purpose of control. Computers have built-in clocks, so they are able to give the concept of "now" substance by using a process that is rather like looking at your watch to find out the time and date. So when figure 17.3 reveals that payment has not yet been made, the computer will find no reason for comment on this fact until after April 14. But on April 15 the claim will occur in a list of "threatened claims" if it has still not yet been paid.

We conclude this chapter by underlining the simplicity of the financial database. We simply use this database to ensure chronological basic registration of data and the protection of this data. The process involved is straightforward, and using modern technology as a tool makes it even easier.

But the financial database is important even though it is simple. Because if we carry out reliable and logically complete basic registration, and if we use computers to organize and print the data registered, we will obtain an up-to-date and reliable picture of the financial position of any given enterprise at any given time. This need for updated information about financial situations has been called "desperate" by practicing accountants. But this desperate need can now be met.

18 THE FUTURE OF ACCOUNTING

Here they are, one people with a single language, and now they have started to do this; henceforward nothing they have a mind to do will be beyond their reach.

—*Genesis chapter 11, verse 6*

The future started in 1912, when people's overoptimistic and almost blind faith in the blessings of technology received its first serious blow with the sinking of the *Titanic*. The two world wars of the twentieth century can be seen in an entirely new light using modern chaos theories. Economics is unpredictable, so theoretical attempts to explain future economic developments must be regarded as mere speculation. If only economists were able to produce a consistent theory about their profession, such attempts would no longer be necessary. Modern chaos theories reveal the impossibility and danger of linear philosophies, but if we are willing to abandon traditional myths and dogma there is a hope that the twenty-first century will witness great progress in the world of economics. This progress will be based on a new system and a new reliability. We shall gain greater insight and argue less amongst ourselves. Information technology will be used to register financial data, just as telescopes are used by astronomers, microscopes by biologists and x-ray cameras by doctors. We may be able to view accounting as a science. Instead of relying on speculation and blind faith, we may be able to truly understand the nature of accounting. Changes in financial positions cannot be described using linear mathematics, but they can be described using nonlinear mathematics. Financial positions are like living organisms, and like the lives of human beings, they cannot be predicted. But they can be described in meaningful and scientifically viable fashion all the same. Biologists can teach us theories about open, interactive, living systems. And we may also be able to learn that as long as there is life, there is hope.

Managers can never claim to know anything about the financial position of their enterprises *right now*. As long as this type of information is not available, managers will be forced to rely on guesswork when making decisions. All the facts indicate that modern day managers do not have access to reliable real-time information about the financial position of their enterprises.

Readers who are familiar with accounting practice, and who respect realism, common sense and logic, will now realize that as far as management and financial control are concerned, managers are forced to rely on estimates and guesswork when reaching agreements that commit their enterprises and others to take certain actions in the future. And if managers know nothing about the current financial position, who else can be expected to do so?

The undeniable conclusion must be that at the moment everyone depends on blind faith, speculation, guesswork, fantasy and imagination when it comes to describing financial positions. But no one can claim to have true insight. Managers, employees, accountants, bank managers, stockholders, trade union leaders, journalists, economists and politicians are all forced to rely on their own particular theories. And this may well be the reason why so many theoretical and practical conflicts arise. Because if no one knows anything for certain, any explanation that sounds plausible can be accepted—even explanations that subsequently prove to be impossible. People are often prepared to believe what they are told if it sounds plausible. It is easy enough to present various theories about a financial position, and it is easy enough to turn people into enthusiastic supporters of such theories. This has been proved on many occasions during this century. But luckily most people are now starting to realize that the conflicts arising when supporters of different theories clash can never be won. In such conflicts, there are no winners—only losers.

Readers may recall a seemingly provocative remark from one of the earliest chapters in this book to the effect that in terms of cognition, current accounting theory is at the stage medicine was at several centuries ago. We should like to explain briefly why this remark should not be seen as provocative. Instead, it should be regarded as a highly realistic analogy.

In the Middle Ages there were two types of doctor—physicians and surgeons. Physicians were trained at university, and were regarded as superior. They were the theorists of their profession. Surgeons had no university training, and were the practitioners of their profession. Doctors with a university training were expected not to treat patients, but to explain the nature of illness to surgeons. There was a clear distinction between doctors who claimed to know about the nature of illness, and doctors who tried to cure illness. Theory and practice were placed in entirely different hands, and this was regarded as the correct way to deal with medical science for 1,500 years. Surgery was considered inferior to medicine, and it was only to be performed by persons of inferior class. So operations were left to barbers, executioners, bathing attendants and traveling quacks. The view that medicine was fine and surgery simple was retained well on into the seventeenth and eighteenth centuries.

In a previous chapter we quoted Bertrand Russell's views about the scientifically barren and dangerous nature of teleological explanations. We also know that plausible systems of explanation are in great demand, particularly when uncertainty and fear are in evidence. Explanations that sound convincing tend to be accepted in such situations. Medical science remained static for 1,500 years, one of the main reasons for this being people's blind orthodoxy and the complete but almost entirely erroneous system of explanation put forward by one particular doctor who was convinced he was right.

The name of this doctor was Galen, and in *Medicinens Historie (A History of Medicine),* Professor Edvard Gotfredsen describes his importance as follows:

The ancient history of medicine starts with one big name—Hippocrates—and finishes with another name of equal significance—Galen (A.D. 130–201). The significance of Galen can be traced right down to modern times. . . . The unique authority of Galen is due to the fact that he constructed a fixed, well-organized system with everything in its place. He was aware of his own importance, and always put forward his theories with great certainty and conviction. For him judgment was not difficult, and experience not disappointing. "Anyone who wishes to be famous," he said, "only needs to understand the things I have been studying throughout my life." Posterity took Galen at his word, and for centuries research focused on his writings, which attained almost the same significance for the world of medicine as the Holy Scriptures had for theologians.[1]

Galen's works survived longer than those of most other doctors. His name was repeated time after time in the centuries after his death, and he was always described as an authority who could never be wrong. As late as the sixteenth century, when the Belgian Vesalius wrote his first true anatomy of the human body, he was opposed from many sides because he described the human body differently from Galen. When William Harvey discovered in the seventeenth century that blood circulates through the human body, he thought he must be mistaken because Galen had said something different. Galen was so sure of himself that he never doubted the truth of what he said. He could explain any type of illness, and he had the rare talent of being able to make his explanations plausible. People who lack scientific training always love plausible explanations, because they remove all doubt and save us from thinking for ourselves. Hippocrates was never entirely certain about anything that he had not proved to his own satisfaction. He knew that human thinking was a very incomplete tool. One of his sayings will still be recognized by many people today: "Life is short, but Art endures." The continuation of this saying is "Experience is disappointing, and it is difficult to evaluate." Hippocrates said, "Observe and discover things for yourself, then prove your discoveries by many observations." Galen, on the other hand, seemed to say "I can explain that."

In our day there are a number of different theoretical systems used to explain any current financial position, each of which claims to contain everything worth thinking and knowing. Let us now read a little more about Galen, comparing him with certain modern financial and accounting theorists:

The aim of Galen's works was to systematize all branches of medical science, and prove that everything had been created to serve mankind. He started with the works of Hippocrates, and he admired Hippocrates as well as regarding him as sadly out of date. He wished to add to the works of Hippocrates all the medical knowledge that had been learned during the 600 years since his death. And he wished to gather it all into a single system, a theory, an explanation of everything that could happen to Man. . . . He included not only the new medical knowledge, but also all the theories and speculations that had been put forward. Actual facts and observations were placed side-by-side with Pythagorean mathematics, the theory of the four humors, and the balance between various states—cold, hot, wet and dry. . . . Galen also believed in the balance between humors and states. For instance, some vegetables were hot, others cold, some wet, others dry. Cucumber seed was cool to the fourth degree—and the expression "cool as a cucumber" is still common today. So Galen could give a patient suffering from fever cucumber seed to counterbalance the heat that was making him ill. The system was extremely simple, and seen with our eyes extremely foolish. . . . Indeed, it would be amusing if it were not for the sad fact that 14 or 15 centuries after Galen's death sick people were still being treated with the useless herbal remedies he recommended. . . . If anyone ever committed the sin of ignorance mentioned by Hippocrates, it was Galen. And his ignorance, which was presented with such great authority, has done serious damage. . . . When you think of the thousands upon thousands of people who suffered and even died of infection quite meaninglessly simply because the great Galen had said that suppuration was necessary to heal wounds, it is a little difficult to regard his works sympathetically.[2]

Similarly convinced, some modern theoretical economists can be accused of sinning with regard to the acquisition of knowledge about their profession. Hippocrates expressed it as follows: "It is one thing to know, but quite another to know that one knows. Knowledge is science, but the mere belief that one has knowledge reveals a lack of knowledge." Many modern economic theories contain apparently comprehensive "knowledge" about the actions of the management with regard to price policies, salaries, interest and so on. But managers themselves have no up-to-date and reliable knowledge about the current financial position of their enterprises. Even the managers of small artisan or agricultural enterprises are unable to understand financial statements. And if it is impossible to understand a simple situation, how can we expect to understand complex situations? The tragic impotency of accounting can no longer be ignored or explained away.

The nearest anyone can get at the moment to an up-to-date and reliable description of the current financial position of any enterprise involves the use of what might be described in friendly terms as *intelligent imagination*. So it would be interesting to discover where modern theoretical economists obtain their information about the financial position of society as a whole. Because any description of the financial position of an enterprise is always a vital feature of any description of the financial position of society.

The Canadian American economist John Kenneth Galbraith makes the following remarks, which clearly show that the science of economics is still largely based on *faith* rather than on *knowledge*. The fact that economists have a number of cognitive problems in defining their profession as a science, that the outside world is changing all the time, and that consequently, people react by clinging to an increasingly unrealistic and impotent tradition, is revealed with all possible clarity:

Accomodation to changing reality is also resisted, as in the past, because of the desire to view economics as a science. In the academic world, where economics is taught, the standard of intellectual precision is set by the hard sciences. . . . It is the paradox of the discipline that it is the wish so to see itself (as a science) that commits economics to an obsolescence in a changing world that, by any scientific standard, is to be deplored.[3]

We note that the term "paradox" is used to refer to economics as a whole. Readers may recall a remark made in a previous chapter that when logical paradoxes are examined, they often may prove to be the springboard leading to new understanding.

Economists are, of course, not happy to be chained to the past in a world of change. Naturally, they wish to regard and develop their profession as a modern, dynamic science. They wish to view basic philosophies, observations of reality and theories in a clear and logical context, and they also wish to be consistent. If economists were capable of presenting a single consistent theory about their profession, all the various economic theories to which people adhere would no longer be necessary.

But unfortunately economists have been forced to work with hypotheses without being able to test these hypotheses using up-to-date and reliable data. No one has yet been able to claim true *knowledge* of the current financial position. When an economic hypothesis can be tested using data, even though this may involve great and even insurmountable difficulties, attention is focused on its internal logic. And at this point mathematics becomes the most important tool. The possible applications of the hypothesis can be drawn up mathematically and discussed as sophisticated suppositions, but they can never be tested. Economists study each other's theories and discover new details to debate among themselves. Each economist has great respect for his or her own particular theory, and great indulgence or disdain for the theories of others. Economic theories are like religions, and each major religion can be divided into sects. Debate rages, particularly when it comes to explaining why predictions about the future economic situation of society so often prove false. And all the nonprofessionals whose lives and daily work are at stake, but who cannot understand the mathematical formulae being debated, regard the economists involved as economic *experts*. Naturally, our hope for the future lies in retaining a healthy skepticism and searching for scientific reliability. Fortunately, not all economists adhere to particular theories, and even though their explanations may not sound as convincing as those provided by their more convinced brethren, our hope for the future rests in them.

Galbraith does not fall for the temptation to provide easy and impressive answers. Instead, he is uncompromisingly honest, and like Hippocrates he is aware that we simply do not have sufficient knowledge to make confident predictions about future financial positions:

The most common qualification of the economic forecaster is not in knowing but in not knowing that he does not know. His greatest advantage is that all predictions, right or wrong, are soon forgotten.[4]

If economics is to be regarded as a science, it must be the science of something that is alive and constantly changing, involving the exchange of information, goods, services and money between people. The task of economics must be to provide a description of the financial consequences of such interactions. There is no disagreement on this point. All the current theories agree that it is a good idea to produce goods to meet people's requirements. The disagreement between economic theories lies elsewhere. For instance, should we be producing butter or cannons? Who should be allowed to eat their fill, and who should starve to death?

What we need is a cognitive explanation and a scientifically reliable procedure to describe economics. The current theories are all obsolete, says Galbraith. And he continues as follows:

Also holding the subject to the past and to the classical model is, as it may be called, the technical escape from reality. The central assumption of classical economics— pure competition in the market extending on from the prices of products to the pricing of the factors of production—lends itself admirably to technical and mathematical refinement. This, in turn, is tested not by its representations of the real world but by its internal logic and the theoretical and mathematical competence that is brougt to bear in analysis and exposition. From this closed intellectual exercise, which is fascinating to its participants, intruders and critics are excluded, often by their own choice, as being technically unqualified. And, a more significant matter, so is the reality of economic life, which, alas, is not, in its varied disorder, suitable for mathematical replication.[5]

The parallel drawn with the teleological systems of explanation of the Middle Ages can no longer be rejected. The distinction between university-trained physicians (accounting theorists) who may well have spoken for centuries about GAMP (Generally Accepted Medical Principles) and untrained surgeons (bookkeepers) is clear.

The points demonstrated by Karl Popper many years ago using philosophy and logic can now be confirmed by the experiments performed by chaos theorists. Our new scientific philosophy is as follows: The physical system known as "the financial position of an enterprise" is unpredictable beyond a short term. All attempts at long-term prediction will fail. And if the financial position of individual enterprises is unpredictable, we must conclude that the financial position of society as a whole is also unpredictable. All attempts at prediction will fail.

The era of long-term predictions of the future must surely now be over. Anyone offering predictions in the worlds of accounting or economics is a victim of his or her own vague habits or wishful thinking. Anyone looking at predictions of the future (no matter how mathematically sophisticated these predictions may be) is looking at chaos. And anyone using chaos for practical purposes in the real world may cause a catastrophe.

Karl Popper and the historian Paul Johnson both use the expression *social engineering* to describe the attempts of politicians to mold the society of the future, based on ideas supplied by well-intentioned economists adhering to their own particular economic theories. A *social engineer* is a person who uses vague religious/moral ideas to set himself or herself up as a god on behalf of others, using the predictions supplied by economic theories to light the way into the future. Adolf Hitler and Josef Stalin were both social engineers of the twentieth century. But surely the judgment of posterity will be that neither of them met with absolutely convincing success.

The new chaos theories may well lead to entirely new insight into the concept of economics. It can no longer be denied that the financial position of enterprises is always unpredictable. So it cannot be denied that the financial position of society as a whole is also unpredictable. But no one has said that the financial position cannot be described. As we have seen, it can be described. But it can never be predicted beyond a short period of time—just like the weather. Galbraith claims that the lack of order in any financial position means that no financial position is a suitable object for mathematical description. Our reply is that although financial positions cannot be described using linear mathematics, they can be described using nonlinear mathematics. Modern chaos theories show that even though the individual elements of any system are straightforward and predictable, this is not the case as soon as we try to predict the future of such systems. But what is the relationship between these mathematical models and reality? Is there a connection between systems and models, between reality and pictures of reality?

We must find the answer to this question ourselves. Let us now consider the first occasion in the twentieth century on which international affairs went seriously wrong. We invite readers to compare modern chaos theories with the following quotations. We have chosen to quote from *The First World War* by the English historian A.J.P. Taylor, from the chapter in which he describes the outbreak of the war. The First World War lasted from 1914 to 1918, and there were no winners. It was the first "technological" war, and a total of 64 million soldiers were mobilized in it. Ten million people lost their lives. The wounded numbered 20 million; seven million of them were so seriously injured that they were handicapped for life.

The First World War and its results have been described many times. But Taylor tries to explain *how* and *why* the war started. His answer to the question "how?" fits uncomfortably well into chaos theories, although the term "butterfly effect" sounds somewhat macabre when used in this connection. But the question "why?" remains unanswered. The war had no objectives. No one wanted it to happen, but no one had sufficient control of the situation to prevent it from happening. The system started the war of its own accord:

Men are reluctant to believe that great events have small causes. Therefore, once the Great War started, they were convinced that it must be the outcome of profound forces. It is hard to discover these when we examine the details. Nowhere was there conscious determination to provoke a war. Statesmen miscalculated. They used the instruments of bluff and threat which had proved effective on previous occasions. This time things went wrong. The deterrent on which they relied failed to deter; the statesmen became the prisoners of their own weapons. The great armies, accumulated to provide security and preserve the peace, carried the nations to war by their own weight. . . . All the European Powers had built up vast armies of conscripts. The plans for mobilizing these millions rested on railways; and railway timetables cannot be improvised. Once started, the wagons and carriages must roll remorselessly and inevitably forward to their predestined goal. Horses can be swapped crossing a stream; railway carriages cannot. The Austrians had already discovered that, if they mobilized against Serbia, they could not then mobilize against Russia. . . . Now the Russians found out, if they mobilized against Austria-Hungary, they would be defenceless against Germany. General mobilization—not for war, but to keep their standing in the diplomatic conflict—was their only course. On 30 July they resolved upon it. The Russians did not want a war, or plan one. They merely wanted to show that, when the Austrians threatened, they could threaten too. One bluff was piled on top of another. . . . The First World War had begun—imposed on the statesmen of Europe by railway timetables. It was an unexpected climax to the railway age. . . . The men slogged along on foot once they reached railhead. Hence the extraordinary contrast of the war: fast in delivering men to the battlefield; slow when they got there.[6]

Generals are often accused of fighting wars using the strategies of the past, and the generals of the First World War failed to take developments in weapons into account. They failed to understand that they would never win the war by attacking enemy lines bravely, and so they continued to do so. The politicians could not understand why the war had started, so they were forced to invent myths about the madness and evil of the enemy to justify their actions. Meanwhile, the soldiers died:

One man with a machine gun, protected by mounds of earth, was more powerful than advancing masses. Trench warfare had begun. The war of movement ended when men dug themselves in. They could be dislodged only by massive bombardment and the accumulation of reserves—warnings which always gave the other side time to bring up reinforcements. The machine gun completed the contrast between the speed with which men could arrive at the battlefield by rail, and the slowness with which they moved once they were there. Indeed they did not move at all. The opposing lines congealed. The generals on both sides stared at these lines impotently and without understanding. They went on staring for nearly four years.[7]

The war ended not by careful thought or negotiation, but simply when one side had used all its resources. When the shooting finally stopped in 1918, the survivors naturally asked the question "Who was to blame?" Taylor's answer is "No one," but this would not have been accepted in 1918. So the peace was made in a way that would have made the ancient Romans shrug and say *vae victis* (woe to the vanquished). The Second World War did not begin in 1939. It started in 1919.

The British economist John Maynard Keynes (1883–1946) is regarded as one of the most important economic theorists of the twentieth century. During the First World War he worked at the British Ministry of Finance, and he suggested in 1916 that the reparations demanded following the war should be either small or nonexistent. His reason was that the achievement of a lasting peace would depend on the rapid resumption of trade, industry and employment, and that revenge and punishment would not achieve this. He also suggested that the countries involved cancel all debts arising between them as a result of the war. The American Ministry of Finance regarded Keynes's suggestion as outrageous, and its employees were forbidden to discuss the issue with him. This made Keynes despise the Americans: "They had the chance to demonstrate a magnanimous or at least humane view of the world, but without hesitating they allowed the opportunity to pass." Marshall Aid came 30 years too late, even though it was a good thing it came when it did.

Keynes described the peace that was *dictated* instead of being *agreed* at Versailles in 1919 as "a recipe for economic disaster and future war." This is one of the few examples of predictions being fulfilled. Keynes repudiated what he called "the tragic farce," and in his anger wrote the book entitled *The Economic Consequences of the Peace*. Paul Johnson describes this book as a classic illustration of the law of unintentional effects, which is the same as the "butterfly effect." Keynes was not the only person trying to appeal to reason in a world of anger. One French participant at Versailles pointed out that the aim was to achieve "a just and lasting peace." But he agreed with Keynes, and bitterly condemned the Treaty of Versailles as forming the basis of "a just and lasting war" (une guerre juste et durable) instead. Adolf Hitler, of course, took the same view of the Treaty of Versailles. It is true that he believed the just war could be completed by rapid Blitzkrieg, but the British, Americans and Russians did not agree with him. The Second World War lasted longer than the First, and cost more than 50 million lives. And like the First World War, it did not end as the result of insight and negotiation—if insight and negotiation had been employed it could have ended in 1943. Like the First World War, the Second World War only ended when one of the sides collapsed completely.

A.J.P. Taylor and many other historians have analyzed the interwar years, and there is general agreement that the inflation that ruined almost the entire German middle class a few years after the Treaty of Versailles was an important and perhaps decisive reason why totalitarianism was able to conquer democracy in Germany in the 1930s. Keynes was proved right, and the result of the Treaty of Versailles was that the lives of millions of ordinary people were lost 20 years later.

In January 1923, when the Germans had fallen behind with their payments (of reparations, which were impossible to repay owing to their size), the French and Belgian troops crossed the border and occupied the Ruhr District in order to exert pressure on the German debtor. The occupation caused a storm of protest in Germany. The people of the Ruhr answered with passive resistance. At the companies taken over by the French as "productive collateral" the workers went on strike. There were several bloody clashes between the occupying troops and the civilian population. However, the main impact of the Ruhr Occupation was felt by the German monetary system. It led to inflation which escalated into sheer madness. . . . When the French troops occupied the Ruhr an American dollar cost just over 10,000 marks. Three weeks later a dollar cost 50,000 marks. The occupation of Germany's most important industrial region . . . completely destroyed the damaged German economy. During the summer of 1923 the rate of exchange against the dollar rose to 100,000 marks, to 1,000,000 marks, to 10,000,000 marks. By the autumn the rate had climbed to 160 million marks. . . . As soon as people received their wages they bought goods with the money, because prices rose each day and each hour. In the end inflation was so far out of control that the exchange rate against the dollar on the Berlin stock exchange rose by 613,000 marks *per second*. . . . Basically, inflation meant that the First World War was paid for by German savers. . . . The middle class were the main losers, and it was among this group that a fanatic named Adolf Hitler now started to attract his most loyal supporters.[8]

Keynes could not predict the Second World War. But he could describe the consequences of the First, and his description of these consequences proved to be an accurate prediction. The huge reparations imposed by the Treaty of Versailles were so impossible to repay, and so imbued with emotional/moral feelings of revenge, that they inevitably led to disaster 20 years later. Of course it is easy to be wise after the event, but it is impossible to deny that emotions ruled the politicians at Versailles instead of common sense, and that the demand for one side to pay for a war that no one had wanted led to despair, hate and—only a few years later—a new holocaust.

Some readers may find it instructive to compare the theories of economists about trade cycles with chaos theories and our new knowledge about unpredictability. The economic collapse in the United States in 1929 and the depression in the 1930s have never been explained satisfactorily by economists. But the emotional explanations provided at the time seemed plausible enough, even though they varied. People believed them, and many died as a result.

Modern chaos theories tell us that these disastrous events were caused by previous developments, but that they were impossible to predict. In other words, it is pointless to discuss who was to blame for them.

Many people find it hard to accept that this is the case. As Taylor points out, people are generally reluctant to believe that great events have small causes. We seem to believe or wish that there is a proportional ratio between cause and effect. We believe that it must be possible to blame someone when major financial disasters occur, in order to have someone to hate and fight against. And we also believe that it must be possible to praise someone when major financial triumphs occur, in order to have someone to thank and worship. The assumption that there must be a proportional ratio between cause and effect allows us to find both God and the Devil among human beings. But the distinction is not always easy to draw, because sometimes the same people are regarded as fulfilling both roles at different times. Hitler and Stalin were both worshiped as gods by their subjects, and by many others with nothing better to believe in. But Hitler and Stalin, of course, are no longer regarded as gods.

Is this type of linear thinking something we have taught each other? The fact that mathematics requires rational, logical but empirically closed thinking may mean that we start expecting to find linear mathematics in the real world. But this assumption would be dangerous, and might even prove fatal:

In 1953 I realized that the straight line leads to the downfall of mankind. But the straight line has become an absolute tyranny. The straight line is something cowardly drawn with a rule, without thought or feeling; it is the line which does not exist in nature. And that line is the rotten foundation of our doomed civilization. Even if there are places where it is recognized that this line is leading to rapid perdition, its course continues to be plotted. . . . Any design undertaken with the straight line will be stillborn. Today we are witnessing the triumph of rationalist knowhow and yet, at the same time, we find ourselves confronted with emptiness. An esthetic void, desert of uniformity, criminal sterility, loss of creative power. Even creativity is prefabricated. We have become impotent. We are no longer able to create. That is our real illiteracy.[9]

Once again we ask readers whether they think this quotation was made by a scientist or an artist. The answer cannot be guessed. In a previous chapter we quoted the scientist Albert Einstein as saying that the doctrines of mathematics bear no relation to reality if they are certain, and that they can never be certain if they bear any relation to reality. This latter quotation contains a somewhat sharper criticism of any belief in linear mathematics and barren rationalism.

The quotation comes from the artist Friedensreich Hundertwasser, and is contained in the preface to a strange book on mathematics written in 1986, entitled *The Beauty of Fractals*. This book demonstrates the results of an entirely new form of mathematics that was not possible until the advent of modern computers. The term *fractals* was introduced by the mathematician Benoit Mandelbrot, after whom a particular mathematical unit of quantity has been named. Like other fractal units, the Mandelbrot unit is surprising because it enables a simple nonlinear mathematical function to create images of amazing beauty when a computer carries out a large number of calculations and reproduces the results in the form of color graphics. These images never end, and they can be calculated using a random number of calculations. They never repeat themselves in exactly the same way, and yet there are undoubted similarities between calculations on a large and small scale. The geometry of fractals fascinates and challenges students, and fractals are a major feature of the experiments carried out by chaos theorists.

The only demand made on a fractal calculation is that it should be an iteration—an ongoing series of calculations with the same nonlinear ratio between input and output data. Output data from calculation stage N is used as input data at stage $N + 1$. The system is almost unbelievably simple.

We shall only make one point with regard to fractals. Fractals deal with images of *complex, dynamic systems*, that is, of complex systems that change constantly. In the real world, the physical system we have called "the financial position of an enterprise" is also a *complex, dynamic system*, a complex system that changes constantly. So we are forced to ask the following questions: Is it possible that the new form of mathematics is somehow related to the description of financial positions? Will the accounting systems of the future contain an element that could be described as beautiful? And is it possible to recover the lost reality and creativity of accounting by using this new form of mathematics?

The fact that fractals and the physical system we call "the financial system of an enterprise" are both complex and dynamic does not, of course, mean that fractals and financial statements are connected in any way. But we cannot deny that they are related, either. We cannot deny that there may be a connection. So it is certainly worth pursuing this line of thought for a little while.

There are a number of undoubted similarities between fractals and financial statements—enough to arouse our curiosity. But we must retain a healthy skepticism and remember that there are clear differences, too.

One decisive difference is that financial statements reflect reality, whereas fractals are images. It is vital to acknowledge the difference between an object being considered and an image. It is vital to distinguish between "Peter" and "an image of Peter." But even though this distinction is essential, it is often overlooked. Many images are regarded as reality, but this is never the case—although at best images may represent part of reality.

So let us distinguish clearly between our *object* and our *image*. Our object is the financial position, or to be more precise the physical system known as *the financial position of an enterprise*. And our image is *the management account*, a system of information that we can regard as a symbolic reflection of the physical system in question. The vital question now is whether there is any isomorphy (i.e., structural similarity) between this object and this image.

It is immediately apparent that although the images produced by the Mandelbrot unit and fractals are fascinating and beautiful, they are no more than sophisticated calculations. No one claims that they reflect reality. The images produced are dynamic and complex, but they reflect a closed system. They do not interact with the outside world, because no one claims that they are images of anything physical. But there certainly seems to be a resemblance with a number of familiar physical structures. And the isomorphy (or structural similarity) cannot be denied in some respects. Complexity and dynamism are properties that are also present in financial systems in the real world. Let us consider this point in greater detail.

As mentioned earlier, we regard the object of "the financial position of an enterprise" as complex and dynamic. We are also familiar with a systematic model that reproduces these properties, and that is based on the use of nonlinear mathematics. This familiar system is double entry bookkeeping, an information system that has been used for 500 years. It is still used all over the world to systematically describe the financial positions of organizations. Invented by Venetian merchants, double entry bookkeeping has played a leading role in the history of accounting.

Double entry bookkeeping reflects the complexity of financial positions. The items entered may reflect transactions that differ entirely in terms of their nature, location and time. The register of an organization undoubtedly provides a complex image. It describes in persuasive, unambiguous fashion the way claims and debts arise as a result of trade between people, as well as describing equally persuasively and unambiguously the way claims and debts are paid *after the lapse of a certain period of time*. The totals calculated by computer automatically and rapidly will always differ, because they describe the sum of all the many items entered, which change constantly.

As far as basic registration and bookkeeping in T-shaped accounts is concerned, double entry bookkeeping is based on the use of nonlinear mathematics. Anyone with basic knowledge of accounting will accept the truth of this remark. Many strange things can be found in double entry bookkeeping, but bookkeepers have never yet found a coefficient of inclination.

Double entry bookkeeping provides an empirically open systematic image. It describes reality, because otherwise no one would ever use it. It provides an image of an organization set in the context of the world around it, an organism in an environment, and the boundaries between the organization and the world outside are open. Otherwise there would be no exchange between the two. The information contained in double entry bookkeeping is also open, since it can all be checked and criticized.

Finally, double entry bookkeeping provides an image of an interactive system. It describes what happens at the interface between an organization and the world outside. The transaction called a sale by the organization is known as a purchase by the customer, but the same transaction is involved nonetheless.

In other words, for the past 500 years or so it has been possible to describe the financial position of organizations using a model, an information system that is *dynamic, complex, open and interactive.* The description is carried out using nonlinear mathematics, and the information contained consists of measurements that are also empirically open. In principle, the term "an organization" covers all types of organization, ranging from individual projects to the financial position of society as a whole. The overall image is formed by adding the individual elements together. Double entry bookkeeping is used all over the world to describe financial positions.

But why do so many financial problems arise? There should not be any such difficulties. Why are there so many cognitive problems with regard to financial positions? Why does John Kenneth Galbraith, one of the most famous and highly regarded economists in the Western world, say that economics is "chained to the past"? Why do Robert N. Anthony and Robert S. Kaplan, two of the most respected accounting professors in the Western world, say that we have "a desperate need" for a new accounting theory, and that accounting has "lost its relevance," its connection with reality? Why do experienced practitioners say that in their capacity as responsible managers they find themselves "in no-man's land in terms of control," and that they have "a desperate need for up-to-date financial information"?

The answer may be that the description of financial positions used until now has been logically incomplete.

Readers may recall a sentence from a previous chapter to the effect that "the difference between static and dynamic concepts of accounting is enormous." Perhaps readers thought this was a somewhat exaggerated claim. But we shall now try to show that the difference concerned is certainly appreciable.

We refer again to project X in chapter 16, and assume that readers are prepared to accept the following claim:

If reliable basic registration is carried out using modern technology as a tool, and if good data discipline is exhibited, it is possible at any time to produce a real-time, clear, logically complete and therefore reliable financial statement for individual projects.

The term "real-time" is used here to describe a delay that is so short that it does not represent a problem for the users of financial statements.

We know that all accounting items are descriptions of the financial consequences of the actions of organizations, and that management accounts only contain items and no other logical elements. We also know that the concepts of projects and the dynamic account can be used to describe the purchase of goods, services, machines (investments), agreements concerning the appointment of employees, rent, telephone expenses, loan agreements, leasing contracts and so on. In other words, we can produce a complete classification and description of all types of payment. We have also seen that in order to be comprehensible, descriptions of the liquidity contribution/financing requirement of individual projects must be formed as a data string containing a certain amount of information about payments organized chronologically.

In a previous chapter we emphasized that logic is the strongest intellectual weapon available to man. We shall now use this weapon. What follows is entirely new, and may appear incredible at first sight. But readers must reach their own conclusions about the new theory. The basic data contained in the new accounting system is all based on a common denominator, which means that the addition of different items can take place without problems arising. Computers can perform the addition at great speed, and the results can be communicated at great speed, too, thanks to modern network technology. Combining all the data strings containing details of individual projects at an enterprise means that the following can also be claimed:

If reliable basic registration is carried out using modern technology as a tool, and if good data discipline is exhibited, it is possible at any time to produce a real-time, clear, logically complete and therefore reliable financial statement for any enterprise.

The term "enterprise" is used here to refer to any organization in the private sector. But we should emphasize that the concepts involved are generally applicable. For instance, the claim can also be applied to schools, hospitals or other organizations, whose "income" consist of "subsidies from the government." So for schools, the following claim can be made:

If reliable basic registration is carried out using modern technology as a tool, and if good data discipline is exhibited, it is possible at any time to produce a real-time, clear, logically complete and therefore reliable financial statement for any school.

We return now to the private sector. In many cases, the same person is the legal owner of several different enterprises that are formally separated from each other. We use the terms parent company/subsidiary for such constructions, and the financial statements produced are called consolidated financial statements. In such circumstances, traditional accounting theory has a number of skeletons in its closet, procedures that look good but that actually only describe empty, superficial details. For instance, serious consideration is given to the issue of which optimum transfer pricing procedures should be adopted between enterprises within the same corporation. This is like discussing whether you should keep your pocket money in your left or right pocket. If subsidiary A purchases a service at a cost of $100 from subsidiary B, two identical predictions of payment are registered in the financial statements of the two enterprises (–$100 for enterprise A, and +$100 for enterprise B). Asking readers what the combination of the two figures is would be an insult to their intelligence.

As far as traditional consolidated financial statements are concerned, we are forced to conclude that the recommended methods are simply inexplicable. They are beyond comprehension, and consist of completely useless rituals involving juggling of figures. The problem with traditional financial statements is that they ignore the factor of time. They are static, and can only reflect situations that are dead.

However, the use of the new system of accounting means that the following claim can be made for consolidated financial statements:

If reliable basic registration is carried out using modern technology as a tool, and if good data discipline is exhibited, it is possible at any time to produce a real-time, clear, logically complete and therefore reliable consolidated financial statement.

Need we say more? Assuming that the basic philosophy, definitions and coherence of the new accounting system can withstand all criticism, the conclusion on a wider scale is unavoidable:

If reliable basic registration is carried out using modern technology as a tool, and if good data discipline is exhibited, it is possible at any time to produce a real-time, clear, logically complete and therefore reliable financial statement for society as a whole.

This means that in the future economists will be able to consider the economy as a phenomenon, instead of being forced to make more or less educated guesses about it. In the future, modern information technology will be the descriptive tool of economists, just as telescopes are used by astronomers, microscopes by biologists and x-ray cameras by doctors. Blind faith and speculation about the economy will gradually be replaced by true knowledge. The "chains to the past" mentioned by John Kenneth Galbraith can be broken, and readers are invited to be among the first to do so.

Let us now conclude our description of the main features of management accounting, the new accounting model. Readers will no doubt appreciate that the new model is very different from the old one, but also that it has retained traditional double entry bookkeeping as part of its overall basic registration method.

Double entry bookkeeping has been used for the past 500 years, but even the old Venetian merchants would probably feel that the time has now come at the end of the twentieth century to make further progress and abandon traditional practices that have proved inadequate. What does the future of accounting hold?

There are only two possible answers to this question, which we shall call "the X answer" and "the Y answer." To demonstrate the X answer, we return again to the world of medicine to find an example of the way specialists react when new, surprising ideas or observations occur.

In Umberto Eco and G.B. Zorzoli's book entitled *A History of Inventions*, there is an excellent example dating back to the Renaissance, a period of history in which people started to make their own observations instead of blindly accepting the views of the authorities. Many centuries of tradition gradually began to be doubted:

Galileo tells us about an episode that he witnessed in Padua, where people had started to use dissection as a means of gaining insight into the human anatomy. Dissection was a new technique, and had previously been forbidden by the church. The following account, written by Galileo, is a typical example of the way change is always resisted: "One day I was visiting a widely respected doctor in Venice. He had several other visitors, people who occasionally came along to witness a dissection; some out of interest, others out of curiosity. He tried to explain where nerves originate, a problem about which Galen's disciples and peripatetics (Aristotle's disciples) were in great disagreement. The anatomist demonstrated that a big cluster of nerves originating in the brain passed through the neck and spinal column to all parts of the body, but that only a very thin nerve led to the heart. He turned to a gentleman known as a peripatetic philosopher, and asked him whether he was now convinced that the nerves originated in the brain and not in the heart. The philosopher thought about this for a moment, and then replied 'You have shown me this so clearly and sensibly that if Aristotle had not explicitly stated that the nerves originated in the heart, I would have to believe what you say.'"

This is the prototype of the X answer. The example is not the only one of its kind. People have often said *video sed non credo* ("I see it, but I do not believe it"). In the example just given, Galen is regarded as the authority instead of Aristotle, but Galen's so-called "knowledge" was also subsequently modified in certain respects. The event described by Galileo took place when Galen had been dead for only 1,200 years, so Galen was a much more recent authority than Aristotle at that time.

Readers must draw their own conclusions about accounting traditions that are only a few hundred years old, but that have become thoroughly well-established in that time. The X answer is easy enough. You simply have to deny the evidence of your own eyes. You reject the obvious problems and ideas as being nonexistent, and continue to observe the beliefs that you and everyone else have held for some time. You reject the idea that accounting has demonstrated its impotence, and refuse to accept that the credibility of accountants has suffered. You believe that unexpected collapses in trade and industry never occur, and that banks never go bankrupt. You believe that traditional financial statements really do convey a true and fair view, and you continue to draw up such financial statements based on assumptions of going concern, continuity, the principle of prudence and so on. You are sure that readers of financial statements have no difficulty in understanding the contents, and that if they do experience any difficulties it must be their own fault. You are convinced that *there are no problems in the world of accounting.*

The X answer to the new challenge facing the world of accounting is easy enough. But what is the Y answer?

This book does not contain the Y answer, because the Y answer can only be provided by readers themselves. Accounting specialists do not need to ask the question "Is current accounting practice really acceptable?" because all the many users of traditional financial statements have already provided the answer. The really important question is "*Are we prepared* to accept that so-called Generally Accepted Accounting Principles could well be criticized and called Locally Applied Accounting Dogma?" Ultimately, this is a question of ethics.

The distinction drawn in the Middle Ages between physicians and surgeons no longer applies. These days, surgeons have considerable theoretical expertise in their field, and physicians have realized that it is an advantage to do more than just talk and produce theories. A similar change may occur in the world of economics in the future. But whatever happens, it will be an advantage to know what you are talking about when discussing economics. The people who draw up financial statements create and maintain a description of the financial position of their enterprises. But they often lack insight into the overall picture. And the people who are looking for insight into the overall picture have so far suffered from a lack of reliable descriptions of the financial position, and have thus been forced to depend on blind faith instead of true knowledge. But this dilemma is no longer insoluble. Computers and communication technology have been invented.

So what happens if doubts arise? What can accountants do to obtain extra safeguards for their actions? The principle of due caution could perhaps be applied, and readers might choose to react by saying to themselves "I can see that the situation is a little uncertain. Something is wrong, but none of the others appear to be worried. So I shall wait and see. There's safety in numbers, after all."

This is exactly what the passengers aboard the *Titanic* said on the night of April 14–15, 1912.

Few disasters have attracted the fascination of posterity in the same way as the loss of the *Titanic*. And it is impossible to find a better example of the butterfly effect (small causes, great effects) than this event. The sinking of the *Titanic* can be seen as the prelude to two disastrous world wars, a reflection of the blind faith of the twentieth century in technology, rationalism and linear thinking, and of the results of this blind faith. The very name of the ship reflects an attempt to emulate the gods, since the Titans of Greek mythology were huge, strong, evil giants who were defeated by Zeus and cast into a bottomless pit.

The *Titanic* was the largest passenger vessel of its day. It was 269 meters long, which is nine-tenths of the height of the Eiffel Tower in Paris. It was new, it was luxuriously appointed, and the brochure announced that it was unsinkable. The hull was partitioned into 16 compartments, each of which could be sealed with watertight doors. Even though four of these compartments were filled with water, the ship would remain afloat. During testing a top speed of almost 24 knots was achieved, and the ship could stop in the space of 800 meters.

The lifeboats had room for 1,178 passengers. There were 2,227 passengers on board for the maiden voyage on April 10, 1912. On April 14 at 11:39 P.M. the ship was moving at a speed of 21 knots in waters where icebergs had already been reported. Two seamen kept a chilly lookout from the forward mast, but they could not see very far because there was no searchlight in the bow of the ship. The sea was calm as a millpond, and the night was cold and starry. The moon was not visible.

The seamen caught sight of an iceberg dead ahead and announced the fact to the first officer. The ship changed course and the engines were set at full astern. They almost escaped. The *Titanic* did not hit the iceberg above the water line, but there was a scraping sound, which few people even noticed, and water started pouring in. There was no drama. Slowly the vertically partitioned compartments filled with water, as with an ice cube tray. Once the front compartment was full the water overflowed into the next compartment. The *Titanic* stayed afloat for almost three hours, until 2:18 A.M. There were 705 survivors, and 1,522 died.

Because the lifeboats had room for 1,178 passengers, 473 more people could perhaps have been saved. But some people refused to get into the lifeboats, and the first few lifeboats were lowered and sailed away from the sinking ship half empty. Everyone thought the *Titanic* was unsinkable, and the tiny lifeboats seemed a very risky option compared with the safety, light and warmth of the huge ship. It was a dark night, it was very cold on deck, and the lifeboats were being lowered 21 meters from the deck down into a black sea below. People preferred to wait and see. One Danish woman who survived was 19 years old at the time, and recounted that there was no panic on board. Everyone remained calm because everyone thought the ship was unsinkable. She was awakened between 1:00 and 1:30 A.M., and when she reached the deck she could see that the bow of the ship was already under water, and that the water had almost reached the first of the ship's four funnels. But everyone was calm. "We knew the ship was unsinkable, so there was no reason to panic. As I got into a lifeboat my uncle said 'I'll see you in New York. We might be a few days late, but just you wait for us there.'"

But her uncle never got to New York. At 2:18 A.M. he and 1,521 others finally realized that the *Titanic* was not completely unsinkable after all. Still there was no panic, and only when the ship split open, with the bow disappearing and the stern tipping into almost vertical position before sinking beneath the waves, was there a terrible scream from the largest passenger ship in the world—a scream that none of the survivors ever forgot. Then there was silence. The unsinkable ship had sunk.

A story arose later that the ship's orchestra played a beautiful hymn to help everyone approach death in dignified fashion. It is true that the orchestra continued to play, but their aim was not to help people meet their doom calmly, but to encourage people to dance. The whole episode was regarded as an exercise that could be called off at any time.

In March 1912 anyone who said that the *Titanic* was sinkable was regarded as ignorant or mad. In May 1912 anyone who said that it was unsinkable was regarded as ignorant or mad. Does this remind readers of the assumption that enterprises are going concerns until financial disasters occur?

We are deceived by linear thinking. We *refuse* to believe that the world tomorrow will not be the same as the world today. We *refuse* to accept that even small causes may have huge effects. Perhaps it is high time that we economists got hold of a searchlight and then persuaded the first officer to sail a little more slowly, enabling us to adjust our speed to suit our chances of changing course if necessary.

How is major scientific progress made? This question was asked on Swedish television a few years ago, and a group of researchers who had just received the Nobel Prize was asked for an answer. Naturally, it is an extremely difficult question to answer, but one of the Nobel Prize winners made the attempt. He said "The main thing is to make mistakes in an interesting way."

If we now abandon linear thinking and accept that change is the normal state of affairs, the sentence "The main thing is to make mistakes in an interesting way" could be seen as a new philosophy for "strategic planning." We need to focus our attention on *the philosophy of learning by trial and error:*

The noble art of losing face
may one day save the human race
and turn into eternal merit
what weaker minds would call disgrace.

This was written by the Danish mathematician and philosopher Piet Hein. The world changes constantly. The latest information is the only valid information, even though it is different from the old information—in fact precisely *because* it is different. It is a paradox that politicians who admit mistakes are often despised and sometimes fired. A few years ago the Danish prime minister said "I always keep one particular point of view until I adopt a new one." He was much criticized for saying this, but perhaps it is one of the most sensible things any politician could say.

There are two types of fool—the fools who never make mistakes because they never learn anything, and the fools who make the same mistakes several times because they never learn anything even though given the chance to do so. But the fools who never make any mistakes can persuade themselves that they are wiser than the sensible people who make one mistake once and learn from it, because these fools believe that they make fewer mistakes than anyone.

The historian Paul Johnson concludes his book entitled *A History of the Modern World* by demonstrating that *politics* has replaced *religion* in the twentieth century as the implement of fanaticism and orthodoxy. And he points out that blind faith has a very high price indeed:

by the turn of the century politics was replacing religion as the chief form of zealotry. To archetypes of the new class, such as Lenin, Hitler and Mao Tse-tung, politics—by which they meant the engineering of society for lofty purposes—was the only legitimate form of moral activity, the only sure means of improving humanity. This view, which would have struck an earlier age as fantastic, became to some extent, the orthodoxy everywhere. . . . They marched across the decades and the hemispheres: mountebanks, charismatics, *exaltés*, secular saints, mass murderers, united by their belief that politics was the cure for human ills: Sun Yat-sen and Ataturk, Stalin and Mussolini, Khrushchev, Ho Chi Minh, Pol Pot, Castro, Nehru, U Nu and Sukarno, Perón and Allende, Nkrumah and Nyerere, Nasser, Shah Pahlevi and Gadafy, usually bringing death and poverty in their train.[10]

In a previous chapter we outlined the postulate of impotency, but applied it only to accounting theory. We have also seen in this chapter that Galbraith believes that economic reality is being excluded and that economics itself is chained to the past. Does the postulate of impotency also apply to economics as a profession? Paul Johnson seems to believe this to be the case, and the fact that it is not yet possible to regard economics as an exact science is also apparently a serious problem with major consequences:

A related development was a growing disesteem for the social sciences, which had done so much to usher in the age of politics and to advance its illusory claims. Economics, sociology, psychology and other inexact sciences—scarcely sciences in the light of modern experience—had constructed the juggernaut of social engineering, which had crushed beneath it so much wealth and so many lives. . . . But its influence will steadily diminish and never again, perhaps, will humanity put so much trust in this modern metaphysic. . . . By contrast, the exact sciences fulfilled all their purposes.[11]

Metaphysical things lie outside the physical world, so it is impossible to gain experience of them. Johnson uses the term "metaphysics" to cover empirically unclear or incomprehensible information that can be discussed endlessly, with one opinion being just as valid as any other opinion—a logical morass. Characterizing the social sciences as being metaphysical is the opposite of expressing respect for them.

Paul Johnson concludes his book by referring to his hope for a new, interdisciplinary science that he calls *sociobiology*. Sociobiology is the study of human behavior in society based on material indicating that almost all differences between human societies can be explained in terms of training and socialization, and that consequently it may be possible to abandon the visions of total revolution of the social engineers and instead focus on evolution. The importance of the biological process of improvement has been discovered and emphasized, a process that never stops, and that is a vital component of all human progress. In this respect we shall simply say that the new theory of financial measurement presented here is also based on a fundamentally biological philosophy. Enterprises are regarded as living organisms. So there is no contradiction in basic philosophy here.

It is not really important what label we attach to our theories. But it is important that a precise and critical scientific method can be used in the social sciences, to help us escape from the shadows of metaphysics:

it should be studied by empirical science, not metaphysics, and by the methodology so brilliantly categorized by Karl Popper, in which theory is made narrow, specific and falsifiable by empirical data, as opposed to the all-purpose, untestable and self-modifying explanations of Marx, Freud . . . and other prophets.[12]

Naturally, Paul Johnson takes the broad view here, because these quotations are taken from the end of his book. They are used to conclude a work comprising over 700 pages. But the message is clear. It is more necessary than ever before to recognize the difference between science and pseudoscience. There are undoubtedly methodological problems involved in economics as a science.

But it is too early to write off the social sciences as being inexact. It is hard to deny, for instance, that psychologists have worked slowly but surely away from a primarily metaphysical standpoint towards modern behavioral psychology, which is empirical in its basic assumptions. For instance, the American psychologist A.H. Maslow seems to have made an extremely well-founded and valuable contribution to the idea of a possible new *human economy*, based on well-founded knowledge, which can be scientifically falsified, about individual needs and experiences, instead of being based on speculation about the future.

It is highly probable that in a few years' time the science of economics will escape from its chains and thus recover its lost respect. Readers who are unable to disprove the new accounting theory presented here will be able to disagree with Paul Johnson and place economics among the modern sciences. It is true that the mathematics used is nonlinear, and that a great number of calculations and recalculations are necessary all the time, because the image of the accounting system is as alive as the system itself. The ideas are new, and they may seem strange at first sight. But this is true of all new ideas. It is not easy to describe the current financial position. But it is possible to do so.

John Kenneth Galbraith also points out that economic theories are always products of their own time. Whether or not we like the theories and the people who produce them, we should never forget that they are all written in an attempt to acknowledge problems with a view to solving them. To some extent, even mad theories deserve consideration. They should always be preferred to having no theories at all. Passivity is only the answer when the outside world is passive—but the outside world is never passive.

The new interdisciplinary approach, which is supported by chaos theories in simple, comprehensible and thus irrefutable fashion, is of great interest to economists. It closes the door on dogma, but it opens other doors. We now know that it is impossible to predict the financial position beyond a relatively short period of time, so we must focus on describing the current financial position instead. Figures are almost too easy to work with, and they have been used to communicate a great deal of misleading information in the past. The time for linear thinking is past, because as Hundertwasser says, linear thinking is unnatural and far too dangerous.

A nonlinear description of financial positions has not yet been researched to the full, but the assumptions on which it is based are reassuring. The information dealt with lies within the limits of our own experience, so we dare to believe in it. We are interested in reasons and in quality, we use ordinary language, and we leave the task of calculation to computers. This will allow us to devote ourselves to the most important things—observation of the real world, careful thought, meaningful dialog with others and the resulting hope that new insight and knowledge of the financial consequences of our actions can thereby be gained.

This book is more or less complete now. But I hope readers will allow me to make a few final remarks based on the idea that economic theories are the result of the age in which they are produced.

These words were written on July 14, 1989, which is exactly 200 years after the start of the French Revolution. And this book was written by a man born in 1938, who has thus (to his surprise) experienced more than a quarter of the two centuries that have elapsed since 1789. The passage of time never ceases to amaze.

The French Revolution started due to economic developments that threatened the lives and welfare of the underprivileged classes. When it broke out, *hunger* was the greatest enemy. The 1788 harvest was the worst for many years. The price of bread rose, and people were unable to pay. The storming of the Bastille was an example of desperation at work. The psychologist A.H. Maslow might even claim that it could have been predicted.

At first the progress of the Revolution was moderate, and the new ideas aroused a certain amount of sympathy. The slogan *Liberty, Equality and Fraternity* attracted support. But it proved impossible to continue in moderation. The fiery tempers of the French people could not be restrained. In the summer of 1789 the English philosopher and proponent of freedom Edmund Burke wrote to a French friend that "You have carried out a revolution, but not a reformation. You have suppressed the monarchy, but not yet introduced freedom. If you distinguish between freedom and justice, then in my opinion neither of the two is certain."

The slogans of the French Revolution have still not been introduced internationally 200 years later. Robespierre, and others such as Adolf Hitler and Ayatollah Khomeiny, have all tried to shape the processes of revolution, resulting in terrible consequences. Naturally, the French Revolution was celebrated once more in France in 1989. But not everyone realized exactly what was being celebrated. The guillotine was still part of the picture. The wrong people have to be found and executed to enable the right people to live on. This has been seen many times before.

The guillotine was originally invented for humanitarian reasons, to ensure a painless and gentle death (une mort douce). When the Paris executioner first saw it, he said it was a beautiful machine (une belle machine), but expressed doubts concerning the possible misuse of its capacity. And its capacity was misused. The Terror arrived, and the Revolution devoured its own children. The gods were thirsty.

They may prove thirsty again. If we demand full economic liberty, the weakest will die of hunger. If we demand full economic equality, we might as well erect the guillotine once again. And if we demand full economic fraternity, we might as well either give up hope or demand fraternity on behalf of our own particular group.

The wonderful old French slogans are fatal, because they can so easily be perverted to reflect the opposite. Each new generation must seek understanding of its own times. This is not easy, but it is the nature of democracy. In Plato's state, government was dealt with by philosophers, the wise, those who loved knowledge. If you believe that those who govern require knowledge, you must also ask how the people elected to govern today can be elected without knowledge. In a democracy it is the task of each individual to seek understanding of his or her own times. This is difficult. I think it was Winston Churchill who said that democracy was the worst possible form of government, apart from the alternatives, of course.

In the spring of 1989 there were three events in the same week that will probably only be footnotes in future history books, but that all made a great impression when they appeared on the front pages of the newspapers. In Iran the guardian of the true faith, Ayatollah Khomeiny, died, and was followed to his last resting place by screaming, illiterate fanatics seeking to tear off a piece of his shroud to retain some of the power that sent hundreds of thousands of young men into war against Iraq. In the People's Republic of China students demonstrated peacefully in Beijing in favor of political reform, but the army was turned against them, and the result was a massacre. The hand killed the mind. The people's soldiers shot the people's students, and the location bore a name that hardly seemed appropriate for such an event (Tiananmen Square means the Square of Heavenly Peace in Chinese).

In West Germany the President of the USSR, Mikhail Gorbachev, was received with delight by the German people, most of whom could remember soldiers who died in the war against Russia from 1941 to 1945. The new policy advocated by Gorbachev was regarded as a step in the right direction after more than 40 years of carelessness and ideological warfare resulting in armed conflict on more than one occasion.

Europeans learnt two Russian words from Gorbachev—Glasnost and Perestroika. Negotiations for disarmament met with considerable success, and the European powers started to abandon the idea that war could be used as a means to an end. To some extent, the philosopher Clausewitz has been proved wrong in his claim that war is nothing more than the continuation of politics by other means.

If economists wish to break the chains binding their profession to the past, it may be a good idea to do so while the window is open that leads to a new era. In the future we can expect increasing numbers of changes in circumstances, and our task is to acknowledge this fact and discuss ways of ensuring openness and readiness for change. The new circumstances will reward those who are prepared to change. But no one can predict or prevent the developments of a changeable and exciting future.

And so we have reached the end of the road. Thank you for bearing with me for so long. You are now invited to decide the best way of answering the question we asked at the very start of this book.

The question was "Can future payments appear from balance sheets?"

NOTES

1. E. Gotfredsen, *Medicinens Historie*, p. 86.
2. H. W. Haggard, *Lægen gennem tiderne*, p. 79.
3. J. K. Galbraith, *Economics in Perspective*, p. 248.
4. Ibid., p. 4.
5. Ibid., p. 284.
6. A. J. P. Taylor, *The First World War*, p. 19.
7. Ibid., p. 20.
8. C. Grimberg, *Verdenshistorien*, Vol. 16, p. 142.
9. H.-O. Peitgen and P. H. Richter, *The Beauty of Fractals*, p.7.
10. P. Johnson, *A History of The Modern World*, p. 729.
11. Ibid., p. 730.
12. Ibid., p. 734.

REFERENCES

Ackoff, Russell L. *Scientific Method—optimizing applied research decisions.* John Wiley and Sons, New York 1962.

AICPA. *Objectives of Financial Statements.* AICPA, New York 1973.

Andersen, Arthur and Co. *Objectives of Financial Statements for Business Enterprises.* 1984.

Anthony, Robert N. "We don't have the accounting concepts that we need." *Harvard Business Review* 1987.1.

Beer, Stafford. *Decision and Control. The Meaning of Operational Research and Management Cybernetics.* John Wiley and Sons, London 1966

Carlzon, Jan. *Riv Pyramiderne ned!* Gyldendal, Copenhagen 1985.

Churchman, C. West. *The Systems Approach.* Delta, New York 1968.

Coveney, Peter and Highfield, Roger. *The Arrow of Time.* W. H. Allen, London 1990.

Crutchfield, James P. et al. "Chaos." *Scientific American* 1989.

Cyert, R. M. and March, J. G. *A Behavioral Theory of the Firm.* Prentice-Hall, Englewood Cliffs, NJ 1963.

Danish Institute of Certified Public Accountants. *Årsregnskabet.* FSR Forlag, Copenhagen 1984.

Dearden, John. *Cost Accounting and Financial Control Systems.* London 1973.

DICPA Regnskabsvejledning nr. 1 FSR Forlag, Copenhagen 1988.

Drucker, Peter F. *The Practice of Management.* Harper and Brothers, New York, 1956.

Drucker, Peter F. *The Age of Discontinuity.* Harper and Row, New York 1968.

Drucker, Peter F. *Managing in Turbulent Times.* Harper and Row, New York 1980.

Eco, Umberto and Zorzoli, G. B. *Opfindelsernes Historie.* Gyldendal, Copenhagen 1965.

Forrester, David A. *Schmalenbach and After.* Glasgow 1977.

Forrester, Jay. *Industrial Dynamics.* MIT Press, Cambridge, MA 1961.

Frisch, Hartvig. *Europas Kulturhistorie*. Politikens Forlag, Copenhagen 1962.

Galbraith, John K. *Economics in Perspective*. Houghton Mifflin, Boston 1987.

Gleick, James. *Chaos. The Making of A New Science*. Viking Penguin 1987.

Gotfredsen, E. *Medicinens Historie*. Nyt Nordisk Forlag, Copenhagen 1973.

Greve, Vagn. *"Er tiden moden til en ny straffelov?"* Juristen 1984.

Grimberg, C. *Grimbergs Verdenshistorie*. Politikens Forlag, Copenhagen 1961.

Gruning, P. E. "Revisors position i konkurstruede virksomheder." *Artikler om Konkurs og Tvangsakkord*, ed. by Niels Ørgaard, Copenhagen 1984.

Guy, Dan M. and Alderman, C. W. *Auditing*. Dryden Press, Fort Worth 1993.

Haggard, H. W. *Lægen gennem tiderne*. C. A. Reitzels Forlag, Copenhagen 1936.

Hansen, Palle. *The Accounting Concept of Profit*. Nyt Nordisk Forlag, Copenhagen 1972.

Hartnack, Justus. *Tænkning og virkelighed*. Berlingske Leksikon Bibliotek, Copenhagen 1961.

Hasselager, O. and Runge Johansen, A. *Årsregnskabsloven af 1981 med kommentarer*. G. E. C. Gad, Copenhagen 1987.

Hawking, Stephen W. *A Brief History of Time*. Bantam Books, New York 1988.

Hendriksen, Eldon S. and M. F. Van Breda, *Accounting Theory*. Irwin, Homewood, IL 1992.

Hicks, James O., Jr. and Leininger, Wayne E. *Accounting Information Systems*. West Publishing Company, St. Paul 1981.

Hildebrandt, Steen. *Om systemer og systemtænkning*. Samfundslitteratur, Copenhagen 1981.

Hofstede, G. *Cultures and Organizations—Software of the Mind*. McGraw-Hill, Amsterdam 1984.

Ijiri, Yuji. *The Foundations of Accounting Measurement*. Prentice-Hall, Englewood Cliffs, NJ 1967.

Ijiri, Yuji. *Theory of Accounting Measurement*. American Accounting Association 1975.

Ijiri, Yuji. *Momentum Accounting and Triple-Entry Bookkeeping*. American Accounting Association 1989.

Johnsen, Erik. *Studies in Multiobjective Decision Models*. Studentlitteratur, Lund 1968.

Johnson, Paul. *A History of The Modern World*. Weidenfeld and Nicholson, London 1984.

Jørgensen, Ole Ravn. *Virksomhedsfilosofi, ledelsesfilosofi. Fra Metode til forståelse*. Schultz Forlag, Copenhagen 1986.

Jørgensen, Jørgen. *Psykologi på biologisk grundlag*. Munksgaard, Copenhagen 1962.

Jørgensen, Jørgen. *Indledning til logikken og metodelæren*. Munksgaard, Copenhagen 1966.

Kam, Vernon. *Accounting Theory*. John Wiley and Sons, New York 1986.

Kaplan, Robert S. *Advanced Management Accounting*. Prentice-Hall, Englewood Cliffs, NJ 1982.

Kaplan, Robert S. "The Evolution of Management Accounting." *Accounting Review* 1984.

Kaplan, Robert S. and Johnson, H. Thomas. *Relevance Lost. The Rise and Fall of Management Accounting*. Harvard Business School Press, Boston, MA 1987.

Kilger, Wolfgang. *Einführug in die Kostenrechnung*. Gabler, Wiesbaden 1980.

Kirkegaard, Henning. *Ledelsesregnskabet. Idé & Metode.* Civiløkonomernes Forlag, Copenhagen 1987.

Kirkegaard, Henning. *REBUS-konceptet.* Civiløkonomernes Forlag, Copenhagen 1987.

Kristensen, Svend Høgsberg. *Revisor og going concern-princippet.* FSR Forlag, Copenhagen 1985.

Kristensen, Thorkil. *Statusteori.* Nyt Nordisk Forlag, Aarhus 1943.

Kuhn, Thomas S. *The Structure of Scientific Revolutions.* The University of Chicago Press, 1972.

Langen, Heinz. *"Die Prognose von Zahlungseingängen."* Zeitschrift für Betriebswirtschaft 1964.5.

Langen, Heinz. *"Der Betriebsprozess in dynamischer Darstellung."* Zeitschrift für Betriebswirtschaft 1966.1.

Langen, Heinz. *"Grundzüge einer betriebswirtschaftlichen Dispositionsrechnung."* Zeitschrift für Betriebswirtschaft 1968.12.

Lehmann W. *Die dynamische Bilanz Schmalenbachs. Darstellung, Vertiefung und Weiterentwicklung.* Wiesbaden 1963.

Madsen, Vagn. *Regnskabsvæsenets opgaver og problemer i ny belysning.* Gyldendal, Copenhagen 1959.

March, J. and Simon H. *Organizations.* John Wiley and Sons, New York 1958.

Mattessich, Richard. *Die Wissenschaftlichen Grundlagen des Rechnungswesens.* Bertelsmann Universitätsverlag, Düsseldorf 1970.

Minzberg, Henry. *Lederens og hans Job.* Nyt fra Samfundsvidenskaberne, Copenhagen 1976.

Minzberg, Henry. *Structures in Five.* Prentice-Hall, New York 1983.

Mock, Theodore J. *Measurement and Accounting Information Criteria.* American Accounting Association 1976.

Moonitz, Maurice. *The Basic Postulates of Accounting.* AICPA, New York 1961.

Munch, Mogens. *Konkursloven med kommentarer* (5th edition). GadJura. Copenhagen 1987.

Munk, Anders. *Om menneskets natur.* Politikens Forlag, Copenhagen 1976.

National Geographic Society. *National Geographic Magazine,* volumes. 168.6, 170.6 and 172.4.

Nielsen, Aksel C. Wiin. *Forudsigelighed. Om grænserne for videnskab.* Munksgaard, Copenhagen 1987.

Nørretranders, Tor. *Det udelelige.* Gyldendal, Copenhagen 1988.

Ørgaard, Niels. *Konkursret.* Jurist-og Økonomforbundets Forlag, Copenhagen 1989.

Ørgaard, Niels (ed.). *Artikler om konkurs og tvangsakkord.* FSR Forlag, Copenhagen 1984.

Pacioli, Luca. *Summa de Aritmetica Geometria Proportioni et Proportionalita.* Venice 1494.

Peitgen, H.-O. and Richter, P. H. *The Beauty of Fractals.* Springer-Verlag, Berlin 1986.

Popper, Karl R. *Conjectures and Refutations, The Growth of Scientific Knowledge.* Routledge and Kegan, London 1972.

Popper, Karl R. *The Logic of Scientific Discovery.* Harper Torchbooks, New York 1959.

Popper, Karl R. *The Open Society and Its Enemies.* Routledge and Kegan, London 1974.

Popper, Karl R. *The Poverty of Historicism.* Ark Edition, London 1986.

Rhenman, E. and Stymne, B. *Virksomhedsledelse i en foranderlig verden.* Hasselbalch, Copenhagen 1969.

Riebel, Paul. *Einzelkosten und Deckungsbeitragsrechnung.* Gabler Verlag, Wiesbaden 1985.

Robertson, J. and Mills, Roger W. "Company Failure or Company Health." *Long Range Planning* 1987.

Ross, Alf. *Om ret og retfærdighed.* Nyt Nordisk Forlag, Copenhagen 1966.

Russell, Bertrand. *A History of Western Philosophy.* George Allen and Unwin, London 1948.

Schmalenbach, Eugen. *Der Kontenrahmen.* Leipzig 1939.

Schmalenbach, Eugen. *Dynamische Bilanz* (7th edition). G. A. Gloeckner, Leipzig 1939.

Schneider, Erich. "*Kapitalbehov, kapitaldækning og likviditet i handels-og industrivirksomheder.*" Nationaløkonomisk, Tidsskrift 1941.

Schon, Donald A. *Efter den stabile tilstand.* Lindhard og Ringhoff, Copenhagen 1972.

Shillinglaw, Gordon. *Managerial Cost Accounting.* Irwin, Homewood, IL 1982.

Simon, H. A. *Administrative Behaviour.* Macmillan, New York 1957.

Simon, H. A. *The Shape of Automation for Men and Management.* Harper and Row, New York 1960.

Skogsvik, Kenth. *Prognos av finansiell kris med redovisningsmŒtt.* Stockholm 1988.

Sobel, Robert. *Dangerous Dreamers.* John Wiley and Sons, New York 1993.

Speer, Albert. *Fra triumf til katastrofe.* Copenhagen 1970.

Sprouse and Moonitz. *A Tentative Set of Broad Accounting Principles for Business Enterprises.* AICPA Accounting Research Study no. 3, 1962.

Stalk, George Jr. and Hout, Thomas M. *Competing Against Time.* The Free Press, London 1990.

Staubus, George J. "An Induced Theory of Accounting Measurement." *The Accounting Review* 1985.

Sveistrup, Poul. "*Systembegrebet og virksomheden som system.*" Erhvervsøkonomisk tidsskrift. 1965.4.

Taylor, A. J. P. *The First World War.* Harmondsworth, London 1966.

Toffler, Alvin. *Den tredie Bølge.* Chr. Eriksen, Copenhagen 1981.

Waaben, Knud. *Strafferettens Ansvarslære.* Gads Forlag, Copenhagen 1987.

Weekes, William. *A General Systems Approach to Management Accounting.* Seaside, CA 1984.

Wiin-Nielsen, A. *Forudsigelighed. Om grænserne for videnskab.* Munksgaard 1987.

Witt-Hansen, Johannes. *Filosofi. Videnskabernes historie i det 20. århundrede.* Gyldendal, Copenhagen 1985.

Worre, Zakken. *Nøglefaktorer i virksomhedens økonomiske tilpasningsproces.* Nyt Nordisk Forlag, Copenhagen 1967.

Yordon, Edward. *Managing the System Life Cycle.* New York 1982.

Zinkernagel, Peter. *Virkelighed.* Munksgaard, Copenhagen 1988.

INDEX

About the Author

HENNING KIRKEGAARD is a researcher and Associate Professor at the Copenhagen Business School. Author of numerous journal articles in Danish and English and ten earlier books published in Danish (including a version of this book under a different title), he has broad, practical experience in the design and use of financial and management information systems. He is also credited with the rediscovery, in 1984, of the original nature of double entry bookkeeping.